SAS® System for Linear Models

Third Edition

SAS Institute Inc.
SAS Campus Drive
Cary, NC 27513

Editing:	Jeffrey Lopes, Philip R. Shelton
Composition:	Candy R. Farrell, Gail C. Freeman, Cynthia M. Hopkins, Lee N. Lai, Nancy Mitchell, Lucy W. Myatt, Blanche W. Phillips, Pamela A. Troutman, David S. Tyree
Proofreading:	Patsy P. Blessis, Carey H. Cox, Paramita Ghosh, Hanna P. Hicks, Josephine P. Pope, Toni P. Sherrill, John M. West, Susan E. Willard, Linda Rudd Wooten
Graphic Design:	Creative Services Department

The correct bibliographic citation for this manual is as follows: SAS Institute Inc., *SAS® System for Linear Models, Third Edition,* Cary, NC: SAS Institute Inc., 1991. 329 pp.

SAS® System for Linear Models, Third Edition

The SAS® System is an integrated system of software providing complete control over data access, management, analysis, and presentation. Base SAS software is the foundation of the SAS System. Products within the SAS System include SAS/ACCESS® SAS/AF® SAS/ASSIST® SAS/CPE® SAS/DMI® SAS/ETS® SAS/FSP® SAS/GRAPH® SAS/IML® SAS/IMS-DL/I® SAS/OR® SAS/QC® SAS/REPLAY-CICS® SAS/SHARE® SAS/STAT® SAS/CONNECT™ SAS/DB2™ SAS/INSIGHT™ SAS/SQL-DS™ and SAS/TOOLKIT™ software. Other SAS Institute products are SYSTEM 2000® Data Management Software, with basic SYSTEM 2000, CREATE™ Multi-User™ QueX™ Screen Writer™ and CICS interface software; NeoVisuals® software; JMP® JMP IN® and JMP Serve™ software; SAS/RTERM® software; and the SAS/C® Compiler. MultiVendor Architecture™ and MVA™ are trademarks of SAS Institute Inc. *SAS Communications® SAS Training® SAS Views®* and the SASware Ballot® are published by SAS Institute Inc. All trademarks above are registered trademarks or trademarks, as indicated by their mark, of SAS Institute Inc.

A footnote must accompany the first use of each Institute registered trademark or trademark and must state that the referenced trademark is used to identify products or services of SAS Institute Inc.

The Institute is a private company devoted to the support and further development of its software and related services.

SAS Institute does not assume responsibility for the accuracy of any material presented in this book.

Doc S19N, Ver 1.01, 07FEB91

Contents

Reference Aids   vii

Acknowledgments   ix

About the Authors   xi

Using This Book   xiii

Chapter 1 · Regression   1

1.1 Statistical Background   1

1.2 Regression with the SAS System   7

1.3 Using the REG Procedure   9

1.4 Polynomial Models   31

1.5 Weighted Regression   37

1.6 Creating Data Sets   39

1.7 Exact Collinearity: Linear Dependency   48

1.8 Diagnostic Measures   49

Chapter 2 · Analysis of Variance for Balanced Data   51

2.1 Introduction   52

2.2 One- and Two-Sample Tests and Statistics   52

2.3 Comparison of Several Means: Analysis of Variance   59

Chapter 3 · Analyzing Data with Random Effects   105

3.1 Introduction   105

3.2 Nested Classifications   106

3.3 Two-Way Mixed Model   115

3.4 A Classification with Both Crossed and Nested Effects   120

3.5 Split-Plot Experiments   130

Chapter 4 · Details of the Linear Model: Understanding GLM Concepts   137

4.1 Introduction   137

4.2 The Dummy-Variable Model   138

4.3 Two-Way Classification: Unbalanced Data   153

4.4 Proper Error Terms   191

Chapter 5 · Examples of Special Applications 199

5.1 Introduction 199

5.2 Confounding in a Factorial Experiment 199

5.3 A Balanced Incomplete Blocks Design 203

5.4 A Crossover Design to Estimate Residual Effects 205

5.5 Experiments with Qualitative and Quantitative Variables 209

5.6 Lack-of-Fit Analysis 214

5.7 Unbalanced Nested Structure 216

5.8 Absorbing Nesting Effects 220

Chapter 6 · Covariance and the Heterogeneity of Slopes 229

6.1 Introduction 229

6.2 A One-Way Structure 230

6.3 Two-Way Structure without Interaction 235

6.4 Two-Way Structure with Interaction 238

6.5 Heterogeneity of Slopes 243

Chapter 7 · Multivariate Linear Models 247

7.1 Introduction 247

7.2 Statistical Background 248

7.3 A One-Way Multivariate Analysis of Variance 249

7.4 Hotelling's T^2 Test 252

7.5 A Two-Factor Factorial 255

7.6 Multivariate Analysis of Covariance 260

7.7 Contrasts in Multivariate Analyses 263

Chapter 8 · Repeated-Measures Analysis of Variance 265

8.1 Introduction 265

8.2 Multivariate Repeated-Measures Analysis Using the MANOVA Statement 266

8.3 Multivariate Repeated-Measures Analysis Using the REPEATED Statement 269

8.4 Univariate Repeated-Measures Analysis As a Split-Plot Design 272

8.5 Univariate Repeated-Measures Analysis Using the REPEATED Statement 274

8.6 Contrasts among Dependent Variables: SUMMARY Option 278

8.7 Two Repeated-Measures Factors: Multivariate and Univariate Analysis 282

Appendix · Example Code 293

Chapter 1 293

Chapter 2 296

Chapter 3   301

Chapter 4   304

Chapter 5   307

Chapter 6   311

Chapter 7   314

Chapter 8   317

References   321

Index   323

vi

Reference Aids

Tables

3.1   Coefficients of Expected Mean Squares   110

3.2   Q(*effect*) in Expected Mean Squares   124

3.3   Summary of *F* Test Results from CONTRAST Statements   128

3.4   Results of Analysis of Variance for Split-Plot Experiment   133

4.1   Interpretation of Sums of Squares in μ-Model Notation   160

4.2   General Form of Estimable Functions   170

4.3   Estimable Functions for Factor A   171

4.4   Estimable Functions for Factor B   174

4.5   Estimable Functions for A*B   175

4.6   General Form of Estimable Functions   179

4.7   Estimable Functions for Factor A   179

4.8   Estimable Functions for Factor B   180

4.9   Sums of Squares and Estimates for B Effect   184

4.10 Estimable Functions for A*B   184

4.11 Coefficients Produced by the ESTIMATE Statement   188

4.12 Summary of Results from CONTRAST, ESTIMATE, and LSMEANS Output for Two-Way Layout with Empty Cell and No Interaction   190

5.1   Type I Estimable Functions for Treatments   204

5.2   Means and Least-Squares Means   220

Acknowledgments

We would like to acknowledge several persons at SAS Institute whose efforts have contributed to the completion of this book. First of all, we are grateful to Jim Goodnight who originally encouraged us to write the book. Several persons reviewed the chapters and contributed many useful comments. The reviewers were Jim Ashton, Donna Fulenwider, and Jenny Kendall.

The work of several persons has influenced our writing. In particular, we acknowledge Professors Walt Harvey of Ohio State University, Ron Hocking of Texas A&M University, George Milliken and Dallas Johnson of Kansas State University, Bill Sanders of the University of Tennessee, Shayle Searle of Cornell University, and David Weeks of Oklahoma State University.

x

About the Authors

Ramon C. Littell, Ph.D.

Dr. Ramon C. Littell has the rank of professor of statistics at the University of Florida in Gainesville. He received his graduate training at Oklahoma State University earning an M.S. degree in mathematics in 1966 and a Ph.D. degree in statistics in 1970. Dr. Littell teaches graduate courses in linear models, a course in matrix algebra for statisticians, and courses in statistical methods.

Rudolf J. Freund, Ph.D.

Rudolf J. Freund is a professor of statistics in the Department of Statistics at Texas A&M University, where he served as associate director and cofounder of the Institute of Statistics from 1962 to 1977. He received an M.A. degree in economics from the University of Chicago in 1951 and a Ph.D. in statistics at North Carolina State University in 1955. He was associate professor of statistics at Virginia Polytechnic Institute from 1955 until 1962 and was also the first director of the computing center for that university.

Dr. Freund is coauthor (with Paul D. Minton) of *Regression Methods* and *SAS System for Regression, Second Edition* (with Ramon Littell), and is currently writing (with William J. Wilson) a textbook on statistical methods for publication in 1991. He has also written a course supplement, *Learning Statistics with the SAS System*.

Currently, Freund teaches basic statistical methods and regression analysis courses for graduate students.

Freund and Littell, both SAS users since 1972 and former SUGI chairmen, were closely associated with the Southern Regional Project that funded continued SAS development at North Carolina State University. In addition to their university positions, both authors publish widely in statistical and applied journals, consult in industry, and serve as Consulting Statisticians to their state Agricultural Experiment Stations. They are both fellows of the American Statistical Association.

Philip C. Spector, Ph.D.

Dr. Philip C. Spector is Applications Manager of the Statistical Computing Facility in the Department of Statistics at the University of California at Berkeley. He received a B.A. in chemistry from the University of Rochester and an M.S. and a Ph.D. in statistics from Texas A & M University and was formerly a Senior Research Statistician at SAS Institute Inc.

Using This Book

Purpose

Most statistical analyses are based on linear models, and most analyses of linear models can be performed by three SAS procedures: REG, ANOVA, and GLM. Unlike statistical packages that need different programs for each type of analysis, these procedures provide the power and flexibility for almost all linear model analyses.

To use these procedures properly, you should understand the statistics you need for the analysis and know how to instruct the procedures to carry out the computations. *SAS System for Linear Models, Third Edition* is written to make it easier for you to apply these procedures to your data analysis problems. In this book, a wide variety of data is used to illustrate the basic kinds of linear models that can be analyzed with these SAS procedures.

Audience

SAS System for Linear Models is intended to assist data analysts who use SAS/STAT software to analyze data using regression analysis and analysis of variance. This book assumes you are familiar with basic SAS System concepts such as creating SAS data sets with the DATA step and manipulating SAS data sets with the procedures in base SAS software.

Prerequisites

The following table summarizes the SAS System concepts that you need to understand in order to use SAS/STAT software.

You need to know how to	Refer to
invoke the SAS System at your site	instructions provided by the SAS Software Consultant at your site
use base SAS software	*SAS Language and Procedures: Introduction, Version 6, First Edition* for a brief introduction, or *SAS Language and Procedures: Usage, Version 6, First Edition* for a more thorough introduction
create and read SAS data sets	*SAS Language: Reference, Version 6, First Edition*
use SAS/STAT software	*SAS/STAT User's Guide, Version 6, Fourth Edition, Volume 1* and *Volume 2*

How to Use This Book

The following sections provide an overview of the information contained in this book and how it is organized.

Organization

SAS System for Linear Models represents an introduction to analyzing linear models with the SAS System. In addition to the most current programming conventions for both Version 5 and Version 6 of the SAS System, this volume contains information about new features and capabilities of several SAS procedures. Here is a summary of the information contained in each chapter:

Chapter 1, "Regression"
covers the statistical background for linear models. It reviews a wide range of topics, including simple and multiple linear regression, polynomial models, weighted least squares regression, output data sets, and multicollinearity.

Chapter 2, "Analysis of Variance for Balanced Data"
discusses topics related to balanced designs. Topics covered include one-sample and two-sample *t*-tests, one-way analysis of variance, contrasts, estimation of linear combinations of means, randomized block designs, two-way factorials, and multiple comparison procedures.

Chapter 3, "Analyzing Data with Random Effects"
discusses random effects models. Topics discussed include nested designs, two-way mixed models, split-plot designs, models with both crossed and nested factors, and expected mean squares.

Chapter 4, "Details of the Linear Model: Understanding GLM Concepts"
provides a detailed discussion of how the GLM procedure works. Topics covered include dummy-variable models, estimable functions, parameterization, Type I, II, III, and IV sums of squares, μ-models and their corresponding overparameterized models, least-squares means, contrasts, empty cells, and proper error terms for mixed models.

Chapter 5, "Examples of Special Applications"
provides several complete analyses of experimental data. Topics presented include confounding in a factorial experiment, balanced incomplete block designs, cross-over designs, experiments with qualitative and quantitative data, and unbalanced nested designs.

Chapter 6, "Covariance and Heterogeneity of Slopes"
covers analysis of covariance. Topics discussed include one-way analysis of covariance, two-way analysis of covariance models with no interaction, two-way analysis of covariance models with interaction, and tests for equality of slopes.

Chapter 7, "Multivariate Linear Models"
covers analysis of data where the response is a vector of dependent variables. Topics covered include one-way multivariate analysis of variance, Hotelling's T^2 test, two-way factorials, multivariate analysis of covariance, and contrasts in multivariate analyses.

Chapter 8, "Repeated-Measures Analysis of Variance"
  covers the analysis of repeated-measures data. Topics presented include multivariate approaches to analyzing data with repeated measures, univariate approaches to analyzing repeated-measures data, contrasts, and two-factors repeated designs.

Appendix, "Example Code"
  provides a summary of SAS code used in the examples.

Conventions

This section covers the conventions this book uses, including typographical conventions and syntax conventions.

Typographical Conventions

This book uses several type styles. The following list summarizes style conventions:

roman	is the basic type style used for most text.
UPPERCASE ROMAN	is used for references in text to SAS language elements.
italic	is used in margin notes to provide cautionary information, in text to define terms, and in formulas.
bold	is used in headings, in text to indicate very important points, and in formulas to indicate matrices and vectors.
bold italic	is used in headings to refer to syntax elements that you supply.
`monospace`	is used to show examples of programming code. In most cases, this book uses lowercase type for SAS code. You can enter your own SAS code in lowercase, uppercase, or a mixture of the two. The SAS System changes your variable names to uppercase, but character variable values remain in lowercase if you have entered them that way. Enter the case for titles, notes, and footnotes exactly as you want them to appear in your output.

Syntax Conventions

Syntax conventions are used to show the basic format of a SAS statement. This book uses the following conventions for syntax:

UPPERCASE BOLD   indicates the names of functions and statements. These must be spelled as shown.

UPPERCASE ROMAN   indicates elements that must be spelled as shown.

italic   indicates elements (such as variable names) that you supply. In some cases, the procedure accepts a limited set of values, such as values between 0 and 1 for an option that provides probability values. In other cases, the procedure accepts any value you supply, such as the name of a data set.

| (vertical bar)   indicates a choice of one of the items from a group. Items separated by bars are either mutually exclusive or aliases.

. . . (ellipsis)   indicates items that can be repeated indefinitely.

The following example illustrates these points:

TEST *'label' equation* <, . . . ,*equation*>;

TEST is in bold uppercase because it is a SAS statement, while *label* and *equation* are in italic because you supply the values. In this TEST statement, a *label* and at least one *equation* are required. Additional *equation* specifications are optional. Commas must appear between each *equation*.

Conventions for Output

All SAS code in the book was run through Release 6.06 of the SAS System under the MVS operating system.

Additional Documentation

The *Publications Catalog*, published twice a year, gives detailed information on the many publications available from SAS Institute. To obtain a free catalog, please send your request to the following address:

SAS Institute Inc.
Book Sales Department
SAS Campus Drive
Cary, NC 27513

SAS Series in Statistical Applications

SAS System for Linear Models is one in a series of statistical applications guides developed by SAS Institute. Each book in the SAS series in statistical applications covers a well-defined statistical topic by describing and illustrating relevant SAS procedures.

Other books currently available include

☐ *SAS System for Regression, Second Edition* (order #A56141) describes SAS procedures for performing regression analyses. Simple regression (a single independent variable) and multiple variable models are discussed as well as polynomial models, log-linear models, nonlinear models, spline functions, and restricted linear models. Features of the AUTOREG, GPLOT, NLIN, PLOT, PRINCOMP, REG, and RSREG procedures are covered.

☐ *SAS System for Forecasting Time Series, 1986 Edition* (order #A5629) describes how SAS/ETS software can be used to perform univariate and multivariate time-series analyses. Early chapters introduce linear regression and autoregression using simple models. Later chapters discuss the ARIMA model and its special applications, state space modeling, spectral analysis, and cross-spectral analysis. The SAS procedures ARIMA, STATESPACE, and SPECTRA are featured, with mention of the simpler procedures FORECAST, AUTOREG, and X11.

☐ *SAS System for Elementary Statistical Analysis* (order #A5619) teaches you how to perform a variety of data analysis tasks and interpret your results. Written in tutorial style, the guide provides the essential information you need, without overwhelming you with extraneous details. This approach makes the book a ready guide for the business user and an excellent tool for teaching fundamental statistical concepts. Topics include comparing two or more groups, simple regression and basic diagnostics, as well as basic DATA steps.

This series is designed to aid data analysts who use the SAS System and students in statistics courses who want to see more practical applications of the methods discussed in textbooks, lectures, and primary SAS statistical documentation. These manuals are intended to supplement the references you are using now; they will not take the place of a good statistics book and should be used with appropriate SAS user's guides.

Documentation for Other
SAS Software

You will find these other books helpful when using SAS/STAT software.

☐ *SAS Language and Procedures: Introduction, Version 6, First Edition* (order #56074) provides information if you are unfamiliar with the SAS System or any other programming language.

☐ *SAS Language and Procedures: Usage, Version 6, First Edition* (order #A56075) provides task-oriented examples of the major features of base SAS software.

☐ *SAS Language: Reference, Version 6, First Edition* (order #A56076) provides detailed reference information about SAS language statements, functions, formats, and informats; the SAS Display Manager System; the SAS Text Editor; or any other element of base SAS software except for procedures.

☐ The *SAS/STAT User's Guide, Version 6, Fourth Edition, Volume 1* and *Volume 2* (order #A56045) provides reference and usage material for SAS/STAT software.

Chapter **1** Regression

1.1 *Statistical Background 1*
    1.1.1 Terminology and Notation 2
    1.1.2 Partitioning the Sums of Squares 3
    1.1.3 Hypothesis Testing 4
    1.1.4 Using the Generalized Inverse 6

1.2 *Regression with the SAS System 7*

1.3 *Using the REG Procedure 9*
    1.3.1 A Model with One Independent Variable 10
    1.3.2 A Model with Several Independent Variables 15
    *1.3.3 The P, CLM, and CLI Options: Predicted Values and
        Confidence Limits 17*
    *1.3.4 The SS1 and SS2 Options: Two Types of Sums of
        Squares 20*
    *1.3.5 Tests of Subsets and Linear Combinations of
        Coefficients 22*
    *1.3.6 Fitting Restricted Models: RESTRICT Statement and
        NOINT Option 25*
    1.3.7 Miscellaneous Option Specifications 27
    1.3.8 Multiple Models 30

1.4 *Polynomial Models 31*

1.5 *Weighted Regression 37*

1.6 *Creating Data Sets 39*
    1.6.1 Plotting Residuals 40
    1.6.2 Plotting Regression Curves 41
    1.6.3 Plotting Other Statistics 43
    1.6.4 Predicting to a Different Set of Data 44
    1.6.5 Plotting with Transformed Variables 47

1.7 *Exact Collinearity: Linear Dependency 48*

1.8 *Diagnostic Measures 49*

1.1 Statistical Background

The REG and GLM procedures implement a multiple linear regression analysis
according to the model

$$y = \beta_0 + \beta_1 x_1 + \beta_2 x_2 + \ldots + \beta_m x_m + \varepsilon$$

which relates the behavior of a dependent variable y to a linear function of the set
of independent variables $x_1, x_2, \ldots, x_m$. The β_j's are the parameters that specify
the nature of the relationship, and ε is the random error term. Although it is
assumed that you have a basic understanding of regression analysis, it may be
helpful to review regression principles, terminology, notation, and procedures. If

you don't need the review, you can read ahead to Section 1.3.1, "A Model with One Independent Variable," for an illustration of using PROC REG.

1.1.1 Terminology and Notation

The principle of least squares is applied to a set of n observed values of y and the associated x_j to obtain estimates $\hat{\beta}_0, \hat{\beta}_1, \ldots, \hat{\beta}_m$ of the respective parameters $\beta_0, \beta_1, \ldots, \beta_m$. These estimates are then used to construct the fitted model

$$\hat{y} = \hat{\beta}_0 + \hat{\beta}_1 x_1 + \ldots + \hat{\beta}_m x_m \quad .$$

Many regression computations are illustrated conveniently in matrix notation. Letting y_i, x_{ij}, and ε_i denote the values of y, x_j, and ε, respectively, in the ith observation, the **Y** vector, the **X** matrix, and the ε vector can be defined as

$$\mathbf{Y} = \begin{bmatrix} y_1 \\ \cdot \\ \cdot \\ \cdot \\ y_n \end{bmatrix} \quad \mathbf{X} = \begin{bmatrix} 1 & x_{11} & \ldots & x_{1m} \\ \cdot & \cdot & & \cdot \\ \cdot & \cdot & & \cdot \\ \cdot & \cdot & & \cdot \\ 1 & x_{n1} & \ldots & x_{nm} \end{bmatrix} \quad \varepsilon = \begin{bmatrix} \varepsilon_1 \\ \cdot \\ \cdot \\ \cdot \\ \varepsilon_n \end{bmatrix} \quad .$$

Then the model in matrix notation is

$$\mathbf{Y} = \mathbf{X}\boldsymbol{\beta} + \boldsymbol{\varepsilon}$$

where $\boldsymbol{\beta}' = (\beta_0, \beta_1, \ldots, \beta_m)$ is the parameter vector.

The vector of least-squares estimates, $\hat{\boldsymbol{\beta}}' = (\hat{\beta}_0, \hat{\beta}_1, \ldots, \hat{\beta}_m)$, is obtained by solving the set of normal equations

$$\mathbf{X'X}\hat{\boldsymbol{\beta}} = \mathbf{X'Y} \quad .$$

Assuming that **X'X** has full rank, there is a unique solution to the normal equations given by

$$\hat{\boldsymbol{\beta}} = (\mathbf{X'X})^{-1}\mathbf{X'Y} \quad .$$

The matrix $(\mathbf{X'X})^{-1}$ is useful in regression analysis and is often denoted by

$$(\mathbf{X'X})^{-1} = \mathbf{C} = \begin{bmatrix} c_{00} & c_{01} & \ldots & c_{0m} \\ c_{10} & c_{11} & \ldots & c_{1m} \\ \cdot & \cdot & & \cdot \\ \cdot & \cdot & & \cdot \\ \cdot & \cdot & & \cdot \\ c_{m0} & c_{m1} & \ldots & c_{mm} \end{bmatrix} \quad .$$

The **C** matrix provides the variances and covariances of the regression parameter estimates $V(\hat{\beta})=\sigma^2\mathbf{C}$, where $\sigma^2=V(\varepsilon_i)$.

1.1.2 Partitioning the Sums of Squares

A basic identity results from least squares, specifically,

$$\Sigma\,(y-\bar{y})^2 = \Sigma\,(\hat{y}-\bar{y})^2 + \Sigma\,(y-\hat{y})^2 \quad .$$

This identity shows that the total sum of squared deviations from the mean, $\Sigma(y-\bar{y})^2$, can be partitioned into two parts: the sum of squared deviations from the regression line to the overall mean, $\Sigma(\hat{y}-\bar{y})^2$, and the sum of squared deviations from the observed y values to the regression line, $\Sigma(y-\hat{y})^2$. These two parts are called the sum of squares due to *regression* (or *model*) and the *residual* (or *error*) sum of squares. Thus,

TOTAL SS = MODEL SS + ERROR SS .

TOTAL SS always has the same value for a given set of data, regardless of the model that is fitted; however, partitioning into MODEL SS and ERROR SS depends on the model. Generally, the addition of a new x variable to a model will increase MODEL SS and, correspondingly, reduce the RESIDUAL SS. The residual or error sum of squares is computed as follows:

$$\begin{aligned} \text{ERROR SS} &= \mathbf{Y'(I - X(X'X)^{-1}X')Y} \\ &= \mathbf{Y'Y - Y'X(X'X)^{-1}X'Y} \\ &= \mathbf{Y'Y - \hat{\beta}'X'Y} \quad . \end{aligned}$$

The error mean square

$$s^2 = \text{MSE} = \text{ERROR SS}\,/\,(n-m-1)$$

is an unbiased estimate of σ^2, the variance of ε_i.

PROC REG and PROC GLM compute several sums of squares. Each sum of squares can be expressed as the difference between the regression sums of squares for two models, which are called *complete* and *reduced* models. This approach relates a given sum of squares to the comparison of two regression models.

Denote by MODEL SS$_1$ the MODEL SS for a regression with $m=5$ x variables:

$$y = \beta_0 + \beta_1 x_1 + \beta_2 x_2 + \beta_3 x_3 + \beta_4 x_4 + \beta_5 x_5 + \varepsilon$$

and by MODEL SS$_2$ the MODEL SS for a reduced model not containing x_4 and x_5:

$$y = \beta_0 + \beta_1 x_1 + \beta_2 x_2 + \beta_3 x_3 + \varepsilon \quad .$$

Reduction notation can be used to represent the difference between regression sums of squares for the two models. For example,

$$R(\beta_4,\,\beta_5 \mid \beta_0,\,\beta_1,\,\beta_2,\,\beta_3) = \text{MODEL SS}_1 - \text{MODEL SS}_2 \quad .$$

The difference, or reduction in error, $R(\beta_4, \beta_5 \mid \beta_0, \beta_1, \beta_2, \beta_3)$ indicates the increase in regression sums of squares due to the addition of β_4 and β_5 to the reduced model. It follows that

$$R(\beta_4, \beta_5 \mid \beta_0, \beta_1, \beta_2, \beta_3) = \text{MODEL SS}_1 - \text{MODEL SS}_2 \quad .$$

Since TOTAL SS = MODEL SS + ERROR SS, it follows that

$$R(\beta_4, \beta_5 \mid \beta_0, \beta_1, \beta_2, \beta_3) = \text{ERROR SS}_2 - \text{ERROR SS}_1 \quad .$$

The expression $R(\beta_4, \beta_5 \mid \beta_0, \beta_1, \beta_2, \beta_3)$ is also commonly referred to as

□ the sum of squares due to β_4 and β_5 (or x_4 and x_5) adjusted for $\beta_0, \beta_1, \beta_2, \beta_3$ (or the intercept and x_1, x_2, x_3)

□ the sum of squares due to fitting x_4 and x_5 after fitting the intercept and x_1, x_2, x_3

□ the effects of x_4 and x_5 above and beyond, or partial of, the effects of the intercept and x_1, x_2, x_3.

1.1.3 Hypothesis Testing

Inferences about model parameters are highly dependent on the other parameters in the model under consideration. Therefore, in hypothesis testing it is important to emphasize the parameters for which inferences have been adjusted. For example, tests based on $R(\beta_3 \mid \beta_0, \beta_1, \beta_2)$ and $R(\beta_3 \mid \beta_0, \beta_1)$ may measure entirely different concepts. Consequently, a test of $H_0: \beta_3 = 0$ versus $H_0: \beta_3 \neq 0$ may have one result for the model $y = \beta_0 + \beta_1 x_1 + \beta_2 x_2 + \beta_3 x_3 + \varepsilon$ and another result for the model $y = \beta_0 + \beta_1 x_1 + \beta_3 x_3 + \varepsilon$. Differences reflect actual physical dependencies among parameters in the model rather than inconsistencies in statistical methodology.

Statistical inferences can also be made in terms of linear functions of the parameters in the form

$$H_0: \ell_0 \beta_0 + \ell_1 \beta_1 + \ldots + \ell_m \beta_m = 0 \quad .$$

where the ℓ_i are constants chosen to correspond to a specified hypothesis. Such functions are estimated by the corresponding linear function

$$\mathbf{L}\hat{\boldsymbol{\beta}} = \ell_0 \hat{\beta}_0 + \ell_1 \hat{\beta}_1 + \ldots + \ell_m \hat{\beta}_m$$

of the least-squares estimates $\hat{\boldsymbol{\beta}}$. The variance of $\mathbf{L}\hat{\boldsymbol{\beta}}$ is

$$V(\mathbf{L}\hat{\boldsymbol{\beta}}) = (\mathbf{L}(\mathbf{X'X})^{-1}\mathbf{L'})\sigma^2 \quad .$$

A t test or F test is then used to test $H_0: (\mathbf{L}\boldsymbol{\beta}) = 0$. The denominator usually uses the error mean square MSE as the estimate of σ^2. Because the variance of the estimated function is based on statistics computed for the entire model, the test of the hypothesis is made in the presence of all model parameters. These tests can be generalized to simultaneous tests of several linear functions. Confidence intervals can be constructed to correspond to the tests.

Three common types of statistical inference are

□   a test that all parameters $(\beta_1, \beta_2, \ldots, \beta_m)$ are 0.
This test compares the fit of the complete model to the model containing only the mean, using the statistic

$$F = (\text{MODEL SS} / m) / \text{MSE}$$

where

$$\text{MODEL SS} = R(\beta_1, \beta_2, \ldots, \beta_m \mid \beta_0) \quad .^*$$

The F statistic has $(m, n-m-1)$ degrees of freedom (DF).

□   a test that the parameters in a subset are 0.
This test compares the fit of the complete model

$$y = \beta_0 + \beta_1 x_1 + \ldots + \beta_g x_g + \beta_{g+1} x_{g+1} + \ldots + \beta_m x_m + \varepsilon$$

with the fit of the reduced model

$$y = \beta_0 + \beta_1 x_1 + \ldots + \beta_g x_g + \varepsilon \quad .$$

An F statistic is used to perform the test:

$$F = (R(\beta_{g+1}, \ldots, \beta_m \mid \beta_0, \beta_1, \ldots, \beta_g) / (m - g)) / \text{MSE} \quad .$$

Note that reordering the variables produces a test for any desired subset of parameters. If the subset contains only one parameter, β_m, the test is

$$\begin{aligned} F &= (R(\beta_m \mid \beta_0, \beta_1, \ldots, \beta_{m-1}) / 1) / \text{MSE} \\ &= (\text{partial SS due to } \beta_m) / \text{MSE} \end{aligned}$$

which is equivalent to the t test

$$t = \hat{\beta}_m / \sqrt{c_{mm}\text{MSE}} \quad .$$

The corresponding $(1-\alpha)$ confidence interval about β_m is

$$\hat{\beta}_m \pm t_{\alpha/2} \sqrt{c_{mm}\text{MSE}} \quad .$$

□   an estimate of a subpopulation mean corresponding to a specific **x**. For a given set of x values described by a vector **x**, the subpopulation mean is

$$E(y_\mathbf{x}) = \beta_0 + \beta_1 x_1 + \ldots + \beta_m x_m = \mathbf{x}'\boldsymbol{\beta} \quad .$$

---

* $R(\beta_0, \beta_1, \ldots, \beta_m)$ is rarely used. For more information, see Section 1.3.6, "Fitting Restricted Models: RESTRICT Statement and NOINT Option."

The estimate of $E(y_\mathbf{x})$ is

$$\hat{y}_\mathbf{x} = \hat{\beta}_0 + \hat{\beta}_1 x_1 + \ldots + \hat{\beta}_m x_m = \mathbf{x}'\hat{\boldsymbol{\beta}} \quad .$$

The vector $\mathbf{x}$ is constant; hence, the variance of $\hat{y}_\mathbf{x}$ is

$$V(\hat{y}_x) = \mathbf{x}'(\mathbf{X}'\mathbf{X})^{-1}\mathbf{x}\sigma^2 \quad . \tag{1.1}$$

This is useful for computing the confidence intervals.

A related inference is to predict a future single value of y corresponding to a specified $\mathbf{x}$. The predicted value is $\hat{y}$, the same as the estimate of the subpopulation mean corresponding to $\mathbf{x}$. But the relevant variance is

$$V(y - \hat{y}_x) = (1 + \mathbf{x}'(\mathbf{X}'\mathbf{X})^{-1}\mathbf{x})\sigma^2 \quad .$$

1.1.4 Using the Generalized Inverse

Many applications, especially those involving PROC GLM, involve an $\mathbf{X}'\mathbf{X}$ matrix that is not of full rank and, therefore, has no unique inverse. For such situations, both PROC GLM and PROC REG compute a generalized inverse, $(\mathbf{X}'\mathbf{X})^-$, and use it to compute a regression estimate, $\mathbf{b} = (\mathbf{X}'\mathbf{X})^-\mathbf{X}'\mathbf{Y}$.

A generalized inverse of a matrix $\mathbf{A}$ is any matrix $\mathbf{G}$ such that $\mathbf{AGA} = \mathbf{A}$. Note that this also identifies the inverse of a full-rank matrix.

If $\mathbf{X}'\mathbf{X}$ is not of full rank, then there is an infinite number of generalized inverses. Different generalized inverses lead to different solutions to the normal equations that will have different expected values. That is, $E(\mathbf{b}) = (\mathbf{X}'\mathbf{X})^-\mathbf{X}'\mathbf{X}\boldsymbol{\beta}$ depends on the particular generalized inverse used to obtain $\mathbf{b}$. Thus, it is important to understand what is being estimated by a particular solution.

Fortunately, not all computations in regression analysis depend on the particular solution obtained. For example, the error sum of squares has the same value for all choices of $(\mathbf{X}'\mathbf{X})^-$ and is given by

$$\text{SSE} = \mathbf{Y}'(\mathbf{I} - \mathbf{X}(\mathbf{X}'\mathbf{X})^-\mathbf{X}')\mathbf{Y} \quad .$$

Hence, the model sum of squares also does not depend on the particular generalized inverse obtained.

The generalized inverse has played a major role in the presentation of the theory of linear statistical models, such as in the books of Graybill (1976) and Searle (1971). In a theoretical setting, it is often possible, and even desirable, to avoid specifying a particular generalized inverse. To apply the generalized inverse to statistical data with computer programs, however, a generalized inverse must actually be calculated. Therefore, it is necessary to declare the specific generalized inverse being computed. Consider, for example, an $\mathbf{X}'\mathbf{X}$ matrix of rank k that can be partitioned as

$$\mathbf{X}'\mathbf{X} = \begin{bmatrix} \mathbf{A}_{11} & \mathbf{A}_{12} \\ \mathbf{A}_{21} & \mathbf{A}_{22} \end{bmatrix}$$

where $\mathbf{A}_{11}$ is $k \times k$ and of rank k. Then $\mathbf{A}_{11}^{-1}$ exists, and a generalized inverse of $\mathbf{X'X}$ is

$$(\mathbf{X'X})^- = \begin{bmatrix} \mathbf{A}_{11}^{-1} & \mathbf{\Phi}_{12} \\ \mathbf{\Phi}_{21} & \mathbf{\Phi}_{22} \end{bmatrix}$$

where each $\mathbf{\Phi}_{ij}$ is a matrix of zeros of the same dimensions as $\mathbf{A}_{ij}$.

This approach for obtaining a generalized inverse can be extended indefinitely by partitioning a singular matrix into several sets of matrices, as shown above. Note that the resulting solution to the normal equations, $\mathbf{b} = (\mathbf{X'X})^- \mathbf{X'Y}$, has zeros in the positions corresponding to the rows filled with zeros in $(\mathbf{X'X})^-$. This is the solution printed by PROC GLM and PROC REG and is regarded as a biased estimate of β.

Because $\mathbf{b}$ is not unique, a linear function, $\mathbf{Lb}$, and its variance are generally not unique either. However, there is a class of linear functions called *estimable functions*, and they have the following properties:

□ **Lb** and its variance are invariant through all possible generalized inverses. In other words, **Lb** and V(**Lb**) are unique.

□ **Lb** is an unbiased estimate of $\mathbf{L\beta}$.

□ The vector **L** is a linear combination of rows of **X**.

Analogous to the full-rank case, the variance of **Lb** is given by

$$V(\mathbf{Lb}) = (\mathbf{L(X'X)}^- \mathbf{L'})\sigma^2 \quad .$$

This expression is used for statistical inference. For example, a test of H_0: $\mathbf{L\beta} = 0$ is given by the t test

$$t = \mathbf{Lb} / \sqrt{(\mathbf{L(X'X)}^- \mathbf{L'})\mathrm{MSE}} \quad .$$

1.2 Regression with the SAS System

This section reviews SAS/STAT software procedures that are used for regression analysis:

CALIS	ORTHOREG
CATMOD	PROBIT
GLM	REG
LIFEREG	RSREG
LOGISTIC	TRANSREG
NLIN	

PROC REG provides the most general analysis capabilities; the other procedures give more specialized analyses. This section also briefly mentions several procedures in SAS/ETS software.

Many SAS/STAT procedures, each with special features, perform regression analysis. The following procedures perform at least one type of regression analysis:

CALIS
: fits systems of linear structural equations with latent variables and path analysis.

CATMOD
: analyzes data that can be represented by a contingency table. PROC CATMOD fits linear models to functions of response frequencies and can be used for log-linear models and logistic regression.

GLM
: uses the method of least squares to fit general linear models. In addition to many other analyses, PROC GLM can perform simple, multiple, polynomial, and weighted regression. PROC GLM has many of the same input/output capabilities as PROC REG but does not provide as many diagnostic tools or allow interactive changes in the model or data.

LIFEREG
: fits parametric models to failure-time data that may be right-, left-, or interval-censored. These types of models are commonly used in survival analysis.

LOGISTIC
: fits logistic regression models. PROC LOGISTIC can perform stepwise regressions as well as compute regression diagnostics.

NLIN
: builds nonlinear regression models. Several different iterative methods are available.

ORTHOREG
: performs regression using the Gentleman-Givens computational method. For ill-conditioned data, PROC ORTHOREG can produce more accurate parameter estimates than other procedures such as PROC GLM and PROC REG.

PROBIT
: performs probit regression as well as logistic regression and ordinal logistic regression. The PROBIT procedure is useful when the dependent variable is either dichotomous or polychotomous and the independent variables are continuous.

REG
: performs linear regression with many diagnostic capabilities, selects models using one of nine selection methods, produces scatter plots of raw data and statistics, highlights scatter plots to identify particular observations, and allows interactive changes in both the regression model and the data used to fit the model.

The REG procedure provides options for special estimates, outlier and specification error detection (row diagnostics), collinearity statistics (column diagnostics), and tests of linear functions of parameter estimates. It can perform restricted least-squares estimation and multivariate tests. It can also produce SAS data sets containing the parameter estimates and most of the statistics produced by the procedure.

RSREG   builds quadratic response-surface regression models. PROC
                 RSREG analyzes the fitted response surface to determine the
                 factor levels of optimum response and performs a ridge analysis
                 to search for the region of optimum response.

TRANSREG   obtains optimal linear and nonlinear transformations of
                 variables using alternating least squares. PROC TRANSREG
                 creates an output data set containing the transformed variables.

Several SAS/ETS procedures also perform regression. The procedures listed
below are documented in the *SAS/ETS User's Guide, Version 6, First Edition*:

AUTOREG   implements regression models using time series data where the
                 errors are autocorrelated.

MODEL   handles nonlinear simultaneous systems of equations, such as
                 econometric models.

PDLREG   performs regression analysis with polynomial distributed lags.

SYSLIN   handles linear simultaneous systems of equations, such as
                 econometric models.

Finally, if a regression method cannot be performed by any of the SAS
procedures mentioned here, you can use SAS/IML software, which provides an
interactive matrix language. Some SAS System users may also find PROC IML an
excellent instructional tool. For more information, see *SAS/IML Software: Usage
and Reference, Version 6, First Edition*.

1.3 Using the REG Procedure

The basic use of PROC REG is to obtain an analysis of data based on a linear
regression model, as specified in Section 1.1, "Statistical Background." The
following SAS statements invoke PROC REG:

```
proc reg;
   model list-of-dependent-variables=list-of-independent-variables;
```

PROC REG can perform a regression of a single dependent variable Y on a
single independent variable X using the following SAS statements:

```
proc reg;
   model y=x;
```

The results of a simple linear regression of this type are shown in Output 1.2.

Many options are available in PROC REG. Some of these are specified
following a slash (/) at the end of the MODEL statement (see Section 1.3.3, "The
P, CLM, and CLI Options: Predicted Values and Confidence Limits," for examples).
Other options are specified as separate SAS statements (see Section 1.3.5, "Tests
of Subsets and Linear Combinations of Coefficients" and Section 1.3.6 for
examples).

1.3.1 A Model with One Independent Variable

This section illustrates a model with one independent variable. Consider an experiment designed to assess the production of methane gas resulting from decomposition of an organic material. Fifteen samples of the material are prepared and stored for different lengths of time. Three samples are stored for one day, three samples are stored for two days, three for three days, three for four days, and three for five days. At the conclusion of the storage times, the amounts of methane gas produced are measured for all the samples. Samples stored for the longer periods of time are expected to produce more gas than those stored for shorter periods of time. There are two primary objectives in the experiment:

□ to estimate the rate of gas production (GAS), that is, how much gas is produced per day of storage time (STORTIME)

□ to estimate the average amount of gas that would be produced for any specified storage time between 1 and 5 days.

The data are in a SAS data set named METHANE with variables STORTIME and GAS. The data set appears in Output 1.1.

Output 1.1
Data Set
METHANE

```
                        The SAS System                          1

                  OBS    STORTIME     GAS

                   1         1        8.2
                   2         1        6.6
                   3         1        9.8
                   4         2       19.7
                   5         2       15.7
                   6         2       16.0
                   7         3       28.6
                   8         3       25.0
                   9         3       31.9
                  10         4       30.8
                  11         4       37.8
                  12         4       40.2
                  13         5       40.3
                  14         5       42.9
                  15         5       32.6
```

A simple linear regression model is used in the initial attempt to analyze the data. The equation for the simple linear regression model is

$$GAS = \beta_0 + \beta_1(STORTIME) + \varepsilon \quad . \tag{1.2}$$

This model uses a straight line with slope β_1 and intercept β_0 to represent the relationship between mean GAS production and STORTIME over the range from STORTIME=1 to STORTIME=5. If the true relationship between mean GAS production and STORTIME is essentially linear over this range, then the parameter β_1 measures the rate of gas production. The parameter β_0, however, has questionable practical value because the true GAS production corresponding to a STORTIME of 0 is 0. The straight line might well provide a good approximation over the range from STORTIME=1 to STORTIME=5, but might not be of much use outside this range. Finally, the ε term in the model is a random quantity, commonly called an error term, that accounts for variation among GAS production values corresponding to the same STORTIME.

Use the following SAS statements to perform a simple linear regression with PROC REG:

```
proc reg data=methane;
   model gas=stortime;
```

The PROC statement invokes PROC REG, and DATA=METHANE tells the SAS System to apply PROC REG to the data set named METHANE. In the remainder of this book, you should assume that the data set to be used is the last data set created unless DATA= *data-set-name* is specified.

The MODEL statement contains the equation GAS=STORTIME, which corresponds to the statistical model of equation 1.2. The left side specifies the dependent variable (in this case GAS) and the right side specifies the independent variable (in this case STORTIME). Note that no term is specified in the MODEL statement corresponding to the intercept (β_0) because an intercept term is automatically assumed by PROC REG unless indicated otherwise with the NOINT option (see Section 1.3.6). In addition, no term is indicated in the MODEL statement corresponding to the error term (ε). PROC REG produces ordinary least-squares estimates of the parameters, which are optimal if the errors are independent and have equal variances. The optional WEIGHT statement is illustrated in Section 1.5, "Weighted Regression," to accommodate unequal error variances. The results from PROC REG appear in Output 1.2.

Output 1.2
Results of Regression with One Independent Variable

```
                              The SAS System                              1

Model: MODEL1
Dependent Variable: GAS
1
                           Analysis of Variance

                        2      3 Sum of      4 Mean
      Source           DF      Squares        Square     5 F Value    6 Prob>F

      Model             1    1916.80133     1916.80133    111.365       0.0001
      Error            13     223.75467       17.21190
      C Total          14    2140.55600

         7 Root MSE        4.14872    10 R-square      0.8955
         8 Dep Mean       25.74000    11 Adj R-sq      0.8874
         9 C.V.           16.11780

                           Parameter Estimates

                      13 Parameter    14 Standard  15 T for H0:
     12 Variable  DF      Estimate        Error    Parameter=0    Prob > |T|

        INTERCEP   1      1.760000     2.51217616      0.701        0.4959
        STORTIME   1      7.993333     0.75744961     10.553        0.0001
```

The bold-faced numbers have been added to the output to key the descriptions that follow:

1. The name of the Dependent Variable (GAS). This is especially useful if the MODEL statement specifies more than one dependent variable (see Section 1.3.8, "Multiple Models").

2. The degrees of freedom (DF) associated with the sums of squares (SS).

3. The Regression SS (called MODEL SS) is 1916.80133, and the Residual SS (called ERROR SS) is 223.75467. The sum of these two sums of squares is the C TOTAL (corrected total) SS=2140.55600. This illustrates the basic identity in regression analysis that TOTAL SS=MODEL SS+ERROR SS. Usually, good models result in the MODEL SS being a large fraction of the C TOTAL SS.

4. The corresponding Mean Squares are the Sum of Squares divided by the respective DF. The MS for ERROR (MSE) is an unbiased estimate of σ^2, provided the model is correctly specified.

5. The value of the F statistic, 111.365, is the ratio of the MODEL Mean Square divided by the ERROR Mean Square. It is used to test the hypothesis that all coefficients in the model, except the intercept, are 0. In the present case, this hypothesis is H_0: $\beta_1=0$.

6. The p value (Prob>F) of 0.0001 indicates that there is less than one chance in 10,000 of obtaining an F this large or larger by chance alone if, in fact, $\beta_1=0$. Thus, you can conclude that β_1 is not equal to 0.*

7. Root MSE=4.14872 is the square root of the ERROR MS and estimates the error standard deviation, σ (if the model is adequate).

8. Dep Mean=25.74 is simply the average of the values of the variable GAS over all observations in the data set.

9. C.V.=16.1178 is the coefficient of variation expressed as a percentage. This measure of relative variation is the ratio of Root MSE to Dep Mean, multiplied by 100. In this example, the error standard deviation is 16.1178% of the overall average value of GAS. The C.V. is sometimes used as a standard to gauge the relative magnitude of error variation compared with that from similar studies.

10. R-SQUARE=0.8955 is the square of the multiple correlation coefficient. It is also the ratio of MODEL SS divided by TOTAL SS and, thereby, represents the fraction of the total variation in the values of GAS due to the linear relationship to STORTIME.

11. ADJ R-SQ is an alternative to R-SQUARE and is discussed in Section 1.3.2, "A Model with Several Independent Variables."

12. The labels INTERCEP and STORTIME identify the coefficient estimates.

13. The number 1.760 to the right of the label INTERCEP is the estimate of β_0, and the number 7.993 found to the right of the label STORTIME is the estimate of β_1. These give the fitted model

$$GAS = 1.760 + 7.993(STORTIME) \quad .$$

These parameter estimates and this equation provide the information sought from the experiment. The quantity 7.993 is the estimated daily rate of gas production. The equation can be used to estimate the amount of gas produced for any prescribed length of storage time. For example, the amount of gas produced in 2.5 days is estimated to be 1.760+7.993(2.5)=15.742 units.

---

* Because it is known that GAS will increase as STORTIME is increased, it is clear that $\beta_1>0$. Therefore, testing H_0: $\beta_1=0$ has little practical value. It is more meaningful in this case to construct a confidence interval for β_1. See number 14 later in this list.

Section 1.3.3 shows how PROC REG can provide this estimate directly, compute its standard error, and construct confidence limits.

14. The (estimated) Standard Errors of the estimates of β_0 and β_1 are 2.512 and 0.757. These can be used to construct confidence intervals for the model parameters. For example, a 95% confidence interval for β_1 is

$$(7.993 - 2.160(0.757),\ 7.993 + 2.160(0.757)) = (6.36,\ 9.63)$$

where 2.160 is the .05 level tabulated t value with 13 degrees of freedom. Thus, you can infer, with 95% confidence, that the true rate of gas production is somewhere between 6.36 and 9.63 units per day.

15. The t statistic for testing the null hypothesis that $\beta_0=0$ is $t=0.701$ with p value (Prob > $|T|$) of 0.4959. The statistic for testing the null hypothesis that $\beta_1=0$ is $t=10.553$ with a p value of 0.0001. Note that for this one-variable model, the t test is equivalent to the F test for the model because $F=t^2$.

In this example, a simple linear regression model is fitted using ordinary least squares. There are two assumptions that are necessary (but not sufficient) for inferences to be valid. These assumptions are listed below:

□ The true relationship between GAS production and STORTIME is linear.

□ The amount of variation between observations within a particular storage time is the same for all storage times.

These assumptions are typically not completely met in real applications. If they are only slightly violated, then inferences are valid for most practical purposes. In this case, however, by examining Output 1.3, which is produced by the following statements, you can see that both assumptions are violated:

```
proc plot;
   plot gas*stortime;
run;
```

Output 1.3
Plot of METHANE
Data

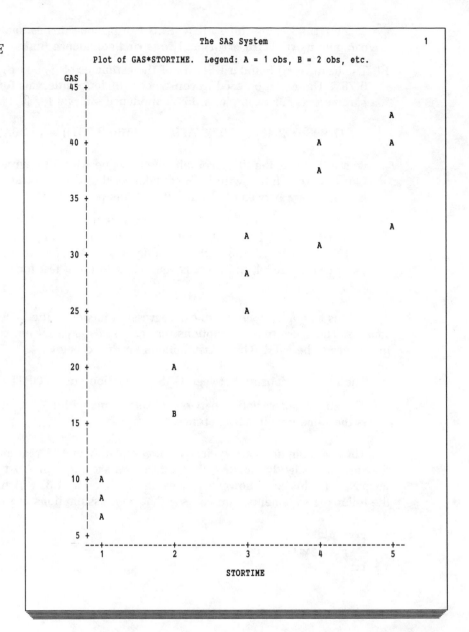

From the plot in Output 1.3, it is apparent that

□   although the amount of gas production increases throughout the range from
    STORTIME=1 to STORTIME=5, the rate of increase tends to diminish with
    increasing STORTIME. Thus, the relationship between GAS and STORTIME
    does not appear to be linear.

□   the variation within STORTIME groups tends to increase with increasing
    STORTIME.

Subsequent sections of this chapter illustrate methods using PROC REG that
can be used to obtain valid inferences. Sections 1.4, "Polynomial Models," and 1.5
deal with fitting a curve other than a straight line and using weighted least
squares to fit the curve. Additional plotting techniques are presented in Section
1.6, "Creating Data Sets."

1.3.2 A Model with Several Independent Variables

This section illustrates regression analyses of data with several independent variables. A data set that has several independent variables appears in Output 1.4.

Output 1.4
Data for
Regression with
Several
Independent
Variables

```
                                  The SAS System                              1

   OBS   MKT   CATTLE   CALVES    HOGS    SHEEP     COST    VOLUME   TYPE

    1     1     3.437    5.791    3.268   10.649   27.698   23.145    O
    2     2    12.801    4.558    5.751   14.375   57.634   37.485    O
    3     3     6.136    6.223   15.175    2.811   47.172   30.345    O
    4     4    11.685    3.212    0.639    0.694   49.295   16.230    B
    5     5     5.733    3.220    0.534    2.052   24.115   11.539    B
    6     6     3.021    4.348    0.839    2.356   33.612   10.564    B
    7     7     1.689    0.634    0.318    2.209    9.512    4.850    O
    8     8     2.339    1.895    0.610    0.605   14.755    5.449    B
    9     9     1.025    0.834    0.734    2.825   10.570    5.418    O
   10    10     2.936    1.419    0.331    0.231   15.394    4.917    B
   11    11     5.049    4.195    1.589    1.957   27.843   12.790    B
   12    12     1.693    3.602    0.837    1.582   17.717    7.714    B
   13    13     1.187    2.679    0.459   18.837   20.253   23.162    O
   14    14     9.730    3.951    3.780    0.524   37.465   17.985    B
   15    15    14.325    4.300   10.781   36.863  101.334   66.269    O
   16    16     7.737    9.043    1.394    1.524   47.427   19.698    B
   17    17     7.538    4.538    2.565    5.109   35.944   19.750    B
   18    18    10.211    4.994    3.081    3.681   45.945   21.967    B
   19    19     8.697    3.005    1.378    3.338   46.890   16.418    B
```

The data set contains data from 19 livestock auction markets and is named AUCTION. The objective is to relate the annual cost (in thousands of dollars) of operating a livestock market (COST) to the numbers (in thousands) of livestock in various classes (CATTLE, CALVES, HOGS, SHEEP) that were sold in each market. This is done with a multiple regression analysis. The variables TYPE and VOLUME are used later.

The multiple regression model

$$COST = \beta_0 + \beta_1(CATTLE) + \beta_2(CALVES) + \beta_3(HOGS) + \beta_4(SHEEP) + \varepsilon$$

relates COST to the four predictor variables. To fit this model, use the following SAS statements:

```
proc reg;
   model cost=cattle calves hogs sheep;
```

The results appear in Output 1.5.

Output 1.5
Results for
Regression with
Several
Independent
Variables

```
                              The SAS System                              1

        Model: MODEL1
        Dependent Variable: COST

                              Analysis of Variance

                                Sum of          Mean
        Source          DF     Squares         Square   1  F Value  2  Prob>F

        Model            4   7936.73649     1984.18412       52.310     0.0001
        Error           14    531.03865       37.93133
        C Total         18   8467.77514

                Root MSE        6.15884   3  R-square      0.9373
                Dep Mean       35.29342   4  Adj R-sq      0.9194
                C.V.           17.45040

                              Parameter Estimates

                      5  Parameter   6  Standard   7 T for H0:
        Variable   DF    Estimate       Error      Parameter=0  8  Prob > |T|

        INTERCEP    1    2.288425    3.38737222       0.676        0.5103
        CATTLE      1    3.215525    0.42215239       7.617        0.0001
        CALVES      1    1.613148    0.85167539       1.894        0.0791
        HOGS        1    0.814849    0.47073855       1.731        0.1054
        SHEEP       1    0.802579    0.18981766       4.228        0.0008
```

The upper portion of the output, as in Output 1.2, contains the partitioning of TOTAL SS, labeled C Total, into MODEL SS and ERROR SS, along with the corresponding mean squares. The bold-faced numbers have been added to the output to key the descriptions that follow:

1. The *F* value of 52.310 is used to test the null hypothesis

   $$H_0: \beta_1 = \beta_2 = \beta_3 = \beta_4 = 0 \quad .$$

2. The associated *p* value (Prob>F) of 0.0001 leads to a rejection of this hypothesis and to the conclusion that some of the βs are not 0.

3. R-SQUARE=0.9373 shows that a large portion of the variation in COST can be explained by variation in the independent variables in the model.

4. ADJ R-SQ=0.9194 is an alternative to R-SQUARE that is adjusted for the number of parameters in the model according to the formula

   $$\text{ADJ R-SQ} = 1 - (1 - \text{R-SQUARE})((n - 1) / (n - m - 1))$$

   where *n* is the number of observations in the data set and *m* is the number of regression parameters in the model, excluding the intercept. This adjustment is used to overcome an objection to R-SQUARE as a measure of goodness of fit of the model. This objection stems from the fact that R-SQUARE can be driven to 1 simply by adding superfluous variables to the model with no real improvement in fit. This is not the case with ADJ R-SQ, which tends to stabilize to a certain value when an adequate set of variables is included in the model.

5. The Parameter Estimates give the fitted model

$$COST = 2.29 + 3.22(CATTLE) + 1.61(CALVES) + 0.81(HOGS)$$
$$+ 0.80(SHEEP) \quad .$$

Thus, for example, one head of CATTLE contributes \$3.22 to the COST of operating a market, if all other numbers of livestock are held fixed. Remember that the COST of operating the markets was given in \$1000 units, whereas the numbers of animals were given in 1000-head units.

6. These are the (estimated) standard errors of the parameter estimates and are useful for constructing confidence intervals for the parameters, as shown in Section 1.3.1.

7. The *t* tests (T for H0 : Parameter=0) are used for testing hypotheses about individual parameters. It is important that you clearly understand the interpretation of these tests. This can be explained in terms of comparing the fits of complete and reduced models. (Review Section 1.1.2, "Partitioning the Sums of Squares.") The complete model for all of these *t* tests contains all the variables on the right side of the MODEL statement. The reduced model for a particular test contains all these variables except the one being tested. Thus, the *t* statistic=1.894 for testing the hypothesis $H_0: \beta_2 = 0$ is actually testing whether the complete model containing CATTLE, CALVES, HOGS, and SHEEP fits better than the reduced model containing only CATTLE, HOGS, and SHEEP.

8. The *p* value (Prob > | T |) for this test is $p = 0.0791$.

1.3.3 The P, CLM, and CLI Options: Predicted Values and Confidence Limits

A common objective of regression analysis is to compute the predicted value

$$\hat{y} = \hat{\beta}_0 + \hat{\beta}_1 x_1 + \ldots + \hat{\beta}_k x_k$$

for some selected values of $x_1, \ldots, x_k$. You can do this in several ways using PROC REG or other regression procedures in the SAS System. In PROC REG, the most direct way is to use the P (for predicted) option in the MODEL statement. Output 1.6 shows output produced with the following SAS statements:

```
proc reg data=methane;
   id stortime;
   model gas=stortime / p clm cli;
```

Output 1.6
PROC REG with P,
CLM, and CLI
Options

```
                            The SAS System                              1
Model: MODEL1
Dependent Variable: GAS

                         Analysis of Variance

                              Sum of          Mean
        Source        DF     Squares        Square     F Value    Prob>F

        Model          1   1916.80133    1916.80133    111.365    0.0001
        Error         13    223.75467      17.21190
        C Total       14   2140.55600

              Root MSE      4.14872     R-square      0.8955
              Dep Mean     25.74000     Adj R-sq      0.8874
              C.V.         16.11780

                         Parameter Estimates

                    Parameter      Standard    T for H0:
        Variable  DF   Estimate        Error  Parameter=0   Prob > |T|

        INTERCEP   1   1.760000   2.51217616        0.701       0.4959
        STORTIME   1   7.993333   0.75744961       10.553       0.0001
```

```
                                                                        2

                       Dep Var   Predict   Std Err  Lower95%  Upper95%
    Obs    STORTIME       GAS     Value    Predict     Mean      Mean

     1        1        8.2000    9.7533     1.855    5.7451   13.7616
     2        1        6.6000    9.7533     1.855    5.7451   13.7616
     3        1        9.8000    9.7533     1.855    5.7451   13.7616
     4        2       19.7000   17.7467     1.312   14.9124   20.5809
     5        2       15.7000   17.7467     1.312   14.9124   20.5809
     6        2       16.0000   17.7467     1.312   14.9124   20.5809
     7        3       28.6000   25.7400     1.071   23.4258   28.0542
     8        3       25.0000   25.7400     1.071   23.4258   28.0542
     9        3       31.9000   25.7400     1.071   23.4258   28.0542
    10        4       30.8000   33.7333     1.312   30.8991   36.5676
    11        4       37.8000   33.7333     1.312   30.8991   36.5676
    12        4       40.2000   33.7333     1.312   30.8991   36.5676
    13        5       40.3000   41.7267     1.855   37.7184   45.7349
    14        5       42.9000   41.7267     1.855   37.7184   45.7349
    15        5       32.6000   41.7267     1.855   37.7184   45.7349
    16      2.5            .     21.7433     1.136   19.2888   24.1979

                       Lower95%  Upper95%
    Obs    STORTIME     Predict   Predict   Residual

     1        1        -0.0649   19.5715    -1.5533
     2        1        -0.0649   19.5715    -3.1533
     3        1        -0.0649   19.5715     0.0467
     4        2         8.3464   27.1469     1.9533
     5        2         8.3464   27.1469    -2.0467
     6        2         8.3464   27.1469    -1.7467
     7        3        16.4833   34.9967     2.8600
     8        3        16.4833   34.9967    -0.7400
     9        3        16.4833   34.9967     6.1600
    10        4        24.3331   43.1336    -2.9333
    11        4        24.3331   43.1336     4.0667
    12        4        24.3331   43.1336     6.4667
    13        5        31.9085   51.5449    -1.4267
    14        5        31.9085   51.5449     1.1733
    15        5        31.9085   51.5449    -9.1267
    16      2.5        12.4505   31.0361         .

    Sum of Residuals                     0
    Sum of Squared Residuals      223.7547
    Predicted Resid SS (Press)    304.6852
```

Specifying the P option in the MODEL statement causes PROC REG to compute predicted values corresponding to each observation in the data set. These computations are printed following the basic PROC REG output under the heading Predict Value. The P option also causes the observed *y* values (in this case, GAS)

to be printed under the heading Dep Var GAS, along with the
residuals, where

Residual = Dep Var GAS − Predict Value   .

The estimated standard errors of the predicted values are also printed as a
result of the P option. These are computed according to the formula

$$\text{Std Err Predict} = \sqrt{(\mathbf{x}'(\mathbf{X}'\mathbf{X})^{-1}\mathbf{x})(\text{MSE})}$$

which is equal to the square root of $V(\hat{y})$ given in equation 1.1 in Section 1.1.3,
"Hypothesis Testing."

A useful feature of PROC REG is that the $\hat{y}$ values can be computed for
observations in the data set even if the observed values of the dependent variable
are missing, as long as data are present for all values of the independent
variables. To illustrate this feature, the data set METHANE has been augmented
with one additional observation that has the value 2.5 for STORTIME and a
missing value for GAS. (The results appear as OBS 16 in Output 1.6.)

Note that Std Err Predict is computed (1.1362) for the observation with a
missing value for GAS because it depends only on the value of the independent
variable in this observation (the **X** matrix) and the error mean square. The
residual value is not computed, however, because it depends on the value of the
dependent variable.

The ID statement identifies each observation according to the value of the
variable indicated in the statement, in this case, STORTIME. This enables you to
relate the observed and predicted values to the values of another variable.
Usually, one of the independent variables is the most meaningful ID variable.

The CLM option in the MODEL statement gives upper and lower 95%
confidence limits for the mean of the subpopulation corresponding to specific
values of the independent variables. The CLM option makes the following
computation:

$$(\hat{y} - t_{\alpha/2}(\text{STD ERR PREDICT}), \hat{y} + t_{\alpha/2}(\text{STD ERR PREDICT}))   .$$

The CLI option in the MODEL statement gives upper and lower 95%
prediction intervals for a future observation. The CLI option makes the following
computation.

$$(\hat{y} - t_{\alpha/2}\sqrt{\hat{V}(y - \hat{y})} , \hat{y} + t_{\alpha/2}\sqrt{\hat{V}(y - \hat{y})})   .$$

$\hat{V}(y-\hat{y})$ is given in equation 1.2 in Section 1.1.3, with σ^2 replaced by MSE.

Consider OBS 10, which has STORTIME=4 (see Output 1.1). The predicted
value for OBS 10 is 33.7333 (see Output 1.6). This number is used to estimate
the mean GAS production corresponding to STORTIME=4. The 95% confidence
limits for this mean are (30.8991, 36.5676). The predicted value of 33.7333 is
also used to predict GAS production (not yet measured) of some other randomly
drawn sample that has STORTIME=4. The 95% prediction limits for this
individual sample are (24.3331, 43.1336).

In short, the CLM option yields a confidence interval for the subpopulation
mean, and the CLI option yields a prediction interval for an independent value to
be drawn at random from the subpopulation. The CLI limits are always wider
than the CLM limits, because the CLM limits accommodate only variability in $\hat{y}$,

whereas the CLI limits accommodate variability in $\hat{y}$ and variability in the future value of y. This is true even though $\hat{y}$ is used as an estimate of the subpopulation mean as well as a predictor of the future value.

1.3.4 The SS1 and SS2 Options: Two Types of Sums of Squares

PROC REG can compute two types of sums of squares associated with the estimated coefficients in the model. These are referred to as Type I and Type II sums of squares and are computed by specifying SS1 or SS2, or both, as MODEL statement options. For example, the following SAS statements produce Output 1.7:

```
proc reg;
   model cost=cattle calves hogs sheep / ss1 ss2;
run;
```

Output 1.7
PROC REG with
SS1 and SS2
MODEL Statement
Options

```
                              The SAS System                              1

Model: MODEL1
Dependent Variable: COST
                           Analysis of Variance

                              Sum of       Mean
        Source       DF      Squares      Square    F Value     Prob>F

        Model         4    7936.73649   1984.18412    52.310     0.0001
        Error        14     531.03865     37.93133
        C Total      18    8467.77514

            Root MSE      6.15884     R-square      0.9373
            Dep Mean     35.29342     Adj R-sq      0.9194
            C.V.         17.45040

                           Parameter Estimates

                     Parameter    Standard    T for H0:
        Variable  DF   Estimate      Error    Parameter=0   Prob > |T|

        INTERCEP   1   2.288425    3.38737222      0.676      0.5103
        CATTLE     1   3.215525    0.42215239      7.617      0.0001
        CALVES     1   1.613148    0.85167539      1.894      0.0791
        HOGS       1   0.814849    0.47073855      1.731      0.1054
        SHEEP      1   0.802579    0.18981766      4.228      0.0008


        Variable  DF    Type I SS    Type II SS

        INTERCEP   1        23667    17.311929
        CATTLE     1   6582.091806   2200.712494
        CALVES     1    186.671101    136.081196
        HOGS       1    489.863790    113.656260
        SHEEP      1    678.109792    678.109792
```

These sums of squares are printed as additional columns and are labeled Type I SS and Type II SS. You may find it helpful at this point to review the material in Section 1.1.2. In particular, the concepts of partitioning sums of squares, complete and reduced models, and reduction notation are useful in understanding the different types of sums of squares.

The Type I SS are commonly called sequential sums of squares. They represent a partitioning of the MODEL SS into component sums of squares due to each variable as it is added sequentially to the model in the order prescribed by the MODEL statement.

The Type I SS for the INTERCEP is simply $n\bar{y}^2$, which is commonly called the correction for the mean. The Type I SS for CATTLE (6582.09181) is the MODEL SS for a regression equation that contains only CATTLE. The Type I SS for CALVES (186.67110) is the increase in MODEL SS due to adding CALVES to the model that already contains CATTLE. In general, the Type I SS for a particular variable is the sums of squares due to adding that variable to a model that already contains all the variables that preceded the particular variable in the MODEL statement. Continuing the pattern, you see that the Type I SS for HOGS (489.86379) is the increase in MODEL SS due to adding HOGS to a model that already contains CATTLE and CALVES. Finally, the Type I SS for SHEEP (678.10979) is the increase in MODEL SS due to adding SHEEP to a model that already contains CATTLE, CALVES, and HOGS. Note that

MODEL SS = 7936.7 = 6582.1 + 186.7 + 489.9 + 678.1

illustrating the sequential partitioning of the MODEL SS into the Type I components that correspond to the variables in the model.

The Type II SS are commonly called the partial sums of squares. For a given variable, the Type II SS is equivalent to the Type I SS for that variable if it were the last variable in the MODEL statement. (Note that the Type I SS and Type II SS for SHEEP are equal in Output 1.7.) In other words, the Type II SS for a particular variable is the increase in MODEL SS due to adding the variable to a model that already contains all the other variables in the MODEL statement. The Type II SS, therefore, do not depend on the order in which the independent variables are listed in the MODEL statement. Furthermore, they do not yield a partitioning of the MODEL SS unless the independent variables are uncorrelated.

The Type I SS and Type II SS are shown in the table below in reduction notation:

	Type I (Sequential)	Type II (Partial)
CATTLE	$R(\beta_1 \mid \beta_0)$	$R(\beta_1 \mid \beta_0, \beta_2, \beta_3, \beta_4)$
CALVES	$R(\beta_2 \mid \beta_0, \beta_1)$	$R(\beta_2 \mid \beta_0, \beta_1, \beta_3, \beta_4)$
HOGS	$R(\beta_3 \mid \beta_0, \beta_1, \beta_2)$	$R(\beta_3 \mid \beta_0, \beta_1, \beta_2, \beta_4)$
SHEEP	$R(\beta_4 \mid \beta_0, \beta_1, \beta_2, \beta_3)$	$R(\beta_4 \mid \beta_0, \beta_1, \beta_2, \beta_3)$

The reduction notation provides a convenient device to determine the complete and reduced models that are compared if you construct an F test using one of these sums of squares. First, note that each sum of squares for a particular variable has one degree of freedom, so that the sums of squares are also mean squares. Thus, for example, a Type I F test for CALVES is given by

$$F = \frac{\text{Type I SS for CALVES}}{\text{MSE}} = \frac{186.7}{37.9} = 4.92 \quad .$$

The reduction notation shows that this F value would be used to test whether the complete model containing CATTLE and CALVES fits the data significantly better than the reduced model containing only CATTLE. Similarly, a Type II F statistic for CALVES is given by

$$F = \frac{\text{Type II SS for CALVES}}{\text{MSE}} = \frac{136.1}{37.9} = 3.59$$

and would be used to test whether the complete model containing CATTLE, CALVES, HOGS, and SHEEP fits significantly better than the reduced model containing CATTLE, HOGS, and SHEEP. In this example, the difference between these two F values is not great. The difference between Type I and Type II F values for HOGS is considerably greater. The variation due to HOGS that is not due to CATTLE and CALVES is 489.86379, but the variation due to HOGS that is not due to CATTLE, CALVES, and SHEEP is only 113.65626. The former is significant at the 0.003 level, whereas the latter is significant only at the 0.105 level. Thus, a model containing CATTLE and CALVES is significantly improved by adding HOGS, but a model containing CATTLE, CALVES, and SHEEP is improved much less significantly by adding HOGS.

PROC REG does not compute F values for the Type I and Type II sums of squares, nor does it compute the corresponding significance probabilities. However, you can use PROC GLM to make the same computations discussed in this chapter. You should note that there are several other distinctions between the capabilities of PROC REG and PROC GLM; not all analyses using PROC REG can be easily performed by PROC GLM. Some of these distinctions are discussed in subsequent sections.

It is now appropriate to note that the Type II F tests are exactly equivalent to the t tests for the parameters because they are comparing the same complete and reduced models. In fact, the Type II F statistic for a given variable is equal to the square of the t statistic for the same variable.

For most applications, the desired test for a single parameter is based on the Type II sums of squares, which are equivalent to the t tests for the parameter estimates. Type I sums of squares, however, are useful if there is need for a specific sequencing of tests on individual coefficients as, for example, in polynomial models (see Section 1.4).

1.3.5 Tests of Subsets and Linear Combinations of Coefficients

Tests of hypotheses that individual coefficients are equal to 0 are given by the t tests on the parameters in the basic PROC REG output, as discussed in Section 1.3.2. In this section, a direct procedure is demonstrated for testing that subsets of coefficients are equal to 0. These tests are specified in the optional TEST statement in PROC REG. The TEST statement can also be used to test that linear functions of parameters are equal to specified constants.

The TEST statement must follow a MODEL statement in PROC REG. Several TEST statements can follow one MODEL statement. The general form of the TEST statement is

label: **TEST** *equation* $<, \ldots,$ *equation*$> <$ / *option*$>$;

The label is optional and serves only to identify results in the output. The equations provide the technical information that PROC REG uses to determine what hypotheses are to be tested. These tests can be interpreted in terms of comparing complete and reduced (or restricted) models in the same manner as discussed in previous sections. The complete model for all tests specified by a TEST statement is the model containing all variables on the right side of the MODEL statement. The reduced model is derived from the complete model by imposing the conditions implied by the equations indicated in the TEST statement.

The algebraic expressions that are computed as a result of the TEST statement are described in "TEST Statement," in Chapter 36, "The REG Procedure," in the *SAS/STAT User's Guide, Version 6, Fourth Edition, Volume 2.*

For illustration, recall the AUCTION data set in Section 1.3.2 and the SAS statement

```
model cost=cattle calves hogs sheep;
```

which fits the complete regression model

$$COST = \beta_0 + \beta_1(CATTLE) + \beta_2(CALVES) + \beta_3(HOGS) + \beta_4(SHEEP) + \varepsilon \quad .$$

To test the hypothesis H_0: $\beta_3 = 0$, use the following statement:

```
hogs:  test hogs=0;
```

This statement tells PROC REG to construct an F test to compare the complete model with the reduced model

$$COST = \beta_0 + \beta_1(CATTLE) + \beta_2(CALVES) + \beta_4(SHEEP) + \varepsilon \quad .$$

Similarly, to test the hypothesis H_0: $\beta_3 = \beta_4 = 0$, which is equivalent to H_0: ($\beta_3 = 0$ and $\beta_4 = 0$), use the following statement:

```
hogsheep:  test hogs=0, sheep=0;
```

The hypothesis of a 0 intercept, H_0: $\beta_0 = 0$, is specified with the following statement:

```
intercep:  test intercept=0;
```

If the right side of an equation in a TEST statement is 0, you don't need to specify it. PROC REG will assume a right-side value of 0 by default.

More general linear functions are tested in a similar fashion. For example, to test that the average cost of selling one hog is one dollar, you test the hypothesis H_0: $\beta_3 = 1$. This hypothesis is specified in the following TEST statement:

```
hogone:  test hogs=1;
```

Another possible linear function of interest is to test whether the average cost of selling one hog differs from the average cost of selling one sheep. The null hypothesis is H_0: $\beta_3 = \beta_4$, which is equivalent to H_0: $\beta_3 - \beta_4 = 0$, and is specified by the following statement:

```
hequals:  test  hogs-sheep=0;
```

The results of all five of these TEST statements appear in Output 1.8.

Output 1.8
Results of the
TEST Statement

```
                                  The SAS System                              1
          Dependent Variable: COST
          Test: HOGS      Numerator:   113.6563  DF:    1   F value:   2.9964
                          Denominator:  37.93133  DF:   14   Prob>F:    0.1054


          Dependent Variable: COST
          Test: HOGSHEEP  Numerator:   583.9868  DF:    2   F value:  15.3959
                          Denominator:  37.93133  DF:   14   Prob>F:    0.0003


          Dependent Variable: COST
          Test: INTERCEP  Numerator:    17.3119  DF:    1   F value:   0.4564
                          Denominator:  37.93133  DF:   14   Prob>F:    0.5103


          Dependent Variable: COST
          Test: HOGONE    Numerator:     5.8680  DF:    1   F value:   0.1547
                          Denominator:  37.93133  DF:   14   Prob>F:    0.7000


          Dependent Variable: COST
          Test: HEQUALS   Numerator:     0.0176  DF:    1   F value:   0.0005
                          Denominator:  37.93133  DF:   14   Prob>F:    0.9831
```

For each TEST statement indicated, a sum of squares is computed with degrees of freedom equal to the number of equations in the TEST statement. From these quantities, a mean square that forms the numerator of an F statistic is computed. The denominator of the F ratio is the mean square for error. The value of F is printed, along with its p value. The test labeled HOGS is, of course, the equivalent of the t test for HOGS in Output 1.5.

Note: If there are linear dependencies or inconsistencies among the equations in a TEST statement, then PROC REG prints a message that the test failed, and no F ratio is computed.

1.3.6 Fitting Restricted Models: RESTRICT Statement and NOINT Option

Subject to linear restrictions on the parameters, models can be fitted by using the RESTRICT statement in PROC REG. The RESTRICT statement follows a MODEL statement and has the general form

RESTRICT *equation* <, . . ., *equation*>;

where each equation is a linear combination of the model parameters set equal to a constant.

Consider again the data set AUCTION and the following MODEL statement:

```
model cost=cattle calves hogs sheep;
```

This model is fitted in Section 1.3.2. Inspection of Output 1.5 shows that the INTERCEP estimate is close to 0 and that the Parameter Estimates for HOGS and SHEEP are similar in value. Hypotheses pertaining to these conditions are tested in Section 1.3.5. The results suggest a model that has 0 intercept and equal coefficients for HOGS and SHEEP, namely

$$COST = \beta_1(CATTLE) + \beta_2(CALVES) + \beta(HOGS) + \beta(SHEEP) + \varepsilon$$

where β is the common value of β_3 and β_4.

This model can be fitted with the following RESTRICT statement:

```
restrict intercept=0, hogs-sheep=0;
```

The results of these statements appear in Output 1.9.

Output 1.9
Results of the
RESTRICT
Statement

```
                              The SAS System                              1

Model: MODEL1
NOTE: Restrictions have been applied to parameter estimates.
Dependent Variable: COST

                        Analysis of Variance

                          Sum of         Mean
   Source          DF    Squares       Square    F Value     Prob>F

   Model            2  7918.75621   3959.37811    115.388     0.0001
   Error           16   549.01893     34.31368
   C Total         18  8467.77514

       Root MSE        5.85779      R-square      0.9352
       Dep Mean       35.29342      Adj R-sq      0.9271
       C.V.           16.59739

                        Parameter Estimates

                  Parameter      Standard     T for H0:
   Variable   DF   Estimate         Error   Parameter=0    Prob > |T|

   INTERCEP    1  1.110223E-15   0.00000000         .            .
   CATTLE      1     3.300043    0.38314175       8.613       0.0001
   CALVES      1     1.967171    0.59107649       3.328       0.0043
   HOGS        1     0.806825    0.13799841       5.847       0.0001
   SHEEP       1     0.806825    0.13799841       5.847       0.0001
   RESTRICT   -1     7.905632   10.92658296       0.724       0.4798
   RESTRICT   -1    -9.059424   64.91322402      -0.140       0.8907
```

Note that the INTERCEP parameter estimate is 0 (except for round off error) and the parameter estimates for HOGS and SHEEP have the common value .806825. Note also that there are parameter estimates and associated t tests for the two equations in the RESTRICT statement. These pertain to the Lagrangian parameters that are incorporated in the restricted minimization of the Error SS. For more information see "RESTRICT Statement" in Chapter 36 of the *SAS/STAT User's Guide, Volume 2*.

You will find it useful to compare Output 1.9 with results obtained by invoking the restrictions explicitly. The model with the RESTRICT statement is equivalent to the model

$$COST = \beta_1(CATTLE) + \beta_2(CALVES) + \beta(SHEEP + HOGS) + \varepsilon \quad .$$

This is a three-variable model with an intercept of 0. The variables are CATTLE, CALVES, and HS, where the variable HS=HOGS+SHEEP. The model is then fitted using PROC REG with the MODEL statement

```
model cost=cattle calves hs / noint;
```

where NOINT is the option that specifies that no intercept be included. In other words, the fitted regression plane is forced to pass through the origin. The results appear in Output 1.10, from which the following fitted equation is obtained:

$$
\begin{aligned}
COST &= 3.300(CATTLE) + 1.967(CALVES) + 0.807(HS) \\
     &= 3.300(CATTLE) + 1.967(CALVES) + 0.807(HOGS) \\
     &\quad + 0.807(SHEEP) \quad .
\end{aligned}
$$

Output 1.10
Results of
Regression with
Implicit
Restrictions

```
                              The SAS System                           1

Model: MODEL1
NOTE: No intercept in model. R-square is redefined.
Dependent Variable: COST

                          Analysis of Variance

                            Sum of         Mean
        Source      DF     Squares        Square     F Value    Prob>F

        Model        3   31585.64204   10528.54735   306.832    0.0001
        Error       16     549.01893      34.31368
        U Total     19   32134.66096

            Root MSE       5.85779     R-square      0.9829
            Dep Mean      35.29342     Adj R-sq      0.9797
            C.V.          16.59739

                          Parameter Estimates

                     Parameter      Standard    T for H0:
        Variable DF   Estimate         Error    Parameter=0   Prob > |T|

        CATTLE    1   3.300043     0.38314175      8.613        0.0001
        CALVES    1   1.967171     0.59107649      3.328        0.0043
        HS        1   0.806825     0.13799841      5.847        0.0001
```

This is the same fitted model obtained in Output 1.9 by using the RESTRICT statements.

As just pointed out, equivalent restrictions can be imposed in different ways using PROC REG. When the NOINT option is used to restrict β_0 to be 0, however, caution is advised in trying to interpret the sums of squares, F values, and R-SQUARES. Notice, for instance, that the MODEL SS do not agree in Output

1.9 and Output 1.10. The ERROR SS and degrees of freedom do agree. In Output 1.9, the MODEL SS and ERROR SS sum to the Corrected TOTAL SS (C TOTAL), whereas in Output 1.10 they sum to the Uncorrected TOTAL SS (U TOTAL). In Output 1.10, the MODEL F statistic is testing whether the fitted model fits better than a model containing no parameters, a test that has little or no practical value.

Corresponding complications arise regarding the R-SQUARE statistic with no-intercept models. Note that R-SQUARE=0.9829 for the no-intercept model in Output 1.10 is greater than R-SQUARE=0.9373 for the model in Output 1.5, although the latter has two more parameters than the former. This seems contrary to the general phenomenon that adding terms to a model causes the R-SQUARE to increase. This seeming contradiction occurs because the denominator of the R-SQUARE is the Uncorrected Total SS when the NOINT option is used. This is the reason for the message that R-SQUARE is redefined at the top of Output 1.10. It is, therefore, not meaningful to compare an R-SQUARE for a model that contains an intercept with an R-SQUARE for a model that does not contain an intercept.

1.3.7 Miscellaneous Option Specifications

In addition to MODEL statement options illustrated in Sections 1.3.3 and 1.3.4, there are numerous options you can use to obtain additional information from PROC REG or to modify the output of PROC REG. These options can appear in one of three places:

□ in the PROC REG statement

□ in the MODEL statement

□ as separate SAS statements that accompany the PROC REG and MODEL statements.

Some options are not illustrated in this book. Other options are illustrated in other sections of this chapter, such as Sections 1.5, 1.6, and 1.7, "Exact Collinearity: Linear Dependency."

Section 1.3.1 shows the DATA= option specified within the PROC REG statement. Two other options that are requested in the PROC REG statement are SIMPLE and USSCP. The SIMPLE option prints descriptive statistics for each variable indicated in the procedure, and the USSCP option prints uncorrected sums of squares and crossproducts. A number of other PROC options, including the creation of data sets containing parameter estimates and other statistics, are described in Chapter 36 of the *SAS/STAT User's Guide, Volume 2.*

Several additional options are requested in the MODEL statement. These include the STB, XPX, and I options.

The STB option produces the set of standardized regression coefficients. Output 1.11 contains the modified portion of the output from the following SAS statements:

```
proc reg;
   model cost=cattle calves hogs sheep / stb;
run;
```

Output 1.11
Results of the STB
Option

```
                                    The SAS System                          1
Model: MODEL1
Dependent Variable: COST

                            Analysis of Variance

                               Sum of         Mean
        Source        DF      Squares        Square     F Value      Prob>F

        Model          4    7936.73649    1984.18412      52.310      0.0001
        Error         14     531.03865      37.93133
        C Total       18    8467.77514

            Root MSE        6.15884     R-square       0.9373
            Dep Mean       35.29342     Adj R-sq       0.9194
            C.V.           17.45040

                            Parameter Estimates

                      Parameter      Standard     T for H0:
        Variable  DF   Estimate         Error    Parameter=0    Prob > |T|

        INTERCEP   1   2.288425    3.38737222         0.676        0.5103
        CATTLE     1   3.215525    0.42215239         7.617        0.0001
        CALVES     1   1.613148    0.85167539         1.894        0.0791
        HOGS       1   0.814849    0.47073855         1.731        0.1054
        SHEEP      1   0.802579    0.18981766         4.228        0.0008

                      Standardized
        Variable  DF    Estimate

        INTERCEP   1   0.00000000
        CATTLE     1   0.62116599
        CALVES     1   0.14804950
        HOGS       1   0.14726883
        SHEEP      1   0.33349355
```

The coefficients labeled Standardized Estimate are the estimates that would be obtained if all variables were standardized to 0 mean and unit variance prior to performing the regression computations. Standardization of the variables is done by subtracting their means and dividing by their standard deviations. Thus, these coefficients are independent of the scales of measurement of the independent variables and might offer a comparison of the magnitude of the effects of the variables.

The XPX and I options are available to specify printing of various matrices used in the regression computations. (See Sections 1.1.1 and 1.1.2.) The XPX option prints the following matrix:

$$\begin{bmatrix} \mathbf{X'X} & \mathbf{X'Y} \\ \mathbf{Y'X} & \mathbf{Y'Y} \end{bmatrix}$$

The I option prints this matrix:

$$\begin{bmatrix} (\mathbf{X'X})^{-1} & \hat{\beta} \\ \hat{\beta}' & \text{ERROR SS} \end{bmatrix}$$

The additional results from the following statements appear in Output 1.12:

```
proc reg;
    model cost=cattle calves hogs sheep / xpx i;
run;
```

Output 1.12
Results of the XPX
and I Options

```
                              The SAS System                              1
Model: MODEL1


                    Model Crossproducts X'X X'Y Y'Y

        X'X         INTERCEP          CATTLE           CALVES

      INTERCEP            19         116.969           72.441
      CATTLE        116.969     1036.087471       507.887804
      CALVES         72.441      507.887804       347.518545
      HOGS           54.063      469.482146       265.408184
      SHEEP         112.222      958.574043       459.327042
      COST          670.575     5570.426016      2944.414095


        X'X            HOGS           SHEEP             COST

      INTERCEP       54.063         112.222          670.575
      CATTLE     469.482146      958.574043      5570.426016
      CALVES     265.408184      459.327042      2944.414095
      HOGS       430.421827      610.516602      2902.209741
      SHEEP      610.516602     2124.903264      6282.97359
      COST      2902.209741     6282.97359     32134.660961



               X'X Inverse, Parameter Estimates, and SSE
                    INTERCEP          CATTLE           CALVES

      INTERCEP   0.3025016496    -0.011264453     -0.049765128
      CATTLE    -0.011264453     0.0046982965     -0.002922723
      CALVES    -0.049765128    -0.002922723      0.0191227392
      HOGS       0.0087290688   -0.001082336      -0.00352373
      SHEEP     -0.002644968    -0.000581803      0.0008254932
      COST       2.2884245768    3.2155248027     1.6131476138


                       HOGS           SHEEP             COST

      INTERCEP   0.0087290688   -0.002644968      2.2884245768
      CATTLE    -0.001082336    -0.000581803      3.2155248027
      CALVES     -0.00352373     0.0008254932     1.6131476138
      HOGS       0.0058419984    -0.00088954      0.814849491
      SHEEP      -0.00088954     0.000949894      0.8025786215
      COST       0.814849491     0.8025786215    531.03864957
```

```
                                                                         2


Dependent Variable: COST

                        Analysis of Variance

                           Sum of         Mean
      Source       DF      Squares        Square      F Value     Prob>F

      Model         4    7936.73649    1984.18412      52.310     0.0001
      Error        14     531.03865      37.93133
      C Total      18    8467.77514

           Root MSE        6.15884    R-square      0.9373
           Dep Mean       35.29342    Adj R-sq      0.9194
           C.V.           17.45040
```

(continued on next page)

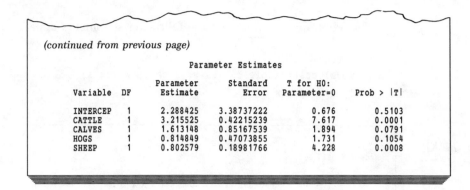

(continued from previous page)

Parameter Estimates

Variable	DF	Parameter Estimate	Standard Error	T for H0: Parameter=0	Prob > |T|
INTERCEP	1	2.288425	3.38737222	0.676	0.5103
CATTLE	1	3.215525	0.42215239	7.617	0.0001
CALVES	1	1.613148	0.85167539	1.894	0.0791
HOGS	1	0.814849	0.47073855	1.731	0.1054
SHEEP	1	0.802579	0.18981766	4.228	0.0008

Because PROC REG uses a dummy variable called INTERCEP (whose value is equal to 1 for all observations) as the first column of the **X** matrix, the **X′X** matrix is uncorrected for the mean and is bordered by a row and column of sample size and sums of observed values.

The additional options, COVB and CORRB, print the matrix of variances and covariances, and the matrix of correlations of the estimated coefficients, respectively.

1.3.8 Multiple Models

A MODEL statement can contain several dependent variables. The following statement performs the four separate regression analyses of Y1, Y2, Y3, and Y4 on the set of variables X1, X2, . . . , X5:

```
model y1 y2 y3 y4=x1 x2 x3 x4 x5;
```

If a value is missing for any variable in the MODEL statement, PROC REG deletes the observation from the process of estimating the coefficients. However, the observation does remain in the data set (see Sections 1.4 and 1.5).

Multiple MODEL statements are permitted in PROC REG (but not in PROC GLM). Some features of the implementation of multiple models are listed below:

□ PROC REG calculates one set of sums of squares and crossproducts (**X′X** and **Y′Y**) for the variables in all models. If the models overlap, that is, many of the same variables appear in several models, the use of multiple models can save considerable computer time. On the other hand, if models overlap very little, the procedure computes a number of unnecessary sums of crossproducts.

□ Sums of squares and crossproducts are calculated once for all variables in all models; therefore, the procedure deletes from these calculations any observation having missing values for any variable in any model.

□ The SIMPLE and USSCP options can print summary statistics and sums of squares and crossproducts for variables in all models. Specify the SIMPLE and USSCP options in the PROC REG statement.

1.4 Polynomial Models

Inspection of Output 1.3 suggests that the simple linear regression model is not adequate because the mean GAS production does not appear to be a linear function of STORTIME. This section illustrates models that attempt to overcome this problem.

The mathematical functions most commonly used to model curvature in plots are polynomials. A polynomial regression model has an equation of the form

$$y = \beta_0 + \beta_1 x + \beta_2 x^2 + \ldots + \beta_k x^k + \varepsilon \quad .$$

The polynomial regression model is actually a multiple linear regression model with $x_1 = x$, $x_2 = x^2$, ..., $x_k = x^k$. Therefore, the methodology for the multiple regression model can be applied directly to the polynomial model. You should be aware that the term linear refers to linearity in the parameters (the βs) and not the independent variable x.

The polynomial model is of degree k, corresponding to the degree of its highest order term. Generally, the higher the degree of the polynomial, the more complex is the trend that its graph can represent. In selecting a polynomial model, the goal is usually to select the polynomial model of lowest order that adequately represents the trend in the plot. The simple linear regression model is of degree 1 and cannot represent curvature. The second-degree polynomial is called a quadratic and has a curve with only one bend. The third-degree polynomial is called a cubic and has a curve with two bends. In general, the kth-degree polynomial has a curve with at most $k-1$ bends. Output 1.3 reveals a trend with no more than two bends, which suggests a polynomial model of, at most, degree 3. Therefore, a third-degree polynomial is fitted and then tested to decide if a lower degree model could just as well be used.

All variables on the right side of a MODEL statement in a PROC REG step must be variables in the data set to which PROC REG is applied. For the third-degree polynomial, these variables are STORTIME, STORTIME squared, and STORTIME cubed. Therefore, a new data set named NEWMETH, which is the same as the data set METHANE only with two more variables (STORSQ=STORTIME**2 and STORCU=STORTIME**3) is created with the following statements:

```
data newmeth;
   set methane;
   storsq=stortime**2;
   storcu=stortime**3;
```

The cubic model is then fitted with the statements below, using the DATA=NEWMETH option in the PROC statement to emphasize that PROC REG is being applied to the data set NEWMETH. Note that several new options are requested.

```
proc reg data=newmeth;
   id stortime;
   model gas=stortime storsq storcu / p clm ss1 seqb;
```

The results appear in Output 1.13.

Output 1.13
Results from Cubic
Regression

```
                              The SAS System                               1

Model: MODEL1
Dependent Variable: GAS

                           Analysis of Variance

                            Sum of        Mean
        Source       DF    Squares       Square     F Value      Prob>F

        Model         3   1995.84667    665.28222    50.571      0.0001
        Error        11    144.70933     13.15539
        C Total      14   2140.55600

              Root MSE      3.62704     R-square     0.9324
              Dep Mean     25.74000     Adj R-sq     0.9140
              C.V.         14.09105

                           Parameter Estimates

                    Parameter      Standard      T for H0:
        Variable  DF  Estimate        Error     Parameter=0   Prob > |T|

        INTERCEP   1   4.373333    10.30146484      0.425       0.6794
        STORTIME   1  -0.277778    13.46557461     -0.021       0.9839
        STORSQ     1   4.700000     4.99795831      0.940       0.3672
        STORCU     1  -0.655556     0.55183603     -1.188       0.2599


        Variable  DF   Type I SS

        INTERCEP   1   9938.214000
        STORTIME   1   1916.801333
        STORSQ     1     60.480000
        STORCU     1     18.565333


                      Sequential Parameter Estimates

            INTERCEP        STORTIME         STORSQ          STORCU

             25.74             0               0               0
              1.76        7.9933333333         0               0
             -6.64       15.193333333        -1.2              0
        4.3733333333    -0.277777778         4.7        -0.655555556
```

```
                                                                           2

                         Dep Var   Predict   Std Err  Lower95%  Upper95%
        Obs    STORTIME     GAS      Value    Predict    Mean      Mean

          1       1       8.2000    8.1400    2.079    3.5640   12.7160
          2       1       6.6000    8.1400    2.079    3.5640   12.7160
          3       1       9.8000    8.1400    2.079    3.5640   12.7160
          4       2      19.7000   17.3733    1.839   13.3252   21.4215
          5       2      15.7000   17.3733    1.839   13.3252   21.4215
          6       2      16.0000   17.3733    1.839   13.3252   21.4215
          7       3      28.6000   28.1400    1.459   24.9278   31.3522
          8       3      25.0000   28.1400    1.459   24.9278   31.3522
          9       3      31.9000   28.1400    1.459   24.9278   31.3522
         10       4      30.8000   36.5067    1.839   32.4585   40.5548
         11       4      37.8000   36.5067    1.839   32.4585   40.5548
         12       4      40.2000   36.5067    1.839   32.4585   40.5548
         13       5      40.3000   38.5400    2.079   33.9640   43.1160
         14       5      42.9000   38.5400    2.079   33.9640   43.1160
         15       5      32.6000   38.5400    2.079   33.9640   43.1160


        Obs    STORTIME    Residual

          1       1        0.0600
          2       1       -1.5400
          3       1        1.6600
          4       2        2.3267
          5       2       -1.6733
```

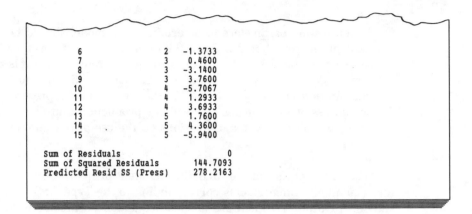

```
          6               2     -1.3733
          7               3      0.4600
          8               3     -3.1400
          9               3      3.7600
         10               4     -5.7067
         11               4      1.2933
         12               4      3.6933
         13               5      1.7600
         14               5      4.3600
         15               5     -5.9400

Sum of Residuals                      0
Sum of Squared Residuals       144.7093
Predicted Resid SS (Press)     278.2163
```

The Type I (sequential) sums of squares are useful for fitting polynomial models. As noted in Section 1.3.4, the Type I SS for any particular term is the amount by which the MODEL SS is increased by adding that particular term to the model that already contains all the terms preceding it in the MODEL statement. To see this, refer to Output 1.13. The Type I SS for INTERCEP is simply the correction for the mean, $n\bar{y}^2 = 9938.214$. The Type I SS for STORTIME (1916.80133) is the MODEL SS for the simple linear regression model (compare to Output 1.2). The Type I SS for STORSQ (60.48) is the increase in MODEL SS due to going from the linear model to the quadratic model. Finally, the Type I SS for STORCU (18.56533) is the increase in MODEL SS due to going from the quadratic to the cubic model.

A general approach to polynomial model building is to fit the highest order model considered appropriate and to use the SS1 option. With these results, you can start at the bottom of the Type I SS and work up until you encounter a term that is significant at, for instance, the .20 level. Then use PROC REG to fit the model of the order given by this first significant term and request whatever optional output is desired. Output 1.13 yields an error mean square of 13.155 and a Type I SS for STORCU of 18.565. An F test based on the Type I SS for STORCU is

$$F = 18.565 / 13.155 = 1.41 \qquad .$$

This F value, with 1 and 11 DF, is not significant at the .20 level. Therefore, you move up to the quadratic term. An F test based on the Type I SS for STORSQ is

$$F = 60.48 / 13.155 = 4.60$$

which is significant at the .20 level. Therefore, you fit a quadratic model.

Before fitting the quadratic model, however, there are two important notes:

□ As illustrated above, the tests of the polynomial terms should be made with F tests, based upon Type I sums of squares, rather than the t tests. (Note: F statistics are not computed by PROC REG, but you can obtain them from PROC GLM using the same MODEL statement.) Except in special cases, only the t test on the highest order term in a polynomial model is useful. The t test for the cubic term in Output 1.13 is equivalent to the Type I F test for the cubic term. None of the other t tests are directly useful. (This is evident since the t tests for the quadratic, linear, and intercept terms are nonsignificant in Output 1.13.)

□   When testing parameters to determine what model should be used for estimation, you should be sure the tests are made at a rather liberal level, such as .20 or .25, rather than at the more traditional levels of .05 or .01. This is done because the use of a level such as .05 tends to lead to models that do not have enough terms. In the context of the present example, this would result in estimates of mean gas production that are excessively biased. See Bancroft (1968) for discussions on the use of preliminary tests in estimation.

The SEQB option in the MODEL statement prints the regression coefficients for sequentially fitted models corresponding to the Type I SS. The results are shown in Output 1.13 and are labeled Sequential Parameter Estimates. Using only the intercept (which is the overall mean for GAS), the fitted equation is

$$GAS = 25.74 \quad .$$

Using a linear model, the fitted equation is

$$GAS = 1.76 + 7.99(STORTIME) \quad .$$

Using a quadratic model, the fitted equation is

$$GAS = -6.64 + 15.19(STORTIME) - 1.2(STORTIME)^2 \quad .$$

Finally, the fitted equation for the cubic model is

$$GAS = 4.37 - 0.28(STORTIME) + 4.7(STORTIME)^2 - 0.66(STORTIME)^3 \quad .$$

The last equation, of course, has the same coefficients as found under the heading Parameter Estimate in Output 1.13. Note how the STORTIME coefficient changes greatly when going from the linear to the quadratic to the cubic model. This illustrates that the coefficient for a given variable in one model does not necessarily tell much about the coefficient for that variable in another model.

At this point you have settled on the quadratic model. You may want more output based on this model, such as predicted values and confidence intervals. These can be obtained with the following statements:

```
proc reg data=newmeth;
   id stortime;
   model gas=stortime storsq / p clm;
```

Results from these statements appear in Output 1.14 and give the following fitted equation:

$$GAS = -6.64 + 15.19(STORTIME) - 1.2(STORTIME)^2 \quad .$$

Output 1.14
Results of
Quadratic
Regression

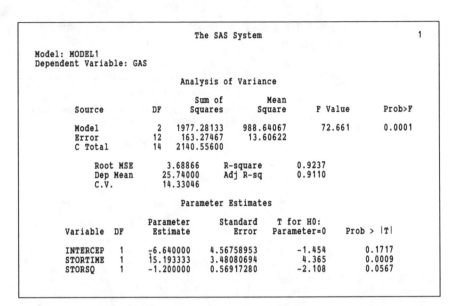

```
                              The SAS System                              1

Model: MODEL1
Dependent Variable: GAS

                          Analysis of Variance

                           Sum of        Mean
      Source       DF      Squares       Square     F Value    Prob>F

      Model         2    1977.28133    988.64067     72.661    0.0001
      Error        12     163.27467     13.60622
      C Total      14    2140.55600

          Root MSE        3.68866     R-square      0.9237
          Dep Mean       25.74000     Adj R-sq      0.9110
          C.V.           14.33046

                          Parameter Estimates

                    Parameter     Standard    T for H0:
      Variable  DF   Estimate       Error    Parameter=0    Prob > |T|

      INTERCEP   1   -6.640000    4.56758953    -1.454       0.1717
      STORTIME   1   15.193333    3.48080694     4.365       0.0009
      STORSQ     1   -1.200000    0.56917280    -2.108       0.0567
```

```
                                                                          2

                   Dep Var    Predict    Std Err   Lower95%   Upper95%
   Obs  STORTIME     GAS       Value     Predict     Mean       Mean

    1      1       8.2000     7.3533      2.004     2.9864     11.7203
    2      1       6.6000     7.3533      2.004     2.9864     11.7203
    3      1       9.8000     7.3533      2.004     2.9864     11.7203
    4      2      19.7000    18.9467      1.298    16.1188     21.7746
    5      2      15.7000    18.9467      1.298    16.1188     21.7746
    6      2      16.0000    18.9467      1.298    16.1188     21.7746
    7      3      28.6000    28.1400      1.484    24.9062     31.3738
    8      3      25.0000    28.1400      1.484    24.9062     31.3738
    9      3      31.9000    28.1400      1.484    24.9062     31.3738
   10      4      30.8000    34.9333      1.298    32.1054     37.7612
   11      4      37.8000    34.9333      1.298    32.1054     37.7612
   12      4      40.2000    34.9333      1.298    32.1054     37.7612
   13      5      40.3000    39.3267      2.004    34.9597     43.6936
   14      5      42.9000    39.3267      2.004    34.9597     43.6936
   15      5      32.6000    39.3267      2.004    34.9597     43.6936


   Obs  STORTIME    Residual

    1      1        0.8467
    2      1       -0.7533
    3      1        2.4467
    4      2        0.7533
    5      2       -3.2467
    6      2       -2.9467
    7      3        0.4600
    8      3       -3.1400
    9      3        3.7600
   10      4       -4.1333
   11      4        2.8667
   12      4        5.2667
   13      5        0.9733
   14      5        3.5733
   15      5       -6.7267


Sum of Residuals                  0
Sum of Squared Residuals      163.2747
Predicted Resid SS (Press)    262.6861
```

Output 1.15 shows the fitted quadratic curve plotted through the GAS production points.

Output 1.15
Plot of Quadratic Curve

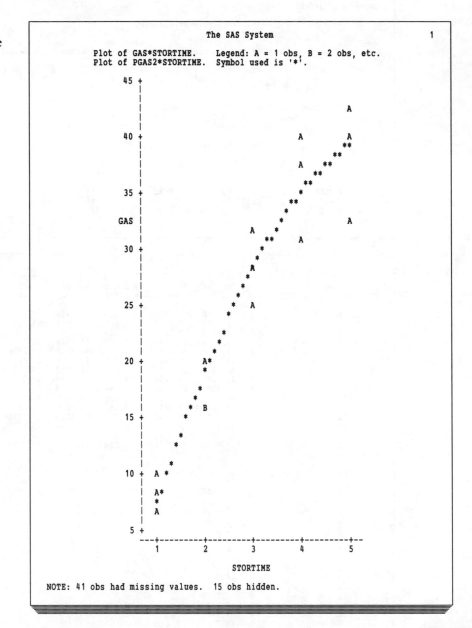

```
                              The SAS System                         1

      Plot of GAS*STORTIME.     Legend: A = 1 obs, B = 2 obs, etc.
      Plot of PGAS2*STORTIME.   Symbol used is '*'.

    45 +
       |
       |
       |                                                       A
       |
    40 +                                   A              A
       |                                                  **
       |                                             **
       |                                A          **
       |                                         **
    35 +                                      **
GAS    |                                    *
       |                              A    *                 A
       |                          A       *
    30 +                           **    *
       |                          A
       |                         *
       |                        *
       |                       *
    25 +                      *    A
       |                     *
       |                    *
       |                   *
    20 +               A*
       |                *
       |              *
       |            *   B
    15 +           *
       |          *
       |         *
       |        *
    10 +   A  *
       |   A*
       |   *
       |   A
       |
     5 +
        ---+---------+---------+---------+---------+--
           1         2         3         4         5

                             STORTIME

   NOTE: 41 obs had missing values.  15 obs hidden.
```

Section 1.6.2, "Plotting Regression Curves," demonstrates how to use PROC REG to create data sets and construct plots of this type.

It is instructive to compare the outputs from the quadratic model (Output 1.14) and the cubic model (Output 1.13). First, note that the error mean squares for the two models are very similar; 13.61 for the quadratic fit and 13.16 for the cubic fit. The cubic model does not fit the data significantly better than the quadratic model, and in this sense is no better. Note also that the confidence intervals from the quadratic model are generally more narrow (and, therefore, more desirable) than those obtained from the cubic model. For example, the confidence interval for STORTIME=2 in Output 1.14 has width

21.775−16.119=5.656, and the confidence interval for STORTIME=2 in Output 1.13 has width 21.422−13.325=8.097. This illustrates that the cubic model, which had the unnecessary third-degree term, produces less precise estimates of mean gas production.

1.5 Weighted Regression

The method of least squares was used to fit all the models in the preceding sections. This method, which is often called ordinary least squares (OLS), yields minimum variance unbiased estimates (MVUEs) of the model parameters if the observations are independent and if they have equal variances. It is often the case, however, that the observations do not have these two properties. This section discusses the use of weighted least squares, which is appropriate when the observations do not have equal variances.

The plot of GAS production versus STORTIME in Output 1.3 indicates that the variation increases with increasing STORTIME. This is a common phenomenon with data; populations with larger means tend to have larger variances. The usual assumptions are therefore not met in these cases. One approach to solving this problem is to make transformations. Another approach is to use weighted least squares (WLS), which gives minimum variance unbiased estimates if appropriate weighting constants can be specified for each term in the sum of squares to be minimized (see Section 1.1.2). The weight for the *j*th term should be proportional to the inverse of the variance of the observation in the term. That is, you should have

$$W_j = K / \sigma_j^2$$

where K is some constant and σ_j^2 is the variance of the *j*th observation.

In practice, parameter estimates can be improved even if the weights specified are only approximately equal to the optimum weights. This section illustrates the use of weighted regression.

The WEIGHT statement, which implements weighted regression in PROC REG, has the form

WEIGHT *variable*;

where *variable* is the name of a variable in the SAS data set whose values are to be used as weighting factors. Values of this variable should be positive. If a weight is negative or 0, the corresponding observation is ignored in the computations. Note that one WEIGHT statement applies to all the MODEL statements in a single PROC REG step and that only one variable may be specified in the WEIGHT statement.

Computation of standard deviations within STORTIME groups for the GAS production data shows that they are roughly proportional to STORTIME. This suggests a weighted regression with weights equal to the reciprocals of the values of STORSQ. The weighted regression uses the following statements:

```
data weighgas;
   set methane;
   storsq=stortime**2;
   ww=1 / storsq;
```

```
proc reg;
    model gas=stortime storsq / clm;
    id stortime;
    weight ww;
```

The results generated by these statements appear in Output 1.16.

Output 1.16
Results of
Weighted
Regression

```
                        The SAS System                              1

Model: MODEL1
Dependent Variable: GAS

                        Analysis of Variance

                        Sum of        Mean
    Source       DF    Squares      Square     F Value     Prob>F

    Model         2   339.05901   169.52950   111.525     0.0001
    Error        12    18.24131     1.52011
    C Total      14   357.30032

        Root MSE      1.23293    R-square    0.9489
        Dep Mean     13.29634    Adj R-sq    0.9404
        C.V.          9.27268

                        Parameter Estimates

                    Parameter     Standard    T for H0:
    Variable   DF    Estimate        Error   Parameter=0    Prob > |T|

    INTERCEP    1   -3.629954    2.53838830     -1.430       0.1782
    STORTIME    1   12.420970    2.67432456      4.645       0.0006
    STORSQ      1   -0.717542    0.52076500     -1.378       0.1934
```

```
                                                                    2

                              Dep Var   Predict   Std Err  Lower95%
Obs    STORTIME   Weight         GAS      Value   Predict     Mean

  1        1      1.0000      8.2000     8.0735     0.705    6.5365
  2        1      1.0000      6.6000     8.0735     0.705    6.5365
  3        1      1.0000      9.8000     8.0735     0.705    6.5365
  4        2      0.2500     19.7000    18.3418     1.061   16.0305
  5        2      0.2500     15.7000    18.3418     1.061   16.0305
  6        2      0.2500     16.0000    18.3418     1.061   16.0305
  7        3      0.1111     28.6000    27.1751     1.339   24.2566
  8        3      0.1111     25.0000    27.1751     1.339   24.2566
  9        3      0.1111     31.9000    27.1751     1.339   24.2566
 10        4      0.0625     30.8000    34.5733     1.575   31.1417
 11        4      0.0625     37.8000    34.5733     1.575   31.1417
 12        4      0.0625     40.2000    34.5733     1.575   31.1417
 13        5      0.0400     40.3000    40.5364     3.110   33.7611
 14        5      0.0400     42.9000    40.5364     3.110   33.7611
 15        5      0.0400     32.6000    40.5364     3.110   33.7611

                       Upper95%
Obs    STORTIME        Mean    Residual

  1        1         9.6104      0.1265
  2        1         9.6104     -1.4735
  3        1         9.6104      1.7265
  4        2        20.6531      1.3582
  5        2        20.6531     -2.6418
  6        2        20.6531     -2.3418
  7        3        30.0935      1.4249
  8        3        30.0935     -2.1751
```

```
         9              3   30.0935    4.7249
        10              4   38.0049   -3.7733
        11              4   38.0049    3.2267
        12              4   38.0049    5.6267
        13              5   47.3116   -0.2364
        14              5   47.3116    2.3636
        15              5   47.3116   -7.9364

Sum of Residuals                      0
Sum of Squared Residuals        18.2413
Predicted Resid SS (Press)      30.3921
NOTE: The above statistics use observation weights or frequencies.
```

You should note the effect of the weighted regression on the relative precision of mean GAS production estimates. This can be seen effectively by observing the width of confidence intervals. When unweighted regression is used, the confidence interval for mean GAS production for STORTIME=1 (5.7451 to 13.7616 from Output 1.6) is as wide as the confidence interval for STORTIME=5 (37.7184 to 45.7349 from Output 1.6), even though GAS production measures are more precise for STORTIME=1 than for STORTIME=5. But when weighted regression is used, the confidence intervals reflect different degrees of precision of the measurements. Compare the widths of the intervals for STORTIME=1 (6.5365 to 9.6104) and STORTIME=5 (33.7611 to 47.3116) in Output 1.16.

A popular application of weighted regression occurs when input data lines are means. Because the variance of a mean of n observations is σ^2/n, a weighted regression using the number of observations per mean as weights provides the correct analysis.

This use of the WEIGHT statement should not be confused with the statement

```
freq n;
```

which is appropriate when a data line represents N actual observations. Using this statement does indeed weight each data line by N, but it also causes the total degrees of freedom to be incremented by N.

1.6 Creating Data Sets

It is often useful to keep the predicted and residual values for further analyses, such as when analyzing residuals for specification error or outliers and plotting predicted values for response surface analysis.

A new data set containing all the variables of the data set input to PROC REG plus the predicted and residual values from the regression analysis can be created. For the AUCTION data set (see Output 1.4), the following statements request PROC REG to produce such a data set:

```
proc reg;
   model cost=cattle calves hogs sheep;
   output out=resplot p=pcost r=rcost;
```

The output data set RESPLOT contains the nine variables in the original data set plus PCOST, the estimated cost $\hat{y}$ of each market and RCOST, the difference between actual and estimated costs ($y-\hat{y}$). The number of variables specified after

P and R (or PREDICTED and RESIDUAL) must be the same as the number of dependent variables in the MODEL statement. However, it is not necessary to create both predicted and residual values. Predicted values, but obviously not residual values, are produced for any observation having missing values of the dependent variable. (See Section 1.6.2 for an example.)

1.6.1   Plotting Residuals

Residual plots are useful as a means of graphically checking the adequacy of a regression model. The residuals versus the predicted variable or independent variable(s) can be plotted to see if there is a dependency between the residuals and one or more of the other variables. If the regression is adequate, then no such dependency should appear in the residual plot. Of course, a residual plot with no apparent dependency does not by itself prove that the model is adequate; it is merely one diagnostic aid.

The data set RESPLOT is used to plot the residuals versus the predicted values and to identify the points according to whether they correspond to a primarily beef market (**B**) or to a market that is primarily of some other type (**O**). (See data set AUCTION in Output 1.4.)

The following statements produce the plot shown in Output 1.17:

```
proc plot data=resplot;
    plot rcost*pcost=type;
run;
```

Output 1.17
Residual Plot

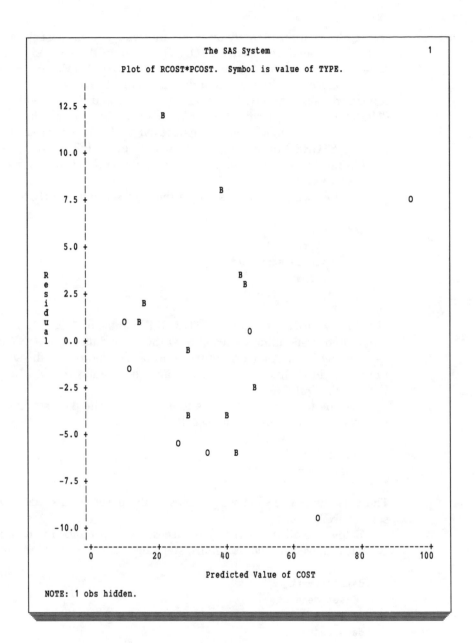

```
                              The SAS System                              1
                 Plot of RCOST*PCOST.  Symbol is value of TYPE.

          |
   12.5 + |                        B
          |
          |
   10.0 + |
          |
          |                              B
    7.5 + |                                                       O
          |
          |
    5.0 + |
          |
 R        |                              B
 e        |                              B
 s  2.5 + |
 i        |               B
 d        |          O  B
 u        |                                 O
 a  0.0 + |
 l        |                 B
          |        O
   -2.5 + |                                    B
          |
          |              B       B
   -5.0 + |             O
          |                O   B
          |
   -7.5 + |
          |
          |                                 O
  -10.0 + |
          |
          -+-------------+-------------+-------------+-------------+-------------+
           0            20            40            60            80           100
                              Predicted Value of COST

 NOTE: 1 obs hidden.
```

In this example, the plot of points appears to be a random scattering, and no pattern is apparent for groups of Bs or Os.

1.6.2 Plotting Regression Curves

Output 1.15 in Section 1.4 shows the quadratic curve fitted to the GAS production data plotted through the GAS production points. This section demonstrates how the plot is obtained.

As noted in Section 1.3.3, PROC REG can compute predicted values for all observations in the data set that have complete data for all variables on the right side of the MODEL statement. You can take advantage of this feature by adding a set of phony observations to the data set that contains values of the independent variables for which you want predicted values. You want to plot predicted values as a smooth curve over the range of the values of STORTIME from 1 to 5, so create observations densely over this interval. You must keep in mind, however, that for the quadratic model, STORSQ is also on the right side of the MODEL statement, so you must create values of both STORTIME and STORSQ.

The basic idea is to create a data set named PHONY that contains the generated values of STORTIME and STORSQ, and then to add the observations in PHONY to the observations in NEWMETH to form a new data set, BOTH. (Recall from Section 1.4 that a data set named NEWMETH was created by adding the variable STORSQ to the original data set named METHANE.) The process of combining the two data sets PHONY and NEWMETH in this manner is called concatenation.

The following statements create the data set named PHONY:

```
data phony;
   do stortime=1 to 5 by .1;
      storsq=stortime**2;
      output;
   end;
```

The data set PHONY contains STORTIME values of 1.0, 1.1, 1.2, . . . , 4.9, and 5.0 and corresponding values of STORSQ. The data set PHONY is created by using a DO loop. For more information on DO loops, see the section "DO, Iterative," in Chapter 9, "SAS Language Statements," in *SAS Language: Reference, Version 6, First Edition.*

Use the following statements to concatenate the data sets NEWMETH and PHONY and to form the data set BOTH:

```
data both;
   set newmeth phony;
```

The variable GAS has missing values in the observations that came from the data set PHONY.

Below are all the DATA steps necessary to produce the data sets PHONY and BOTH, followed by the procedure steps necessary to produce Output 1.15.

```
data newmeth;
   set methane;
   storsq=stortime**2;
data phony;
   do stortime=1 to 5 by .1;
      storsq=stortime**2;
      output;
   end;
data both;
   set newmeth phony;
proc reg data=both;
   model gas=stortime storsq / p;
   output out=gasplot p=pgas2;
proc plot data=gasplot;
   plot gas*stortime pgas2*stortime='*' / overlay;
```

Parameter estimates computed by PROC REG are based on only those observations that have complete data for all variables in the MODEL statement, that is, the variables in the NEWMETH data set. Predicted values (PGAS2) are computed for all observations in the data set BOTH that have complete data for STORTIME and STORSQ.

PROC PLOT produces printer graphics, which are not very sophisticated by modern graphic standards, but are nonetheless useful for data analysis. More sophisticated graphics can be obtained with the GPLOT procedure, which is available in SAS/GRAPH software. For more information about SAS/GRAPH software, consult *SAS/GRAPH Software: Reference, Version 6, First Edition, Volume 1* and *Volume 2*.

1.6.3 Plotting Other Statistics

Other statistics available as MODEL statement options can also be included in the output data set and used for plotting or other analyses. For example, the confidence limits for mean GAS production from the METHANE data can be plotted along with the regression curve using the following statements:

```
proc reg data=both;
   model gas=stortime storsq;
   output out=ciplot p=pgas2 l95m=l u95m=u;
proc plot data=ciplot;
   plot pgas2*stortime='*' l*stortime='-' u*stortime='-' / overlay;
```

The variables L and U have values equal to the lower 95% and upper 95% confidence limits, respectively. The resulting plot appears in Output 1.18. If you want prediction limits instead of confidence limits, use L95 and U95 in place of L95M and U95M in the OUTPUT statement. (See Section 1.3.3 for the distinction between prediction limits and confidence limits.)

Output 1.18
Plotting
Confidence
Intervals

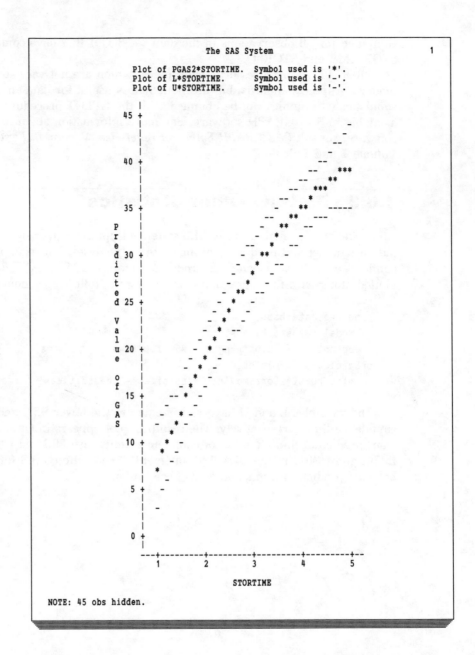

```
            Plot of PGAS2*STORTIME.   Symbol used is '*'.
            Plot of L*STORTIME.       Symbol used is '-'.
            Plot of U*STORTIME.       Symbol used is '-'.
```

NOTE: 45 obs hidden.

1.6.4 Predicting to a Different Set of Data

A regression equation estimated from one set of data can be used to predict values of the dependent variable for another set of similar data. This type of prediction has been used to settle charges of pay discrimination against members of minority groups. An equation relating pay rates to factors like education, performance, and tenure is estimated with data for nonminority employees (usually white males). This equation predicts what salaries should be for minority employees in the absence of discrimination or some other factor; if predicted minority salaries are substantially higher than actual minority salaries, there is cause to suspect a factor like discrimination. This type of analysis is illustrated below with the auction market example from Section 1.3.2.

Remember that in Section 1.6.1 the variable TYPE was created to identify beef and other markets. In this example a new variable, BCOST, is created. This variable's values are the costs of beef markets or a missing value for the other markets. To begin, insert the following additional statements before the CARDS statement:

```
if type='B' then bcost=cost;
else bcost=.;
```

Now analyze the data with PROC REG:

```
proc reg;
    model bcost=cattle calves hogs sheep;
    output out=b p=pbcost;
```

The results generated by these statements appear in Output 1.19.

Output 1.19
Regression for
Beef Markets Only

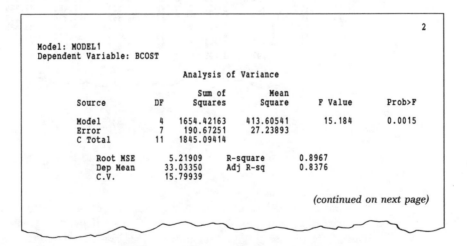

```
                        The SAS System                              1
Model: MODEL1
Dependent Variable: COST

                      Analysis of Variance

                        Sum of        Mean
        Source     DF   Squares      Square     F Value    Prob>F

        Model       4  7936.73649  1984.18412    52.310    0.0001
        Error      14   531.03865    37.93133
        C Total    18  8467.77514

            Root MSE      6.15884   R-square     0.9373
            Dep Mean     35.29342   Adj R-sq     0.9194
            C.V.         17.45040

                      Parameter Estimates

                    Parameter    Standard    T for H0:
        Variable  DF  Estimate      Error   Parameter=0   Prob > |T|

        INTERCEP   1  2.288425   3.38737222     0.676      0.5103
        CATTLE     1  3.215525   0.42215239     7.617      0.0001
        CALVES     1  1.613148   0.85167539     1.894      0.0791
        HOGS       1  0.814849   0.47073855     1.731      0.1054
        SHEEP      1  0.802579   0.18981766     4.228      0.0008
```

```
                                                                    2

Model: MODEL1
Dependent Variable: BCOST

                      Analysis of Variance

                        Sum of        Mean
        Source     DF   Squares      Square     F Value    Prob>F

        Model       4  1654.42163   413.60541    15.184    0.0015
        Error       7   190.67251    27.23893
        C Total    11  1845.09414

            Root MSE      5.21909   R-square     0.8967
            Dep Mean     33.03350   Adj R-sq     0.8376
            C.V.         15.79939

                              (continued on next page)
```

```
(continued from previous page)
                        Parameter Estimates

                      Parameter      Standard     T for H0:
          Variable  DF  Estimate        Error   Parameter=0   Prob > |T|

          INTERCEP   1  4.409175    4.22796743       1.043      0.3317
          CATTLE     1  3.235018    0.57108119       5.665      0.0008
          CALVES     1  2.210468    0.89842181       2.460      0.0434
          HOGS       1 -2.325496    1.82764877      -1.272      0.2439
          SHEEP      1  1.373493    1.17547078       1.168      0.2809
```

The new regression estimates are based on the 12 beef markets only. Note that the coefficients for HOGS and SHEEP are not significantly different from 0. Worse yet, the coefficient for HOGS is negative. Predicted values are generated in data set B for all markets.

In data set C, residuals for all markets are created:

```
data c;
   set b;
   rbcost=cost-pbcost;
proc print;
```

The results appear in Output 1.20.

Output 1.20
*Prediction from
One Data Set to
Another*

```
                              The SAS System                              1

   OBS    MKT    CATTLE    CALVES    HOGS     SHEEP     COST     VOLUME

     1     1      3.437     5.791    3.268    10.649    27.698    23.145
     2     2     12.801     4.558    5.751    14.375    57.634    37.485
     3     3      6.136     6.223   15.175     2.811    47.172    30.345
     4     4     11.685     3.212    0.639     0.694    49.295    16.230
     5     5      5.733     3.220    0.534     2.052    24.115    11.539
     6     6      3.021     4.348    0.839     2.356    33.612    10.564
     7     7      1.689     0.634    0.318     2.209     9.512     4.850
     8     8      2.339     1.895    0.610     0.605    14.755     5.449
     9     9      1.025     0.834    0.734     2.825    10.570     5.418
    10    10      2.936     1.419    0.331     0.231    15.394     4.917
    11    11      5.049     4.195    1.589     1.957    27.843    12.790
    12    12      1.693     3.602    0.837     1.582    17.717     7.714
    13    13      1.187     2.679    0.459    18.837    20.253    23.162
    14    14      9.730     3.951    3.780     0.524    37.465    17.985
    15    15     14.325     4.300   10.781    36.863   101.334    66.269
    16    16      7.737     9.043    1.394     1.524    47.427    19.698
    17    17      7.538     4.538    2.565     5.109    35.944    19.750
    18    18     10.211     4.994    3.081     3.681    45.945    21.967
    19    19      8.697     3.005    1.378     3.338    46.890    16.418
```

OBS	TYPE	PCOST	RCOST	BCOST	PBCOST	RBCOST
1	O	33.8915	-6.1935	.	35.3554	-7.6574
2	O	67.0264	-9.3924	.	62.2660	-4.6320
3	O	46.6789	0.4931	.	6.5865	40.5855
4	B	46.1209	3.1741	49.295	48.7776	0.5174
5	B	27.9994	-3.8844	24.115	31.6498	-7.5348
6	B	21.5910	12.0210	33.612	25.0781	8.5339
7	O	10.7742	-1.2622	.	13.5691	-4.0571
8	B	13.8491	0.9059	14.755	15.5771	-0.8221
9	O	9.7951	0.7749	.	11.7418	-1.1718
10	B	14.4734	0.9206	15.394	16.5914	-1.1974
11	B	28.1562	-0.3132	27.843	29.0084	-1.1654
12	B	15.4946	2.2224	17.717	18.0746	-0.3576
13	O	25.9191	-5.6661	.	38.9761	-18.7231
14	B	43.4497	-5.9847	37.465	36.5488	0.9162
15	O	93.6577	7.6763	.	85.8157	15.5183
16	B	44.1137	3.3133	47.427	48.2792	-0.8522
17	B	40.0380	-4.0940	35.944	39.8781	-3.9341
18	B	48.6431	-2.6981	45.945	46.3720	-0.4270
19	B	38.9032	7.9868	46.890	40.5668	6.3232

The beef markets do not appear to be good predictors for other markets. Output 1.20 shows that for the market represented by OBS 3, a heavy hog market, the negative HOGS coefficient gives a predicted cost of $6,586 (under the variable PBCOST) when the actual cost is $47,172.

1.6.5 Plotting with Transformed Variables

Regression analysis is also useful with transformed values. One popular model takes the logarithm (either base *e* or base 10) of both dependent and independent variables:

$$\log(y) = \beta_0 + \beta_1 \log(x_1) + \beta_2 \log(x_2) + \ldots + \beta_m \log(x_m)$$

as a means of linearizing the multiplicative model (assuming base *e*)

$$y = (e^{\beta 0})(x_1^{\beta 1})(x_2^{\beta 2}) \ldots (x_m^{\beta m}) \quad .$$

This model is easy to implement. If you create the log values in the DATA step and run PROC REG on these transformed values, the predicted and residual values that result are expressed as logs, and the log model can be compared to a linear or polynomial model.

Assume LY and LX have been created as the logarithms of Y and X, respectively. Use the following statements:

```
proc reg;
   model y=x;
   output out=a p=py r=ry;
   model ly=lx;
   output out=b p=ply;
data compare;
   merge a b;
   pey=exp(ply);
   rey=y-pey;
```

```
proc print;
proc plot;
   plot y*x='0' py*x='1' pey*x='*' / overlay;
```

Specific features of these statements are described below:

□ Two MODEL statements with two corresponding OUTPUT statements are used under the same PROC REG. The output data sets are the same as if PROC REG had been called separately for each MODEL statement.

□ The two data sets (A and B) are merged rather than concatenated. That is, they are adjoined side-by-side rather than one stacked on top of the other. Merging is more efficient in this case.

□ In the data set COMPARE, the predicted log values revert to the original scale of Y; these predicted values (PEY) are used to compare residuals (REY).

□ The plot compares the fit of the linear and exponential models.

Note that the values of PEY are biased estimates of Y. In general, the mean of PEY is smaller than the mean of Y; the smaller the value of R^2, the larger the bias.

1.7 Exact Collinearity: Linear Dependency

Linear dependency occurs when exact linear relationships exist among the independent variables, that is, when one or more of the columns of the **X** matrix can be expressed as a linear combination of the other columns. In this event, the **X′X** matrix is singular and cannot be inverted in the usual sense to obtain parameter estimates. If this occurs, PROC REG uses a generalized inverse to compute parameter estimates. However, care must be exercised to determine exactly what parameters are being estimated. More technically, the generalized inverse approach yields one particular solution to the normal equations. The PROC REG computations are illustrated with the auction market data.

Recall the variable VOLUME in Output 1.4. VOLUME represents the total of all major livestock sold in each market. This is an example of exact linear dependency: VOLUME is exactly the sum of the variables CATTLE, CALVES, HOGS, and SHEEP.

The following statements produce the results shown in Output 1.21:

```
proc reg;
   model cost=cattle calves hogs sheep volume;
```

Output 1.21
Results of Exact
Collinearity

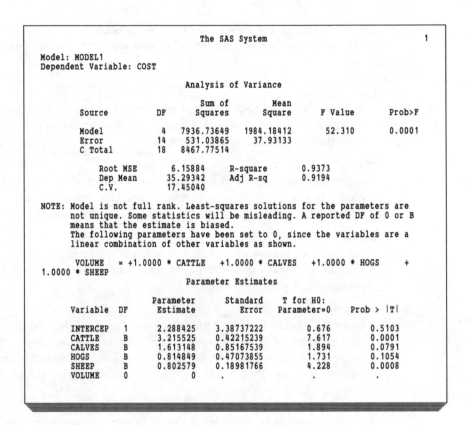

```
                            The SAS System                         1

Model: MODEL1
Dependent Variable: COST

                         Analysis of Variance

                          Sum of        Mean
      Source        DF   Squares       Square     F Value    Prob>F

      Model          4  7936.73649  1984.18412     52.310    0.0001
      Error         14   531.03865    37.93133
      C Total       18  8467.77514

           Root MSE      6.15884    R-square     0.9373
           Dep Mean     35.29342    Adj R-sq     0.9194
           C.V.         17.45040

NOTE: Model is not full rank. Least-squares solutions for the parameters are
      not unique. Some statistics will be misleading. A reported DF of 0 or B
      means that the estimate is biased.
      The following parameters have been set to 0, since the variables are a
      linear combination of other variables as shown.

      VOLUME   = +1.0000 * CATTLE   +1.0000 * CALVES   +1.0000 * HOGS    +
1.0000 * SHEEP
                         Parameter Estimates

                   Parameter     Standard    T for H0:
      Variable DF   Estimate       Error    Parameter=0    Prob > |T|

      INTERCEP  1   2.288425    3.38737222     0.676        0.5103
      CATTLE    B   3.215525    0.42215239     7.617        0.0001
      CALVES    B   1.613148    0.85167539     1.894        0.0791
      HOGS      B   0.814849    0.47073855     1.731        0.1054
      SHEEP     B   0.802579    0.18981766     4.228        0.0008
      VOLUME    0          0          .           .            .
```

In Output 1.21, the existence of the collinearity is indicated by the note in the model summary, followed by the equation describing the collinearity. The parameter estimates that are printed are equivalent to the ones that are obtained if VOLUME were not included in the MODEL statement. A variable, which is a linear combination of other variables that precede it in the MODEL statement, is indicated by 0 under the DF and Parameter Estimate headings. Other variables involved in the linear dependencies are indicated with a B, for bias, under the DF heading. The estimates are, in fact, unbiased estimates of the parameters in a model that does not include the variables indicated with a 0 but are biased for the parameters in the other models. Thus, the parameter estimates printed in Output 1.21 are unbiased estimates for the coefficients in the model

$$COST = \beta_0 + \beta_1(CATTLE) + \beta_2(CALVES) + \beta_3(HOGS) + \beta_4(SHEEP) + \varepsilon \quad .$$

But these estimates are biased for the parameters in a model that included VOLUME but did not include, for example, SHEEP.

1.8 Diagnostic Measures

Statistical measures that are used for detecting problems with regression models and data sets are called diagnostic measures. The problems are of various types and include model misspecification, outliers, influential observations, and collinearity. These are terms that have no precise definitions, and their meanings vary from one author to another. The following are general descriptions of the terms:

misspecification

refers to a model that does not represent the system that gave rise to the data, in terms of either inadequate specification of terms in the model or incorrect specification of the random error.

outlier

refers generally to an observation whose value of the dependent variable is either much larger or much smaller than the values of the dependent variable for other observations with similar values of the independent variables.

influential observation

refers to an observation that, because of its particular values of independent variables, exerts especially heavy influence on the values of parameter estimates or predicted values.

collinearity

refers to nearly linear relationships among the independent variables, that is, one or more of the independent variables are almost linear combinations of other independent variables. Strictly speaking, collinearity refers to the existence of one linear relationship. Multicollinearity refers to the existence of several linear relationships.

Several good regression texts that give various treatments of regression diagnostic measures have been published in recent years. The most extensive treatment is given by Belsley, Kuh, and Welsch (1980). PROC REG computes virtually all of the diagnostic measures discussed by these authors, plus some others. For more information on the capabilities of PROC REG in this area, see Chapter 36 of the *SAS/STAT User's Guide, Volume 2* and Freund and Littell (1991).

Chapter 2 Analysis of Variance for Balanced Data

2.1 *Introduction 52*

2.2 *One- and Two-Sample Tests and Statistics 52*
2.2.1 *One-Sample Statistics 52*
2.2.2 *Two Related Samples 55*
2.2.3 *Two Independent Samples 56*

2.3 *Comparison of Several Means: Analysis of Variance 59*
2.3.1 *Terminology and Notation 59*
2.3.2 *Using the ANOVA Procedure 62*
2.3.3 *Multiple Comparisons and Preplanned
  Comparisons 63*
2.3.4 *Analysis of One-Way Classification of Data 64*
  Computing the ANOVA Table 65
  *Computing Means, Multiple Comparisons of Means,
    and Confidence Intervals 67*
  *Preplanned Comparisons for One-Way Classification:
    the CONTRAST Statement 68*
  Linear Combinations of Model Parameters 72
  Testing Several Contrasts Simultaneously 72
  Orthogonal Contrasts 73
  *Estimating Linear Combinations of Parameters: the
    ESTIMATE Statement 74*
2.3.5 *Randomized-Blocks Design with Multiple
  Comparisons 76*
  Analysis of Variance for Randomized-Blocks Design 77
  Other Methods for Multiple Comparisons 78
2.3.6 *Latin Square Design with Two Response Variables 83*
2.3.7 *Two-Way Factorial Experiment 86*
  ANOVA for a Two-Way Factorial Experiment 87
  Multiple Comparison for Factorial Experiment 91
  *Preplanned Comparisons in a Two-Way Factorial
    Experiment 95*
  Simple Effect Comparisons 97
  Main Effect Comparisons 99
  Simultaneous Contrasts in Two-Way Classification 99
  *Comparing Levels of One Factor within Subgroups of
    Levels of Another Factor 101*
  *An Easier Way to Set Up CONTRAST and ESTIMATE
    Statements 103*

2.1 Introduction

The arithmetic mean is the basic descriptive statistic associated with the linear model. This chapter presents one- and two-sample analyses of means using the MEANS and TTEST procedures. More complex analyses using the ANOVA and GLM procedures are also discussed.[*]

2.2 One- and Two-Sample Tests and Statistics

In addition to a wide selection of descriptive statistics, the SAS System can provide *t* tests for a single sample, for paired samples, and for two independent samples.

2.2.1 One-Sample Statistics

The following single-sample statistics are available with the SAS System:

mean: $\bar{x} = (\Sigma x_i) / n$

standard deviation: $s = \sqrt{\Sigma (x_i - \bar{x})^2 / (n - 1)}$

standard error of the mean: $s_{\bar{x}} = s / \sqrt{n}$

student's *t*: $t = \bar{x} / s_{\bar{x}}$

The statistics $\bar{x}$, s, and $s_{\bar{x}}$ estimate the population parameters μ, σ, and $\sigma_{\bar{x}} = \sigma / \sqrt{n}$, respectively. Student's *t* is used to test the null hypothesis H_0: $\mu = 0$.

PROC MEANS can compute most common descriptive statistics and can calculate *t* tests for a single sample and the associated significance probability. The basic syntax of the MEANS procedure is as follows:

PROC MEANS *options*;
    VAR *variables*;
    BY *variables*;
    CLASS *variables*;
    WHERE *variables*;
    FREQ *variables*;
    WEIGHT *variable*;
    ID *variables*;
    OUTPUT *options*;

The VAR statement is optional. If this statement is not included, PROC MEANS computes statistics for all numeric variables in the data set. The BY, CLASS and WHERE statements enable you to obtain separate computations for subgroups of observations in the data set. The FREQ, WEIGHT, ID, and OUTPUT statements can be used with PROC MEANS to perform functions such as weighting or creating an output data set. For more information on PROC MEANS,

---

[*] The SAS System can provide other descriptive statistics with the UNIVARIATE, MEANS, and SUMMARY procedures. PROC SUMMARY is useful for creating data sets of descriptive statistics.

see Chapter 21, "The MEANS Procedure," in the *SAS Procedures Guide, Version 6, Third Edition.*

The following example below shows a single-sample analysis. In order to design a mechanical harvester for bell peppers, an engineer determined the angle (from a vertical reference) at which 28 peppers hang on the plant (ANGLE). The following statistics are needed:

□   the sample mean $\bar{x}$, an estimate of the population mean, μ

□   the sample standard deviation s, an estimate of the population standard deviation, σ

□   the standard error of the mean $s_{\bar{x}}$, a measure of the precision of the mean.

Using these computations, the engineer can construct a 95% confidence interval for the mean, the endpoints of which are $\bar{x} - t_{.05}s_{\bar{x}}$ and $\bar{x} + t_{.05}s_{\bar{x}}$, where $t_{.05}$ is obtained from a table of t values. The engineer can also use the statistic $t = \bar{x}/s_{\bar{x}}$ to test the hypothesis that the population mean is equal to 0.

The following SAS statements print the data and perform these computations:

```
data peppers;
   input angle aa;
cards;
3 11 -7 2 3 8 -3 -2 13 4 7
-1 4 7 -1 4 12 -3 7 5 3 -1
9 -7 2 4 8 -2
;
proc print;
proc means mean std stderr t prt;
run;
```

This PROC MEANS statement specifically calls for the mean (MEAN), the standard deviation (STD), the standard error of the mean (STDERR), a *t* test of the hypothesis that the population mean is 0 (T), and the significance probability of the *t* test (PRT). These specifications represent only a few of the descriptive statistics that can be requested in a PROC MEANS statement. The data, listed by PROC PRINT, and output from PROC MEANS, appear in Output 2.1.

Output 2.1
PROC MEANS for Single-Sample Analysis

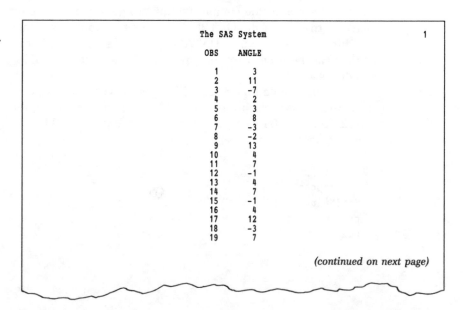

```
                            The SAS System                              1

                        OBS      ANGLE

                          1         3
                          2        11
                          3        -7
                          4         2
                          5         3
                          6         8
                          7        -3
                          8        -2
                          9        13
                         10         4
                         11         7
                         12        -1
                         13         4
                         14         7
                         15        -1
                         16         4
                         17        12
                         18        -3
                         19         7
```

(continued on next page)

```
(continued from previous page)
                                  20      5
                                  21      3
                                  22     -1
                                  23      9
                                  24     -7
                                  25      2
                                  26      4
                                  27      8
                                  28     -2
```

```
                                                                    2
        Analysis Variable : ANGLE


               Mean      Std Dev     Std Error          T   Prob>|T|
        ----------------------------------------------------------------
            3.1785714   5.2988718    1.0013926   3.1741510    0.0037
        ----------------------------------------------------------------
```

A t table shows $t_{.05} = 2.052$ with 27 degrees of freedom (DF). The confidence interval for the mean ANGLE is, therefore, $3.179 \pm 2.052(1.0014) =$ (1.123, 5.333). The value of $t = 3.17$ has a significance probability of $p = 0.0037$, indicating that the engineer can reject the null hypothesis that the mean ANGLE in the population is 0.

You can use the OUTPUT statement, along with other programming statements, to compute the confidence interval.

```
output out=stats
mean=xbar stderr=sxbar;
data stats; set stats;
t=tinv(27,.05);
bound=t*sxbar;
lower=xbar-bound;
upper=xbar+bound;
proc print;
run;
```

This might seem a little complicated just to get a confidence interval. However, it illustrates the use of the OUTPUT statement to obtain computations from a procedure and the use of a DATA step to make additional computations. Similar methods can be used with other procedures, such as the GLM and REG procedures.

You should note that a test of H_0: $\mu = C$, where $C \neq 0$, can be obtained by subtracting C from each x (in the DATA step) and applying the single-sample analysis to the difference $(x_i - C)$. For example, you could test H_0: $\mu = 5$ with the following statements:

```
data peppers;
set peppers;
diff5=angle-5;
proc means t;
run;
```

2.2.2   Two Related Samples

An inference about means from paired samples can be made by applying a single-sample analysis to the difference between the paired measurements. This type of analysis is appropriate for randomized-blocks experiments with two treatments. It is also appropriate in many experiments that use before-treatment and after-treatment responses on the same experimental unit, as shown in the example below.

A combination stimulant-relaxant drug is administered to 15 animals whose pulse rates are measured before (PRE) and after (POST) administration of the drug. The purpose of the experiment is to determine if there is a change in the pulse rate as a result of the drug.

The appropriate t statistic is

$$t = \bar{d} / \sqrt{s_d^2 / n}$$

where $\bar{d}$ is the mean and s_d^2 is the variance of the individual differences between the paired measurements for individual animals.

The t for the paired differences tests the null hypothesis of no change in pulse rate. You can compute the differences, D = PRE − POST, for each subject and the one-sample t test based on the differences with the following SAS statements:

```
data pulse;
   input pre post;
   d=pre-post;
cards;
62 61
63 62
58 59
64 61
64 63
61 58
68 61
66 64
65 62
67 68
69 65
61 60
64 65
61 63
63 62
;
proc print;
proc means mean std stderr t prt;
   var d;
run;
```

In this example, the following SAS statement creates the variable D (the difference in rates):

```
d=pre-post;
```

Remember that a SAS statement that generates a new variable is part of a DATA step.

The PROC MEANS statements here and in the preceding example are identical. The statement

```
var d;
```

following the PROC MEANS statement requests that the PROC MEANS analysis is restricted to the variable D; otherwise, computations would also be performed on PRE and POST. The data, listed by PROC PRINT, and output from PROC MEANS appear in Output 2.2.

Output 2.2
Paired-Difference
Analysis

```
                         The SAS System                         1

                 OBS    PRE    POST    D

                  1      62     61     1
                  2      63     62     1
                  3      58     59    -1
                  4      64     61     3
                  5      64     63     1
                  6      61     58     3
                  7      68     61     7
                  8      66     64     2
                  9      65     62     3
                 10      67     68    -1
                 11      69     65     4
                 12      61     60     1
                 13      64     65    -1
                 14      61     63    -2
                 15      63     62     1
```

```
                                                                2

      Analysis Variable : D


          Mean        Std Dev      Std Error        T    Prob>|T|
      ----------------------------------------------------------------
        1.4666667    2.3258383    0.6005289    2.4422917   0.0285
      ----------------------------------------------------------------
```

The t value of 2.44 with $p = 0.0285$ indicates a change in mean pulse rate. Because the mean of D (1.46) is positive, the drug evidently decreases pulse rate.

2.2.3 Two Independent Samples

You can test the significance of the difference between means from two independent samples with the t statistic

$$t = (\bar{x}_1 - \bar{x}_2) / \sqrt{s^2(1 / n_1 + 1 / n_2)}$$

where $\bar{x}_1$, $\bar{x}_2$ and s_1^2, s_2^2 (in the following equations) refer to the means and variances of the two groups, and

$$s^2 = [(n_1 - 1)s_1^2 + (n_2 - 1)s_2^2] / (n_1 + n_2 - 2)$$
$$= \text{pooled variance estimate} \quad .$$

The pooled variance estimate should be used if it is reasonable to assume $\sigma_1^2 = \sigma_2^2$. If this assumption cannot be justified, then an approximate t statistic is given by

$$t = (\bar{x}_1 - \bar{x}_2) / \sqrt{s_1^2/n_1 + s_2^2/n_2} \quad .$$

Both of these t statistics can be computed by PROC TTEST along with the (folded) F statistic

$$F' = (\text{larger of } s_1^2, s_2^2) / (\text{smaller of } s_1^2, s_2^2)$$

for testing the assumption $\sigma_1^2 = \sigma_2^2$.*

An example of this test is the comparison of muzzle velocities of cartridges made from two types of gunpowder (POWDER). The muzzle velocity (VELOCITY) was measured for eight cartridges made from powder type 1 and ten cartridges from powder type 2.

The two-sample t test is appropriate for testing the null hypothesis that the muzzle velocities are equal. You can obtain such a t test with these SAS statements:

```
data bullets;
   input powder velocity;
cards;
1 27.3
1 28.1
1 27.4
1 27.7
1 28.0
1 28.1
1 27.4
1 27.1
2 28.3
2 27.9
2 28.1
2 28.3
2 27.9
2 27.6
2 28.5
2 27.9
2 28.4
2 27.7
proc print data=bullets;
proc ttest data=bullets; var velocity;
   class powder;
run;
```

PROC TTEST performs the two-sample analysis. The variable POWDER in the CLASS statement identifies the groups (or treatments) for which means are to be compared. CLASS variables may be numeric or character variables. This CLASS statement has the same interpretation in all other procedures that require

---

* PROC ANOVA gives equivalent results but does not test equality of the variances and perform the approximate t test.

identification of groups of treatments. In PROC TTEST, the CLASS variable must have exactly two values; otherwise, the procedure issues an error message and stops processing. The VAR statement identifies the variable whose means you wish to compare. See Section 2.3, "Comparison of Several Means: Analysis of Variance," for comparison of more than two means. Output 2.3 shows the data and results of PROC TTEST.

Output 2.3
PROC TTEST for
Two Independent
Samples

```
                        The SAS System                          1

            OBS      POWDER      VELOCITY

             1          1          27.3
             2          1          28.1
             3          1          27.4
             4          1          27.7
             5          1          28.0
             6          1          28.1
             7          1          27.4
             8          1          27.1
             9          2          28.3
            10          2          27.9
            11          2          28.1
            12          2          28.3
            13          2          27.9
            14          2          27.6
            15          2          28.5
            16          2          27.9
            17          2          28.4
            18          2          27.7
```

```
                                                                2

                         TTEST PROCEDURE

   Variable: VELOCITY

   POWDER      N         Mean      Std Dev    Std Error     Minimum      Maximum
   ------------------------------------------------------------------------------
      1        8    27.63750000   0.39256483  0.13879263  27.10000000  28.10000000
      2       10    28.06000000   0.30623158  0.09683893  27.60000000  28.50000000

   Variances        T       DF     Prob>|T|
   -----------------------------------------
   Unequal      -2.4965    13.1     0.0267
   Equal        -2.5694    16.0     0.0206

   For H0: Variances are equal, F' = 1.64    DF = (7,9)    Prob>F' = 0.4782
```

PROC PRINT produces a listing of the data. PROC TTEST produces the number of observations, mean, standard deviation, and standard error of the mean of VELOCITY for the two levels of POWDER. The headings T, DF, and Prob > |T|, however, correspond to two types of assumptions: the usual two-sample t test that assumes equal variances (Equal) or an approximate t test that does not assume equal variances (Unequal). The approximate t test uses Satterthwaite's approximation for the sum of two mean squares (Satterthwaite 1946) to calculate the significance probability Prob > |T|.

The F test at the bottom of Output 2.3 is used to test the hypothesis of equal variances. An $F' = 1.64$ with a significance probability of $p = 0.4782$ provides insufficient evidence to conclude that the variances are unequal. For the test assuming equal variances, $t = -2.5694$ with a significance level of 0.0206. This is strong evidence of a difference between the mean velocities for the two powder types, with the mean velocity for powder type 2 greater than for powder type 1.

2.3 Comparison of Several Means: Analysis of Variance

When you want to make statistical inferences about a set of more than two means, use analysis of variance. The SAS System offers two general purpose procedures for analysis of variance: PROC ANOVA for balanced or orthogonal data sets and PROC GLM for unbalanced data sets. Other procedures, such as the NESTED and VARCOMP procedures, are available for specialized types of analyses.

2.3.1 Terminology and Notation

Analysis of variance partitions the variation among observations into portions associated with certain factors that are defined by the classification scheme of the data. These factors are called *sources of variation*. For example, variation in prices of houses can be partitioned into portions associated with region differences, house type differences, and other differences. Partitioning is done in terms of sums of squares (SS) with a corresponding partitioning of the associated degrees of freedom (DF). For three sources of variation (A, B, C)

$$\text{TOTAL SS} = \text{SS(A)} + \text{SS(B)} + \text{SS(C)} + \text{RESIDUAL SS} \quad .$$

The term TOTAL SS is normally the sum of the squared deviations of the data values from the overall mean, $\Sigma(y-\bar{y})^2$, where y represents the response variable.

The formula for computing SS(A), SS(B), and SS(C) depends on the situation. Typically, these terms are sums of squared differences between means. The term RESIDUAL SS is simply what is left after subtracting SS(A), SS(B), and SS(C) from TOTAL SS.

Degrees of freedom are numbers associated with sums of squares. They represent the number of independent differences used to compute the sum of squares. For example, $\Sigma(y_i - \bar{y})^2$ is a sum of squares based upon the n differences $y_1-\bar{y}, y_2-\bar{y}, \ldots, y_n-\bar{y}$. There are only $n-1$ independent differences, because any one of these differences is equal to the negative of the sum of the others. For example, consider the following:

$$y_n - \bar{y} = -\left(\sum_{i=1}^{n-1} (y_i - \bar{y}) \right) \quad .$$

Total degrees of freedom are partitioned into degrees of freedom associated with each factor and the residual:

$$\text{TOTAL DF} = \text{DF(A)} + \text{DF(B)} + \text{DF(C)} + \text{RESIDUAL DF} \quad .$$

Mean squares (MS) are computed by dividing each SS by its corresponding DF. Ratios of mean squares, called F ratios, are then used to compare the amount of variability associated with each source of variation. Tests of hypotheses about group means can be based on F ratios. The computations are usually displayed in the familiar tabular form shown below:

Source of Variation	DF	SS	MS	F	p
A	DF(A)	SS(A)	MS(A)	F(A)	p for F(A)
B	DF(B)	SS(B)	MS(B)	F(B)	p for F(B)
C	DF(C)	SS(C)	MS(C)	F(C)	p for F(C)
Residual	RESIDUAL DF	RESIDUAL SS	RESIDUAL MS		
Total	TOTAL DF	TOTAL SS			

Three kinds of effects (sources of variation) in analysis of variance are considered in this chapter: main effects, interaction effects, and nested effects. Each is discussed in terms of its SS computation. Effects can be either fixed or random. These concepts are defined in Chapter 3, "Analyzing Data with Random Effects."

A main effect sum of squares for a factor A is given by

$$SS(A) = \Sigma_i \, n_i (\bar{y}_i - \bar{y}_.)^2 \tag{2.1}$$

or alternatively by

$$SS(A) = \Sigma_i \, y_i^2 / n_i - y_.^2 / n_. \tag{2.2}$$

where

n_i equals the number of observations in level i of factor A.

y_i equals the total of observations in level i of factor A.

$\bar{y}_i$ equals the mean of observations in level i of factor A.

$n_.$ equals the total number of observations ($\Sigma_i \, n_i$).

$y_.$ equals the total of all observations ($\Sigma_i \, y_i$).

$\bar{y}_.$ equals the mean of all observations ($y_./n_.$).

As equation 2.1 implies, the SS for a main effect measures variability among the means corresponding to the levels of the factor. If A has a levels, then SS(A) has $(a-1)$ degrees of freedom.

An *interaction effect* refers to crossed factors, where each level of each factor occurs with each level of the other factors. It measures the failure of the effects of one factor to be the same at all levels of another factor, that is, the failure of $\bar{y}_{ij} - \bar{y}_{ij'}$ to be the same as $\bar{y}_{i'j} - \bar{y}_{i'j'}$ for all i, j, i', j', where $\bar{y}_{ij}$ refers to the mean of the observations in level i of A and level j of B. Calculate the sum of squares for the interaction between the factors A and B with the equation

$$SS(A*B) = \Sigma_{ij} \, n(\bar{y}_{ij} - \bar{y}_{i.} - \bar{y}_{.j} + \bar{y}_{..})^2 \tag{2.3}$$

or alternatively

$$SS(A^*B) = \Sigma_{ij}\, y_{ij}^2 / n - \Sigma_i\, y_{i.}^2 / bn - \Sigma_j\, y_{.j}^2 / an + y_{..}^2 / abn \qquad (2.4)$$

where

n	equals the common number of observations in each ij cell.
a and b	are the numbers of levels of A and B, respectively.
y_{ij}	equals the total of all observations in the ij cell.
$y_{i.}$	is equal to $\Sigma_j\, y_{ij}$
$y_{.j}$	is equal to $\Sigma_i\, y_{ij}$
$y_{..}$	is equal to $\Sigma_{ij}\, y_{ij}$.

The sum of squares for A*B has

$$(a - 1)(b - 1) = ab - a - b + 1$$

degrees of freedom.

A *nested effect* refers to one factor whose levels are nested within the levels of another, that is, a factor with a different set of levels for each level of another factor. The sum of squares of B nested in A, written B(A), is

$$SS(B(A)) = \Sigma_{ij}\, n_{ij}(\bar{y}_{ij} - \bar{y}_{i.})^2 \qquad (2.5)$$

or alternatively

$$SS(B(A)) = \Sigma_{ij}\, y_{ij}^2 / n_{ij} - \Sigma_i\, y_{i.}^2 / n_{i.} \qquad (2.6)$$

where

n_{ij}	equals the number of observations in level j of B in level i of A.
y_{ij}	equals the total of observations in level j of B in level i of A.
$\bar{y}_{ij}$	equals the mean of observations in level j of B in level i of A.
$n_{i.}$	is equal to $\Sigma_j\, n_{ij}$.
$y_{i.}$	is equal to $\Sigma_j\, y_{ij}$.
$\bar{y}_{i.}$	is equal to $y_{i.}/n_{i.}$.

Looking at equation 2.5 as

$$SS(B(A)) = \Sigma_i\, (\Sigma_j\, n_{ij}(\bar{y}_{ij} - \bar{y}_{i.})^2) \qquad (2.7)$$

you see that SS(B(A)) measures the variation among the levels of B within each level of A and then pools, or adds, across the levels of A. If there are b_i levels of B in level i of A, then there are (b_i-1) DF for B in level i of A, and therefore $\Sigma_i\, (b_i-1)$ DF for B(A) altogether.

2.3.2   Using the ANOVA Procedure

In most cases PROC ANOVA is the appropriate SAS procedure for one-way and balanced multiway classifications. The term *balanced* means that each cell of the multiway classification has the same number of observations. Appropriate uses of PROC ANOVA for one-way, crossed, and nested classifications are illustrated by examples for basic experimental designs (completely random, randomized blocks, Latin square) and factorial experiments (including split-plot).

Generally, PROC ANOVA computes the sum of squares for a factor A in the classification according to equation 2.2. Nested effects are computed according to equation 2.6.

A two-factor interaction sum of squares computed by PROC ANOVA follows the formula

$$SS(A^*B) = \Sigma_{ij} \, y_{ij}^2 / n_{ij} - \Sigma_i \, y_{i.}^2 / n_{i.} - \Sigma_j \, y_{.j}^2 / n_{.j} + y_{..}^2 / n_{..} \tag{2.8}$$

where

y_{ij} equals the total for the level i of A and level j of B.

n_{ij} equals the number of observations in y_{ij}.

If n_{ij} has the same value for all ij, then equation 2.8 is the same as equation 2.4. Equation 2.4 is not correct unless all the n_{ij} are equal to the same value, and this formula could even produce a negative value because it would not actually be a sum of squares. If a negative value is obtained, PROC ANOVA prints a value of 0 in its place. Sums of squares for higher-order interactions follow a similar formula.

The basic syntax of the ANOVA procedure is as follows:

PROC ANOVA *options*;
    CLASS *variables*;
    MODEL *dependents=effects / options*;
    MEANS *effects / options*;
    ABSORB *variables*;
    FREQ *variable*;
    TEST H=*effects* E=*effect*;
    MANOVA H=*effects* E=*effect*
            M=*equations / options*;
    REPEATED *factor-name levels / options*;
    BY *variables*;

The PROC ANOVA, CLASS, and MODEL statements are required to produce the ANOVA table. The other statements are optional. Included in the ANOVA output are F tests of all effects in the MODEL statement. All of these F tests use residual mean squares as the error term. The MEANS statement produces tables of the means corresponding to the list of effects. Among the options available in the MEANS statement are several multiple comparison procedures, which are illustrated in "Computing Means, Multiple Comparisons of Means, and Confidence Intervals," and also in "Other Methods for Multiple Comparisons," later in this chapter. The TEST statement tests for effects where the residual mean square is not the appropriate error term, such as certain effects in mixed models and main-plot effects in split-plot experiments (see Chapter 3). There can be multiple MEANS and TEST statements, but, as in PROC GLM, only one MODEL statement.

The ABSORB statement implements the technique of absorption, which saves time and reduces storage requirements for certain types of models. This is illustrated in Chapter 4, "Details of the Linear Model: Understanding GLM Concepts." Use the FREQ statement when you want each observation in a data set to represent n observations, where n is the value of the FREQ variable. The MANOVA statement is used for implementing multivariate analysis of variance (see Chapter 7, "Multivariate Linear Models"). The REPEATED statement is useful for analyzing repeated-measures designs (see Chapter 8, "Repeated-Measures Analysis of Variance"), and the BY statement specifies that separate analyses are performed on observations in groups defined by the BY variables. For more information on PROC ANOVA, see Chapter 13, "The ANOVA Procedure," in the *SAS/STAT User's Guide, Version 6, Fourth Edition, Volume 1*.

2.3.3 Multiple Comparisons and Preplanned Comparisons

The F test for a factor in an analysis of variance tests the null hypothesis that all the factor means are equal. However, the conclusion of such a test is seldom a satisfactory end to the analysis. You usually want to know more about the differences among the means (for example, which means are different from which other means or if any groups of means have common values).

Multiple comparisons of the means are commonly used to answer these questions. There are numerous methods for making multiple comparisons, most of which are available in PROC ANOVA and PROC GLM. In this chapter, only a few of the methods are illustrated.

One method of multiple comparisons is to conduct a series of t tests between pairs of means; this is essentially the method known as least significant difference (LSD). Refer to Steel and Torrie (1980) for examples.

Another method of multiple comparisons is Duncan's multiple-range test. With this test, the means are first ranked from largest to smallest. Then the equality of two means is tested by referring the difference to tabled critical points, the values of which depend on the range of the ranks of the two means tested. The larger the range of the ranks, the larger the tabled critical point (Duncan 1955).

The LSD method and, to a lesser extent, Duncan's method are frequently criticized for inflating the Type I error rate. In other words, the overall probability of falsely declaring some pair of means different, when in fact they are equal, is substantially larger than the specified α value. This overall probability of a Type I error is called the *experimentwise error rate*. The probability of a Type I error for one particular comparison is called the *comparisonwise error rate*. Other methods are available to control the experimentwise error rate, including Tukey's method.

You can request the various multiple comparison tests with options in the MEANS statement in the ANOVA and GLM procedures.

Multiple comparison procedures, as described in the previous paragraphs, are useful when there are no particular comparisons of special interest. But in most situations there is something about the factor that suggests specific comparisons. These are called preplanned comparisons because you can decide to make these comparisons prior to collecting data. Specific hypotheses for preplanned comparisons can be tested by using the CONTRAST, ESTIMATE, or LSMEANS statement in PROC GLM, as discussed in "Preplanned Comparisons for One-Way Classification: the CONTRAST Statement," later in this chapter.

2.3.4 Analysis of One-Way Classification of Data

The expression *one-way classification* refers to data that are grouped according to some criterion, such as the values of the classification variable. The gunpowder data presented in Section 2.2.3, "Two Independent Samples," are an example of a one-way classification; the values of VELOCITY are classified according to POWDER. In this case, there are two levels of the classification variable, 1 and 2. Other examples of one-way classifications might have more than two levels of the classification variable. Populations of U.S. cities could be classified according to the state containing the city, giving a one-way classification with 50 levels (the number of states) of the classification variable. One-way classifications of data can result from sample surveys. For example, wages determined in a survey of migrant farm workers could be classified according to the type of work performed. One-way classifications also result from a completely randomized designed experiment. For example, strengths of monofilament fiber can be classified according to the amount of an experimental chemical used in the manufacturing process, or sales of a new facial soap in a marketing test could be classified according to the color of the soap. The type of statistical analysis that is appropriate for a given one-way classification of data depends on the goals of the investigation that produced the data. However, you can use analysis of variance as a tool for many applications.

The levels of a classification variable are considered to correspond to different populations from which the data were obtained. Let k stand for the number of levels of the classification criterion, so there are data from k populations. Denote the means of the populations $\mu_1, \ldots, \mu_k$. Assume that all the populations have the same variance, σ^2, and that all the populations are normally distributed. Also, consider now those situations for which there are the same number of observations from each population, denoted n, although this is not a critical assumption for the methods of this section. Denote by y_{ij} the jth observation in the ith group of data. Then consider that

$$y_{11}, \ldots, y_{1,n} \text{ is a sample from N}(\mu_1, \sigma^2),$$

$$y_{21}, \ldots, y_{2,n} \text{ is a sample from N}(\mu_2, \sigma^2),$$

$$\vdots$$

$$y_{k1}, \ldots, y_{k,n} \text{ is a sample from N}(\mu_k, \sigma^2) \quad .$$

N(μ, σ^2) refers to a normally distributed population with mean μ and variance σ^2. Sometimes it is useful to express the data in terms of linear models. One way of doing this is to write

$$y_{ij} = \mu_i + \varepsilon_{ij}$$

where μ_i is the mean of the ith population and ε_{ij} is the departure of the observed value y_{ij} from population mean. This is called a *means model*. Another model is called an *effects model*, and is denoted by the equation

$$y_{ij} = \mu + \tau_i + \varepsilon_{ij} \quad .$$

The effects model simply expresses the *i*th population mean as the sum of two components, $\mu_i = \mu + \tau_i$. In both models ε_{ij} is called the *error* and is normally distributed with mean 0 and variance σ^2. Moreover, both of these models are, in fact, regression models. Therefore, results from regression analysis can be used for these models, as discussed in subsequent sections. The following section presents an example of analysis of variance for a one-way classification.

Computing the ANOVA Table

Four specimens of each of five brands (BRAND) of a synthetic wood veneer material are subjected to a friction test. A measure of wear is determined for each specimen. All tests are made on the same machine in completely random order. Data are stored in a SAS data set named VENEER.

```
data veneer;
    input brand $ wear;
cards;
ACME 2.3
ACME 2.1
ACME 2.4
ACME 2.5
CHAMP 2.2
CHAMP 2.3
CHAMP 2.4
CHAMP 2.6
AJAX 2.2
AJAX 2.0
AJAX 1.9
AJAX 2.1
TUFFY 2.4
TUFFY 2.7
TUFFY 2.6
TUFFY 2.7
XTRA 2.3
XTRA 2.5
XTRA 2.3
XTRA 2.4
;
proc print data=veneer;
run;
```

Output 2.4 shows the data.

Output 2.4
Data for One-Way
Classification

```
                        The SAS System                          1

              OBS      BRAND      WEAR

               1       ACME       2.3
               2       ACME       2.1
               3       ACME       2.4
               4       ACME       2.5
               5       CHAMP      2.2
               6       CHAMP      2.3
               7       CHAMP      2.4
               8       CHAMP      2.6

                                        (continued on next page)
```

(continued from previous page)

```
 9    AJAX    2.2
10    AJAX    2.0
11    AJAX    1.9
12    AJAX    2.1
13    TUFFY   2.4
14    TUFFY   2.7
15    TUFFY   2.6
16    TUFFY   2.7
17    XTRA    2.3
18    XTRA    2.5
19    XTRA    2.3
20    XTRA    2.4
```

An appropriate analysis of variance has the sources of variation:

Source of Variation	DF
BRAND	4
Error	15
Total	19

The following SAS statements produce the analysis of variance:

```
proc anova data=veneer; class brand;
  model wear=brand;
run;
```

Since the data are classified only according to the values of BRAND, this is the only variable in the CLASS statement. The variable WEAR is the response variable to be analyzed, so WEAR appears on the left side of the equal sign in the MODEL statement. The only source of variation (effect in the ANOVA table) other than ERROR (residual) and TOTAL is variation due to brands; therefore, BRAND appears on the right side of the equal sign in the MODEL statement.

Output from the MODEL statement appears in Output 2.5.

Output 2.5
Analysis of
Variance for
One-Way
Classification

```
                              The SAS System                          1

                        Analysis of Variance Procedure

Dependent Variable: WEAR
                                  Sum of          Mean
Source             DF           Squares        Square   F Value   Pr > F

Model               4        0.61700000    0.15425000      7.40   0.0017

Error              15        0.31250000    0.02083333

Corrected Total    19        0.92950000

                R-Square          C.V.      Root MSE            WEAR Mean

                0.663798      6.155120     0.1443376            2.3450000


Source             DF         Anova SS   Mean Square   F Value   Pr > F

BRAND               4       0.61700000    0.15425000      7.40   0.0017
```

The results in Output 2.5 are summarized in the following ANOVA table:

Source	DF	SS	MS	F	p
BRAND	4	0.6170	0.1542	7.40	0.0017
ERROR	15	0.3125	0.0208		
TOTAL	19	0.9295			

Note that the sum of squares for BRAND (0.6170) appears twice in the output; once for MODEL in the upper section and once for BRAND in the lower section. The distinction between these two SS is discussed in Section 2.3.5, "Randomized-Blocks Design with Multiple Comparisons." The p value of 0.0017 indicates significant differences between BRAND means.

Computing Means, Multiple Comparisons of Means, and Confidence Intervals

You can easily obtain means and multiple comparisons of means by using a MEANS statement after the MODEL statement. For the VENEER data, you get BRAND means and LSD comparisons of the BRAND means with the statements

```
means brand/lsd;
```

Results appear in Output 2.6.

Output 2.6
Least Significant Difference Comparisons of BRAND Means

```
                        The SAS System                          1

                  Analysis of Variance Procedure

                 T tests (LSD) for variable: WEAR

     NOTE: This test controls the type I comparisonwise error rate not the
           experimentwise error rate.

             Alpha= 0.05  df= 15  MSE= 0.020833
                  Critical Value of T= 2.13
             Least Significant Difference= 0.2175

     Means with the same letter are not significantly different.

            T Grouping          Mean     N   BRAND

                     A         2.6000     4   TUFFY

                     B         2.3750     4   XTRA
                     B
                     B         2.3750     4   CHAMP
                     B
                     B         2.3250     4   ACME

                     C         2.0500     4   AJAX
```

Means and the number of observations (N) are produced for each BRAND. Because LSD is specified as an option, the means appear in descending order of magnitude. Under the heading T Grouping are sequences of A's, B's, and C's. Means are joined by the same letter if, according to the *t* test, they are not significantly different. The BRAND means for **XTRA**, **CHAMP**, and **ACME** are not significantly different and are joined by a sequence of B's. The means for **AJAX** and **TUFFY** are found to be significantly different from all other means so they are labeled with a single C and A, respectively, and no other means are labeled with A's or C's.

You obtain confidence intervals about means instead of comparisons of the means if you specify the CLM option, such as

```
means brand/lsd clm;
```

Results in Output 2.7 are self-explanatory.

Output 2.7
Confidence Intervals for BRAND Means

```
                    The SAS System                              1

                Analysis of Variance Procedure

          T Confidence Intervals for variable: WEAR

    Alpha= 0.05  Confidence= 0.95  df= 15  MSE= 0.020833
                  Critical Value of T= 2.13
         Half Width of Confidence Interval= 0.153824

                           Lower                 Upper
        BRAND       N    Confidence    Mean    Confidence
                           Limit                 Limit

        TUFFY       4     2.44618     2.60000    2.75382
        XTRA        4     2.22118     2.37500    2.52882
        CHAMP       4     2.22118     2.37500    2.52882
        ACME        4     2.17118     2.32500    2.47882
        AJAX        4     1.89618     2.05000    2.20382
```

You can also obtain confidence limits for differences between means, as discussed in "Other Methods for Multiple Comparisons" later in this chapter.

Preplanned Comparisons for One-Way Classification: the CONTRAST Statement

Multiple comparison procedures, as demonstrated in the previous section, are useful when there are no particular comparisons of special interest and you want to make all comparisons among the means. But in most situations there is something about the classification criterion that suggests specific comparisons. For example, suppose that you know something about the companies that manufacture the five BRANDS of synthetic wood veneer material. You know that **ACME** and **AJAX** are produced by a U.S. company named A-Line, that **CHAMP** is produced by a U.S. company named C-Line, and that **TUFFY** and **XTRA** are produced by a foreign company. Then you would probably be interested in comparing certain groups of means with other groups of means. For example, you would want to compare the means for the U.S. companies with the means for the foreign companies; you would want to compare the means for the two U.S. companies with each other; you would want to compare the two A-Line means; and you would want to compare the means for the two foreign brands. These would be called *preplanned comparisons*, because they are suggested by the structure of the classification criterion (BRANDS) rather than the data. You know what comparisons you want to make before you look at the data. When this is the case, you ordinarily obtain a more relevant analysis of the data by making the preplanned comparisons rather than using a multiple comparison technique, because the preplanned comparisons are focused on the objectives of the study.

You can make preplanned comparisons in the SAS System with the CONTRAST statement in the GLM procedure. You run the GLM procedure just like you run the ANOVA procedure, with CLASS and MODEL statements, which are required. You use CONTRAST as an optional statement in the same way you used a MEANS statement with PROC ANOVA. As you will see, the same analysis-of-variance computations are obtained from PROC GLM as from PROC ANOVA for the one-way classification. But the CONTRAST statement is not supported in the ANOVA procedure; you must use PROC GLM for CONTRAST statements.

You should first express the comparisons as null hypotheses concerning linear combinations of means to be tested. For the comparisons indicated above, you would have the following null hypotheses:

□ U.S. versus foreign

$$H_0: \quad 1/3(\mu_{ACME} + \mu_{AJAX} + \mu_{CHAMP}) = 1/2(\mu_{TUFFY} + \mu_{XTRA})$$

□ A-Line versus C-Line

$$H_0: \quad 1/2(\mu_{ACME} + \mu_{AJAX}) = \mu_{CHAMP}$$

□ **ACME** versus **AJAX**

$$H_0: \quad \mu_{ACME} = \mu_{AJAX}$$

□ **TUFFY** versus **XTRA**

$$H_0: \quad \mu_{TUFFY} = \mu_{XTRA}$$

The basic form of the CONTRAST statement is

CONTRAST *'label' effect-name effect-coefficients*;

where *label* is a character string used for labeling output, *effect-name* is a term on the right-hand side of the MODEL statement, and *effect-coefficients* is a list of numbers that specifies the linear combination of parameters in the null hypothesis. The ordering of the numbers follows the alphabetical ordering of the levels of the classification variable, unless specified otherwise with an ORDER= option in the PROC GLM statement.

Starting with one of the simpler comparisons, **ACME** versus **AJAX**, you want to test $H_0: \mu_{ACME} = \mu_{AJAX}$. This hypothesis must be expressed as a linear combination of the means equal to 0, that is $H_0: \mu_{ACME} - \mu_{AJAX} = 0$. In terms of all the means, the null hypothesis is

$$H_0: \quad 1 * \mu_{ACME} - 1 * \mu_{AJAX} + 0 * \mu_{CHAMP} + 0 * \mu_{TUFFY} + 0 * \mu_{XTRA} = 0 \quad .$$

Notice that the BRAND means are listed in alphabetical order. All you have to do is insert the coefficients on the BRAND means in the list of effect coefficients in the CONTRAST statement. The coefficients for the levels of BRAND will follow the alphabetical ordering.

```
proc glm; class brand;
   model wear = brand;
      contrast 'ACME vs AJAX'  brand  1 -1  0  0  0;
run;
```

Results appear in Output 2.8.

Output 2.8
Analysis of
Variance and
Contrast with
PROC GLM

```
                             The SAS System                            1

                      General Linear Models Procedure

Dependent Variable: WEAR
                                   Sum of          Mean
Source                 DF        Squares         Square    F Value    Pr > F

Model                   4     0.61700000     0.15425000       7.40    0.0017

Error                  15     0.31250000     0.02083333

Corrected Total        19     0.92950000

                 R-Square            C.V.        Root MSE         WEAR Mean

                 0.663798        6.155120       0.1443376         2.3450000


Source                 DF      Type I SS    Mean Square    F Value    Pr > F

BRAND                   4     0.61700000     0.15425000       7.40    0.0017

Source                 DF    Type III SS    Mean Square    F Value    Pr > F

BRAND                   4     0.61700000     0.15425000       7.40    0.0017

Contrast               DF    Contrast SS    Mean Square    F Value    Pr > F

ACME vs AJAX            1     0.15125000     0.15125000       7.26    0.0166
```

Notice that you get the same computations from PROC GLM as from PROC ANOVA for the analysis of variance, although they are labeled somewhat differently. For one thing, PROC GLM computes Type I and Type III sums of squares for BRAND which, for the one-way classification, are the same as the BRAND sum of squares computed by the ANOVA procedure. (Chapter 4 has further discussion of these different types of sums of squares.) Output from the CONTRAST statement, labeled **ACME** vs **AJAX**, shows a sum of squares for the contrast, and an *F* value for testing the null hypothesis H_0: $\mu_{ACME} = \mu_{AJAX}$. The *p* value tells you the means are significantly different at the 0.0166 level.

Actually, you don't have to include the trailing zeros. You can simply use

```
contrast 'ACME vs AJAX' brand 1 -1;
```

Following the same procedure, to test H_0: $\mu_{TUFFY} = \mu_{XTRA}$, use the statement

```
contrast 'TUFFY vs XTRA' brand 0 0 0 1 -1;
```

The contrast U.S. versus foreign is a little more complicated because it involves fractions. You can use the statement

```
contrast 'US vs FOREIGN' brand .33333 .33333 .33333 -.5 -.5;
```

This is not a problem because the continued fraction for 1/3 is easily written. But for other fractions, such as 1/7, it's more difficult to write the decimal expansion. It is usually easier to multiply all coefficients by the least common denominator to get rid of the fractions. This is legitimate because the hypothesis you are testing with a CONTRAST statement is that a linear combination is equal to 0, and multiplication by a constant does not change whether the hypothesis is true or false. (Something is equal to 0 if and only if a constant times the something is equal to 0.) In the case of U.S. versus foreign, the assertion is that

$$H_0: \quad 1/3(\mu_{ACME} + \mu_{AJAX} + \mu_{CHAMP}) = 1/2(\mu_{TUFFY} + \mu_{XTRA})$$

is equivalent to

$$H_0: \quad 2(\mu_{ACME} + \mu_{AJAX} + \mu_{CHAMP}) - 3(\mu_{TUFFY} + \mu_{XTRA}) = 0 \quad .$$

This tells you the appropriate CONTRAST statement is

```
contrast 'US vs FOREIGN' brand  2 2 2 -3 -3;
```

The GLM procedure enables you to run as many CONTRAST statements as you want, but good statistical practice ordinarily indicates that this number should not exceed the number of degrees of freedom for the effect (in this case, 4). Moreover, you should be aware of the inflation of the overall (experimentwise) Type I error rate when you run several CONTRAST statements.

To see how CONTRAST statements for all four comparisons are used, run the following program:

```
proc glm; class brand;
   model wear = brand;
      contrast 'US vs FOREIGN' brand  2  2  2 -3 -3;
      contrast 'A-L vs C-L'    brand  1  1 -2  0  0;
      contrast 'ACME vs AJAX'  brand  1 -1  0  0  0;
      contrast 'TUFFY vs XTRA' brand  0  0  0  1 -1;
run;
```

Output 2.9
*Contrasts among
BRAND Means*

```
                          The SAS System                          1

                    General Linear Models Procedure

Dependent Variable: WEAR
                            Sum of            Mean

Contrast             DF    Contrast SS     Mean Square   F Value   Pr > F

US vs FOREIGN         1     0.27075000      0.27075000    13.00    0.0026
A-L vs C-L            1     0.09375000      0.09375000     4.50    0.0510
ACME vs AJAX          1     0.15125000      0.15125000     7.26    0.0166
TUFFY vs XTRA         1     0.10125000      0.10125000     4.86    0.0435
```

Results in Output 2.9 indicate statistical significance for each of the contrasts. Notice that the *p* value for **ACME** vs **AJAX** is the same in the presence of other CONTRAST statements as it was when run as a single contrast in Output 2.8. Computations for one CONTRAST statement are unaffected by the presence of other CONTRAST statements. The contrasts in Output 2.9 have a special property called orthogonality, which is discussed in "Orthogonal Contrasts" later in this chapter.

Linear Combinations of Model Parameters

Thus far, the coefficients in a CONTRAST statement have been discussed as coefficients in a linear combination of means. In fact, these are coefficients on the effect parameters in the MODEL statement. It is easier to think in terms of means, but PROC GLM works in terms of model parameters. Therefore, you must be able to translate between the two sets of parameters.

Models are discussed in more depth in Chapter 4. For now, all you need to understand is the relationship between coefficients on a linear combination of means and the corresponding coefficients on linear combinations of model effect parameters. For the linear combinations representing comparisons of means (that is, with coefficients summing to 0), this relationship is very simple for the one-way classification. The coefficient of an effect parameter in a linear combination of effect parameters is equal to the coefficient on the corresponding mean in the linear combination of means. This is because of the fundamental relationship between means and effect parameters, that is, $\mu_i = \mu + \alpha_i$. For example, take the contrast A-Line versus C-Line. The linear combination in terms of means is

$$2\mu_{CHAMP} - \mu_{ACME} - \mu_{AJAX}$$

$$= 2(\mu + \alpha_{CHAMP}) - (\mu + \alpha_{ACME}) - (\mu + \alpha_{AJAX})$$

$$= 2\,\alpha_{CHAMP} - \alpha_{ACME} - \alpha_{AJAX} \ .$$

You see that the coefficient on α_{CHAMP} is the same as the coefficient on μ_{CHAMP}, the coefficient on α_{ACME} is equal to the coefficient on μ_{ACME}, and so on. Moreover, the parameter μ disappears when you convert from means to effect parameters, because the coefficients on the means sum to 0. It follows that, for comparisons in the one-way classification, you may derive coefficients in terms of means and simply insert them as coefficients on model effect parameters in a CONTRAST statement. For more complicated applications, such as two-way classification, the task is not so straightforward. You'll see this in "Preplanned Comparisons in a Two-Way Factorial Experiment" and subsequent sections later in this chapter.

Testing Several Contrasts Simultaneously

Sometimes you need to test several contrasts simultaneously. For example, you might want to test for differences among the three means for U.S. BRANDs. The null hypothesis is

$$H_0: \ \mu_{ACME} = \mu_{AJAX} = \mu_{CHAMP} \ .$$

This hypothesis *equation* actually embodies two equations that can be expressed in several ways. One way to express the hypothesis in terms of two equations is

$$H_0: \quad \mu_{ACME} = \mu_{AJAX} \quad \text{and} \quad \mu_{ACME} = \mu_{CHAMP} \quad .$$

Why are the two hypotheses equivalent? Because the three means are all equal if and only if the first is equal to the second and the first is equal to the third.

You can test this hypothesis by writing a CONTRAST statement that expresses sets of coefficients for the two equations, separated by a comma. An appropriate CONTRAST statement is

```
contrast 'US BRANDS' brand 1 -1 0 0 0,  brand 1 0 -1 0 0;
```

Results appear in Output 2.10.

Output 2.10
Simultaneous Contrasts among US BRAND Means

```
                           The SAS System                              1
                    General Linear Models Procedure
Dependent Variable: WEAR
                              Sum of          Mean
Contrast           DF     Contrast SS     Mean Square    F Value    Pr > F

US BRANDS           2      0.24500000      0.12250000       5.88    0.0130
```

Notice that the sum of squares for the contrast has 2 degrees of freedom. This is because you are testing two equations simultaneously. The F statistic of 5.88 and associated p value tell you the means are different at the 0.0130 level of significance.

Another way to express the hypothesis in terms of two equations is

$$H_0: \mu_{ACME} = \mu_{AJAX} \quad \text{and} \quad 2\,\mu_{CHAMP} = \mu_{ACME} + \mu_{AJAX} \quad .$$

A contrast for this version of the hypothesis is

```
contrast 'US BRANDS'    brand  1 -1  0  0  0,
                        brand  1  1 -2  0  0;
```

Results from this CONTRAST statement, not included here, are identical to Output 2.10.

Orthogonal Contrasts

Notice that the sum of squares of 0.245 in Output 2.10 is equal to the sum of the sums of squares for the two contrasts **ACME** vs **AJAX** (0.15125) and A-L vs C-L (0.09375) in Output 2.9. That is because the two sets of coefficients in this CONTRAST statement are *orthogonal*. Mathematically, this means the sum of products of coefficients for the respective means is 0: that is, $1 \times 1 + (-1) \times 1 + 0 \times (-2) = 0$. Moreover, all four of the contrasts in Output 2.9 form an orthogonal set. (Verify this by multiplying pairs of coefficients and adding the products.) Therefore, the sum of the four contrast sums of squares in Output 2.9 is equal to the overall BRAND SS (0.617) in Output 2.8.

Statistically, *orthogonal* means that the sums of squares for the two contrasts are independent. The outcome of one of them in no way influences the outcome of any other. Sets of orthogonal comparisons are commonly considered desirable, because the result of any one of them tells you (essentially) nothing about what to expect from any other comparison. However, desirable as it is to have independent tests, it is more important to construct sets of contrasts to attain the objectives of the investigation. Practically meaningful contrasts are more desirable than simply orthogonal ones.

Estimating Linear Combinations of Parameters: the ESTIMATE Statement

The CONTRAST statement is used to construct an *F* test for a hypothesis that a linear combination of parameters is equal to 0. In many applications, you want to obtain an estimate of the linear combination of parameters, along with the standard error of the estimate. This can be done with an ESTIMATE statement. The ESTIMATE statement is used in much the same way as a CONTRAST statement. You could estimate the difference $\mu_{ACME} - \mu_{AJAX}$ with the following statement:

```
estimate 'ACME vs AJAX'  brand  1 -1  0  0  0;
```

Output 2.11
Estimating
Difference between
BRAND Means

```
                        The SAS System                            1

                  General Linear Models Procedure

Dependent Variable: WEAR
Parameter                 Estimate    Parameter=0        Estimate

ACME vs AJAX            0.27500000         2.69  0.0166  0.10206207
```

This statement is exactly like the CONTRAST statement for **ACME** vs **AJAX**, with the keyword CONTRAST replaced by the keyword ESTIMATE. Results shown in Output 2.11 include the value of the estimate, a standard error, a *t* statistic for testing whether the estimate is significantly different from 0, and a *p* value for the *t* statistic. Note the *p* value (0.0166) for the *t* test is the same as for the *F* test for the contrast in Output 2.8. This is because the two tests are equivalent; the *F* is equal to the square of the *t*.

For the present application, the estimate of $\mu_{ACME} - \mu_{AJAX}$ can be computed as

$$\bar{y}_{ACME} - \bar{y}_{AJAX} \quad .$$

The standard error is

$$\left((1/n_1 + 1/n_2)\ MS(ERROR)\right)^{1/2} \quad .$$

In more complicated examples, such as two-way classification with unbalanced data, more complicated computations for means are required.

Suppose you want to estimate $\mu_{CHAMP} - 1/2(\mu_{ACME} + \mu_{AJAX})$. You can use the following statement:

```
estimate 'A-L vs C-L' brand -.5 -.5 1 0 0;
```

You can avoid the fractions by using the DIVISOR option:

```
estimate 'A-L vs C-L' brand -1 -1 2 0 0 / divisor=2;
```

Now suppose you want to estimate a linear combination of means that does not represent a comparison of two groups of means. For example, maybe you want to estimate the average of the three U.S. means, $1/3(\mu_{ACME} + \mu_{AJAX} + \mu_{CHAMP})$. The coefficients do not sum to 0, so you can't simply take coefficients off the means and use them in the ESTIMATE statement as coefficients on model effect parameters. The μ parameter does not disappear when you convert from means to effect parameters:

$$1/3(\mu_{ACME} + \mu_{AJAX} + \mu_{CHAMP})$$

$$= 1/3(\mu + \alpha_{ACME} + \mu + \alpha_{AJAX} + \mu + \alpha_{CHAMP})$$

$$= \mu + 1/3(\alpha_{ACME} + \alpha_{AJAX} + \alpha_{CHAMP}) \quad .$$

You see that the parameter μ remains in the linear combination of effect model parameters. This parameter is called INTERCEPT in CONTRAST and ESTIMATE statements. (This is because μ shows up as the intercept in a regression model, as discussed in Chapter 4 where the connection between analysis-of-variance models and regression models is explained.) An appropriate ESTIMATE statement is

```
estimate 'US MEAN' intercept 1 brand .33333 .33333 .33333 0 0;
```

or equivalently

```
estimate 'US MEAN' intercept 3 brand 1 1 1 0 0 / divisor=3;
```

Results from this ESTIMATE statement appear in Output 2.12.

Output 2.12
Estimating Mean
of US BRANDS

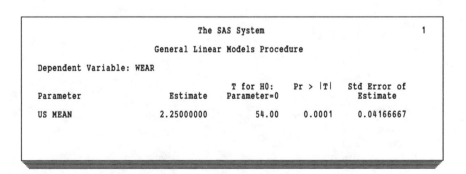

In this application the estimate and its standard error are useful. For example, you can construct a 95% confidence interval:

$$2.25 \pm 2.13(0.0417) \quad .$$

Again, the estimate is $2.25 = 1/3(2.325 + 2.050 + 3.375)$, and the standard error is $((1/4 + 1/4 + 1/4)\text{MS(ERROR)})^{1/2}$. Since MS(ERROR) is the basic variance estimate in this formula, the degrees of freedom for the t statistic are there for MS(ERROR). The t statistic is computed to test the null hypothesis

$$H_0: \quad \mu_{\text{ACME}} + \mu_{\text{AJAX}} + \mu_{\text{CHAMP}} = 0 \quad .$$

Of course, this hypothesis is not of practical interest.

2.3.5 Randomized-Blocks Design with Multiple Comparisons

The randomized-blocks design assumes that a population of experimental units can be divided into a number of relatively homogeneous subpopulations or blocks. The treatments are then randomly assigned to experimental units within the blocks. If all treatments are assigned in each block, the design is called a randomized-complete-blocks design. Blocks usually represent naturally occurring differences not related to the treatments. In analysis of variance, the extraneous variation among blocks can be partitioned out, usually reducing the error mean square. Also, differences between treatment means do not contain block variation. In this sense, the randomized-blocks design controls block variation.

A classic example of blocks is an agricultural field divided into smaller, more homogeneous subfields. Other examples of blocks include days of the week, measuring or recording devices, and operators of a machine.

In the following example, five chemical blends (BLEND) of household insecticide are applied to areas in each of three locations. The locations constitute the blocking factor (BLOCK). Assignment of a blend to an area within each location is random, giving a randomized-complete-blocks design. After one week, the persistence of the pesticides is determined by measuring the percent loss (PCTLOSS) in each location. The objective is to determine if there are differences in percent loss among blends and to rank the blends according to percent loss.

```
data pestcide;
input block blend $ pctloss;
cards;
1 B 18.2
1 A 16.9
1 C 17.0
1 E 18.3
1 D 15.1
2 A 16.5
2 E 18.3
2 B 19.2
2 C 18.1
2 D 16.0
3 B 17.1
```

```
3 D 17.8
3 C 17.3
3 E 19.8
3 A 17.5
;
proc print;
run;
```

Output 2.13 shows the data.

Output 2.13
Data for
Randomized-Blocks
Design

```
                        The SAS System                          1

        OBS    BLOCK    BLEND    PCTLOSS

         1       1        B       18.2
         2       1        A       16.9
         3       1        C       17.0
         4       1        E       18.3
         5       1        D       15.1
         6       2        A       16.5
         7       2        E       18.3
         8       2        B       19.2
         9       2        C       18.1
        10       2        D       16.0
        11       3        B       17.1
        12       3        D       17.8
        13       3        C       17.3
        14       3        E       19.8
        15       3        A       17.5
```

Analysis of Variance for
Randomized-Blocks Design

The following analysis of variance for the randomized-blocks experiment provides a test for differences between blends:

Source	DF
BLOCK	2
BLEND	4
ERROR	8
TOTAL	14

The appropriate SAS statements for this analysis are as follows:

```
proc anova data=pestcide; class block blend;
  model pctloss=block blend;
run;
```

Because the data are classified according to BLOCK and BLEND, these variables appear in the CLASS statement. As specified in the MODEL statement, the response variable to be analyzed is PCTLOSS. The two sources of variation in the analysis-of-variance table (in addition to TOTAL and ERROR) are BLOCK and BLEND, so these variables appear on the right side of the MODEL statement.

Analysis-of-variance output produced by the MODEL statement appears in Output 2.14.

Output 2.14
Analysis of
Variance for
Randomized-Blocks
Design

```
                          The SAS System                              1

                     Analysis of Variance Procedure

Dependent Variable: PCTLOSS
                                 Sum of          Mean
Source              DF          Squares        Square    F Value    Pr > F

Model                6      13.20400000     2.20066667       2.52    0.1133

Error                8       6.99200000     0.87400000

Corrected Total     14      20.19600000

                 R-Square           C.V.       Root MSE       PCTLOSS Mean

                 0.653793       5.329987      0.9348797          17.540000


Source              DF         Anova SS    Mean Square    F Value    Pr > F
BLOCK                2      1.64800000     0.82400000       0.94    0.4289
BLEND                4     11.55600000     2.88900000       3.31    0.0705
```

The top section of the output contains lines labeled MODEL, ERROR, and CORRECTED TOTAL. The total variation, or total sum of squares, is partitioned into two components: variation due to effects in the model (MODEL) and variation not due to effects in the model (ERROR). The bottom section of the output contains lines labeled BLOCK and BLEND. This is a partitioning of the MODEL sums of squares into two components: sums of squares due to differences between BLOCKs and sums of squares due to differences between BLENDs.

The output is summarized in this ANOVA table:

Source	DF	SS	MS	*F*	*p*
BLOCK	2	1.648			
BLEND	4	11.556	2.889	3.31	0.0705
ERROR	8	6.992	0.874		
TOTAL	14	20.196			

Other Methods for Multiple Comparisons

There are many multiple comparison tests available in PROC ANOVA and PROC GLM. In this section the randomized-blocks example shown above is used to illustrate some of these tests. The tests illustrated in this example are summarized below, including information pertaining to their error rates and option keywords.

Least Significant Difference (LSD)
  comparisonwise error rate (ALPHA=probability of Type I error for any one particular comparison)

Duncan's New Multiple Range (DUNCAN)
  error rate comparable to $k-1$ orthogonal comparisons tested simultaneously

Waller-Duncan (WALLER)
  error rate dependent on value of analysis-of-variance F test

Tukey's Honest Significant Difference (TUKEY)
  experimentwise error rate (ALPHA=probability of one or more Type I errors altogether).

A characteristic of multiple comparison tests is their Type I error rate, that is, their probability of incorrectly declaring means to be different.

For the LSD, DUNCAN, and TUKEY options, ALPHA=.05 unless the ALPHA= option is specified. Only ALPHA= values of .01, .05, or .1 are allowed with the Duncan's test. The Waller test is based on Bayesian principles and utilizes the Type I/Type II error seriousness ratio, called the k ratio, instead of an ALPHA= value. In practice, ALPHA=.05 for the DUNCAN option and KRATIO=100 for the WALLER option produce similar results.

The following SAS statements illustrate the options:

```
proc anova;
   class block blend;
   model pctloss=block blend;
   means blend / lsd;
   means blend / duncan;
   means blend / waller;
   means blend / tukey;
   means blend / duncan alpha=.1;
   means blend / tukey alpha=.1;
run;
```

The results appear in Output 2.15 and reveal that, among the methods illustrated, the LSD option tends to declare the most differences, the TUKEY option tends to declare the least, and the DUNCAN option is between LSD and TUKEY in this respect. The WALLER and DUNCAN options produce the same results. Furthermore, specifying ALPHA=.1 results in more declared differences than the default ALPHA=.05. The opposite is true for ALPHA=.01.

Note: Do not confuse the use of A, B, C, D, and E to group the means with the **A, B, C, D,** and **E** used to identify values of BLEND.

Output 2.15
Several Types of
Multiple
Comparison
Procedures

```
                              The SAS System                               1

                        Analysis of Variance Procedure

                        T tests (LSD) for variable: PCTLOSS

    NOTE: This test controls the type I comparisonwise error rate not the
          experimentwise error rate.

                      Alpha= 0.05  df= 8  MSE= 0.874
                        Critical Value of T= 2.31
                      Least Significant Difference= 1.7602

    Means with the same letter are not significantly different.

              T Grouping              Mean      N  BLEND

                           A        18.8000      3  E
                           A
                    B      A        18.1667      3  B
                    B      A
                    B      A   C    17.4667      3  C
                    B          C
                    B          C    16.9667      3  A
                               C
                               C    16.3000      3  D
```

```
                                                                           2

                        Analysis of Variance Procedure

                   Duncan's Multiple Range Test for variable: PCTLOSS

    NOTE: This test controls the type I comparisonwise error rate, not
          the experimentwise error rate

                      Alpha= 0.05  df= 8  MSE= 0.874

              Number of Means     2     3     4     5
              Critical Range   1.758 1.833 1.877 1.899

    Means with the same letter are not significantly different.

              Duncan Grouping          Mean      N  BLEND

                           A        18.8000      3  E
                           A
                    B      A        18.1667      3  B
                    B      A
                    B      A        17.4667      3  C
                    B      A
                    B      A        16.9667      3  A
                    B
                    B               16.3000      3  D
```

```
                                                                    3

                        Analysis of Variance Procedure

            Waller-Duncan K-ratio T test for variable: PCTLOSS

NOTE: This test minimizes the Bayes risk under additive loss and
      certain other assumptions.

            Kratio= 100  df= 8  MSE= 0.874  F= 3.305492
                    Critical Value of T= 2.54613
                Minimum Significant Difference= 1.9435

Means with the same letter are not significantly different.

        Waller Grouping              Mean     N  BLEND

                        A          18.8000     3  E
                        A
                 B      A          18.1667     3  B
                 B      A
                 B      A          17.4667     3  C
                 B      A
                 B      A          16.9667     3  A
                 B
                 B                 16.3000     3  D
```

```
                                                                    4

                        Analysis of Variance Procedure

        Tukey's Studentized Range (HSD) Test for variable: PCTLOSS

NOTE: This test controls the type I experimentwise error rate, but
      generally has a higher type II error rate than REGWQ.

               Alpha= 0.05  df= 8  MSE= 0.874
            Critical Value of Studentized Range= 4.886
               Minimum Significant Difference= 2.6371

Means with the same letter are not significantly different.

        Tukey Grouping               Mean     N  BLEND

                        A          18.8000     3  E
                        A
                        A          18.1667     3  B
                        A
                        A          17.4667     3  C
                        A
                        A          16.9667     3  A
                        A
                        A          16.3000     3  D
```

(continued on next page)

(continued from previous page)

```
                                                                      5

                      Analysis of Variance Procedure

            Duncan's Multiple Range Test for variable: PCTLOSS

     NOTE: This test controls the type I comparisonwise error rate, not
           the experimentwise error rate

                   Alpha= 0.1  df= 8  MSE= 0.874

            Number of Means      2     3     4     5
            Critical Range   1.419 1.479 1.510 1.529

     Means with the same letter are not significantly different.

          Duncan Grouping              Mean     N  BLEND

                         A          18.8000     3  E
                         A
                  B      A          18.1667     3  B
                  B      A
                  B      A    C     17.4667     3  C
                  B           C
                  B           C     16.9667     3  A
                              C
                              C     16.3000     3  D
```

```
                                                                      6

                      Analysis of Variance Procedure

          Tukey's Studentized Range (HSD) Test for variable: PCTLOSS

     NOTE: This test controls the type I experimentwise error rate, but
           generally has a higher type II error rate than REGWQ.

                   Alpha= 0.1  df= 8  MSE= 0.874
            Critical Value of Studentized Range= 4.169
              Minimum Significant Difference= 2.25

     Means with the same letter are not significantly different.

          Tukey Grouping               Mean     N  BLEND

                         A          18.8000     3  E
                         A
                  B      A          18.1667     3  B
                  B      A
                  B      A          17.4667     3  C
                  B      A
                  B      A          16.9667     3  A
                  B
                  B                 16.3000     3  D
```

Some multiple comparison results can be expressed as confidence intervals for differences between pairs of means. This provides more information regarding the differences than simply joining nonsignificantly different means with a common letter, but more space is required to print the results. Specifying the CLDIFF option selects the confidence interval option. For example, the following SAS statement produces Output 2.16:

```
means blend / tukey alpha=.1 cldiff;
```

Output 2.16
Simultaneous
Confidence
Intervals for
Differences

```
                            The SAS System                              1

                       Analysis of Variance Procedure

            Tukey's Studentized Range (HSD) Test for variable: PCTLOSS

            NOTE: This test controls the type I experimentwise error rate.

                 Alpha= 0.1  Confidence= 0.9  df= 8  MSE= 0.874
                   Critical Value of Studentized Range= 4.169
                      Minimum Significant Difference= 2.25

            Comparisons significant at the 0.1 level are indicated by '***'.

                          Simultaneous              Simultaneous
                             Lower      Difference     Upper
                   BLEND    Confidence   Between    Confidence
                 Comparison    Limit      Means        Limit

                  E  - B     -1.6166     0.6333      2.8833
                  E  - C     -0.9166     1.3333      3.5833
                  E  - A     -0.4166     1.8333      4.0833
                  E  - D      0.2500     2.5000      4.7500    ***

                  B  - E     -2.8833    -0.6333      1.6166
                  B  - C     -1.5500     0.7000      2.9500
                  B  - A     -1.0500     1.2000      3.4500
                  B  - D     -0.3833     1.8667      4.1166

                  C  - E     -3.5833    -1.3333      0.9166
                  C  - B     -2.9500    -0.7000      1.5500
                  C  - A     -1.7500     0.5000      2.7500
                  C  - D     -1.0833     1.1667      3.4166

                  A  - E     -4.0833    -1.8333      0.4166
                  A  - B     -3.4500    -1.2000      1.0500
                  A  - C     -2.7500    -0.5000      1.7500
                  A  - D     -1.5833     0.6667      2.9166

                  D  - E     -4.7500    -2.5000     -0.2500    ***
                  D  - B     -4.1166    -1.8667      0.3833
                  D  - C     -3.4166    -1.1667      1.0833
                  D  - A     -2.9166    -0.6667      1.5833
```

The three asterisks (***) to the right of a difference (in this case, **E-D** and **D-E**) in Output 2.16 indicate the difference is significant at the ALPHA rate. The asterisks appear next to differences whose confidence intervals do not include 0.

The confidence interval method of presentation is the default for some methods when the means are based on different numbers of observations because the required difference for significance depends on the numbers of observations in the means.

2.3.6 Latin Square Design with Two Response Variables

As described in Section 2.3.5, the randomized-blocks design controls one source of extraneous variation. It often happens, however, that there are two or more identifiable sources of variation. Such a situation may call for a Latin square design, which controls two sources of extraneous variation, usually referred to as rows and columns. Treatments are randomly assigned to experimental units so that each treatment occurs once in each row and once in each column.

Consider the following example of a Latin square: Four materials (A, B, C, and D) used in permanent press garments are subjected to a test for weight loss and shrinkage. The four materials (MAT) are placed in a heat chamber that has four control settings or positions (POS). The test is conducted in four runs (RUN), with each material assigned to each of the four positions in one execution of the experiment as follows:

	Position			
Run	1	2	3	4
1	B	D	A	C
2	D	B	C	A
3	A	C	B	D
4	C	A	D	B

The weight loss (WTLOSS) and shrinkage (SHRINK) are measured on each sample following each test. The data appear in Output 2.17.

Output 2.17
Data for Latin
Square Design

```
                          The SAS System                              1

      OBS     RUN     POS     MAT     WTLOSS     SHRINK

       1       2       4       A        251        50
       2       2       2       B        241        48
       3       2       1       D        227        45
       4       2       3       C        229        45
       5       3       4       D        234        46
       6       3       2       C        273        54
       7       3       1       A        274        55
       8       3       3       B        226        43
       9       1       4       C        235        45
      10       1       2       D        236        46
      11       1       1       B        218        43
      12       1       3       A        268        51
      13       4       4       B        195        39
      14       4       2       A        270        52
      15       4       1       C        230        48
      16       4       3       D        225        44
```

The following table shows the sources of variation and degrees of freedom for an analysis of variance for the Latin square design:

Source	DF
RUN	3
POS	3
MAT	3
ERROR	6

Use the following SAS statements to obtain the analysis of variance:

```
proc anova data=garments;
  class run pos mat;
  model wtloss shrink = run pos mat;
run;
```

The data are classified according to RUN, POS, and MAT, so these variables appear in the CLASS statement. The response variables to be analyzed are WTLOSS and SHRINK, and the sources of variation in the ANOVA table are RUN, POS, and MAT. Note that one MODEL statement handles both response variables simultaneously. Output 2.18 shows the output.

Output 2.18
Analysis of
Variance for Latin
Square Design

```
                            The SAS System                           1
                      Analysis of Variance Procedure

Dependent Variable: WTLOSS
                                  Sum of           Mean
Source                 DF        Squares         Square   F Value    Pr > F

Model                   9      7076.5000000    786.2777778   12.84    0.0028

Error                   6       367.5000000     61.2500000

Corrected Total        15      7444.0000000

                 R-Square          C.V.       Root MSE        WTLOSS Mean

                 0.950631       3.267740      7.8262379         239.50000


Source                 DF       Anova SS    Mean Square   F Value    Pr > F

RUN                     3      986.5000000    328.8333333    5.37    0.0390
POS                     3     1468.5000000    489.5000000    7.99    0.0162
MAT                     3     4621.5000000   1540.5000000   25.15    0.0008
```

```
                                                                     2
                      Analysis of Variance Procedure

Dependent Variable: SHRINK
                                  Sum of           Mean
Source                 DF        Squares         Square   F Value    Pr > F

Model                   9       265.75000000    29.52777778   9.84    0.0058

Error                   6        18.00000000     3.00000000

Corrected Total        15       283.75000000

                 R-Square          C.V.       Root MSE        SHRINK Mean

                 0.936564       3.675439      1.7320508         47.125000


Source                 DF       Anova SS    Mean Square   F Value    Pr > F

RUN                     3       33.25000000    11.08333333    3.69    0.0813
POS                     3       60.25000000    20.08333333    6.69    0.0242
MAT                     3      172.25000000    57.41666667   19.14    0.0018
```

The table below is a summary of the results.

WTLOSS

Source	DF	SS	MS	F	p
RUN	3	986.5			
POS	3	1468.5			
MAT	3	4621.5	1540.5	25.15	0.0008
ERROR	6	367.5	61.25		
TOTAL	15	7444.0			

SHRINK

Source	DF	SS	MS	F	p
RUN	3	33.25			
POS	3	60.25			
MAT	3	172.25	57.42	19.14	0.0018
ERROR	6	18.00	3.00		
TOTAL	15	283.75			

The *F* tests for MAT indicate differences between materials in both WTLOSS and SHRINK. For a more detailed discussion of Latin square designs, see Steel and Torrie (1980).

2.3.7 Two-Way Factorial Experiment

Two of the basic aspects of experiment design are treatment structure and error control. Choosing between randomization schemes, such as completely randomized, randomized blocks, and so on, is part of error control. The concept of the factorial experiment, on the other hand, concerns the structure of treatments. The factorial treatment structure can be used with any randomization scheme.

A balanced factorial experiment consists of all possible combinations of levels of two or more variables. Levels can refer to numeric quantities of variables, such as pounds of fertilizer ingredients or degrees of temperature, as well as qualitative categories, such as names of breeds or drugs. Variables, which are called factors, can be different fertilizer ingredients (N, P, K), operating conditions (temperature, pressure), biological factors (breeds, varieties), or any combination of the above. An example of a factorial experiment is a study using nitrogen, phosphorus, and potassium, each at three levels. Such an experiment has $3^3 = 27$ treatment combinations.

Factorial experiments are used to investigate not only overall differences between levels of each factor (main effects), but also how levels of one factor affect the response variable across levels of another factor (interactions). For example, suppose three seed growth promoting methods (METHOD) are applied to seed from each of five varieties (VARIETY) of turf grass. Six pots are planted with seed from each METHOD×VARIETY combination. The resulting 90 pots are randomly placed in a uniform growth chamber and the dry matter yields (YIELD) are measured after clipping at the end of four weeks. In this experiment, the concern is only about these five varieties and three growth methods. VARIETY and METHOD are regarded as fixed effects. The experiment is a 3×5 factorial in a completely randomized design. The two factors are METHOD and VARIETY.

Data are recorded in a SAS data set called GRASSES, which appears in Output 2.19. For convenience, the six replicate measurements are recorded as Y1—Y6 in the same observation.

Output 2.19
Data for Factorial Experiment

```
                            The SAS System                              1

   OBS     METHOD    VARIETY    Y1     Y2     Y3     Y4     Y5     Y6    TRT

    1        A          1      22.1   24.1   19.1   22.1   25.1   18.1   A1
    2        A          2      27.1   15.1   20.6   28.6   15.1   24.6   A2
    3        A          3      22.3   25.8   22.8   28.3   21.3   18.3   A3
    4        A          4      19.8   28.3   26.8   27.3   26.8   26.8   A4
    5        A          5      20.0   17.0   24.0   22.5   28.0   22.5   A5
    6        B          1      13.5   14.5   11.5    6.0   27.0   18.0   B1
    7        B          2      16.9   17.4   10.4   19.4   11.9   15.4   B2
    8        B          3      15.7   10.2   16.7   19.7   18.2   12.2   B3
    9        B          4      15.1    6.5   17.1    7.6   13.6   21.1   B4
   10        B          5      21.8   22.8   18.8   21.3   16.3   14.3   B5
   11        C          1      19.0   22.0   20.0   14.5   19.0   16.0   C1
   12        C          2      20.0   22.0   25.5   16.5   18.0   17.5   C2
   13        C          3      16.4   14.4   21.4   19.9   10.4   21.4   C3
   14        C          4      24.5   16.0   11.0    7.5   14.5   15.5   C4
   15        C          5      11.8   14.3   21.3    6.3    7.8   13.8   C5
```

ANOVA for a Two-Way Factorial Experiment

An analysis of variance for the experiment has the following form:

Source	DF
METHOD	2
VARIETY	4
METHOD×VARIETY	8
ERROR	75

The METHOD×VARIETY interaction is a measure of whether differences among METHOD means depend on the VARIETY being used. If the interaction is present, it may be necessary to compare METHOD means separately for each VARIETY. If the interaction is not present, a comparison of METHODs averaged over all levels of VARIETY is appropriate.

Because a single YIELD value is needed for each observation instead of six values, the data in GRASSES (see Output 2.19) must be rearranged for analysis.* Use the following SAS statements to rearrange the data:

```
data fctorial;  set grasses;  drop y1-y6;
  yield=y1; output;
  yield=y2; output;
  yield=y3; output;
  yield=y4; output;
  yield=y5; output;
  yield=y6; output;
run;
```

The rearranged data are put into a SAS data set named FCTORIAL, which is sorted by METHOD and VARIETY. These SAS statements compute and plot means for visual inspection:

```
proc means data=fctorial noprint;
  by method variety;
  output out=factmean mean=yldmean;
proc print data=factmean;
run;

proc plot data=factmean;
  plot yldmean*variety=method / haxis=1 to 5 by 1 vaxis=12 to 26 by 2;
run;
```

The PROC MEANS statement requests computation of means and standard errors of the means of each METHOD×VARIETY combination, but the NOPRINT option suppresses their printing. The OUTPUT statement causes a new SAS data set named FACTMEAN to be created. FACTMEAN contains a variable named YLDMEAN, whose values are the means of the variable YIELD for each combination of the values of the variables METHOD and VARIETY. The data set FACTMEAN appears in Output 2.20.

---

* This data manipulation would not be necessary if the values of YIELD had originally been recorded as single values.

Output 2.20
Cell Means for
Factorial
Experiment

```
                          The SAS System                            1

         OBS    METHOD   VARIETY    _TYPE_    _FREQ_    YLDMEAN

          1       A        1          0         6       21.7667
          2       A        2          0         6       21.8500
          3       A        3          0         6       23.1333
          4       A        4          0         6       25.9667
          5       A        5          0         6       22.3333
          6       B        1          0         6       15.0833
          7       B        2          0         6       15.2333
          8       B        3          0         6       15.4500
          9       B        4          0         6       13.5000
         10       B        5          0         6       19.2167
         11       C        1          0         6       18.4167
         12       C        2          0         6       19.9167
         13       C        3          0         6       17.3167
         14       C        4          0         6       14.8333
         15       C        5          0         6       12.5500
```

Use the following SAS statements to apply PROC PLOT to the data set FACTMEAN:

```
proc plot data=factmean;
   plot yldmean*variety=method;
```

The PLOT statement plots the values of YLDMEAN on the vertical axis versus the VARIETY values on the horizontal axis and labels the points according to METHOD names **A**, **B**, or **C** (see Output 2.21). Apparently, the magnitude of differences between METHOD means depends on which VARIETY is used.

The analysis of variance is obtained with the following SAS statements:

```
proc anova data=fctorial; class method variety;
   model yield=method variety method*variety;
run;
```

These statements request an analysis of variance for the data set FCTORIAL. The data are classified according to METHOD and VARIETY. The MODEL statement specifies that the analysis of YIELD is to contain sources of variation METHOD, VARIETY, and METHOD*VARIETY. Note that the METHOD*VARIETY

interaction in the PROC ANOVA output in Output 2.22 is significant at the
$p=0.0241$ level, confirming the interaction observed in Output 2.21.

Output 2.21
*Plots of Cell
Means for
Factorial
Experiment*

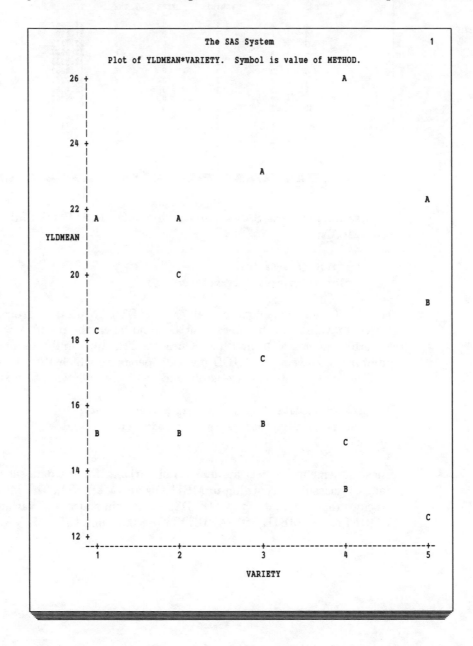

Output 2.22
Analysis of
Variance for
Factorial
Experiment

```
                              The SAS System                        1

                        Analysis of Variance Procedure

Dependent Variable: YIELD
                                     Sum of           Mean
Source                  DF          Squares         Square   F Value    Pr > F

Model                   14      1339.0248889     95.6446349      4.87    0.0001

Error                   75      1473.7666667     19.6502222

Corrected Total         89      2812.7915556

                   R-Square            C.V.       Root MSE         YIELD Mean

                   0.476048        24.04225      4.4328571          18.437778


Source                  DF         Anova SS    Mean Square   F Value    Pr > F

METHOD                   2     953.15622222    476.57811111     24.25    0.0001
VARIETY                  4      11.38044444      2.84511111      0.14    0.9648
METHOD*VARIETY           8     374.48822222     46.81102778      2.38    0.0241
```

You should note that this example contains balanced data because every
METHOD*VARIETY combination contains six observations. The analysis of
variance is, therefore, correctly obtained with PROC ANOVA. If the number of
observations had not been equal in all METHOD*VARIETY combinations, PROC
ANOVA would not necessarily provide valid computations of sums of squares. In
this event, PROC GLM should be used. See Chapter 4 for more information.

Multiple Comparison for Factorial Experiment

Because the interaction is significant, it is appropriate to compare the METHOD
means separately for each VARIETY with Duncan's multiple-range test. This can
be done by using a BY statement in a PROC ANOVA step.

The data set FCTORIAL must be sorted according to VARIETY before the BY
statement is used with PROC ANOVA. PROC ANOVA is then set up to analyze the
data for a single VARIETY. Within each VARIETY, the data are classified
according to METHOD. The SAS statements for the analysis are as follows:

```
proc sort data=fctorial;
   by variety;
proc anova data=fctorial;
   by variety;
   class method;
   model yield=method;
   means method / duncan;
run;
```

The results for VARIETY=1 and VARIETY=5 appear in Output 2.23.

For VARIETY=1, METHODs **A** and **B** are declared to be significantly
different from each other, but not from **C**. Now compare VARIETY=1 with
VARIETY=5. The printout for VARIETY=5 declares METHOD **C** to be different
from both **A** and **B**, but **A** and **B** are not different from each other; thus, the
ranking of the METHOD means is different in VARIETY=1 and VARIETY=5. In
short, the nature of the differences between treatments depends on which

VARIETY is investigated. This phenomenon is reflected in the significant METHOD*VARIETY interaction in the overall analysis of variance.

Output 2.23
Multiple
Comparisons of
METHOD Means
By Variety

```
                         The SAS System                        1
-------------------------------- VARIETY=1 -----------------------------------
                      Analysis of Variance Procedure
                         Class Level Information

                     Class     Levels    Values

                     METHOD        3     A B C


              Number of observations in by group = 18
```

```
                                                               2

-------------------------------- VARIETY=1 -----------------------------------
                     Analysis of Variance Procedure

Dependent Variable: YIELD
                                  Sum of          Mean
Source                 DF         Squares         Square   F Value    Pr > F

Model                   2     134.00111111     67.00055556     3.11    0.0742

Error                  15     323.25000000     21.55000000

Corrected Total        17     457.25111111

               R-Square           C.V.        Root MSE        YIELD Mean

               0.293058        25.19890       4.6421978         18.422222


Source                 DF        Anova SS     Mean Square   F Value    Pr > F

METHOD                  2     134.00111111     67.00055556     3.11    0.0742
```

```
                                                               3

-------------------------------- VARIETY=1 -----------------------------------
                     Analysis of Variance Procedure

             Duncan's Multiple Range Test for variable: YIELD

   NOTE: This test controls the type I comparisonwise error rate, not
         the experimentwise error rate

             Alpha= 0.05  df= 15  MSE= 21.55

                    Number of Means      2      3
                    Critical Range   5.703  5.982

   Means with the same letter are not significantly different.

        Duncan Grouping            Mean     N  METHOD

                           A      21.767     6  A
                           A
                      B    A      18.417     6  C
                      B
                      B           15.083     6  B
```

```
                                                                    4
----------------------------------- VARIETY=5 -----------------------------------
                        Analysis of Variance Procedure
                           Class Level Information

                        Class    Levels    Values

                        METHOD      3      A B C


                  Number of observations in by group = 18
```

```
                                                                    5
----------------------------------- VARIETY=5 -----------------------------------
                        Analysis of Variance Procedure

Dependent Variable: YIELD
                                  Sum of            Mean
Source                  DF        Squares          Square    F Value    Pr > F

Model                    2     299.74333333    149.87166667     8.36    0.0036

Error                   15     268.91666667     17.92777778

Corrected Total         17     568.66000000

                R-Square          C.V.         Root MSE          YIELD Mean

                0.527105        23.47941       4.2341207          18.033333


Source                  DF        Anova SS     Mean Square    F Value    Pr > F

METHOD                   2     299.74333333    149.87166667     8.36    0.0036
```

```
                                                                    6
----------------------------------- VARIETY=5 -----------------------------------
                        Analysis of Variance Procedure

              Duncan's Multiple Range Test for variable: YIELD

      NOTE: This test controls the type I comparisonwise error rate, not
            the experimentwise error rate

                   Alpha= 0.05  df= 15  MSE= 17.92778

                        Number of Means    2     3
                        Critical Range  5.201 5.456

      Means with the same letter are not significantly different.

              Duncan Grouping           Mean      N  METHOD

                            A          22.333     6  A
                            A
                            A          19.217     6  B

                            B          12.550     6  C
```

If the interaction is not significant, multiple comparisons can be performed on the main effect means. Adding the following SAS statement to the PROC ANOVA statement produces the main effect and interaction means as well as Duncan's multiple-range test on main effect means:

```
means method variety method*variety / duncan;
```

However, many statisticians do not consider multiple comparisons appropriate for comparison of the METHOD*VARIETY means; multiple comparisons are not computed by PROC ANOVA. This is not a criticism of Duncan's procedure, but rather a criticism of its frequent misuse. See Chew (1976) and Little (1978) for more detailed explanations.

Other statisticians do not object to this practice. If you want multiple comparisons of the METHOD*VARIETY means, you can create a variable, say TRT, whose values are the combinations of values of METHOD and VARIETY, and then analyze TRT means as if TRT were a one-way classification of the data. For example, you might have A1, A2, . . . , C4, C5 as the values of TRT. Then run the following statements:

```
proc anova data=fctorial;  class trt;
  model yield = trt;
  means trt / duncan;
run;
```

Output 2.24
Multiple Comparisons across Factorial Means

```
                            The SAS System                              1

                       Analysis of Variance Procedure

Dependent Variable: YIELD
                                    Sum of            Mean
Source                DF           Squares          Square    F Value    Pr > F

Model                 14       1339.0248889      95.6446349      4.87    0.0001

Error                 75       1473.7666667      19.6502222

Corrected Total       89       2812.7915556

                   R-Square            C.V.         Root MSE         YIELD Mean

                   0.476048         24.04225        4.4328571         18.437778


Source                DF          Anova SS     Mean Square    F Value    Pr > F

TRT                   14       1339.0248889      95.6446349      4.87    0.0001
```

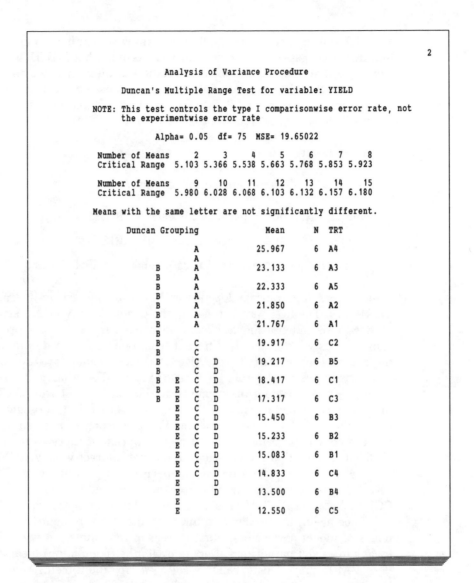

```
                                                                    2
                        Analysis of Variance Procedure

                  Duncan's Multiple Range Test for variable: YIELD

        NOTE: This test controls the type I comparisonwise error rate, not
              the experimentwise error rate

                    Alpha= 0.05  df= 75  MSE= 19.65022

        Number of Means     2     3     4     5     6     7     8
        Critical Range   5.103 5.366 5.538 5.663 5.768 5.853 5.923

        Number of Means     9    10    11    12    13    14    15
        Critical Range   5.980 6.028 6.068 6.103 6.132 6.157 6.180

        Means with the same letter are not significantly different.

                Duncan Grouping              Mean     N  TRT

                              A            25.967     6  A4
                              A
                        B     A            23.133     6  A3
                        B     A
                        B     A            22.333     6  A5
                        B     A
                        B     A            21.850     6  A2
                        B     A
                        B     A            21.767     6  A1
                        B
                        B     C            19.917     6  C2
                        B     C
                        B     C  D         19.217     6  B5
                        B     C  D
                        B  E  C  D         18.417     6  C1
                        B  E  C  D
                        B  E  C  D         17.317     6  C3
                           E  C  D
                           E  C  D         15.450     6  B3
                           E  C  D
                           E  C  D         15.233     6  B2
                           E  C  D
                           E  C  D         15.083     6  B1
                           E  C  D
                           E  C  D         14.833     6  C4
                           E     D
                           E     D         13.500     6  B4
                           E
                           E                12.550     6  C5
```

Output 2.24 shows the multiple comparisons of the TRT means. This type of analysis ignores the structure of the classification as it relates to METHOD and VARIETY. For this reason, it is not focused on the objectives of the study, which are to investigate the effects of METHOD and VARIETY.

Preplanned Comparisons in a Two-Way Factorial Experiment

You can use CONTRAST and ESTIMATE statements to make preplanned comparisons among means in a two-way classification just like you did in the one-way classification. These statements may be used in PROC GLM, along with CLASS and MODEL statements that are essentially the same as the CLASS and MODEL statements used with PROC ANOVA.

In the previous section, METHODs are compared separately for each VARIETY using a multiple comparison procedure. The comparisons were made separately for each variety because of the significant METHOD*VARIETY interaction. The multiple comparison procedure was used because no knowledge of the METHODs was assumed that might suggest specific comparisons among the

METHOD means. Now assume that you know something about the METHODs that might suggest a specific comparison. Assume that METHOD **A** is a new technique that is being evaluated in relation to the industry standard techniques, METHODs **B** and **C**. So you might want to compare a mean for METHOD **A** with the average of means for METHODs **B** and **C**, referred to here as **A** vs **B,C**. In general terms, assume you want to estimate the difference

$$\mu_A - 1/2(\mu_B + \mu_C) \quad .$$

There are several ways to make this comparison:

□ compare **A** vs **B,C** separately for each VARIETY   (simple effect)

□ compare **A** vs **B,C** averaged across all VARIETYs   (main effect)

□ compare **A** vs **B,C** averaged across subsets of VARIETYs   (a compromise)

Which way is appropriate depends on how the comparison interacts with VARIETYs. The first way, estimating the comparison **A** vs **B,C** separately for each VARIETY, is called a *simple effect* comparison. It would be appropriate if the comparisons were generally different from one VARIETY to the next, that is, if the comparison *interacts* with VARIETYs. The second way, estimating the comparison averaged across all VARIETYs, is called a *main effect* comparison. It would be appropriate if the comparison did not interact with VARIETYs, that is, if the comparison had essentially the same value (within the range of random error) for all the VARIETYs. The third way is a compromise between simple effect and main effect comparisons. It would be appropriate if there were subsets of VARIETYs such that the comparison did not interact with VARIETYs within the subsets. Each way of making the comparison can be done with CONTRAST or ESTIMATE statements. This illustrates the tremendous flexibility of the CONTRAST and ESTIMATE statements as tools for statistical analysis.

Once again, it is easier to think in terms of means, but PROC GLM works in terms of model parameters. For this reason some notation is needed to relate means to model parameters. Denote by μ_{ij} the (population) mean for METHOD i with VARIETY j. (This is called a *cell mean* for the i,j cell.) Then, for example, μ_{B3} is the (cell) mean for METHOD **B** with VARIETY 3. A GLM model for this two-way classification would specify that

$$\mu_{ij} = \mu + \alpha_i + \beta_j + (\alpha\beta)_{ij} \quad .$$

This equation is the basic relationship between the means and model parameters. In words, the mean for METHOD i with VARIETY j is equal to a constant μ plus an effect of METHOD i plus an effect of VARIETY j plus an effect due to interaction for METHOD i and VARIETY j. In terms of the data,

$$y_{ijk} = k\text{th observed value in METHOD } i \text{ with VARIETY } j$$
$$= \mu_{ij} + \varepsilon_{ijk}$$
$$= \mu + \alpha_i + \beta_j + (\alpha\beta)_{ij} + \varepsilon_{ijk}$$

where ε_{ijk} is the random error representing the difference between the observed value and the mean of the population from which the observation was obtained.

Writing CONTRAST and ESTIMATE statements can be a little tricky, especially in multiway classifications. You can use the basic relationship between the means and model parameters to construct CONTRAST and ESTIMATE statements. Following is a three-step process that always works. In "An Easier Way to Set Up CONTRAST and ESTIMATE Statements," later in this chapter, a simpler way of accomplishing the same task is presented. It is instructive to go through this three-step approach first to demonstrate how the process works. Here are the steps:

1. Write the linear combination you wish to test or estimate in terms of means.

2. Convert means into model parameters.

3. Gather like terms.

The resulting expression will have coefficients for model parameters that you can directly insert into a CONTRAST or ESTIMATE statement.

Simple Effect Comparisons

To set up a comparison of the first type, a comparison of **A** vs **B,C** in VARIETY 1 use the basic relationship between means and model parameters. This is a *simple effect* comparison because you are comparing METHOD means within a particular VARIETY. Use an ESTIMATE statement to estimate **A** versus **B,C** in VARIETY 1.

1. Writing the linear combination in terms of cell means gives

$$\mu_{A1} - .5(\mu_{B1} + \mu_{C1}) \quad .$$

2. Converting to model parameters gives

$$(\mu + \alpha_A + \beta_1 + (\alpha\beta)_{A1}) - .5[(\mu + \alpha_B + \beta_1 + (\alpha\beta)_{B1}) + (\mu + \alpha_C + \beta_1 + (\alpha\beta)_{C1})] \quad .$$

3. Gathering like terms gives

$$(1 - .5 - .5)\,\mu + \alpha_A - .5\alpha_B - .5\alpha_C + (1 - .5 - .5)\beta_1 + (\alpha\beta)_{A1} - .5(\alpha\beta)_{B1} - .5(\alpha\beta)_{C1}$$
$$= \alpha_A - .5\alpha_B - .5\,\alpha_C + (\alpha\beta)_{A1} - .5(\alpha\beta)_{B1} - .5(\alpha\beta)_{C1} \quad .$$

Now you have the information you need to set up the ESTIMATE statement to go with the PROC GLM model. The required statements are

```
proc glm; class method variety;
  model yield = method variety method*variety
  estimate 'A vs B,C in V1' method 1 -.5 -.5
  method*variety 1 0 0 0 0 -.5 0 0 0 0 -.5 0 0 0 0;
```

Consider the following notes:

□ The μ and β parameters disappeared from the expression, so you don't need INTERCEPT or VARIETY terms in the ESTIMATE statement. Leaving them out is equivalent to setting their coefficients equal to 0.

□ The ordering of the METHOD*VARIETY coefficients is determined by the CLASS statement. In this CLASS statement, METHOD comes before VARIETY. For this reason, VARIETY levels change within METHOD levels.

□ If you only wanted a test of the hypothesis H_0: $\mu_A - .5(\mu_B + \mu_C) = 0$, you would replace the ESTIMATE statement with a CONTRAST statement containing the same coefficients:

```
contrast 'A vs B,C in V1' method 1 -5 -5
  method*variety 1 0 0 0 0 -.5 0 0 0 0 -.5 0 0 0 0;
```

Rather than examine output for the single ESTIMATE statement, make the comparison for all five varieties. You would probably want to estimate the comparison **A** vs **B,C** separately for each VARIETY if the comparison interacts with VARIETYs, that is, if the value of the comparison differs from one VARIETY to the next.

As an exercise, see if you can go through the three-step process to get the coefficients for estimates of **A** vs **B,C** in each of VARIETYs 2, 3, 4, and 5. Here is a complete PROC GLM step with the correct ESTIMATE statements for **A** vs **B,C** in each of the five VARIETYs:

```
proc glm; class method variety;
   model yield=method variety method*variety / ss1;
run;
     estimate 'A vs B,C in V1' method 1 -.5 -.5
       method*variety 1 0 0 0 0  -.5 0 0 0 0  -.5 0 0 0 0;
     estimate 'A vs B,C in V2' method 1 -.5 -.5
       method*variety 0 1 0 0 0  0 -.5 0 0 0  0 -.5 0 0 0;
     estimate 'A vs B,C in V3' method 1 -.5 -.5
       method*variety 0 0 1 0 0  0 0 -.5 0 0  0 0 -.5 0 0;
     estimate 'A vs B,C in V4' method 1 -.5 -.5
       method*variety 0 0 0 1 0  0 0 0 -.5 0  0 0 0 -.5 0;
     estimate 'A vs B,C in V5' method 1 -.5 -.5
       method*variety 0 0 0 0 1  0 0 0 0 -.5  0 0 0 0 -.5;
   run;
```

The results appear in Output 2.25.

Output 2.25
Estimates of
Method
Differences By
Variety

```
                              The SAS System                          1

                        General Linear Models Procedure

Dependent Variable: YIELD

                                      T for H0:   Pr > |T|   Std Error of
Parameter               Estimate    Parameter=0              Estimate

A vs B,C in V1         5.01666667        2.26      0.0265     2.21642856
A vs B,C in V2         4.27500000        1.93      0.0575     2.21642856
A vs B,C in V3         6.75000000        3.05      0.0032     2.21642856
A vs B,C in V4        11.80000000        5.32      0.0001     2.21642856
A vs B,C in V5         6.45000000        2.91      0.0048     2.21642856
```

Notice that the estimates differ considerably between VARIETYs, which indicates interaction between the comparison **A** vs **B,C** and VARIETYs. This is no surprise, because there was interaction between METHODs and VARIETYs in the analysis-of-variance table in "ANOVA for a Two-Way Factorial Experiment," earlier in this chapter. It is possible that VARIETYs could interact with

METHODS in general, but not interact with the comparison **A** vs **B,C**. In "Simultaneous Contrasts in Two-Way Classification," later in this chapter, you see how to set up a test for the statistical significance of the interaction between the comparison **A** vs **B,C** and VARIETYs.

Main Effect Comparisons

If the comparison **A** vs **B,C** did not interact with VARIETYs (that is, if the comparison had essentially the same value across all VARIETYs), then you would want to average all the simple effect estimates to get a better estimate of the common value of the comparison. This is called a main effect comparison. In terms of means, the main effect of **A** vs **B,C** is

$$.2 \{\mu_{A1} - .5[\mu_{B1} + \mu_{C1}]\} + \ldots + .2 \{\mu_{A5} - .5[\mu_{B5} + \mu_{C5}]\} \quad .$$

To estimate this main effect with an ESTIMATE statement, convert to model parameters and simplify. You will obtain

$$\alpha_A - .5\mu_B - .5\alpha + .2(\alpha\beta)_{A1} + \ldots + .2(\alpha\beta)_{A5}$$
$$- .1(\alpha\beta)_{B1} - \ldots - .1(\alpha\beta)_{B5}$$
$$- .1(\alpha\beta)_{C1} - \ldots - .1(\alpha\beta)_{C5} \quad .$$

So an appropriate ESTIMATE statement is

```
estimate 'A vs B,C Overall' method 1 -.5 -.5
method*variety .2 .2 .2 .2 .2  -.1 -.1 -.1 -.1 -.1 -.1 -.1 -.1 -.1 -.1;
```

Results from this statement appear in Output 2.26. You can verify by hand that, in fact, this estimate is the average of all the estimates in Output 2.25. Moreover, the standard error in Output 2.26 is only $1/\sqrt{5}$ times as large as the standard errors in Output 2.25, so you can see the benefit of averaging the estimates if they are all estimates of the same quantity.

Output 2.26
Estimate of A vs B,C Averaged over All VARIETYs

```
                          The SAS System                                1

                    General Linear Models Procedure

Dependent Variable: YIELD

                                  T for H0:   Pr > |T|   Std Error of
Parameter              Estimate  Parameter=0             Estimate

A vs B,C Overall     6.85833333         6.92     0.0001    0.99121698
```

Simultaneous Contrasts in Two-Way Classification

This section illustrates setting up simultaneous contrasts in a two-way classification by constructing a test for significance of interaction between the comparison **A** vs **B,C** and VARIETYs. The hypothesis of no interaction between **A** vs **B,C** and VARIETYs is

$$H_0: \{\mu_{A1} - .5[\mu_{B1} + \mu_{C1}]\} = \ldots = \{\mu_{A5} - .5[\mu_{B5} + \mu_{C5}]\} \quad .$$

This hypothesis is actually a set of four equations, which can be written in different but equivalent ways. One way to express the equality of all the comparisons is to specify that each is equal to the last. This gives the hypothesis in the equations

$$H_0: \quad \{\mu_{A1} - .5[\mu_{B1} + \mu_{C1}]\} = \{\mu_{A5} - .5[\mu_{B5} + \mu_{C5}]\} \quad \text{and}$$
$$\{\mu_{A2} - .5[\mu_{B2} + \mu_{C2}]\} = \{\mu_{A5} - .5[\mu_{B5} + \mu_{C5}]\} \quad \text{and}$$
$$\{\mu_{A3} - .5[\mu_{B3} + \mu_{C3}]\} = \{\mu_{A5} - .5[\mu_{B5} + \mu_{C5}]\} \quad \text{and}$$
$$\{\mu_{A4} - .5[\mu_{B4} + \mu_{C4}]\} = \{\mu_{A5} - .5[\mu_{B5} + \mu_{C5}]\} \quad .$$

Going through the three-step process for each of these equations results in the following CONTRAST statement:

```
contrast 'A vs BC * Varieties'
method * variety 1 0 0 0 -1 -.5 0 0 0 .5  -.5 0 0 0 .5,
method * variety 0 1 0 0 -1  0 -.5 0 0 .5  0 -.5 0 0 .5,
method * variety 0 0 1 0 -1  0 0 -.5 0 .5  0 0 -.5 0 .5,
method * variety 0 0 0 1 -1  0 0 0 -.5 .5  0 0 0 -.5 .5;
```

As mentioned in "Preplanned Comparison for One-Way Classification: the CONTRAST Statement," concerning the CONTRAST statement for simultaneous comparisons in the one-way classification, there are several ways to specify a set of four equations that would be equivalent to the null hypothesis that the comparison A vs B,C is the same in all five VARIETYs. No matter how you set up the four equations, a CONTRAST statement derived from those equations would produce the results in Output 2.27.

Output 2.27
*Test for A vs BC **
Varieties
Interaction

```
                              The SAS System                           1
                      General Linear Models Procedure
Dependent Variable: YIELD

Contrast               DF      Contrast SS     Mean Square   F Value    Pr > F

A vs BC * Varieties     4     138.65555556    34.66388889      1.76     0.1450
```

The *F* test for the A vs B,C * Varieties interaction in Output 2.27 is significant at the $p = 0.145$ level. In many hypothesis testing situations, you might not consider this significant. However, the *F* test for the interaction is a preliminary test in the model-building phase to decide whether simple effects or main effects should be reported for the contrast. The decision should be based on a rather liberal cutoff level of significance, such as .2 or .25. You want to relax the Type I error rate in order to decrease the Type II error rate. It might be a serious mistake to declare there is no interaction when in fact there is interaction (a Type II error); you would then report main effects when you should report simple effects. The estimated main effect might not be a good representation of any of the simple effects. It is usually a less serious mistake to declare there is interaction when in fact there is not (a Type I error); you would then report simple effects when you should report main effects. In this event, you still have unbiased estimates, but you lose precision.

Comparing Levels of One Factor within Subgroups of Levels of Another Factor

There are sometimes good reasons to report simple effects averaged across subgroups of levels of another factor (or factors). This is especially desirable when there are a large number of levels of the second factor. For example, if there were twenty varieties in the example instead of five, it would not be feasible to report a separate comparison of methods for each of the twenty varieties. You might want to consider trying to find subgroups of varieties such that the method comparison does not interact with the varieties within the subgroups. It would be legitimate to report the method comparison averaged across the varieties within the subgroups. You should search for the subgroups with caution, however. Identification of potential subgroups should be on the basis of some prior knowledge of the varieties, such as subgroups that have some property in common.

In our example, suppose that VARIETY 1 and VARIETY 2 have a similar genetic background, and that VARIETY 3 and VARIETY 4 have a similar genetic background. This presents a natural basis for forming subgroups. You might want to group VARIETY 1 and VARIETY 2 together and report a single result for the comparison **A** vs **B,C** averaged across these two varieties, and do the same thing for VARIETY 3 and VARIETY 4. The validity of these groupings, however, is contingent upon there being no interaction between the comparison **A** vs **B,C** and VARIETYs within the groups. A test for the significance of interaction between the comparison and the VARIETYs within the respective subgroups is presented here. If the p value for a test is less than .2, then assume interaction to be sufficiently large to indicate separate comparisons for the two VARIETYs within a group. Otherwise, assume that interaction is negligible, and average the comparison across the VARIETYs within a group.

The null hypothesis of no interaction between the comparison **A** vs **B,C** and VARIETY 1 and VARIETY 2 is

$$H_0: \quad \mu_{A1} - .5[\mu_{B1} + \mu_{C1}] = \mu_{A2} - .5[\mu_{B2} + \mu_{C2}] \quad .$$

You have probably become familiar with the three-step process of converting null hypothesis equations into CONTRAST statements. You can determine that the CONTRAST statement to test this hypothesis is

```
contrast 'A vs B,C * V1,V2'
   method*variety 1 -1 0 0 0  -.5 .5 0 0 0  -.5 .5 0 0 0;
```

Likewise, the null hypothesis of no interaction between **A** vs **B,C** and VARIETY 3 and VARIETY 4 is

$$H_0: \quad \mu_{A3} - .5[\mu_{B3} + \mu_{C3}] = \mu_{A4} - .5[\mu_{B4} + \mu_{C4}]$$

and the associated CONTRAST statement is

```
contrast 'A vs B,C * V3,V4'
      method*variety 0 0 1 -1 0  0 0 -.5 .5 0  0 0 -.5 .5 0;
```

Results of these CONTRAST statements appear in Output 2.28.

Output 2.28
Interaction between A vs B,C and VARIETY Subsets

```
                             The SAS System                              1

                       General Linear Models Procedure

Dependent Variable: YIELD

Contrast                 DF      Contrast SS     Mean Square   F Value   Pr > F

A vs B,C * V1,V2          1       1.10013889      1.10013889     0.06    0.8136
A vs B,C * V3,V4          1      51.00500000     51.00500000     2.60    0.1114
```

You can see that the *F* test for the interaction between **A** vs **B,C** and VARIETY 1 and VARIETY 2 has a *p* value of only 0.8136, which is about as nonsignificant as you can hope to get. Assume that this interaction is negligible, and average the comparison across VARIETY 1 and VARIETY 2. On the other hand, the *F* test for interaction between **A** vs **B,C** and VARIETY 3 and VARIETY 4 has a *p* value of .1114, which can be considered sufficiently significant to require separate estimates of **A** vs **B,C** in each to VARIETY 3 and VARIETY 4. Estimates of **A** vs **B,C** obtained separately for VARIETY 3 and VARIETY 4 are given in "Simple Effect Comparisons," earlier in this chapter. Additionally, you need the comparison **A** vs **B,C** averaged across VARIETY 1 and VARIETY 2.

You want an estimate of

$$.5 \ \{[\mu_{A1} - .5 \ (\mu_{B1} + \mu_{C1})] + [\mu_{A2} - .5(\mu_{B2} + \mu_{C2}) \ ]\} \quad .$$

The three-step process yields the following ESTIMATE statement

```
estimate 'A vs B,C in V1,V2' method 1 -.5 -.5
method*variety .5 .5 0 0 0  -.25 -.25 0 0 0  -.25 -.25 0 0 0;
```

Output 2.29 shows the results.

Output 2.29
Estimate of A vs B,C Averaged over VARIETY 1 and VARIETY 2

```
                             The SAS System                              1

                       General Linear Models Procedure

Dependent Variable: YIELD

                                        T for H0:   Pr > |T|   Std Error of
Parameter                Estimate      Parameter=0             Estimate

A vs B,C in V1,V2        4.64583333        2.96      0.0041     1.56725166
```

Note that the estimate 4.64 is the average of the two estimates 5.02 for VARIETY 1 and 4.27 for VARIETY 2 in Output 2.25.

The advantage of averaging is the smaller standard error of 1.57 for the combined estimate compared with 2.21 (see Output 2.25) for the individual estimates.

An Easier Way to Set Up CONTRAST and ESTIMATE Statements

You have used the three-step process given in "Simple Effect Comparisons" earlier in this chapter to obtain coefficients for a CONTRAST or ESTIMATE statement. This process always works, but it can be tedious. Now that you understand the process, here is a simpler diagrammatic method. This method works because of two basic principles that are easy to understand in terms of a two-way classification with factors A and B having a and b levels, respectively. Recall the relation between the cell means and model parameters $\mu_{ij} = \alpha_i + \beta_j + (\alpha\beta_{ij})$.

When you convert a linear combination of cell means to a linear combination of model parameters, the coefficients on the interaction parameters are equal to the coefficients on the cell means.

Certain conditions must hold regarding coefficients of model parameters:

□ coefficients on the $(\alpha\beta_{ij})$ terms for a fixed i must add up to the coefficient on α_i

□ coefficients on the $(\alpha\beta_{ij})$ terms for a fixed j must add up to the coefficient on β_j

□ coefficients on the α_i's and coefficients on the β_j's must both sum to the coefficient on μ.

Let c_{ij} stand for the coefficient on μ_{ij}. Put the coefficients in a diagram as follows:

		Factor B				
		1	2	. . .	b	subtotals
	1	c_{11}	c_{12}	. . .	c_{1b}	$c_{1.}$
	2	c_{21}	c_{22}	. . .	c_{2b}	$c_{2.}$
Factor A	.	.	.		.	.
	.	.	.	. .	.	
	.	.	.	. .		
	a	c_{a1}	c_{a2}	. . .	c_{ab}	$c_{a.}$
subtotals		$c_{.1}$	$c_{.2}$	. . .	$c_{.b}$	$c_{..}$

Then c_{ij} will also be the coefficient on $(\alpha\beta)_{ij}$, $c_{i.}$ will be the coefficient on α_i, $c_{.j}$ will be the coefficient on β_j, and $c_{..}$ will be the coefficient on μ.

To use this for a particular linear combination, take **A** vs **B,C** in VARIETY 1. The linear combination in terms of cell means is

$$\mu_{A1} - .5(\mu_{B1} + \mu_{C1}) \quad .$$

First put the c_{ij} coefficients into the body of the table, then sum down columns and across rows to get the coefficients on the α's and β's. Finally, sum the coefficients on either the α's or the β's to get the coefficient on μ:

VARIETY

		1	2	3	4	5	
	A	1	0	0	0	0	1
METHOD	**B**	−.5	0	0	0	0	−.5
	C	−.5	0	0	0	0	−.5
		0	0	0	0	0	0

You can see that the linear combination in terms of model parameters is

$$\alpha_A - .5\alpha_B - .5\alpha_C + (\alpha\beta)_{A1} - .5(\alpha\beta)_{B1} - .5(\alpha\beta)_{C1}$$

which we derived using the three-step process discussed earlier in "Simple Effect Comparisons."

Chapter 3 Analyzing Data with Random Effects

3.1   Introduction   105

3.2   Nested Classifications   106
3.2.1   Analysis of Variance for Nested Classification: Using PROC NESTED to Estimate Variance Components   109
3.2.2   Computing Variances of Means from Nested Classifications and Deriving Optimum Sampling Plans   111
3.2.3   Analysis of Variance for Nested Classifications: Using Expected Mean Squares to Obtain Valid Tests of Hypotheses   112
3.2.4   Analysis of Variance for Nested Classification: Using the GLM Procedure to Compute Expected Mean Squares   112

3.3   Two-Way Mixed Model   115
3.3.1   Analysis of Variance for Two-Way Mixed Model: Expected Mean Squares   115

3.4   A Classification with Both Crossed and Nested Effects   120
3.4.1   Analysis of Variance for Crossed-Nested Classification   122
3.4.2   Using Expected Mean Squares to Set Up Several Tests of Hypotheses for Crossed-Nested Classification   122
3.4.3   Satterthwaite's Formula for Approximate Degrees of Freedom   128

3.5   Split-Plot Experiments   130
3.5.1   A Standard Split-Plot Experiment   130
3.5.2   Split-Split-Plot Experiment   134

3.1   Introduction

Many studies incorporate blocking factors to provide replication over a selection of different conditions. Investigators are not specifically interested in individual blocks, but rather what the average across blocks reveals. For example, you might want to test chemical compounds at several laboratories to compare the compounds averaged across all the laboratories. Laboratories are selected to represent some broader possible set of laboratories. You might not be too interested in what happens at specific laboratories. Other studies employ experimental factors in which the levels of the factors are a sample of a much larger collection of possible levels. Interest would typically not be in the specific levels of the factors employed but instead on results averaged across the levels and on the degree of variability among the levels. If you work in industry, you probably have seen experiments that utilize a selection of batches of raw material, or a sample of the workers on an assembly line, or a subset of machines out of a much larger set of machines that are used in a production process. In these examples, interest is in what happens across the broader collection of laboratories or batches or workers or machines rather than in what happens with a particular laboratory or batch or worker or machine that was actually employed in the experiment. The factor (laboratories, batches, workers, machines, or whatever) is called a *random* effect. Theoretically, the levels of the factor that are in the experiment are considered to be a random sample from a broader population of possible levels of the factor.

With balanced data, the presence of random factors does not present a major issue for the estimation of treatment means or differences between treatment means. You simply compute means or differences between means, averaged across the levels of the random factors in the experiment. However, the presence of random effects has a major impact on the use of appropriate statistical techniques for testing hypotheses and constructing standard errors of estimates. It is safe to say that improper attention to the presence of random effects is one of the most common and serious mistakes in statistical analysis of data. Random effects probably occur in one form or another in the majority of statistical studies. The RANDOM statement in the GLM procedure can help you determine correct methods for a large variety of applications.

3.2 Nested Classifications

Nested classifications of data have sampling units which are classified in a hierarchical or *nested* manner. Typically, these samples are taken in several stages:

1. selection of main units

2. selection of subunits from each main unit

3. selection of sub-subunits from the subunits, and so on.

Normally, the classification factors at each stage are considered random effects, but in some cases a classification factor may be considered fixed, especially one corresponding to the first stage of sampling.

Here is an example of a nested classification. Microbial counts are made on samples of ground beef in a study whose objective is to assess sources of variation in numbers of microbes. Twenty packages of ground beef (PACKAGE) are purchased and taken to a laboratory. Three samples (SAMPLE) are drawn from each package, and two replicate counts are made on each sample. Output 3.1 shows the raw data.

Output 3.1
Microbial Counts
in Ground Beef

```
                          The SAS System                               1

     OBS   PACKAGE   CT11    CT12    CT21    CT22    CT31    CT32

       1      1       527     821     107     299    1382    3524
       2      2      2813    2322    3901    4422     383     479
       3      3       703     652     745     995    2202    1298
       4      4      1617    2629     103      96    2103    8814
       5      5      4169    2907    4018     882     768     271
       6      6        67      28      68     111     277     199
       7      7      1612    1680    6619    4028    5625    6507
       8      8       195     127     591     399     275     152
       9      9       619     520     813     956    1219     923
      10     10       436     555      58      54     236     188
      11     11      1682    3235    2963    2249     457    2950
      12     12      6050    3956    2782    7501    1952    1299
```

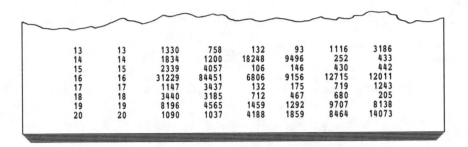

13	13	1330	758	132	93	1116	3186
14	14	1834	1200	18248	9496	252	433
15	15	2339	4057	106	146	430	442
16	16	31229	84451	6806	9156	12715	12011
17	17	1147	3437	132	175	719	1243
18	18	3440	3185	712	467	680	205
19	19	8196	4565	1459	1292	9707	8138
20	20	1090	1037	4188	1859	8464	14073

The data are plotted in Output 3.2, with points identified according to their SAMPLE number.

Output 3.2
Plot of Count versus Package Number

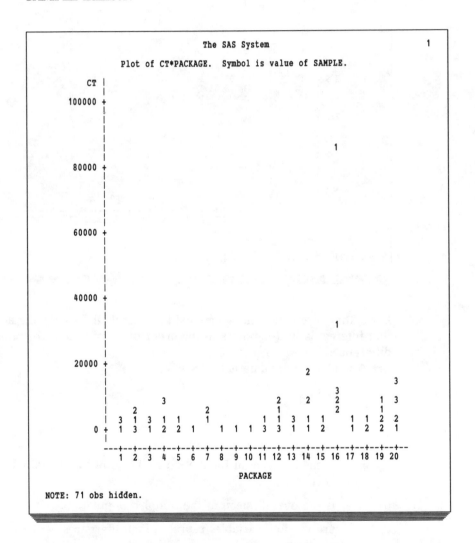

You can see the larger variation among larger counts. In order to stabilize the variance, the logarithm (base 10) of the counts (LOGCT) was computed and serves as the response variable to be analyzed. The plot of LOGCT, which appears in Output 3.3, indicates the transformation was successful in stabilizing the variance.

Output 3.3
Plot of Log Count versus Package Number

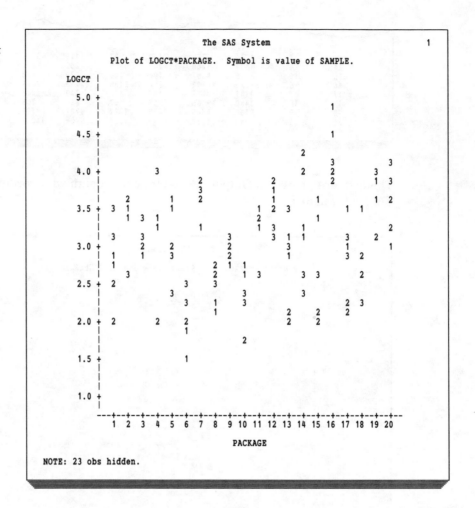

NOTE: 23 obs hidden.

Logarithms are commonly computed for microbial data for the additional reason that interest is in differences in the order of magnitude rather than interval differences.

A model for the data is

$$y_{ijk} = \mu + \alpha_i + \beta_{ij} + \varepsilon_{ijk}$$

where

y_{ijk} is the $\log_{10}$ count for the kth replicate of the jth sample from the ith package.

μ is the overall mean of the sampled population.

α_i are random variables representing differences between packages, with variance σ_P^2, $i=1, \ldots, 20$.

β_{ij} are random variables representing differences between samples in the same package, with variance σ_S^2, $i=1, \ldots, 20$, $j=1,2,3$.

ε_{ijk} are random variables representing differences between replicate counts in the same sample, with variance σ^2, $i=1, \ldots, 20$, $j=1,2,3$, and $k=1,2$.

The random variables α_i, β_{ij}, and ε_{ijk} are assumed independent with means equal to 0. Then the variance (V) of the log counts can be expressed as

$$V(y_{ijk}) = \sigma_y^2$$
$$= \sigma_P^2 + \sigma_S^2 + \sigma^2 \quad .$$

Expressing the equation with words, the variance of the logarithms of microbial count is equal to the sum of the variances due to differences between packages, between samples in the same package, and between replicates in the same sample. These individual variances are therefore called *components of variance*. The first objective is to estimate the variance components, and there are several statistical techniques for doing so, including analysis of variance and maximum likelihood. In this chapter, analysis-of-variance methods are used.

3.2.1 Analysis of Variance for Nested Classification: Using PROC NESTED to Estimate Variance Components

An analysis-of-variance table for the ground beef microbial counts has the following form:

Source of Variation	DF
packages	19
samples in packages	40
replicates in samples	60

You can produce this table using the ANOVA or GLM procedures (see Chapter 2, "Analysis of Variance for Balanced Data"). The NESTED and VARCOMP procedures also produce this table. Which procedure is best to use depends on the objectives of the investigation.

PROC ANOVA and PROC GLM are general purpose procedures that can be used for a broad range of data classifications. In contrast, PROC NESTED is a specialized procedure that is useful only for nested classifications. It provides estimates of the components of variance using the analysis-of-variance method of estimation, which is the purpose here. Later sections discuss some of the features of PROC ANOVA and PROC GLM for nested classifications.

Because PROC NESTED is so specialized, it is very easy to use. You simply list the sources of variation in the proper order in a CLASS statement. This means the CLASS statement in PROC NESTED has a broader purpose than it does in PROC ANOVA and PROC GLM; it encompasses the purpose of the MODEL statement as well. But you must also have the data sorted appropriately, following the same order as the classification scheme. Here are the proper SAS statements:

```
proc sort; by package sample;
proc nested; class package sample;
var logct;
```

Results appear in Output 3.4.

Output 3.4
Nested Analysis of
Variance of Log
Count

```
                              The SAS System                              1
                     Coefficients of Expected Mean Squares

            Source      PACKAGE        SAMPLE        ERROR

            PACKAGE        6             2             1
            SAMPLE         0             2             1
            ERROR          0             0             1
```

```
                                                                          2

         Nested Random Effects Analysis of Variance for Variable LOGCT

                      Degrees
         Variance       of         Sum of                          Error
         Source       Freedom      Squares     F Value   Pr > F     Term

         TOTAL         119        52.772098
         PACKAGE        19        30.529155     3.224    0.0009    SAMPLE
         SAMPLE         40        19.934312    12.952    0.0000    ERROR
         ERROR          60         2.308631

         Variance                            Variance        Percent
         Source       Mean Square            Component        of Total

         TOTAL         0.443463             0.453157        100.0000
         PACKAGE       1.606798             0.184740         40.7673
         SAMPLE        0.498358             0.229940         50.7418
         ERROR         0.038477             0.038477          8.4909

                      Mean                                 3.04945863
                      Standard error of mean               0.11571508
```

First look at the portion of output labeled Coefficients of Expected Mean Squares. This part of the output tells you the expressions for the expected values of the mean squares, that is, what is being estimated by the individual mean squares. Table 3.1 shows you how to interpret the coefficients of expected mean squares.

Table 3.1 *Coefficients of Expected Mean Squares*

Variance Source	Source of Variation	DF	Expected Mean Squares	This tells you:
PACKAGE	packages	19	$\sigma^2 + 2\sigma_S^2 + 6\sigma_P^2$	MS(PACKAGE) estimates $\sigma^2 + 2\sigma_S^2 + 6\sigma_P^2$
SAMPLE	samples in packages	40	$\sigma^2 + 2\sigma_S^2$	MS(SAMPLE) estimates $\sigma^2 + 2\sigma_S^2$
ERROR	replicates in samples	60	σ^2	MS(ERROR) estimates σ^2

From the table of expected mean squares you get the estimates of variance components. These estimates are printed under the heading Variance Component.

□ $\hat{\sigma}^2 = 0.0385 = $ MS(ERROR)

□ $\hat{\sigma}_S^2 = 0.2299 = $ [MS(SAMPLE) $-$ MS(ERROR)]/2

□ $\hat{\sigma}_P^2 = 0.1847 = $ [MS(PACKAGE) $-$ MS(SAMPLE)]/6

The variance of a single microbial count is

$$\hat{\sigma}_y^2 = \text{TOTAL Variance Estimate}$$
$$= \hat{\sigma}^2 + \hat{\sigma}_S^2 + \hat{\sigma}_P^2$$
$$= 0.0385 + 0.2299 + 0.1847$$
$$= 0.4532 \quad .$$

Note: The expression TOTAL Variance Estimate does not refer to MS(TOTAL)$=0.4435$, although the values are similar.

Under the heading Percent of Total you see that

□ 8.49% of TOTAL variance is attributable to ERROR variance

□ 50.74% of TOTAL variance is attributable to SAMPLE variance

□ 40.77% of TOTAL variance is attributable to PACKAGE variance.

3.2.2 Computing Variances of Means from Nested Classifications and Deriving Optimum Sampling Plans

The variance of a mean can also be partitioned into portions attributable to individual sources of variation. The variance of a mean $\bar{y}_{...}$ computed from a sample of n_P packages, n_S samples per package, and n replicates per sample, is estimated to be

$$\hat{\sigma}_{\bar{y}_{...}}^2 = (0.1847) / n_P + (0.2299) / n_P n_S + (0.0385) / n_P n_S n \quad .$$

Output 3.4 shows that the overall mean is 3.0494, with standard error equal to 0.1157. This standard error was computed as the square root of the variance estimate

$$\hat{\sigma}_{\bar{y}_{...}} = [(0.1847) / 20 + (0.2299) / 20 * 3 + (0.0385) / 20 * 3250 * 2]^{(1/2)} \quad .$$

The formula for the variance of a mean can also be used to derive an optimum sampling plan, subject to certain cost constraints. Suppose you are planning a study, for which you have a budget of \$500. Each package costs \$5, each sample costs \$3, and each replicate count costs \$1. Then the total cost is

$$\text{cost} = \$5 * n_P + \$3 * n_P * n_S + \$1 * n_P * n_S * n \quad .$$

You can create a SAS data set taking various combinations of n_P, n_S, and n for which cost $\leq\$500$, and compute the variance estimate for the mean. Then choose the combination of n_P, n_S, and n that minimizes $\sigma_{\bar{y}...}^2$.

3.2.3 Analysis of Variance for Nested Classifications: Using Expected Mean Squares to Obtain Valid Tests of Hypotheses

Expected mean squares tell you how to set up appropriate tests of a hypothesis regarding the variance components. Suppose you want to test the null hypothesis H_0: $\sigma_P^2=0$. If this null hypothesis is true, then the expected mean square for PACKAGE and the expected mean square for SAMPLE (samples in packages) are both equal to $\sigma^2+2\sigma_S^2$. Therefore, MS(PACKAGE) and MS(SAMPLE) should have approximately the same value if H_0: $\sigma_P^2=0$ is true. But if H_0: $\sigma_P^2=0$ is false, then the MS(PACKAGE) should be larger than the MS(SAMPLE). It follows that you can compare the value of MS(PACKAGE) with the value of MS(SAMPLE) to get an indication of whether the null hypothesis is true or false. Formally, you do this with an F statistic; divide MS(PACKAGE) by MS(SAMPLE). The result has an F distribution with n_P-1 DF in the numerator and $n_P{}^*(n_S-1)$ DF in the denominator. For the microbial count data, $F=1.607/0.498=3.224$, with numerator DF$=19$ and denominator DF$=40$, which is significant at the $p=0.0009$ level. Therefore, you reject H_0: $\sigma_P^2=0$, and conclude $\sigma_P^2>0$.

You can go through the same process of using the table of expected mean squares to set up a test of the null hypothesis H_0: $\sigma_S^2=0$. You see that the appropriate test statistic is $F=$MS(SAMPLE)/MS(REPLICATE), with numerator DF$=40$ and denominator DF$=60$. This $F=12.952$ is significant at the $p<0.0001$ level. Again, you conclude $\sigma_S^2>0$.

3.2.4 Analysis of Variance for Nested Classification: Using the GLM Procedure to Compute Expected Mean Squares

You denote a nested effect such as A nested in B in a SAS model with the notation A(B). This is frequently used, but not universal, statistical notation for a nested effect. The analysis-of-variance table for the microbial data is obtained from these statements:

```
proc glm;  class package sample;
  model logct = package sample(package);
run;
```

Output 3.5 shows the results.

Output 3.5
Nested Analysis of Variance from the GLM Procedure

```
                              The SAS System                          1
                      General Linear Models Procedure
Dependent Variable: LOGCT
                                Sum of            Mean
Source              DF         Squares           Square    F Value    Pr > F

Model               59      50.46346700       0.85531300     22.23    0.0001

Error               60       2.30863144       0.03847719

Corrected Total    119      52.77209844

                  R-Square            C.V.        Root MSE          LOGCT Mean

                  0.956253        6.432487       0.1961560          3.0494586


Source              DF         Type I SS     Mean Square   F Value    Pr > F

PACKAGE             19      30.52915506      1.60679763     41.76     0.0001
SAMPLE(PACKAGE)     40      19.93431194      0.49835780     12.95     0.0001

Source              DF         Type III SS   Mean Square   F Value    Pr > F

PACKAGE             19      30.52915506      1.60679763     41.76     0.0001
SAMPLE(PACKAGE)     40      19.93431194      0.49835780     12.95     0.0001
```

Compare the results in Output 3.5 with those from PROC NESTED in Output 3.4.

Note: *F* statistics in the basic PROC GLM output are not necessarily correct. For example, the *F* statistic for PACKAGE (*F*=41.76) does not have the correct denominator. These tests are computed automatically by PROC GLM with MS(ERROR) for denominator. You can use the expected mean squares to determine if the tests are correct; that is, you can determine if MS(ERROR) is the correct denominator.

By adding the RANDOM statement with a list of all random effects in the model, you can obtain a table of expected mean squares:

```
random package sample(package)/test;
run;
```

Results appear in Output 3.6.

Output 3.6
Expected Mean Squares from the GLM Procedure

```
                              The SAS System                          1
                      General Linear Models Procedure
Source              Type III Expected Mean Square

PACKAGE             Var(Error) + 2 Var(SAMPLE(PACKAGE)) + 6 Var(PACKAGE)

SAMPLE(PACKAGE)     Var(Error) + 2 Var(SAMPLE(PACKAGE))
```

(continued on next page)

(continued from previous page)

```
                                                                        2
                      General Linear Models Procedure
              Tests of Hypotheses for Random Model Analysis of Variance

Dependent Variable: LOGCT


Source: PACKAGE
Error: MS(SAMPLE(PACKAGE))
                              Denominator    Denominator
        DF      Type III MS       DF             MS       F Value   Pr > F
        19     1.6067976348       40        0.4983577986   3.224    0.0009

Source: SAMPLE(PACKAGE)
Error: MS(Error)
                              Denominator    Denominator
        DF      Type III MS       DF             MS       F Value   Pr > F
        40     0.4983577986       60        0.0384771907  12.952    0.0001
```

The TEST option in the RANDOM statement causes PROC GLM to compute F (or approximate F) statistics that have an appropriate denominator as determined from the table of expected mean squares. (Compare expected mean squares and F tests in Output 3.6 with those in Output 3.4 from PROC NESTED.)

You can also obtain appropriate F tests from the TEST statement in PROC GLM. In it, you specify H=*numerator-source-of-variation* and E=*denominator-source-of-variation*. The appropriate F statistic for testing H_0: $\sigma_P^2 = 0$ is obtainable using the TEST statement:

```
test h=package  e=sample(package);
run;
```

Results appear in Output 3.7.

Output 3.7
Appropriate F Test for Package Variance Component

```
                          The SAS System                            1

Dependent Variable: LOGCT

Tests of Hypotheses using the Type III MS for SAMPLE(PACKAGE) as an error term

Source            DF      Type III SS      Mean Square   F Value    Pr > F

PACKAGE           19      30.52915506      1.60679763     3.22      0.0009
```

Again, compare results in Output 3.7 with those in Output 3.4.

Here is how you would typically use the RANDOM and TEST statements in PROC GLM: You might not know the appropriate denominator for an F test for a given effect, so you run PROC GLM with the appropriate MODEL statement followed by a RANDOM statement. Look at the expected mean squares from the RANDOM statement to determine an appropriate F statistic. Then run a TEST statement specifying the appropriate numerator and denominator. Alternatively, you can specify the TEST option in the RANDOM statement. This produces F tests automatically.

3.3 Two-Way Mixed Model

Recall the discussion in Section 2.3.7, "Two-Way Factorial Experiment." Assume that you actually had sources of seed from many varieties, perhaps several hundred. And suppose the objective of the experiment was to compare the methods across all the varieties in the population of potential varieties. It is not feasible to run all these varieties in the experiment, so you randomly choose five varieties from the population of varieties. Interest is not in these five particular varieties, but in the population from which they were drawn. This makes VARIETY a random effect. As a consequence, any effect involving VARIETY is also a random effect. In particular, METHOD*VARIETY is a random effect. Interest remains only in the three methods, so METHOD is still a fixed effect. Since both random and fixed effects are involved, the model is *mixed*.

The fact that VARIETY is a random effect alters how you should analyze METHOD differences. First of all, you are not interested in what happens with any particular VARIETY. This means you don't care about simple METHOD effects. You are interested in main effects of METHODs, even in the presence of interaction. Furthermore, as you will see, VARIETY being a random effect determines how you measure experimental error appropriate for comparing varieties. The RANDOM statement in PROC GLM computes a table of expected mean squares, which helps you set up appropriate F tests for these main effects of METHODs.

3.3.1 Analysis of Variance for Two-Way Mixed Model: Expected Mean Squares

A model for the data is

$$y_{ijk} = \mu + \alpha_i + \beta_j + (\alpha\beta)_{ij} + \varepsilon_{ijk}$$

where

$\mu + \alpha_i = \mu_i$	is the mean for method i, averaged across all varieties in the population.
β_j	are random variables representing differences between varieties, with variance σ_V^2, $j=1, \ldots ,5$.
$(\alpha\beta)_{ij}$	are random variables representing interaction between methods and varieties, with variance σ_{MV}^2, $i=1, \ldots ,3$, $j=1, \ldots ,5$.
ε_{ijk}	are random variables representing differences between yields from plants of the same variety using the same method, with variance σ^2, $i=1, \ldots ,3$, $j=1, \ldots ,5$, $k=1, \ldots ,6$.

The random variables β_j, $(\alpha\beta)_{ij}$, and ε_{ijk} are all assumed independent with mean 0.

Note: This formulation of the model is not universally accepted. Other formulations specify other assumptions regarding terms in the model. The main distinction in these formulations pertains to how one defines *VARIETY* variance (Hocking 1973). This is discussed at greater length in Chapter 4, "Details of the

Linear Model: Understanding GLM Concepts." Here, the concern is comparing METHODs. All formulations of the model lead to the same techniques for comparing METHODs, so the issue of alternative model formulations is not of immediate concern.

The data contain the same sources of variation whether VARIETY is fixed or random, so you can compute the same analysis-of-variance table. But you should use computations from the table differently than when VARIETY was considered fixed. The main effect of differences between METHODs, rather than simple effects, even in the presence of interaction between METHOD and VARIETY, is tested here. Also tested is the comparison **A** vs **B,C** between the METHODs. Now, however, the focus is on the main effect of the contrast, even in the presence of interaction.

Run the following statements:

```
proc glm data=fctorial; class method variety;
  model yield = method variety method*variety / ss3;
  contrast 'A vs B,C' method 2 -1 -1;
run;
```

Compare results from PROC GLM in Output 3.8 with results from PROC ANOVA in Output 2.22.

Output 3.8
Analysis of Variance for Two-Way Mixed Model

```
                          The SAS System                          1

                   General Linear Models Procedure

Dependent Variable: YIELD
                              Sum of          Mean
Source              DF       Squares        Square   F Value   Pr > F

Model               14    1339.0248889    95.6446349    4.87   0.0001

Error               75    1473.7666667    19.6502222

Corrected Total     89    2812.7915556

                 R-Square        C.V.      Root MSE        YIELD Mean

                 0.476048     24.04225     4.4328571        18.437778


Source              DF    Type III SS   Mean Square   F Value   Pr > F

METHOD               2    953.15622222  476.57811111    24.25   0.0001
VARIETY              4     11.38044444    2.84511111     0.14   0.9648
METHOD*VARIETY       8    374.48822222   46.81102778     2.38   0.0241

Contrast            DF    Contrast SS   Mean Square   F Value   Pr > F

A vs B,C             1    940.73472222  940.73472222    47.87   0.0001
```

Add the RANDOM statement to specify that VARIETY and METHOD*VARIETY are random effects.

```
random variety method*variety;
```

The RANDOM statement specified here only causes expected mean squares to be computed. It does not affect any of the PROC GLM computations. If you want correct *F* statistics, you have to specify it in a TEST statement or use the TEST option in the RANDOM statement. Output 3.9 shows expected mean squares.

Output 3.9
Expected Mean
Squares for
Two-Way Mixed
Models

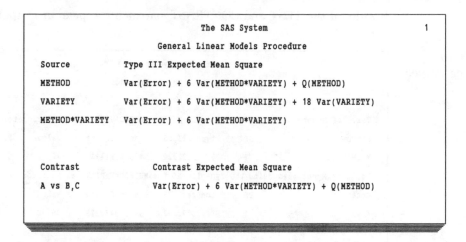

```
                              The SAS System                          1
                        General Linear Models Procedure
     Source             Type III Expected Mean Square

     METHOD             Var(Error) + 6 Var(METHOD*VARIETY) + Q(METHOD)

     VARIETY            Var(Error) + 6 Var(METHOD*VARIETY) + 18 Var(VARIETY)

     METHOD*VARIETY     Var(Error) + 6 Var(METHOD*VARIETY)



     Contrast               Contrast Expected Mean Square

     A vs B,C                Var(Error) + 6 Var(METHOD*VARIETY) + Q(METHOD)
```

In statistical notation, these expected mean squares are as follows:

Source	Expected Mean Squares
METHOD	$\sigma^2 + 6\sigma_{MV}^2 + 30[\Sigma_i(\alpha_i - \bar{\alpha}.)^2/2]$
VARIETY	$\sigma^2 + 6\sigma_{MV}^2 + 18\sigma_V^2$
METHOD*VARIETY	$\sigma^2 + 6\sigma_{MV}^2$
ERROR	σ^2

You can probably see how all of these terms come from Output 3.9 except the expression $30[\Sigma_i(\alpha_i-\bar{\alpha}.)^2/2]$. This is the Q(METHOD) from Output 3.9. How to obtain this algebraic expression is discussed later in this section using the Q option in the RANDOM statement. For now, all you need to know about Q(METHOD) is that it measures differences between the METHOD means. This is true because $\mu_i = \mu + \alpha_i$, and therefore

$$\Sigma_i(\alpha_i - \bar{\alpha}.)^2 = \Sigma_i(\mu_i - \bar{\mu}.)^2 \quad .$$

The null hypothesis H_0: $\mu_A = \mu_B = \mu_C$ is true when Q(METHOD)=0. Therefore, the expected mean square for METHOD is the same as the expected mean square for METHOD*VARIETY, when the null hypothesis is true. This tells you to use $F=$MS(METHOD)/MS(METHOD*VARIETY) to test the null hypothesis, which can be done with the following TEST statement:

```
test h=method  e=method*variety;
```

You also find an expected mean square for the comparison **A** vs **B,C** in Output 3.9 as a result of the CONTRAST statement. It looks like the expected mean square for METHOD, but Q(METHOD) has a different interpretation. For the contrast **A** vs **B,C**, Q(METHOD) stands for $30[\mu_A-.5(\mu_B-\mu_C)]^2$. The same type of reasoning tells you to use $F=$MS (**A** vs **B,C**)/MS(METHOD*VARIETY) to test the null hypothesis H_0: $\mu_A-.5(\mu_B-\mu_C)=0$. You can do this with the E= option in the CONTRAST statement:

```
contrast 'A vs B,C' method 2 -1 -1 / e=method*variety;
```

Results of the TEST and CONTRAST statements appear in Output 3.10.

Output 3.10
Tests Using Proper
Denominator in
the F Statistic

```
                              The SAS System                              1

                       General Linear Models Procedure

Dependent Variable: YIELD

Tests of Hypotheses using the Type III MS for METHOD*VARIETY as an error term

Source              DF      Type III SS     Mean Square   F Value    Pr > F

METHOD               2      953.15622222    476.57811111    10.18    0.0063

Tests of Hypotheses using the Type III MS for METHOD*VARIETY as an error term

Contrast            DF      Contrast SS     Mean Square   F Value    Pr > F

A vs B,C             1      940.73472222    940.73472222    20.10    0.0020
```

The denominator MS(METHOD*VARIETY) of the F values in Output 3.10 is larger than the denominator MS(ERROR) of the F values in Output 3.8. The F tests in Output 3.10 are therefore less significant than the F tests in Output 3.8. Using MS(METHOD*VARIETY) in the denominator makes inference from the tests valid for all varieties in the population, whereas use of MS(ERROR) in the denominator restricts inference to only the five varieties actually employed in the experiment. MS(METHOD*VARIETY) is the *experimental error* for comparing methods across all varieties in the population, whereas MS(ERROR) is the experimental error for comparing methods across only those varieties used in the experiment.

You can obtain detailed information about the meaning of Q(METHOD) by using the Q option at the end of the RANDOM statement. Output 3.11 shows the results of using the Q option.

```
random variety method*variety / q;
```

Output 3.11
Quadratic Forms
for Method Effects
from Q Option

```
                              The SAS System                              1

                       General Linear Models Procedure
                Quadratic Forms of Fixed Effects in the Expected Mean Squares

Source: Type III Mean Square for METHOD

                   METHOD A        METHOD B        METHOD C

METHOD A         20.00000000    -10.00000000    -10.00000000
METHOD B        -10.00000000     20.00000000    -10.00000000
METHOD C        -10.00000000    -10.00000000     20.00000000


Source: Contrast Mean Square for A vs B,C

                   METHOD A        METHOD B        METHOD C

METHOD A         20.00000000    -10.00000000    -10.00000000
METHOD B        -10.00000000      5.00000000      5.00000000
METHOD C        -10.00000000      5.00000000      5.00000000
```

The Q option prints a matrix of the quadratic form for fixed effects, which tells you

$$Q(\text{METHOD}) = (\boldsymbol{\alpha}'\mathbf{A}\boldsymbol{\alpha})/\text{DF}$$

where $\boldsymbol{\alpha}' = (\alpha_A, \alpha_B, \alpha_C)$ is a row vector containing the fixed effect parameters in the model, $\mathbf{A}$ is the matrix of the quadratic form, and DF is the number of degrees of freedom for the effect. You see two matrices printed in Output 3.11, one for the METHOD effect in the analysis-of-variance table and one for the contrast **A** vs **B,C**. For the overall METHOD effect in the analysis-of-variance table, the matrix is

$$\mathbf{A} = \begin{bmatrix} 20 & -10 & -10 \\ -10 & 20 & -10 \\ -10 & -10 & 20 \end{bmatrix}$$

This tells you the matrix algebraic expression for the quadratic form is

$$Q(\text{METHOD}) = (\alpha_A, \alpha_B, \alpha_C) \begin{bmatrix} 20 & -10 & -10 \\ -10 & 20 & -10 \\ -10 & -10 & 20 \end{bmatrix} \begin{bmatrix} \alpha_A \\ \alpha_B \\ \alpha_C \end{bmatrix} (1/2)$$

Some algebraic manipulation reveals that

$$Q(\text{METHOD}) = 30 \, \overline{\Sigma}_i (\alpha_i - \overline{\alpha}_.)^2/2$$

as indicated earlier. You can go through the same process to get the expression for Q(METHOD) for the contrast **A** vs **B,C**.

The quadratic form expressions can be used to tell you the null hypothesis being tested. To do this, determine what values of the fixed parameters make Q(METHOD)=0. For the overall METHOD effect, you have already seen that Q(METHOD)=0 whenever $\alpha_A=\alpha_B=\alpha_C$, or equivalently, whenever $\mu_A=\mu_B=\mu_C$.

You also find a matrix for the contrast **A** vs **B,C** in Output 3.11. Some straightforward but tedious matrix algebra reveals, as indicated above, that

$$Q(\text{METHOD}) = 30[\mu_A - .5(\mu_B - \mu_C)]^2 \quad .$$

3.4 A Classification with Both Crossed and Nested Effects

Some classifications involve both crossed and nested factors. The example in this section is typical of a study design that is common to many fields of investigation.

An engineer in a semiconductor plant investigated the effect of several modes of a process condition (ET) on the resistance in computer chips. Twelve silicon wafers (WAFER) were drawn from a lot, and three wafers were randomly assigned to each of four modes of ET. Resistance in chips was measured in four positions (POS) on each wafer after processing. The measurement was recorded as the variable RESISTA in a SAS data set named CHIPS. The data appear in Output 3.12.

Output 3.12
Semiconductor
Resistance Data

```
                        The SAS System                      1

        OBS     RESISTA     ET      WAFER      POS

          1      5.22       1        1          1
          2      5.61       1        1          2
          3      6.11       1        1          3
          4      6.33       1        1          4
          5      6.13       1        2          1
          6      6.14       1        2          2
          7      5.60       1        2          3
          8      5.91       1        2          4
          9      5.49       1        3          1
         10      4.60       1        3          2
         11      4.95       1        3          3
         12      5.42       1        3          4
         13      5.78       2        1          1
         14      6.52       2        1          2
         15      5.90       2        1          3
         16      5.67       2        1          4
         17      5.77       2        2          1
         18      6.23       2        2          2
         19      5.57       2        2          3
         20      5.96       2        2          4
         21      6.43       2        3          1
         22      5.81       2        3          2
         23      5.83       2        3          3
         24      6.12       2        3          4
         25      5.66       3        1          1
         26      6.25       3        1          2
         27      5.46       3        1          3
         28      5.08       3        1          4
         29      6.53       3        2          1
         30      6.50       3        2          2
         31      6.23       3        2          3
         32      6.84       3        2          4
         33      6.22       3        3          1
         34      6.29       3        3          2
         35      5.63       3        3          3
         36      6.36       3        3          4
         37      6.75       4        1          1
         38      6.97       4        1          2
         39      6.02       4        1          3
         40      6.88       4        1          4
         41      6.22       4        2          1
         42      6.54       4        2          2
         43      6.12       4        2          3
         44      6.61       4        2          4
         45      6.05       4        3          1
         46      6.15       4        3          2
         47      5.55       4        3          3
         48      6.13       4        3          4
```

Here are some features of this experiment:

1. There are two experimental factors, ET and POS, which appear together in all combinations. These factors are *crossed* because the POS labels 1,2,3, and 4 have the same meaning for all levels of ET; POS 1 refers to the same location on a wafer in ET 1 as it does on a wafer in ET 2. The engineer wants to compare mean resistance between levels of ET and between levels of POS. He also wants to determine if differences between levels of ET depend on the value of POS at which they are measured. The data are analyzed in terms of either simple effects or main effects of ET and POS, depending on the presence or absence of interaction between ET and POS. How to set up appropriate tests for several types of effects is discussed in Section 3.4.2, "Using Expected Mean Squares to Set Up Several Tests of Hypotheses for Crossed-Nested Classification," later in this chapter.

2. ET levels are assigned to wafers in a completely randomized design, making WAFER the experimental unit for comparing levels of ET. Wafers are *nested* within levels of ET.

3. Levels of POS change between chips on the same wafer, whereas levels of ET change between wafers. So a different measure of experimental error is required to compare positions than is used to compare levels of ET. This is the primary feature that distinguishes this experiment from a standard factorial.

This data set has features of both crossed and nested classification, so it is referred to as *crossed-nested*. It is similar to a *split-plot* experiment, with wafer taken as the main-plot unit and chips on a wafer as the sub-plot unit. It also has features in common with repeated-measures experiments, which are discussed in Chapter 8.

A model for the data is

$$y_{ijk} = \mu + \alpha_i + \delta_{ij} + \beta_k + (\alpha\beta)_{ik} + \varepsilon_{ijk}$$

where

y_{ijk}	is the measured resistance at the kth position on the jth wafer in the ith level of ET.
$\mu + \alpha_i + \beta_k + (\alpha\beta)_{ik} = \mu_{ik}$	is the mean resistance in position k with ET level i.
δ_{ij}	are random variables representing differences between wafers assigned to the same level of ET, $i=1,\ldots,4$, $j=1,\ldots,3$, with variance σ_W^2.
ε_{ijk}	are random variables representing differences between chips on the same wafer, $i=1,\ldots,4$, $j=1,\ldots,3$, $k=1,\ldots,4$, with variance σ^2. These ε_{ijk} random variables are assumed to be independent. This is a potentially flawed assumption because correlation between chips could depend on their relative proximity on the wafer. If this is the case, then the data should be analyzed using methods appropriate for repeated-measures experiments (see Chapter 8).

3.4.1   Analysis of Variance for Crossed-Nested Classification

An analysis-of-variance table has the form

Source of Variation	DF
ET	3
WAFER(ET)	8
POS	3
ET*POS	9
ERROR = POS*WAFER(ET)	24

3.4.2   Using Expected Mean Squares to Set Up Several Tests of Hypotheses for Crossed-Nested Classification

This section illustrates how to set up several types of tests of hypothesis for an experiment of this type. These include tests of the following null hypotheses:

□   overall main effect of ET $H_0: \mu_{1.} = \mu_{2.} = \mu_{3.} = \mu_{4.}$

□   overall main effect of POS $H_0: \mu_{.1} = \mu_{.2} = \mu_{.3} = \mu_{.4}$

□   main effect contrast of ET (ET1 vs ET2) $H_0: \mu_{1.} = \mu_{2.}$

□   main effect contrast of POS (POS1 vs POS2) $H_0: \mu_{.1} = \mu_{.2}$

□   simple effect contrast of POS (POS1 vs POS2 in ET1) $H_0: \mu_{11} = \mu_{12}$

□   simple effect contrast of ET (ET1 vs ET2 in POS1) $H_0: \mu_{11} = \mu_{21}$

CONTRAST and RANDOM statements in PROC GLM are used to obtain appropriate tests for these effects. This example illustrates the flexibility and generality of PROC GLM for complicated data structures.

The following SAS statements produce the analysis-of-variance table and contrasts with expected mean squares:

```
proc glm data=chips;
   class et wafer pos;
   model resista = et wafer(et) pos et*pos / ss3;
   contrast 'ET1 vs ET2'        et 1 -1 0 0;
   contrast 'POS1 vs POS2'      pos 1 -1 0 0;
   contrast 'POS1 vs POS2 in ET1'  pos 1 -1 0 0 et*pos 1 -1;
   contrast 'ET1 vs ET2 in POS1'   et 1 -1 0 0 et*pos 1 0 0 0 -1;
   run;
```

The analysis-of-variance table and CONTRAST statement results appear in Output 3.13.

Output 3.13
Analysis of Variance for Semiconductor Resistance Data

```
                          The SAS System                            1

                   General Linear Models Procedure

Dependent Variable: RESISTA
                                 Sum of           Mean
Source                 DF       Squares         Square    F Value    Pr > F

Model                  23    9.32500833     0.40543514       3.65    0.0013

Error                  24    2.66758333     0.11114931

Corrected Total        47   11.99259167

                 R-Square           C.V.       Root MSE        RESISTA Mean

                 0.777564       5.553811      0.3333906           6.0029167


Source                 DF    Type III SS    Mean Square    F Value    Pr > F

ET                      3     3.11215833     1.03738611       9.33    0.0003
WAFER(ET)               8     4.27448333     0.53431042       4.81    0.0013
POS                     3     1.12889167     0.37629722       3.39    0.0345
ET*POS                  9     0.80947500     0.08994167       0.81    0.6125

Contrast               DF    Contrast SS    Mean Square    F Value    Pr > F

ET1 vs ET2              1     0.69360000     0.69360000       6.24    0.0197
POS1 vs POS2            1     0.07706667     0.07706667       0.69    0.4132
POS1 vs POS2 in ET1     1     0.04001667     0.04001667       0.36    0.5541
ET1 vs ET2 in POS1      1     0.21660000     0.21660000       1.95    0.1755
```

F statistics are computed for all effects in the MODEL statement as well as for all of the effects in the CONTRAST statements. These *F* statistics are computed using MS(ERROR) in the denominator. Remember that the *F* statistics that are computed automatically in the analysis-of-variance table are unaffected by the RANDOM statement. You must examine the expected mean squares to determine which of these automatically computed *F* statistics are valid, and for which of them you must specify an appropriate error term (denominator of the *F*). You can specify appropriate error terms for the effects in the analysis-of-variance table with a TEST statement or with a TEST option at the end of the RANDOM statement. Appropriate error terms for the contrast *F* statistics can be specified with the E= option in a CONTRAST statement. These features are illustrated later in this section.

Now, obtain tests for the fixed effects of ET, POS, and ET*POS in the analysis-of-variance table and tests for the effects specified in the CONTRAST statements. The following statement gives expected mean squares for all effects in Output 3.14:

```
random wafer(et);
```

Output 3.14
Expected Mean
Squares for
Semiconductor
Data

```
                              The SAS System                              1
                        General Linear Models Procedure
   Source      Type III Expected Mean Square

   ET          Var(Error) + 4 Var(WAFER(ET)) + Q(ET,ET*POS)

   WAFER(ET)   Var(Error) + 4 Var(WAFER(ET))

   POS         Var(Error) + Q(POS,ET*POS)

   ET*POS      Var(Error) + Q(ET*POS)



   Contrast              Contrast Expected Mean Square

   ET1 vs ET2            Var(Error) + 4 Var(WAFER(ET)) + Q(ET,ET*POS)

   POS1 vs POS2          Var(Error) + Q(POS,ET*POS)

   POS1 vs POS2 in ET1   Var(Error) + Q(POS,ET*POS)

   ET1 vs ET2 in POS1    Var(Error) + Var(WAFER(ET)) + Q(ET,ET*POS)
```

You could use the Q option at the end of the RANDOM statement to get an interpretation of Q(*effect*) in the expected mean squares. Table 3.2 relates the Q(*effect*) with the corresponding algebraic expressions in terms of model parameters and means model.

Table 3.2
Q(effect) in
Expected Mean
Squares

Effect Name	Expression in Output	Algebraic Expression for Q(*effect*)
ET	Q(ET,ET*POS)	$= 12 \, \Sigma_i [\alpha_i + \overline{(\alpha\beta)}_{i.} - \overline{\alpha}. - \overline{(\alpha\beta)}_{..}]^2$ $= 4 \, \Sigma_i [\mu_{i.} - \mu_{..}]^2$
POS	Q(POS,ET*POS)	$= 12 \, \Sigma_j [\beta_j + \overline{(\alpha\beta)}_{.j} - \overline{\beta}. - \overline{(\alpha\beta)}_{..}]^2$ $= 4 \, \Sigma_j [\mu_{.j} - \mu_{..}]^2$
ET*POS	Q(ET*POS)	$= 12 \, \Sigma_{ij} [(\alpha\beta)_{ij} - \overline{(\alpha\beta)}_{i.} - \overline{(\alpha\beta)}_{.j} + \overline{(\alpha\beta)}_{..}]^2$ $= 12 \, \Sigma_{ij} [\mu_{ij} - \mu_{i.} - \mu_{.j} - \mu_{..}]^2$
ET1 vs ET2	Q(ET,ET*POS)	$= 12 \, [\alpha_1 + \overline{(\alpha\beta)}_{1.} - \alpha_2 - \overline{(\alpha\beta)}_{2.}]^2$ $= 4 \, [\mu_{1.} - \mu_{2.}]^2$
POS1 vs POS2	Q(POS,ET*POS)	$= 12 \, [\beta_1 + \overline{(\alpha\beta)}_{.1} - \beta_2 - \overline{(\alpha\beta)}_{.2}]^2$ $= 4 \, [\mu_{.1} - \mu_{.2}]^2$
POS1 vs POS2 in ET1	Q(POS,ET*POS)	$= 12 \, [\beta_1 + (\alpha\beta)_{11} - \beta_2 - (\alpha\beta)_{12}]^2$ $= 4 \, [\mu_{11} - \mu_{12}]^2$
ET1 vs ET2 in POS1	Q(ET,ET*POS)	$= 12 \, [\alpha_1 + (\alpha\beta)_{11} - \alpha_2 - (\alpha\beta)_{21}]^2$ $= 4 \, [\mu_{11} - \mu_{21}]^2$

Note: It may seem strange that the Q(*effect*) for ET main effects contains the expression ET*POS within the parentheses. The ET*POS expression is present because the quadratic form is a function of the $(\alpha\beta)$ parameters as well as the α_i parameters. This is because PROC GLM imposes no assumptions on the model parameters, so that $\mu_{i.}=\mu+\alpha_i+\beta_{.}+(\alpha\beta)_{i.}$ and $\mu_{..}=\mu+\alpha_{.}+\beta_{.}+(\alpha\beta)_{..}$. Consequently, $\mu_{i.}-\mu_{..}=\alpha_i+(\alpha\beta)_{i.}-\alpha_{.}-(\alpha\beta)_{..}$; that is, differences between means for two levels of ET are functions of the $(\alpha\beta)_{ik}$ parameters as well as the α_i parameters. The same type of phenomenon holds true for the main effect of POS and the effects in the CONTRAST statements.

In each case, you see from the algebraic expression for Q(*effect*) that the null hypothesis you want to test is H_0: Q(*effect*)=0. The expected mean squares tell you to use the denominators in the F statistics as indicated in this table:

Effect	Appropriate Denominator for F Statistic
ET	MS(WAFER(ET))
POS	MS(ERROR)
ET*POS	MS(ERROR)
ET1 vs ET2	MS(WAFER(ET))
POS1 vs POS2	MS(ERROR)
POS1 vs POS2 in ET1	MS(ERR0R)
ET1 vs ET2 in POS1	Not directly available

Automatically computed F statistics are valid for all of these effects for which MS(ERROR) is the appropriate denominator.

Appropriate F tests for ET main effect and ET1 vs ET2 contrast are obtained with the statements

```
test h=et  e=wafer(et);
contrast 'ET1 vs ET2'  et 1 -1 0 0 / e=wafer(et);
```

Results appear in Output 3.15.

Output 3.15
F Tests for ET Effects

```
                        The SAS System                              1
                  General Linear Models Procedure
Dependent Variable: RESISTA

Tests of Hypotheses using the Type III MS for WAFER(ET) as an error term

Source             DF     Type III SS     Mean Square    F Value    Pr > F

ET                  3      3.11215833      1.03738611       1.94    0.2015

Tests of Hypotheses using the Type III MS for WAFER(ET) as an error term

Contrast           DF     Contrast SS     Mean Square    F Value    Pr > F

ET1 vs ET2          1      0.69360000      0.69360000       1.30    0.2875
```

Compare *F* statistics in Output 3.15 with those in Output 3.13 for these effects. Alternatively, you can obtain test statistics for effects in the analysis-of-variance table with the TEST option in the RANDOM statement, as follows:

```
random wafer(et) / test;
```

Output 3.16 shows the results.

Output 3.16
F Tests from the TEST Option

```
                              The SAS System                              1

                         General Linear Models Procedure
                Tests of Hypotheses for Mixed Model Analysis of Variance

Dependent Variable: RESISTA


Source: ET *
Error: MS(WAFER(ET))
                              Denominator     Denominator
     DF      Type III MS          DF              MS       F Value    Pr > F
      3    1.0373861111            8        0.5343104167     1.942    0.2015
* - This test assumes one or more other fixed effects are zero.


Source: WAFER(ET)
Error: MS(Error)
                              Denominator     Denominator
     DF      Type III MS          DF              MS       F Value    Pr > F
      8    0.5343104167           24        0.1111493056     4.807    0.0013

Source: POS *
Error: MS(Error)
                              Denominator     Denominator
     DF      Type III MS          DF              MS       F Value    Pr > F
      3    0.3762972222           24        0.1111493056     3.386    0.0345
* - This test assumes one or more other fixed effects are zero.


Source: ET*POS
Error: MS(Error)
                              Denominator     Denominator
     DF      Type III MS          DF              MS       F Value    Pr > F
      9    0.0899416667           24        0.1111493056     0.809    0.6125




Contrast                   Contrast Expected Mean Square

ET1 vs ET2                 Var(Error) + 4 Var(WAFER(ET)) + Q(ET,ET*POS)

POS1 vs POS2               Var(Error) + Q(POS,ET*POS)

POS1 vs POS2 in ET1        Var(Error) + Q(POS,ET*POS)

ET1 vs ET2 in POS1         Var(Error) + Var(WAFER(ET)) + Q(ET,ET*POS)

ET1 vs ET2                 Var(Error) + 4 Var(WAFER(ET)) + Q(ET,ET*POS)
```

```
                                                                              2

Dependent Variable: RESISTA

Tests of Hypotheses using the Type III MS for WAFER(ET) as an error term

Source                    DF     Type III SS    Mean Square    F Value    Pr > F

ET                         3      3.11215833     1.03738611       1.94    0.2015

Tests of Hypotheses using the Type III MS for WAFER(ET) as an error term

Contrast                  DF     Contrast SS     Mean Square    F Value    Pr > F

ET1 vs ET2                 1      0.69360000      0.69360000       1.30    0.2875
```

Compare results in Output 3.16 with those in Outputs 3.13 and 3.15. Unfortunately, the TEST option does not compute appropriate tests for effects in CONTRAST statements.

There is no directly available, or appropriate, F test for the contrast ET1 vs ET2 in POS1. An appropriate denominator for this F statistic would be an estimate of $\sigma^2 + \sigma_W^2$. There is no source of variation in the analysis-of-variance table whose expected mean square is equal to $\sigma^2 + \sigma_W^2$. But you can combine MS(ERROR) and MS(WAFER(ET)) to get an estimate of $\sigma^2 + \sigma_W^2$. You need amounts of both σ^2 and σ_W^2 in an appropriate denominator for the F test; you need one unit of each. Of the expected mean squares for ERROR and WAFER(ET), only the expected mean square for WAFER(ET) contains any σ_W^2; in fact, it contains four units of it. You need to multiply MS(WAFER(ET)) by the appropriate constant to produce one unit of $\sigma^2{}_W$, which, of course, is 1/4. This gives $.25\sigma^2 + \sigma_W^2$, so you need an additional $.75\sigma^2$, which you can get by adding $.75$MS(ERROR). So an appropriate denominator of the F statistic for testing for the effect of ET1 vs ET2 in POS1 is

$$\widehat{\sigma^2 + \sigma_W^2} = .75\text{MS(ERROR)} + .25\text{MS(WAFER(ET))}$$
$$= .75(0.111) + .25(0.534)$$
$$= 0.217 \quad .$$

An appropriate F statistic for testing $H_0: \mu_{11} - \mu_{21} = 0$ is then

$$F = \text{MS(ET1 vs ET2 in POS1)} / \widehat{(\sigma^2 + \sigma_W^2)}$$
$$= 0.2166 / 0.217$$
$$= 1.0 \quad .$$

Here, F is essentially equal to 1.0, indicating that it is nonsignificant. You do not need to refer it to an F distribution to calculate a p value to determine its significance, because F must be substantially larger than 1.0 in order to be significant at any meaningful level. Thus, you don't need to know degrees of freedom for the denominator mean square. Normally, however, you would need degrees of freedom in order to assess the level of significance. They can be approximated using Satterthwaite's formula, which is demonstrated in Section 3.4.3, "Satterthwaite's Formula for Approximate Degrees of Freedom," later in this chapter.

But first, Table 3.3 gives a summary of all the appropriate F tests from the analysis-of-variance table and CONTRAST statements:

Table 3.3
Summary of F Test Results from CONTRAST Statements

Effect	Appropriate F Statistic	Level of Significance
ET	$1.037/0.534 = 1.94$	0.202
POS	$0.376/0.111 = 3.39$	0.034
ET*POS	$0.090/0.111 = 0.81$	0.612
ET1 vs ET2	$0.694/0.534 = 1.30$	0.287
POS1 vs POS2	$0.077/0.111 = 0.69$	0.413
POS1 vs POS2 in ET1	$0.040/0.111 = 0.36$	0.554
ET1 vs ET2 in POS1	$0.217/0.217 = 1.00$	NS

3.4.3 Satterthwaite's Formula for Approximate Degrees of Freedom

The denominator of the F statistic for the contrast ET1 vs ET2 in POS1 is a linear combination of mean squares from the analysis-of-variance table. In general, such a linear combination has properties that approximate those of actual mean squares. The number of degrees of freedom for the linear combination of mean squares can be approximated using a formula attributed to Satterthwaite (1946). This is the subject of the following discussion.

Let $MS_1, \ldots, MS_k$ be a set of independent mean squares with respective degrees of freedom $DF_1, \ldots, DF_k$, and let $a_1, \ldots, a_k$ be a set of known constants. Then the linear combination

$$MS = a_1\, MS_1 + \ldots + a_k\, MS_k$$

is a *synthetic mean square* with approximate degrees of freedom equal to

$$DF = \frac{(MS)^2}{\dfrac{(MS_1)^2}{DF_1} + \ldots + \dfrac{(MS_2)^2}{DF_2}}$$

Applying Satterthwaite's formula, you get

$$\widehat{\sigma^2 + \sigma_W^2} = .75MS(ERROR) + .25MS(WAFER(ET)) \quad .$$

The data used here yield

$$MS_1 = MS(ERROR) = 0.111 \qquad DF_1 = 24 \qquad a_1 = .75$$

$$MS_2 = MS(WAFER(ET)) = 0.534 \qquad DF_2 = 8 \qquad a_2 = .25$$

so

$$DF = \frac{(0.217)^2}{\dfrac{(0.083)^2}{24} + \dfrac{(0.134)^2}{8}}$$

$$= \frac{0.0471}{0.000287 + 0.002245}$$

$$= 18.6 \quad .$$

Round down to DF=18. This synthetic mean square with DF=18 is useful for several applications. It is an appropriate denominator for any contrast among levels of ET at a given level of POS, such as the comparison ET1 vs ET2 at POS1 shown above. Other examples include the CONTRAST statement

```
contrast 'ET1,ET2 vs ET3,ET4 at POS2' et 1 1 -1 -1
                        et*pos 0 0 0 0  1 1 -1 -1;
```

In addition to providing appropriate denominators for F statistics, it is equally important to use appropriate mean squares when you compute confidence intervals for means or differences between means. Suppose you wanted a confidence interval on the overall mean for ET1, averaged across WAFER and POS. This mean is

$$\bar{y}_{1..} = \mu + \alpha_1 + \bar{\delta}_{1.} + \bar{B}_. + \overline{(\alpha\beta)}_{1.} + \bar{\varepsilon}_{1..} \quad .$$

The random parts are $\bar{\delta}_{1.}$ and $\bar{\varepsilon}_{1..}$. Now $\bar{\delta}_{1.}$ is the mean of three δ's (δ_{11}, δ_{12}, and δ_{13}), so $V(\bar{\delta}_{1.})=\sigma_w^2/B$. Additionally, $\bar{\varepsilon}_{1..}$ is the mean of twelve ε's, so $V(\bar{\varepsilon}_{1..})=\sigma^2/12$. Therefore, the variance of $\bar{y}_{1..}$ is

$$\begin{aligned}
V(\bar{y}_{1..}) &= V(\bar{\delta}_{1.}) + V(\bar{\varepsilon}_{1..}) \\
&= \sigma_w^2/3 + \sigma^2/12 \\
&= (\sigma^2 + 4\sigma_w^2)/12 \quad .
\end{aligned}$$

From the table of expected mean squares you have seen that an estimate of $V(\bar{y}_{1..})$ is MS(WAFER(ET))/12. So a 95% confidence interval for the mean is

$$\bar{y}_{1..} \pm t_{8,0.025}[MS\ (WAFER(ET))/12]^{1/2}$$

$$= 5.63 \pm 2.30(0.210)$$

$$= (5.14, 6.12) \quad .$$

Similarly, the mean for POS1 averaged across POS and WAFER is

$$\bar{y}_{..1} = \mu + \bar{\alpha}_. + \bar{\delta}_{.1} + \beta_1 + \overline{(\alpha\beta)}_{.1} + \bar{\epsilon}_{.1} \quad .$$

The variance of $y_{..1}$ is

$$\begin{aligned}
V(\bar{y}_{..1}) &= V(\bar{\delta}_{.1}) + V(\bar{\epsilon}_{..1}) \\
&= \sigma^2_W / 12 + \sigma^2 / 12 \\
&= (\sigma^2 + \sigma^2_W) / 12 \quad .
\end{aligned}$$

If you look back at the synthetic mean square we computed, you see that an estimate of $V(y_{..1})$ is $(.75 \text{ MS(ERROR)} + .25 \text{ MS(WAFER(ET)))}/12$. So an approximate 95% confidence interval for $y_{..1}$ is

$$\begin{aligned}
y_{..1} &\pm t_{18,0.025}[(.75 \text{ MS(ERROR)} + .25 \text{ MS(WAFER(ET)))} / 12]^{1/2} \\
&= 6.02 \pm 2.10(0.134) \\
&= (5.74, 6.30) \quad .
\end{aligned}$$

3.5   Split-Plot Experiments

The split-plot design results from a specialized randomization scheme for a factorial experiment. It is often used when one factor is more readily applied to large experimental units, or main plots, and when another factor can be applied to smaller units, or subplots, within the larger unit. A split-plot design is also useful when more information is needed for comparing the levels of one factor than for comparing the levels of the other factor. In this case, the factor for which more information is needed should be the subplot factor.

A classic example of a split plot is an irrigation experiment where irrigation levels are applied to large areas, and factors like varieties and fertilizers are assigned to smaller areas within a particular irrigation treatment. The proper analysis of a split-plot design recognizes that treatments applied to main plots are subject to larger experimental error than those applied to subplots; hence, different mean squares are used as denominators for the corresponding F ratios. This concept is discussed in terms of expected mean squares in this section.

3.5.1   A Standard Split-Plot Experiment

The split-plot example below analyzes the effect on dry weight yields of three bacterial inoculation treatments applied to two cultivars of grasses (**A** and **B**). The experiment is a split-plot design with CULT (cultivar) as the main-plot factor and INOC (inoculi) as the subplot factor. INOC has the values **CON** for control, **LIV** for live, and **DEA** for dead. This provides more information for comparing levels of INOC than for comparing levels of CULT. This is desirable because INOC is the factor of primary interest in the experiment.

Data for the experiment appear in Output 3.17.

Output 3.17
Data for Split-Plot
Experiment

```
                        The SAS System                              1

          OBS    REP    CULT    INOC    DRYWT

            1     1      A      CON     27.4
            2     1      A      DEA     29.7
            3     1      A      LIV     34.5
            4     1      B      CON     29.4
            5     1      B      DEA     32.5
            6     1      B      LIV     34.4
            7     2      A      CON     28.9
            8     2      A      DEA     28.7
            9     2      A      LIV     33.4
           10     2      B      CON     28.7
           11     2      B      DEA     32.4
           12     2      B      LIV     36.4
           13     3      A      CON     28.6
           14     3      A      DEA     29.7
           15     3      A      LIV     32.9
           16     3      B      CON     27.2
           17     3      B      DEA     29.1
           18     3      B      LIV     32.6
           19     4      A      CON     26.7
           20     4      A      DEA     28.9
           21     4      A      LIV     31.8
           22     4      B      CON     26.8
           23     4      B      DEA     28.6
           24     4      B      LIV     30.7
```

A standard analysis of variance for this experiment is as follows:

Source	DF
replication	3
cultivar	1
replication × cultivar (Error A)	3
inoculi	2
cultivar × inoculi	2
replication × inoculi + replication × inoculi × cultivar (Error B)	12

Error A (main-plot error) is computationally equivalent to the replication×cultivar interaction and is the appropriate error term in testing for differences among cultivars. Error B (subplot error) is computationally equivalent to the replication×inoculi+replication×inoculi×cultivar interaction. The Error B mean square is the appropriate error term for testing for inoculi and cultivar×inoculi effects.

The following SAS statements are needed for this analysis:

```
proc anova;
    class rep cult inoc;
    model drywt=rep cult rep*cult inoc cult*inoc;
    test h=cult e=rep*cult;
run;
```

Note: You can add the following RANDOM statement to obtain expected mean squares to verify the appropriate tests.

```
random rep rep*cult;
```

Results of the analysis of variance appear in Output 3.18.

Output 3.18
Analysis of
Variance for
Split-Plot
Experiment

```
                              The SAS System                              1
                         Analysis of Variance Procedure

Dependent Variable: DRYWT
                                    Sum of           Mean
Source                  DF          Squares          Square    F Value    Pr > F

Model                   11      157.20833333      14.29166667     20.26    0.0001

Error                   12        8.46500000       0.70541667

Corrected Total         23      165.67333333

                   R-Square             C.V.        Root MSE        DRYWT Mean

                   0.948905          2.761285       0.8398909        30.416667


Source                  DF          Anova SS     Mean Square    F Value    Pr > F

REP                      3        25.32000000     8.44000000      11.96    0.0006
CULT                     1         2.40666667     2.40666667       3.41    0.0895
REP*CULT                 3         9.48000000     3.16000000       4.48    0.0249
INOC                     2       118.17583333    59.08791667      83.76    0.0001
CULT*INOC                2         1.82583333     0.91291667       1.29    0.3098

Tests of Hypotheses using the Anova MS for REP*CULT as an error term

Source                  DF          Anova SS     Mean Square    F Value    Pr > F

CULT                     1         2.40666667     2.40666667       0.76    0.4471
```

The data are classified according to REP, CULT, and INOC, so these variables are specified in the CLASS statement. The response variable DRYWT appears on the left side of the equation in the MODEL statement, and the terms corresponding to lines in the analysis-of-variance table appear on the right side. It is not necessary to specify Error B because it is the residual.

The TEST statement specifies that the hypothesis concerning cultivars (H=CULT) is tested using REP*CULT as the error term (E=REP*CULT). This statement requests an *F* test whose numerator is the CULT mean square and whose denominator is the REP*CULT mean square. The TEST statement is necessary in a split-plot analysis because all the default *F* tests use the residual mean square in the denominator. This technique is not statistically valid when testing main-plot effects.

The analysis-of-variance table appears as follows:

Table 3.4
Results of Analysis of Variance for Split-Plot Experiment

Source	DF	SS	MS	F	p
REP	3	25.32			
CULT	1	2.41	2.41	0.76	.4471
REP*CULT (Error A)	3	9.48	3.16		
INOC	2	118.18	59.09	83.76	.0001
CULT*INOC	2	1.83	0.91	1.29	.3098
REP*INOC+					
REP*INOC*CULT (Error B)	12	8.47	0.71		

The degrees of freedom and sums of squares are obtained directly from the output, with Error A=REP*CULT and Error B=Error. The F values for INOC and CULT*INOC, along with their associated significance probabilities, also come directly from the output. These F values indicate no significant CULT*INOC interaction ($p=0.3098$) and highly significant differences between INOC means ($p=0.0001$).

The appropriate F value for CULT comes from the bottom of the output instead of from the output ANOVA table. Note that the appropriate F value shows no evidence of differences between CULT means ($p=0.4471$). Do *not* use the inappropriate F value of 3.41 from the ANOVA table, which declares differences among CULT means significant at the $p=0.0895$ level.

Similarly, a valid comparison of CULT means with Duncan's test requires the appropriate error variance. (Duncan's test is only used with more than two cultivars.) This is done by using the following MEANS statement after the TEST statement:

```
means cult / duncan e=rep*cult;
```

3.5.2 Split-Split-Plot Experiment

A split-split-plot design with a main-plot factor A, subplot factor B, and sub-subplot factor C illustrates some principles of sums of squares computations with PROC ANOVA. A standard analysis of variance is shown in the table below:

Source

Replications

A

Replications × A (Error A)

B

A × B

Replications × B
+ Replications × A × B } (Error B)

C

A × C

B × C

A × B × C

Replications × C
+ Replications × A × C
+ Replications × B × C } (Error C)
+ Replications × A × B × C

Computationally, Error A is equal to

Replications × A .

Error B is equal to

Replications × B + Replications × A × B .

Error C is equal to

Replications × C + Replications × A × C + Replications × B × C
+ Replications × A × B × C .

Obviously, Error A can be computed directly by specifying REP*A in a MODEL statement, and Error C is the residual sum of squares, labeled Error by PROC ANOVA. Computing Error B requires more effort and an understanding of the computational principles employed by PROC ANOVA.

Generally, if X and Y are two effects in an analysis of variance, then, computationally, the sum of squares for X(Y) is equal to the sum of squares for X plus the sum of squares for X×Y. With X=Replications×B and Y=A, it follows that

Error B = Replications × B + Replications × B × A
= Replications × B(A)   .

Thus, you can compute Error B directly with PROC ANOVA by specifying REP*B(A).

Another feature of PROC ANOVA (and PROC GLM) is that MODEL statements containing interaction terms without one or more of the corresponding main-effect terms produce sums of squares that contain the nonspecified main-effect sums of squares. For example, the SAS statement

```
model y=a*b;
```

produces a SS labeled A*B that is actually

SS(A) + SS(B) + SS(A*B)   .

However, the statement

```
model y=a a*b;
```

produces a SS labeled A*B that is actually

SS(B) + SS(A*B)   .

Thus, in the split-split-plot experiment above, Error B can be obtained by specifying either

Replications × B(A)

or

Replications × B × A   .

The following SAS statements produce an analysis of variance and correct tests.

```
proc anova;
   classes rep a b c;
   model response=rep a rep*a
                 b a*b rep*b(a)
                 c a*c b*c a*b*c;
   test h=a e=rep*a;
   test h=b a*b e=rep*b(a);
```

Chapter 4 Details of the Linear Model: Understanding GLM Concepts

4.1 *Introduction*   *137*

4.2 *The Dummy-Variable Model*   *138*
    4.2.1   *The Simplest Case: One-Way Classification*   *138*
    4.2.2   *Parameter Estimates for One-Way Classification*   *141*
    4.2.3   *Using PROC GLM for Analysis of Variance*   *143*
    4.2.4   *Estimable Functions in the One-Way Classification*   *148*

4.3 *Two-Way Classification: Unbalanced Data*   *153*
    4.3.1   *General Considerations*   *153*
    4.3.2   *Sums of Squares Computed by PROC GLM*   *155*
    4.3.3   *Interpreting Sums of Squares in Reduction*
    Notation   *157*
    4.3.4   *Interpreting Sums of Squares in μ-Model Notation*   *159*
    4.3.5   *Example of Unbalanced Two-Way Classification*   *161*
    4.3.6   *MEANS, LSMEANS, CONTRAST, and ESTIMATE*
    Statements in the Two-Way Layout   *164*
    4.3.7   *Estimable Functions for Two-Way Classification*   *169*
    General Form of Estimable Functions   *169*
    Interpreting Sums of Squares Using Estimable
      Functions   *170*
    Estimating Estimable Functions   *175*
    Interpreting LSMEANS, CONTRAST, and ESTIMATE
      Results Using Estimable Functions   *176*
    4.3.8   *Empty Cells*   *178*

4.4 *Proper Error Terms*   *191*
    4.4.1   *More On Expected Mean Squares*   *193*

4.1 Introduction

The general linear model approach to analysis of variance uses dummy or indicator variables in a regression model. Although this technique is useful in all situations, it is primarily applied to analysis of variance with *unbalanced* data, where the direct computation of sums of squares fails, and to analysis of covariance and associated techniques.

While this approach is capable of handling a vast array of applications, it also presents some complications that must be overcome. Two of the principal complications are

☐   specifying model parameters and their estimates

☐   setting up meaningful combinations of parameters for testing and estimation.

Both of these are concerned with estimable functions. These complications must be dealt with in computer programs using general linear models. The purpose of this chapter is to explain, with the use of fairly simple examples, how the GLM procedure deals with the complications. A more technical description of GLM features is given in Chapter 24, "The GLM Procedure," in the *SAS/STAT User's Guide, Version 6, Fourth Edition, Volume 2.*

This chapter describes the essence of GLM computation. It is more or less self-contained, and you will notice some overlap with previous and subsequent chapters. In particular, the CONTRAST and ESTIMATE statements are discussed in Chapter 2, "Analysis of Variance for Balanced Data," and the RANDOM statement is discussed in Chapter 3, "Analyzing Data with Random Effects." This chapter delves more deeply into some of the same topics.

4.2   The Dummy-Variable Model

This section presents the analysis-of-variance model using dummy variables, methods for specifying model parameters, and the methods used by PROC GLM. For simplicity, an analysis-of-variance model with one-way classification that results from a completely randomized design illustrates the discussion. In application, however, such a structure might be adequately (and more efficiently) analyzed by using the ANOVA procedure (see Section 2.3.4, "Analysis of One-Way Classification of Data").

4.2.1   The Simplest Case: One-Way Classification

Data for the one-way classification consist of measurements classified according to a one-dimensional criterion. An example of this kind of structure is a set of student exam scores, where each student is taught by one of three teachers. The exam scores are thus grouped or classified according to TEACHER. The most straightforward model for data of this type is

$$y_{ij} = \mu_i + \varepsilon_{ij}$$

where

y_{ij}	represents the jth measurement in the ith group.
μ_i	represents the population mean for the ith group.
ε_{ij}	represents the random error with mean$=0$ and variance$=\sigma^2$.
$i=1, \ldots, t$	where t equals the number of groups.
$j=1, \ldots, n_i$	where n_i equals the number of observations in the ith group.

This is called the means or μ-model because it uses the means $\mu_1, \ldots, \mu_t$ as the basic parameters in the mathematical expression for the model (Hocking and Speed 1975). The corresponding estimates of these parameters are

$$\hat{\mu}_1 = \bar{y}_{1.}$$
$$\vdots$$
$$\hat{\mu}_t = \bar{y}_{t.}$$

where $\bar{y}_{i.} = (\Sigma_j y_{ij})/n_i$ is the mean of n_i observations in group i.

In these situations, the statistical inference of interest is often about differences between the means of the form $(\mu_i - \mu_{i'})$ or between the means and some reference or baseline value μ. Therefore, many statistical textbooks present a model for the one-way structure that employs these differences as basic parameters. This is the familiar analysis-of-variance model illustrated in Section 2.3.4:

$$y_{ij} = \mu + \tau_i + \varepsilon_{ij}$$

where μ equals the reference value and

$$\tau_i = \mu_i - \mu \quad .$$

Thus, the means can be expressed as

$$\mu_i = \mu + \tau_i \quad .$$

This relates the set of t means $\mu_i, \ldots, \mu_t$ to a set of $t+1$ parameters $\mu, \tau_1, \ldots, \tau_t$. Therefore, this model is said to be *overspecified*. Consequently, the parameters $\mu, \tau_i, \ldots, \tau_t$ are not well defined. For any set of values of $\mu_1, \ldots, \mu_t$, there are infinitely many choices for $\mu, \tau_1, \ldots, \tau_t$, which satisfy the basic equations $\mu_i = \mu + \tau_i$, $i = 1, \ldots, t$. The choice may depend on the situation at hand, or it may not be necessary to fully define the parameters.

For the implementation of the dummy-variable model, the analysis-of-variance model

$$y_{ij} = \mu + \tau_i + \varepsilon_{ij}$$

is rewritten as a regression model

$$y_{ij} = \mu + \tau_1 x_1 + \ldots + \tau_t x_t + \varepsilon_{ij}$$

where the dummy variables $x_1, \ldots, x_t$ are defined as follows:

x_1 equals 1 for an observation in group 1 and 0 otherwise.

x_2 equals 1 for an observation in group 2 and 0 otherwise.

.

.

.

x_t equals 1 for an observation in group t and 0 otherwise.

In matrix notation, the model equations for the data become

$$
\mathbf{Y} =
\begin{bmatrix}
y_{11} \\
\cdot \\
\cdot \\
\cdot \\
y_{1n_1} \\
y_{21} \\
\cdot \\
\cdot \\
y_{2n_2} \\
\cdot \\
\cdot \\
\cdot \\
y_{t1} \\
\cdot \\
\cdot \\
\cdot \\
y_{tn_t}
\end{bmatrix}
=
\begin{bmatrix}
1 & 1 & 0 & \ldots & 0 \\
\cdot & \cdot & \cdot & & \cdot \\
\cdot & \cdot & \cdot & & \cdot \\
1 & 1 & 0 & \ldots & 0 \\
1 & 0 & 1 & \ldots & 0 \\
\cdot & \cdot & \cdot & & \cdot \\
\cdot & \cdot & \cdot & & \cdot \\
1 & 0 & 1 & \ldots & 0 \\
\cdot & \cdot & \cdot & & \cdot \\
\cdot & \cdot & \cdot & & \cdot \\
1 & 0 & 0 & \ldots & 1 \\
\cdot & \cdot & \cdot & & \cdot \\
\cdot & \cdot & \cdot & & \cdot \\
1 & 0 & 0 & \ldots & 1
\end{bmatrix}
\begin{bmatrix}
\beta_0 \\
\beta_1 \\
\cdot \\
\cdot \\
\cdot \\
\beta_t
\end{bmatrix}
+
\begin{bmatrix}
\varepsilon_{11} \\
\cdot \\
\cdot \\
\cdot \\
\varepsilon_{1n_1} \\
\varepsilon_{21} \\
\cdot \\
\cdot \\
\varepsilon_{2n_2} \\
\cdot \\
\cdot \\
\cdot \\
\varepsilon_{t1} \\
\cdot \\
\cdot \\
\cdot \\
\varepsilon_{tn_t}
\end{bmatrix}
= \mathbf{X}\beta + \varepsilon
$$

Thus, the matrices of the normal equations are

$$
\mathbf{X'X} =
\begin{bmatrix}
n_. & n_1 & n_2 & \ldots & n_t \\
n_1 & n_1 & 0 & \ldots & 0 \\
n_2 & 0 & n_2 & \ldots & 0 \\
\cdot & \cdot & \cdot & & \cdot \\
\cdot & \cdot & \cdot & & \cdot \\
\cdot & \cdot & \cdot & & \cdot \\
n_t & 0 & 0 & \ldots & n_t
\end{bmatrix},
\quad
\mathbf{X'Y} =
\begin{bmatrix}
Y_{..} \\
Y_{1.} \\
Y_{2.} \\
\cdot \\
\cdot \\
Y_{t.}
\end{bmatrix}
$$

where $Y_{i.}$ and $Y_{..}$ are totals corresponding to $\bar{y}_{i.}$ and $\bar{y}_{..}$. The normal equations $(\mathbf{X'X})\hat{\beta} = \mathbf{X'Y}$ are equivalent to the set

$$\hat{\mu} + \hat{\tau}_1 = \bar{y}_{1.}$$
$$\hat{\mu} + \hat{\tau}_2 = \bar{y}_{2.}$$
$$\cdot$$
$$\cdot$$
$$\cdot$$
$$\hat{\mu} + \hat{\tau}_t = \bar{y}_{t.} \ .$$

Because there are only t equations, there is no unique solution for the $(t+1)$ estimates $\hat{\mu}, \hat{\tau}_1, \ldots, \hat{\tau}_t$. Corresponding to this, the $\mathbf{X'X}$ matrix describing the set of normal equations is of dimension $(t+1) \times (t+1)$ and of rank t. In this model the first row of $\mathbf{X'X}$ is equal to the sum of the other t rows. The same relationship exists among the columns of $\mathbf{X'X}$. Therefore, $\mathbf{X'X}$ is said to be of less than full rank.

4.2.2 Parameter Estimates for One-Way Classification

There are two popular methods for obtaining estimates with a less-than-full-rank model. Restrictions can be imposed on the parameters to obtain a full-rank model, or a generalized inverse can be obtained of $X'X$. PROC GLM uses the latter method. This section reviews both methods in order to put the approach used by PROC GLM into perspective.

The restrictions method is based on the fact that any definition of one of the parameters in the model (say the reference parameter) causes the other parameters to be uniquely defined. The definition can be restated in the form of a restriction. Another view of the term restriction is to define the parameters to have a unique interpretation. The corresponding estimates are then required to coincide with the definition of the parameters.

One type of restriction is to define one of the τ_i equal to 0, say $\tau_t = 0$. In this case, μ becomes the mean of the tth group $\mu_\tau = \mu + \tau_t = \mu$, and τ_i becomes the difference between the mean for the ith group and the mean for the tth group, $\tau_i = \mu_i - \mu = \mu_i - \mu_t$.

The corresponding restriction on the solution to the normal equations is to require $\hat{\tau}_t = 0$. Requiring $\hat{\tau}_t = 0$ leads automatically to a unique set of values for the remaining set of estimates $\hat{\mu}, \hat{\tau}_1, \ldots, \hat{\tau}_{t-1}$. This occurs because τ_t is dropped from the linear model. Consequently, the column corresponding to τ_t is dropped from the X matrix, producing the following model equation:

$$
\begin{bmatrix}
y_{11} \\
\cdot \\
\cdot \\
y_{1n_1} \\
\cdot \\
\cdot \\
y_{t-1,1} \\
\cdot \\
\cdot \\
y_{t-1,n_{t-1}} \\
y_{t1} \\
\cdot \\
\cdot \\
y_{tn_t}
\end{bmatrix}
=
\begin{bmatrix}
1 & 1 & \ldots & 0 \\
\cdot & \cdot & & \cdot \\
\cdot & \cdot & & \cdot \\
1 & 1 & \ldots & 0 \\
\cdot & \cdot & & \cdot \\
\cdot & \cdot & & \cdot \\
1 & 0 & \ldots & 1 \\
\cdot & \cdot & & \cdot \\
\cdot & \cdot & & \cdot \\
1 & 0 & \ldots & 1 \\
1 & 0 & \ldots & 0 \\
\cdot & \cdot & & \cdot \\
\cdot & \cdot & & \cdot \\
1 & 0 & \ldots & 0
\end{bmatrix}
\begin{bmatrix}
\mu \\
\tau_1 \\
\cdot \\
\cdot \\
\tau_{t-1}
\end{bmatrix}
+
\begin{bmatrix}
\varepsilon_{11} \\
\cdot \\
\cdot \\
\varepsilon_{1n_1} \\
\cdot \\
\cdot \\
\varepsilon_{t-1,1} \\
\cdot \\
\cdot \\
\varepsilon_{t-1,n_{t-1}} \\
\varepsilon_{t1} \\
\cdot \\
\cdot \\
\varepsilon_{tn_t}
\end{bmatrix}
$$

The solution to the corresponding normal equation $(X'X)\hat{\beta} = X'Y$, where $X'X$ is now nonsingular, results in

$$\hat{\mu} = \bar{y}_{t.}$$
$$\hat{\tau}_1 = \bar{y}_{1.} - \bar{y}_{t.}$$
$$\hat{\tau}_2 = \bar{y}_{2.} - \bar{y}_{t.}$$
$$\cdot$$
$$\cdot$$
$$\cdot$$
$$\hat{\tau}_{(t-1)} = \bar{y}_{(t-1).} - \bar{y}_{t.} \quad .$$

Another approach defines μ to be equal to the mean of $\mu_1, \mu_2, \ldots, \mu_t$; that is, $\mu = (\mu_1 + \mu_2 + \ldots + \mu_t)/t$. Then μ is called the *grand mean* and the τ_i are called the *group effects*. From this definition of μ, it follows that $\Sigma_i \tau_i = 0$. Consequently,

$$\tau_t = -\tau_1 - \tau_2 - \ldots - \tau_{t-1} \quad.$$

Therefore, observations $y_{tj} = \mu + \tau_t + \varepsilon_{ij}$ in the tth group can be written

$$y_{tj} = \mu - \tau_1 - \tau_2 - \ldots - \tau_{t-1} + \varepsilon_{ij} \quad.$$

The parameter τ_t is dropped from the model, which now becomes

$$
\begin{bmatrix} y_{11} \\ \cdot \\ \cdot \\ \cdot \\ y_{1n_1} \\ \cdot \\ \cdot \\ \cdot \\ y_{t-1,1} \\ \cdot \\ \cdot \\ \cdot \\ y_{t-1,n_{t-1}} \\ y_{t1} \\ \cdot \\ \cdot \\ \cdot \\ y_{tn_t} \end{bmatrix}
=
\begin{bmatrix}
1 & 1 & 0 & \ldots & 0 \\
\cdot & \cdot & \cdot & & \cdot \\
\cdot & \cdot & \cdot & & \cdot \\
\cdot & \cdot & \cdot & & \cdot \\
1 & 1 & 0 & \ldots & 0 \\
\cdot & \cdot & \cdot & & \cdot \\
\cdot & \cdot & \cdot & & \cdot \\
\cdot & \cdot & \cdot & & \cdot \\
1 & 0 & 0 & \ldots & 1 \\
\cdot & \cdot & \cdot & & \cdot \\
\cdot & \cdot & \cdot & & \cdot \\
\cdot & \cdot & \cdot & & \cdot \\
1 & 0 & 0 & \ldots & 1 \\
1 & -1 & -1 & \ldots & -1 \\
\cdot & \cdot & \cdot & & \cdot \\
\cdot & \cdot & \cdot & & \cdot \\
\cdot & \cdot & \cdot & & \cdot \\
1 & -1 & -1 & \ldots & -1
\end{bmatrix}
\begin{bmatrix} \mu \\ \tau_1 \\ \tau_2 \\ \cdot \\ \cdot \\ \cdot \\ \tau_{t-1} \end{bmatrix}
+
\begin{bmatrix} \varepsilon_{11} \\ \cdot \\ \cdot \\ \cdot \\ \varepsilon_{1n_1} \\ \cdot \\ \cdot \\ \cdot \\ \varepsilon_{t-1,1} \\ \cdot \\ \cdot \\ \cdot \\ \varepsilon_{t-1,n_{t-1}} \\ \varepsilon_{t1} \\ \cdot \\ \cdot \\ \cdot \\ \varepsilon_{tn_t} \end{bmatrix}
$$

The solution to the corresponding normal equation yields

$$\hat{\mu} = (\bar{y}_{1.} + \ldots + \bar{y}_{t.})\,/\,t$$
$$\hat{\tau}_1 = \bar{y}_{1.} - \bar{y}_{..}$$
$$\hat{\tau}_2 = \bar{y}_{2.} - \bar{y}_{..}$$
$$\cdot$$
$$\cdot$$
$$\cdot$$
$$\hat{\tau}_{t-1} = \bar{y}_{(t-1).} - \bar{y}_{..}$$

and the implementation of the condition $\tau_t = -\tau_1 - \ldots - \tau_{t-1}$ yields

$$\hat{\tau}_t = \bar{y}_{t.} - \bar{y}_{..} \quad.$$

The use of generalized inverses and estimable functions may be preferable for a variety of reasons. In the restrictions method, it might not be clear which particular restriction is desired. In cases of empty cells in multiway classifications, it can be difficult to define the parameters. In fact, it is often hard to identify the empty cells in large, multiway classifications, let alone to define a set of parameters that adequately describe all pertinent effects and interactions. The generalized-inverse approach partially removes the burden of defining parameters from the data analyst.

Section 1.1.4, "Using the Generalized Inverse," shows that there is no unique solution to a system of equations with a less-than-full-rank coefficient matrix and introduces the generalized inverse to obtain a nonunique solution. Although the set of parameter estimates produced using the generalized inverse is not unique, there is a class of linear functions of parameters called *estimable functions* for which unique estimates do exist. For example, the function $(\tau_i - \tau_j)$ is estimable: its least-squares estimate is the same regardless of the particular solution obtained for the normal equations. For a discussion of the definition of estimable functions as it relates to the theory of linear models, see Graybill (1976) or Searle (1971).

PROC GLM uses a generalized inverse to obtain a solution that produces one set of estimates. The technique, in some respects, is parallel to using a set of restrictions that set some of the parameter estimates to 0. Quantities to be estimated or comparisons to be made are specified, and PROC GLM determines whether or not the estimates or comparisons represent estimable functions. PROC GLM then provides estimates, standard errors, and test statistics.

For certain applications, there is more than one set of hypotheses that can be tested. To cover these situations, PROC GLM provides four types of sums of squares and associated F statistics and also gives additional information to assist in interpreting the hypotheses tested.

4.2.3 Using PROC GLM for Analysis of Variance

Using PROC GLM for analysis of variance is similar to using PROC ANOVA; the statements listed for PROC ANOVA in Section 2.3.2, "Using the ANOVA Procedure," are also used for PROC GLM. In addition to the statements listed for PROC ANOVA, the following SAS statements can be used with PROC GLM:

CONTRAST *'label' effect values*< . . . *effect values*> < / *options*>;
ESTIMATE *'label' effect values*< . . . *effect values*> < / *options*>;
ID *variables*;
LSMEANS *effects*< / *options*>;
OUTPUT <OUT=*SAS-data-set*> *keyword*= *names* < . . . *keyword*=*names*>;
RANDOM *effects*< / *options*>;
WEIGHT *variable*;

The CONTRAST statement provides a way for obtaining custom hypotheses tests. The ESTIMATE statement can be used to estimate linear functions of the parameters. The LSMEANS (least-squares means) statement specifies effects for which least-squares estimates of means are computed. The uses of these statements are illustrated in Section 4.2.4, "Estimable Functions in the One-Way Classification," and Section 4.3.6, "MEANS, LSMEANS, CONTRAST, and ESTIMATE Statements in the Two-Way Layout." The RANDOM statement specifies which effects in the model are random (see Section 4.4, "Proper Error Terms"). When predicted values are requested as a MODEL statement option, values of the variable specified in the ID statement are printed for identification beside each observed, predicted, and residual value. The OUTPUT statement produces an output data set that contains the original data set values along with predicted and residual values. The WEIGHT statement is used when a weighted residual sum of squares is needed. For more information, refer to Chapter 24 in the *SAS/STAT User's Guide, Volume 2*.

Implementing PROC GLM for an analysis-of-variance model is illustrated by an example of test scores made by students in three classes taught by three different teachers; the data appear in Output 4.1.

Output 4.1
Data for One-Way Analysis of Variance

```
                      The SAS System                          1

         OBS    TEACH    SCORE1    SCORE2

          1     JAY        69        75
          2     JAY        69        70
          3     JAY        71        73
          4     JAY        78        82
          5     JAY        79        81
          6     JAY        73        75
          7     PAT        69        70
          8     PAT        68        74
          9     PAT        75        80
         10     PAT        78        85
         11     PAT        68        68
         12     PAT        63        68
         13     PAT        72        74
         14     PAT        63        66
         15     PAT        71        76
         16     PAT        72        78
         17     PAT        71        73
         18     PAT        70        73
         19     PAT        56        59
         20     PAT        77        83
         21     ROBIN      72        79
         22     ROBIN      64        65
         23     ROBIN      74        74
         24     ROBIN      72        75
         25     ROBIN      82        84
         26     ROBIN      69        68
         27     ROBIN      76        76
         28     ROBIN      68        65
         29     ROBIN      78        79
         30     ROBIN      70        71
         31     ROBIN      60        61
```

In terms of the analysis-of-variance model described above, the τ_i are the parameters associated with the different teachers (TEACH); τ_1 is associated with **JAY**, τ_2 with **PAT**, and τ_3 with **ROBIN**. The following SAS statements are used to analyze SCORE2:

```
proc glm;
   class teach;
   model score2=teach / solution xpx i;
```

In this example, the CLASS variable TEACH identifies the three classes. In effect, PROC GLM establishes a dummy variable (1 for presence, 0 for absence) for each level of each CLASS variable. In this example, the CLASS statement causes PROC GLM to create dummy variables corresponding to JAY, PAT, and ROBIN, resulting in the following **X** matrix:

INTERCEPT JAY PAT ROBIN

$$
\mathbf{X} = \begin{bmatrix}
\mu & \tau_1 & \tau_2 & \tau_3 \\
1 & 1 & 0 & 0 \\
\cdot & \cdot & \cdot & \cdot \\
\cdot & \cdot & \cdot & \cdot \\
\cdot & \cdot & \cdot & \cdot \\
1 & 1 & 0 & 0 \\
1 & 0 & 1 & 0 \\
\cdot & \cdot & \cdot & \cdot \\
\cdot & \cdot & \cdot & \cdot \\
\cdot & \cdot & \cdot & \cdot \\
1 & 0 & 1 & 0 \\
1 & 0 & 0 & 1 \\
\cdot & \cdot & \cdot & \cdot \\
\cdot & \cdot & \cdot & \cdot \\
\cdot & \cdot & \cdot & \cdot \\
1 & 0 & 0 & 1
\end{bmatrix}
\begin{array}{l}
\\ \\ \\
\text{6 rows for Jay's group} \\ \\ \\ \\ \\
\text{14 rows for Pat's group} \\ \\ \\ \\ \\
\text{11 rows for Robin's group} \\ \\
\end{array}
$$

Note that the columns for the dummy variables are in alphabetical order; the column positioning depends only on the values of the CLASS variable. For example, the column for JAY would appear after the columns for PAT and ROBIN if the value JAY were replaced by ZJAY.*

The MODEL statement has the same purpose in PROC GLM as it does in PROC REG and PROC ANOVA. Note that the MODEL statement contains the SOLUTION option. This option is used because PROC GLM does not automatically print the estimated parameter vector when a model contains a CLASS statement. The results of the SAS statements shown above appear in Output 4.2.

Output 4.2
One-Way Analysis of Variance from PROC GLM

```
                           The SAS System                           1
                    General Linear Models Procedure
Dependent Variable: SCORE2
                                Sum of          Mean
Source              DF        Squares         Square    F Value    Pr > F

Model                2     49.73586091    24.86793046       0.56    0.5776

Error               28   1243.94155844    44.42648423

Corrected Total     30   1293.67741935

                                            (continued on next page)
```

---

* You can use the ORDER= option in the PROC GLM statement to alter the column position.

(continued from previous page)

	R-Square	C.V.	Root MSE	SCORE2 Mean
	0.038445	9.062496	6.6653195	73.548387

Source	DF	Type I SS	Mean Square	F Value	Pr > F
TEACH	2	49.73586091	24.86793046	0.56	0.5776

Source	DF	Type III SS	Mean Square	F Value	Pr > F
TEACH	2	49.73586091	24.86793046	0.56	0.5776

Parameter		Estimate	T for H0: Parameter=0	Pr > |T|	Std Error of Estimate
INTERCEPT		72.45454545 B	36.05	0.0001	2.00966945
TEACH	JAY	3.54545455 B	1.05	0.3036	3.38277775
	PAT	0.90259740 B	0.34	0.7393	2.68553376
	ROBIN	0.00000000 B	.	.	.

NOTE: The X'X matrix has been found to be singular and a generalized inverse was used to solve the normal equations. Estimates followed by the letter 'B' are biased, and are not unique estimators of the parameters.

The first portion of the output, as in previous examples, shows the statistics for the overall model.

The second portion partitions the model sum of squares (MODEL SS) into portions corresponding to factors defined by the list of variables in the MODEL statement. In this model there is only one factor, TEACH, so the Type I and Type III SS are the same as the MODEL SS. Type II and Type IV have no special meaning here and would be the same as Type I and Type III.

The final portion of the output contains the parameter estimates obtained with the generalized inverses. Specifying XPX and I in the list of options in the MODEL statement causes the **X′X** and **(X′X)** ¯ matrices to be printed. Results appear in Output 4.3.

Output 4.3
X′X and (X′X)⁻
Matrices for
One-Way
Classification

```
                                    The SAS System                          1
                            General Linear Models Procedure

                                   The X'X Matrix

                    INTERCEPT     TEACH JAY    TEACH PAT   TEACH ROBIN     SCORE2

    INTERCEPT            31             6           14            11       2280
    TEACH JAY            6              6            0             0        456
    TEACH PAT           14              0           14             0       1027
    TEACH ROBIN         11              0            0            11        797
    SCORE2            2280            456         1027           797     168984
```

```
                                                                            2
                            General Linear Models Procedure

                             X'X Generalized Inverse (g2)

                    INTERCEPT      TEACH JAY      TEACH PAT   TEACH ROBIN       SCORE2

  INTERCEPT       0.0909090909 -0.090909091 -0.090909091        0  72.454545455
  TEACH JAY      -0.090909091  0.2575757576  0.0909090909        0   3.5454545455
  TEACH PAT      -0.090909091  0.0909090909  0.1623376623        0   0.9025974026
  TEACH ROBIN         0             0             0              0        0
  SCORE2         72.454545455  3.5454545455  0.9025974026        0  1243.9415584
```

For this example, the matrix **X′Y** is

$$\mathbf{X'Y} = \begin{bmatrix} \text{SCORE2 total overall} \\ \text{SCORE2 total for } \textsf{JAY} \\ \text{SCORE2 total for } \textsf{PAT} \\ \text{SCORE2 total for } \textsf{ROBIN} \end{bmatrix} = \begin{bmatrix} 2280 \\ 456 \\ 1027 \\ 797 \end{bmatrix}$$

Taking $(\mathbf{X'X})^-$ from the PROC GLM output and using **X′Y** above, the solution $\hat{\boldsymbol{\beta}} = (\mathbf{X'X})^- \mathbf{X'Y}$ is

$$\begin{bmatrix} \hat{\beta}_0 \\ \hat{\beta}_1 \\ \hat{\beta}_2 \\ \hat{\beta}_3 \end{bmatrix} = \begin{bmatrix} .0909 & -.0909 & -.0909 & .0000 \\ -.0909 & .2575 & .0909 & .0000 \\ -.0909 & .0909 & .1623 & .0000 \\ .0000 & .0000 & .0000 & .0000 \end{bmatrix} \begin{bmatrix} 2280 \\ 456 \\ 1027 \\ 797 \end{bmatrix} = \begin{bmatrix} 72.45 \\ 3.54 \\ 0.90 \\ 0.00 \end{bmatrix}$$

As pointed out in Section 1.1.4, the particular generalized inverse used by PROC GLM causes the last row and column of $(\mathbf{X'X})^-$ to be set to 0. This yields a set of parameter estimates equivalent in this example to the set given by the restriction that $\tau_3 = 0$. Using the principles discussed in Section 4.2.2, "Parameter Estimates for One-Way Classification," it follows that the INTERCEPT μ is actually the mean for the reference group ROBIN. The estimate $\hat{\tau}_1$ labeled JAY is the difference between the mean for Jay's group and the mean for Robin's group, and, similarly, the estimate $\hat{\tau}_2$ labeled PAT is the mean for Pat's group minus the mean for Robin's group. Finally, the estimate $\hat{\tau}_3$ labeled ROBIN, which is set to 0, can be viewed as the mean for Robin's group minus the mean for Robin's group.

Remember that these estimates are not unique; that is, they depend on the alphabetical order of the values of the CLASS variable. This fact is recognized in the output by denoting the estimates as biased, which is explained in the note after the listing of estimates.

The other MODEL statement options (P, CLM, CLI, and TOLERANCE), as well as the BY, ID, WEIGHT, FREQ, and OUTPUT statements, are not affected by the use of CLASS variables and may be used as described in Section 1.3.4, "The SS1 and SS2 Options: Two Types of Sums of Squares" and Section 1.3.5, "Tests of Subsets and Linear Combinations of Coefficients."

4.2.4   Estimable Functions in the One-Way Classification

It is often the case that the particular parameter estimates obtained by the SOLUTION option in PROC GLM are not the estimates of interest, or there may be additional functions of the parameters that you want to estimate. You can specify such other estimates with PROC GLM.

An estimable function is a member of a special class of linear functions of parameters (see Section 1.1.4). Basically, an estimable function of the parameters has a definite interpretation regardless of how the parameters themselves are specified. Denote with $\mathbf{L}$ a vector of coefficients $(L_1, L_2, \ldots, L_t, L_{t+1})$. Then $\mathbf{L}\boldsymbol{\beta}=L_1\mu+L_2\tau_1+\ldots+L_{t+1}\tau_t$ is a linear function of the model parameters and is estimable (for this example) if it can be expressed as a linear function of the means $\mu_1, \ldots, \mu_t$. Let $\hat{\boldsymbol{\beta}}$ be a solution to the normal equation. The function $\mathbf{L}\boldsymbol{\beta}$ is estimated by $\mathbf{L}\hat{\boldsymbol{\beta}}$, the corresponding linear function of the parameters. If $\mathbf{L}\boldsymbol{\beta}$ is estimable, then $\mathbf{L}\hat{\boldsymbol{\beta}}$ will have the same value regardless of the solution obtained to the normal equations. In the example,

$$\hat{\boldsymbol{\beta}} = \begin{bmatrix} \bar{\mu} \\ \hat{\tau}_1 \\ \hat{\tau}_2 \\ \hat{\tau}_3 \end{bmatrix} = \begin{bmatrix} 72.454 \\ 3.545 \\ 0.902 \\ 0.000 \end{bmatrix} \begin{matrix} \text{INTERCEPT} \\ \text{JAY} \\ \text{PAT} \\ \text{ROBIN} \end{matrix}$$

To illustrate, define

$$\mathbf{L} = \begin{bmatrix} 1 & 1 & 0 & 0 \end{bmatrix}$$

Then $\mathbf{L}\hat{\boldsymbol{\beta}}=\hat{\mu}+\hat{\tau}_1=\hat{\mu}_1=76.0$, which is the estimate of the mean score of Jay's class. Alternately, let

$$\mathbf{L} = \begin{bmatrix} 0 & +1 & -1 & 0 \end{bmatrix}$$

Then $\mathbf{L}\hat{\boldsymbol{\beta}}=(\hat{\tau}_1-\hat{\tau}_2)=\hat{\mu}_1-\hat{\mu}_2=2.643$, the estimated mean difference between Jay's and Pat's sections. Because both of these are estimable functions, identical estimates would be obtained using a different generalized inverse, for example, if different names for the teachers changed the order of the dummy variables.

Variances of these estimates can be readily obtained with standard formulas that involve elements of the generalized inverse (see Section 1.1.4).

You can obtain the general form of the estimable functions with the E option in the MODEL statement

```
model score2 = teach / e ;
```

Output 4.4 shows you that L4, the coefficient or τ_3, must be equal to $L1-L2-L3$. Equivalently, $L1=L2+L3+L4$. That is, the coefficient on μ must be the sum of the coefficients on τ_1, τ_2 and τ_3.

Output 4.4
Obtaining the
General Form of
Estimable
Functions Using
the E Option

```
                              The SAS System                              1

                       General Linear Models Procedure
                       General Form of Estimable Functions

       Effect              Coefficients

       INTERCEPT           L1

       TEACH      JAY      L2
                  PAT      L3
                  ROBIN    L1-L2-L3
```

```
                                                                          2

                      General Linear Models Procedure

     Dependent Variable: SCORE2
                                     Sum of            Mean
     Source              DF          Squares           Square    F Value   Pr > F

     Model                2       49.73586091      24.86793046     0.56    0.5776

     Error               28     1243.94155844      44.42648423

     Corrected Total     30     1293.67741935

                       R-Square              C.V.        Root MSE        SCORE2 Mean

                       0.038445          9.062496       6.6653195         73.548387


     Source              DF       Type I SS      Mean Square   F Value   Pr > F

     TEACH                2     49.73586091      24.86793046     0.56    0.5776

     Source              DF     Type III SS      Mean Square   F Value   Pr > F

     TEACH                2     49.73586091      24.86793046     0.56    0.5776
```

PROC GLM calculates estimates and variances for several special types of estimable functions with LSMEANS, CONTRAST, or ESTIMATE statements as well as estimates of user-supplied functions.

The LSMEANS statement produces the least-squares estimates of CLASS variable means; these are sometimes referred to as adjusted means. For the one-way structure, these are simply the ordinary means. In terms of model parameter estimates, they are $\hat{\mu}+\hat{\tau}_i$. The following SAS statement lists the least-squares means for the three teachers for all dependent variables in the MODEL statement:

```
lsmeans teach / options;
```

The available options in the LSMEANS statement are

STDERR   prints the standard errors of each estimated least-squares mean and the *t* statistic for a test of the hypothesis that the mean is 0.

PDIFF   prints the *p* values for the tests of equality of all pairs of CLASS means.

E   prints a description of the linear function used to obtain each least-squares mean; this has importance in more complex situations.

E=   specifies an effect in the model to use as an error term.

ETYPE=   specifies the type (1, 2, 3, or 4) of the effect specified in the E= option.

SINGULAR=   tunes the estimability checking.

For more information, refer to Chapter 24 in the *SAS/STAT User's Guide, Volume 2*. Output 4.5 shows results from the following SAS statement:

```
lsmeans teach / stderr pdiff;
```

Output 4.5
Results of
LSMEANS
Statement

```
                              The SAS System                              1

                        General Linear Models Procedure
                              Least Squares Means

            TEACH      SCORE2        Std Err    Pr > |T|    LSMEAN
                       LSMEAN         LSMEAN   H0:LSMEAN=0   Number

            JAY      76.0000000     2.7211053     0.0001       1
            PAT      73.3571429     1.7813816     0.0001       2
            ROBIN    72.4545455     2.0096694     0.0001       3

                    Pr > |T| H0: LSMEAN(i)=LSMEAN(j)

                      i/j     1        2        3
                       1      .      0.4233   0.3036
                       2    0.4233     .      0.7393
                       3    0.3036   0.7393     .

    NOTE: To ensure overall protection level, only probabilities associated with
          pre-planned comparisons should be used.
```

The least-squares mean for **JAY** is computed as $\hat{\mu}+\hat{\tau}_1=72.45+3.54$. Note that this linear function has coefficients L1=1, L2=1, L3=0 and L4=0, so it meets the estimability condition L1=L2+L3+L4.

Least-squares means should not, in general, be confused with ordinary means, which are available with a MEANS statement. The MEANS statement produces simple, unadjusted means of all observations in each class or treatment. Except for one-way designs and some nested and balanced factorial structures that are normally analyzed with PROC ANOVA, these unadjusted means are generally not equal to the least-squares means. Note that for this example, the least-squares means are the same as the means obtained with the MEANS statement. (The MEANS statement is discussed in Section 2.3.2.)

A contrast is a linear function such that the elements of the coefficient vector sum to 0 for each effect. PROC GLM can be instructed to calculate a sum of squares and associated F test due to one or more contrasts.

As an example, assume that teacher **JAY** used a special teaching method. You might then be interested in testing whether Jay's students had mean scores different from those of other teachers and whether **PAT** and **ROBIN**, using the same method, produced different mean scores. The corresponding contrasts are shown below:

	Multipliers for TEACH		
Contrast	**JAY**	**PAT**	**ROBIN**
JAY vs others	-2	$+1$	$+1$
PAT vs **ROBIN**	0	-1	$+1$

Taking $\boldsymbol{\beta} = (\mu, \tau_1, \tau_2, \tau_3)'$, the contrasts are

$$\begin{aligned} \mathbf{L}\boldsymbol{\beta} &= -2\mu_1 + \mu_2 + \mu_3 \quad \text{(\textbf{JAY} vs others)} \\ &= -2\tau_1 + \tau_2 + \tau_3 \end{aligned}$$

and

$$\begin{aligned} \mathbf{L}\boldsymbol{\beta} &= -\mu_2 + \mu_3 \quad \text{(\textbf{PAT} vs \textbf{ROBIN})} \\ &= -\tau_2 + \tau_3 \end{aligned}$$

The corresponding CONTRAST statements are as follows:

```
contrast 'JAY vs others' teach -2 1 1;
contrast 'PAT vs ROBIN' teach 0 -1 1;
```

The results appear in Output 4.6.

Output 4.6
Results of CONTRAST and ESTIMATE Statements

```
                            The SAS System                              1

                    General Linear Models Procedure

      Contrast          DF     Contrast SS      Mean Square   F Value    Pr > F

      JAY vs others      1     46.19421179      46.19421179     1.04     0.3166
      PAT vs ROBIN       1      5.01844156       5.01844156     0.11     0.7393

                                          T for H0:    Pr > |T|   Std Error of
      Parameter              Estimate   Parameter=0                 Estimate

      LSM JAY             76.00000000       27.93      0.0001      2.72110530
      LSM PAT             73.35714286       41.18      0.0001      1.78138157
      LSM ROBIN           72.45454545       36.05      0.0001      2.00966945
```

The following are points you should keep in mind when using the CONTRAST statement:

□ You must know how many classes (categories) are present in the effect and in what order they are sorted by PROC GLM. If there are more effects (classes) in the data than the number of coefficients specified in the CONTRAST statement, PROC GLM adds trailing zeros. In other words, there is no check to see if the proper number of classes has been specified.

□ The name or label of the contrast must be twenty characters or less.

□ Available CONTRAST statement options are

E   prints the entire **L** vector.

E=*effect*   specifies an alternate error term.

ETYPE=*n*   specifies the type (1, 2, 3, or 4) of the E=*effect*.

□ Multiple degrees-of-freedom contrasts can be specified by repeating the effect name and coefficients as needed. Thus, the statement

```
contrast 'ALL' teach -2 1 1, teach 0 -1 1;
```

produces a two DF sum of squares due to both contrasts. This feature can be used to obtain partial sums of squares for effects through the reduction principle, using sums of squares from multiple degrees-of-freedom contrasts that include and exclude the desired contrasts.

□ If a nonestimable contrast has been specified, a message to that effect appears in the SAS log.

□ Although only $(t-1)$ linearly independent contrasts exist for t classes, any number of contrasts can be specified.

□ The contrast sums of squares are not partial of (adjusted for) other contrasts that may be specified for the same effect (see number 4 above).

□ The CONTRAST statement is not available with PROC ANOVA; thus, the computational inefficiency of PROC GLM for analyzing balanced data may be justified if contrasts are required. However, contrast variables can be defined in a DATA step and estimates and statistics can be obtained by a full-rank regression analysis.

The ESTIMATE statement is used to obtain statistics for estimable functions other than least-squares means and contrasts, although it can also be used for these. For the current example, the ESTIMATE statement is used to reestimate the least-squares means.

The respective least-squares means for **JAY**, **PAT**, and **ROBIN** estimate $\mu_1=\mu+\tau_1$, $\mu_2=\mu+\tau_2$, and $\mu_3=\mu+\tau_3$. The following statements duplicate the least-squares means:

```
estimate 'LSM JAY' intercept 1 teach 1;
estimate 'LSM PAT' intercept 1 teach 0 1;
estimate 'LSM ROBIN' intercept 1 teach 0 0 1;
```

Note the use of the term INTERCEPT (referring to μ) and the fact that the procedure supplies trailing zero-valued coefficients. The results of these statements appear after the listing of parameter estimates at the bottom of Output 4.6 for convenient comparison with the results of the LSMEANS statement.

4.3 Two-Way Classification: Unbalanced Data

The major applications of the two-way structure are the two-factor factorial experiment and the randomized-blocks design (see Section 2.3.5, "Randomized-Blocks Design with Multiple Comparisons"). These applications have balanced data. In this section, the two-way classification with unbalanced data is explored. This introduces new questions, such as how means and sums of squares should be computed.

4.3.1 General Considerations

The two-way classification model is

$$y_{ijk} = \mu + \alpha_i + \beta_j + \alpha\beta_{ij} + \varepsilon_{ijk}$$

where

y_{ijk} equals the kth observed score for the (i,j)th cell.

α_i equals the effect of the ith level of factor A.

β_j equals an effect of the jth level of factor B.

$\alpha\beta_{ij}$ equals the interaction effect for the ith level of factor A and the jth level of factor B.

ε_{ijk} equals the random error associated with individual observations.

The model can be defined without the interaction term when appropriate. Let n_{ij} denote the number of observations in the cell for level i of A and level j of B. If μ_{ij} denotes the population cell mean for level i of A and level j of B, then

$$\mu_{ij} = \mu + \alpha_i + \beta_j + \alpha\beta_{ij} \quad .$$

At this point, no further restrictions on the parameters are assumed.

The computational formulas for PROC ANOVA that use the various treatment means provide correct statistics for balanced data, that is, data with an equal number of observations ($n_{ij}=n$ for all i, j) for each treatment combination. When data are not balanced, sums of squares computed by PROC ANOVA can contain functions of the other parameters of the model, and thereby produce biased results.

To illustrate the effects of unbalanced data on the estimation of differences between means and computation of sums of squares, consider the data in this two-way table:

	B	
	1	2
A 1	7,9	5
2	8	4,6

Within level 1 of B, the cell mean for each level of A is 8; that is, $\bar{y}_{11.}=(7+9)/2=8$ and $\bar{y}_{21.}=8$. Hence, there is no evidence of a difference between the levels of A within level 1 of B. Similarly, there is no evidence of a difference between levels of A within level 2 of B, because $\bar{y}_{12.}=5$ and $\bar{y}_{22.}=(4+6)/2=5$. Therefore, you may conclude that there is no evidence in the table of a difference between the levels of A. However, the marginal means for A are

$$\bar{y}_{1..} = (7 + 9 + 5)/3 = 7$$

and

$$\bar{y}_{2..} = (8 + 4 + 6)/3 = 6 \quad .$$

The difference of $7-6=1$ between these marginal means may be erroneously interpreted as measuring an overall effect of the factor A. Actually, the observed difference between the marginal means for the two levels of A measures the effect of factor B in addition to the effect of factor A. This can be verified by expressing the observations in terms of the analysis-of-variance model $y_{ijk}=\mu+\alpha_i+\beta_j$. (For simplicity, the interaction and error terms have been left out of the model.)

		B	
		1	2
A	1	$7 = \mu + \alpha_1 + \beta_1$	$5 = \mu + \alpha_1 + \beta_1$
		$9 = \mu + \alpha_1 + \beta_2$	$4 = \mu + \alpha_2 + \beta_2$
	2	$8 = \mu + \alpha_2 + \beta_1$	$6 = \mu + \alpha_2 + \beta_2$

The difference between marginal means for A_1 and A_2 is shown to be

$$\bar{y}_{1..} - \bar{y}_{2..} = (1/3)[(\alpha_1 + \beta_1) + (\alpha_1 + \beta_1) + (\alpha_1 + \beta_2)]$$
$$- (1/3)[(\alpha_2 + \beta_1) + (\alpha_2 + \beta_2) + (\alpha_2 + \beta_2)]$$
$$= (\alpha_1 - \alpha_2) + (1/3)(\beta_1 - \beta_2) \quad .$$

Thus, instead of estimating $(\alpha_1 - \alpha_2)$, the difference between the marginal means of A estimates $(\alpha_1 - \alpha_2)$ plus a function of the factor B parameters $(\beta_1 - \beta_2)/3$. In other words, the difference between the A marginal means is biased by factor B effects.

The null hypothesis about A that would normally be tested is

$$H_0: \alpha_1 - \alpha_2 = 0 \quad .$$

However, for this example, the sum of squares for A computed by PROC ANOVA can be shown to equal $3(\bar{y}_{1..} - \bar{y}_{2..})^2/2$. Hence, the PROC ANOVA F test for A actually tests the hypothesis

$$H_0: (\alpha_1 - \alpha_2) + (\beta_1 - \beta_2)/3 = 0$$

which involves the factor B difference $(\beta_1 - \beta_2)$ in addition to the factor A difference $(\alpha_1 - \alpha_2)$.

In terms of the μ model $y_{ijk} = \mu_{ij} + \varepsilon_{ijk}$, you usually want to estimate $(\mu_{11} + \mu_{12})/2$ and $(\mu_{21} + \mu_{22})/2$ or the difference between these quantities. However, the A marginal means for the example are

$$\bar{y}_{1..} = (2\mu_{11} + \mu_{12})/3 + \bar{\varepsilon}_{1..}$$

and

$$\bar{y}_{2..} = (\mu_{21} + 2\mu_{22})/3 + \bar{\varepsilon}_{2..} \quad .$$

These means estimate $(2\mu_{11} + \mu_{22})/3$ and $(\mu_{21} + 2\mu_{22})/3$, which are functions of the cell frequencies and might not be meaningful.

In summary, a major problem in the analysis of unbalanced data is the contamination of differences between factor means by effects of other factors. The solution to this problem is to adjust the means to remove the contaminating effects.

4.3.2 Sums of Squares Computed by PROC GLM

PROC GLM recognizes different theoretical approaches to analysis of variance by providing four types of sums of squares and associated statistics. The four types of sums of squares in PROC GLM are called Type I, Type II, Type III, and Type IV (Goodnight 1978). The four types of sums of squares are explained in general, conceptual terms, followed by more technical descriptions.

Type I sums of squares functions retain the properties discussed in Chapter 1, "Regression." They correspond to adding each source (factor) sequentially to the model in the order listed. For example, the Type I sum of squares for the first factor listed is the same as PROC ANOVA would compute for that effect. It reflects differences between unadjusted means of that factor as if the data consist of a one-way structure. The Type I SS may not be particularly useful for analysis of unbalanced multiway structures but may be useful for nested models, polynomial models, and certain tests involving the homogeneity of regression coefficients (see Chapter 6, "Covariance and the Heterogeneity of Slopes"). Also, comparing Type I and other types of sums of squares provides some information on the effect of the lack of balance.

Type II sums of squares are more difficult to understand. Generally, the Type II SS for an effect U, which may be a main effect or interaction, is adjusted for an effect V if and only if V does not contain U. Specifically, for a two-factor structure with interaction, the main effects, A and B, are not adjusted for the A*B interactions because the symbol A*B contains both A and B. Factor A is adjusted for B because the symbol B does not contain A. Similarly, B is adjusted for A, and the A*B interaction is adjusted for the two main effects.

Type II sums of squares for the main effects A and B are mainly appropriate for situations in which no interaction is present. These are the sums of squares presented in many major statistical textbooks. Their method of computation is often referred to as the method of fitting constants.

The Type II analysis relates to the following general guidelines often given in applied statistical texts. First, test for the significance of the A*B interaction. If A*B is insignificant, delete it from the model and analyze main effects, each adjusted for the other. If A*B is significant, then abandon main-effects analysis and focus your attention on simple effects.

Note that for full-rank regression models, the Type II sums of squares are adjusted for crossproduct terms. This occurs because, for example,

$$y = \beta_0 + \beta_1 x_1 + \beta_2 x_2 + \beta_3 x_1 x_2 + \varepsilon$$

where the product $x_1 x_2$ is dealt with simply as another independent variable with no concept of order of the term.

The Type III sums of squares correspond to Yates' weighted squares of means analysis. Their principal use is in situations that require a comparison of main effects even in the presence of interaction. Type III sums of squares are partial sums of squares. In this sense, each effect is adjusted for all other effects. In particular, main effects A and B are adjusted for the interaction A*B if all these terms are in the model. If the model contains only main effects, then Type II and Type III analyses are the same. See Steel and Torrie (1980), Searle (1971), and Speed, Hocking, and Hackney (1978) for further discussion of the method of fitting constants and the method of weighted squares of means.

The Type IV functions were designed primarily for situations where there are empty cells. The principles underlying the Type IV sums of squares are quite involved and can be discussed only in a framework using the general construction of estimable functions. It should be noted that the Type IV functions are not necessarily unique when there are empty cells but are identical to those provided by Type III when there are no empty cells.

You can request four sums of squares in PROC GLM as options in the MODEL statement. For example, the following SAS statement specifies the printing of Type I and Type IV sums of squares:

```
model . . . / ss1 ss4;
```

Any or all types may be requested. If no sums of squares are specified, PROC GLM computes the Type I and Type III sums of squares by default.

The next two sections interpret the different sums of squares in terms of reduction notation and the μ-model.

4.3.3 Interpreting Sums of Squares in Reduction Notation

The types of sums of squares can be explained in terms of the reduction notation that is developed for regression models in Chapter 2. This requires writing the model as a regression model using dummy variables, with certain restrictions imposed on the parameters to give them unique interpretation.

As an example, consider a 2×3 factorial structure with n_{ij} observations in the cell in row i, column j. The equation for the model is

$$y_{ijk} = \mu + \alpha_i + \beta_j + \alpha\beta_{ij} + \varepsilon_{ijk}$$

where $i=1,2$, $j=1,2,3$, and $k=1, \ldots, n_{ij}$. Assume $n_{ij}>0$ for all i, j. An expression of the form $R(\alpha \mid \mu, \beta)$ means the same as $R(\alpha_1, \alpha_2 \mid \mu, \beta_1, \beta_2, \beta_3)$. The sums of squares printed by PROC GLM can be interpreted in reduction notation most easily under the restrictions

$$\Sigma_i \, \alpha_i = \Sigma_j \, \beta_j = \Sigma_i \, \alpha\beta_{ij} = \Sigma_j \, \alpha\beta_{ij} = 0 \qquad (4.1)$$

that is, by taking an **X** matrix with full column rank given by

$$
\begin{array}{cccccc}
\mu & \alpha_1 & \beta_1 & \beta_2 & \alpha\beta_{11} & \alpha\beta_{12}
\end{array}
$$

$$
\mathbf{X} =
\left[
\begin{array}{cccccc}
1 & 1 & 1 & 0 & 1 & 0 \\
\cdot & \cdot & \cdot & \cdot & \cdot & \cdot \\
\cdot & \cdot & \cdot & \cdot & \cdot & \cdot \\
1 & 1 & 1 & 0 & 1 & 0 \\
1 & 1 & 0 & 1 & 0 & 1 \\
\cdot & \cdot & \cdot & \cdot & \cdot & \cdot \\
\cdot & \cdot & \cdot & \cdot & \cdot & \cdot \\
1 & 1 & 0 & 1 & 0 & 1 \\
1 & 1 & -1 & -1 & -1 & -1 \\
\cdot & \cdot & \cdot & \cdot & \cdot & \cdot \\
\cdot & \cdot & \cdot & \cdot & \cdot & \cdot \\
1 & 1 & -1 & -1 & -1 & -1 \\
1 & -1 & 1 & 0 & -1 & 0 \\
\cdot & \cdot & \cdot & \cdot & \cdot & \cdot \\
\cdot & \cdot & \cdot & \cdot & \cdot & \cdot \\
1 & -1 & 1 & 0 & -1 & 0 \\
1 & -1 & 0 & 1 & 0 & -1 \\
\cdot & \cdot & \cdot & \cdot & \cdot & \cdot \\
\cdot & \cdot & \cdot & \cdot & \cdot & \cdot \\
1 & -1 & 0 & 1 & 0 & -1 \\
1 & -1 & -1 & -1 & 1 & 1 \\
\cdot & \cdot & \cdot & \cdot & \vdots & \cdot \\
\cdot & \cdot & \cdot & \cdot & \cdot & \cdot \\
1 & -1 & -1 & -1 & 1 & 1
\end{array}
\right]
$$

- n_{11} rows for observations in cell 11
- n_{12} rows for observations in cell 12
- n_{13} rows for observations in cell 13
- n_{21} rows for observations in cell 21
- n_{22} rows for observations in cell 22
- n_{23} rows for observations in cell 23

With this set of restrictions or definitions of the parameters, the sums of squares that result from the following MODEL statement are summarized below:

```
model y=a b a*b / ss1 ss2 ss3 ss4;
```

Effect	Type I	Type II	Type III = Type IV
A	$R(\alpha \mid \mu)$	$R(\alpha \mid \mu, \beta)$	$R(\alpha \mid \mu, \beta, \alpha\beta)$
B	$R(\beta \mid \mu, \alpha)$	$R(\beta \mid \mu, \alpha)$	$R(\beta \mid \mu, \alpha, \alpha\beta)$
A*B	$R(\alpha\beta \mid \mu, \alpha, \beta)$	$R(\alpha\beta \mid \mu, \alpha, \beta)$	$R(\alpha\beta \mid \mu, \alpha, \beta)$

You should be careful when using reduction notation with less-than-full-rank models. If no restrictions had been specified on the model for the two-way structure above, then $R(\alpha \mid \mu, \beta, \alpha\beta)=0$ because the columns of the $\mathbf{X}$ matrix corresponding to the α_i would be linearly dependent on the columns corresponding to μ and the $\alpha\beta_{ij}$.

In addition, the dependence of reduction notation on the restrictions imposed cannot be overemphasized. For example, imposing the restriction

$$\alpha_2 = \beta_3 = \alpha\beta_{21} = \alpha\beta_{22} = \alpha\beta_{13} = \alpha\beta_{23} = 0 \qquad (4.2)$$

results in a different value for $R(\alpha \mid \mu, \beta, \alpha\beta)$. Although the restrictions of equation 4.1 are those that correspond to the sums of squares computed by PROC GLM, the restrictions of equation 4.2 are those that correspond to the (biased) parameter estimates computed by PROC GLM.

There is a relationship between the four types of sums of squares and four types of data structures in a two-way classification. The relationship derives from the principles of adjustment that the sums of squares types obey. Letting n_{ij} denote the number of observations in level i of factor A and level j of factor B, the four types of data structures are listed below:

□ equal cell frequencies: n_{ij}=common value for all i, j

□ proportionate cell frequencies: $n_{ij}/n_{il}=n_{kj}/n_{kl}$ for all i, j, k, l

□ disproportionate, nonzero cell frequencies: $n_{ij}/n_{il} \neq n_{kj}/n_{kl}$ for some i, j, k, l, but $n_{ij}>0$ for all i, j

□ empty cell(s): $n_{ij}=0$ for some i, j.

The display below shows the relationship between sums of squares types and data structure types pertaining to the following MODEL statement:

```
model y=a b a*b / ss1 ss2 ss3 ss4;
```

For example, writing III=IV indicates that Type III is equal to Type IV.

	Data Structure Type			
	1	2	3	4
	(Equal n_{ij})	(Proportionate n_{ij})	(Disproportionate, nonzero n_{ij})	(Empty Cell)
A	I=II=III=IV	I=II, III=IV	III=IV	
B	I=II=III=IV	I=II, III=IV	I=II, III=IV	I=II
A*B	I=II=III=IV	I=II=III=IV	I=II=III=IV	I=II=III=IV

4.3.4 Interpreting Sums of Squares in μ-Model Notation

The μ model for the two-way structure takes the form

$$y_{ijk} = \mu_{ij} + \varepsilon_{ijk} \quad . \qquad (4.3)$$

The parameters of the μ model relate to the parameters of the standard analysis-of-variance model according to the equation

$$\mu_{ij} = \mu + \alpha_i + \beta_j + \alpha\beta_{ij} \quad .$$

This relation holds regardless of any restriction that may be imposed upon the α, β, and $\alpha\beta$ parameters. The advantage of using μ-model notation over standard analysis-of-variance notation is that all of the μ_{ij} parameters are clearly defined without specifying restrictions; thus, a hypothesis stated in terms of the μ_{ij} can be easily understood.

Speed, Hocking, and Hackney (1978) give interpretations of the different types of sums of squares (I, II, III, and IV) computed by PROC GLM using μ-model notation. It is assumed that all $n_{ij} > 0$, making Type III equal to Type IV.

Using their results, the sums of squares obtained from the following MODEL statement are expressed in terms of the μ_{ij}, as given in Table 4.1.

```
model response = a b a*b / ss1 ss2 ss3 ss4;
```

Table 4.1
Interpretation of Sums of Squares in μ-Model Notation

Type	Effect
	Effect A
I	$(\Sigma_j n_{1j}\mu_{1j}) / n_{1.} = \ldots = (\Sigma_j n_{aj}\mu_{aj}) / n_{a.}$
II	$\Sigma_j n_{1j}\mu_{1j} = \Sigma_i \Sigma_j (n_{1j}n_{ij}\mu_{ij} / n_{.j}), \ldots, \Sigma_j n_{aj}\mu_{aj}$ $= \Sigma_i \Sigma_j (n_{aj}n_{ij}\mu_{ij} / n_{.j})$
III & IV	$\mu_{11} + \ldots + \mu_{1b} = \ldots = \mu_{a1} + \ldots + \mu_{ab}$
	that is, $\overline{\mu}_{1.} = \ldots = \overline{\mu}_{a.}$
	where $\overline{\mu}_{i.} = \Sigma_j \mu_{ij} / b$
	Effect B
I & II	$\Sigma_i n_{i1}\mu_{i1} = \Sigma_i \Sigma_j (n_{i1}n_{ij}\mu_{ij} / n_{i.}, \ldots, \Sigma_i n_{ib}\mu_{ib} = \Sigma_i \Sigma_j (n_{ib}n_{ij}\mu_{ij}) / n_{i.})$
III & IV	$\mu_{11} + \ldots + \mu_{a1} = \ldots \mu_{1b} + \ldots + \mu_{ab}$
	that is, $\overline{\mu}_{.1} = \ldots = \overline{\mu}_{.b}$
	where $\overline{\mu}_{ij} = \Sigma_i \mu_{ij} / a$
	Effect A*B
I, II, III, IV	$\mu_{ij} - \mu_{im} - \mu_{lj} + \mu_{lm} = 0$ for all i, j, l, m

Table 4.1 shows that the tests can be expressed in terms of equalities of weighted cell means, only some of which are easily interpretable. Considering the Type I A effect, the weights $n_{ij}/n_{i.}$ attached to μ_{ij} are simply the fraction of the $n_{i.}$ observations in level i of A that were in level j of B. If these weights reflect the distribution across the levels of B in the population of units in level i of A, then the Type I test may have meaningful interpretation. That is, suppose the population of units in level i of A is made up of a fraction ρ_{i1} of units in level 1 of B, of a fraction ρ_{i2} of units in level 2 of B, and so on, where $\rho_{i1} + \ldots + \rho_{ib} = 1$. Then it may be reasonable to test

$$H_0: \Sigma_j \rho_{1j}\mu_{1j} = \ldots = \Sigma_j \rho_{aj}\mu_{aj}$$

which would be the Type I test in case $n_{ij}/n_{i.} = \rho_{ij.}$.

Practical interpretation of the Type II weights is more difficult; refer to "Interpreting Sums of Squares Using Estimable Functions" later in this chapter. Recall that the Type II tests are primarily for main effects with no interaction. You can see from Table 4.1 that the Type II hypothesis clearly depends on the n_{ij}, the numbers of observations in the cells.

The interpretation of Type III and Type IV tests is clear because all weights are unity. When the hypotheses are stated in terms of the μ-model, the benefit of the Type III test is more apparent because the Type III hypothesis does not depend on the n_{ij}, the numbers of observations in the cells. Type I and Type II hypotheses do depend on the n_{ij}, and this may not be desirable.

For example, suppose a scientist sets up an experiment with ten plants in each combination of four levels of nitrogen (N) and three levels of lime (P). Suppose also that some plants die in some of the cells for reasons unrelated to the effects of N and P, leaving some cells with $n_{ij} < 10$. An hypothesis test concerning the effects of N and P, which depends on the values of n_{ij}, would be contaminated by the accidental variation in the n_{ij}. The scientific method declares that the hypotheses to be tested should be stated before data are collected. It would be impossible to state Type I and Type II hypotheses prior to data collection because the hypotheses depend on the n_{ij}, which are known only after data are collected.

Note that the Type I and Type II hypotheses are different for effect A but the same for effect B. This occurs because the Type I sums of squares are model-order dependent. Being sequential, the Type I sums of squares are A (unadjusted), B (adjusted for A), and A*B (adjusted for A and B). Thus, the Type I sums of squares for the effects A and B listed in the MODEL statement in the order A, B, A*B would not be the same as in the order B, A, A*B. The Type II hypotheses are not model-order dependent because for the two-way structure, both Type II main-effect sums of squares are adjusted for each other, that is, A (adjusted for B), B (adjusted for A), and A*B (adjusted for A and B). These Type II sums of squares are the partial sums of squares if no A*B interaction is specified in the model, in which case Type II, Type III, and Type IV would be the same.

Another interpretation of these tests is given by Hocking and Speed (1980), who point out that Type I, Type II, and Type III=Type IV tests for effect A each represent a test of

$$H_0: \mu_{11} + \ldots + \mu_{1b} = \ldots = \mu_{a1} + \ldots + \mu_{ab}$$

subject to certain conditions on the cell means. The conditions are

Type I	no B effect, $\mu_{.1} = \ldots = \mu_{.k}$, and no A*B effect, $\mu_{ij} - \mu_{im} - \mu_{lj} + \mu_{lm} = 0$ for all i, j, l, m
Type II	no A*B effect, $\mu_{ij} - \mu_{im} - \mu_{lj} + \mu_{lm} = 0$ for all i, j, l, m
Type III=Type IV	none (provided $n_{ij} > 0$ for all ij).

4.3.5 Example of Unbalanced Two-Way Classification

This example is a two-factor layout with data presented by Harvey (1975). Two types of feed rations (variable A) are given to calves from three different sires (variable B). The observed dependent variable y_{ijk} (variable Y) is the coded amount of weight gained by each calf. Because unequal numbers of calves of each sire are fed each ration, this is an unbalanced experiment. However, there are observations for each ration-sire combination; that is, there are no empty cells. The data appear in Output 4.7.

Output 4.7
Data for
Unbalanced
Two-Way
Classification

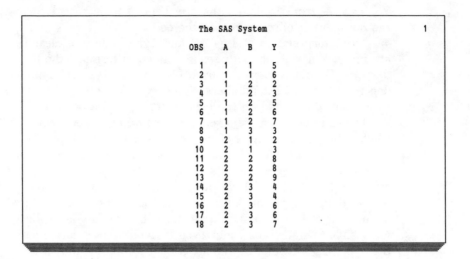

```
                              The SAS System                              1

                        OBS    A    B    Y

                         1     1    1    5
                         2     1    1    6
                         3     1    2    2
                         4     1    2    3
                         5     1    2    5
                         6     1    2    6
                         7     1    2    7
                         8     1    3    3
                         9     2    1    2
                        10     2    1    3
                        11     2    2    8
                        12     2    2    8
                        13     2    2    9
                        14     2    3    4
                        15     2    3    4
                        16     2    3    6
                        17     2    3    6
                        18     2    3    7
```

The analysis-of-variance model for these data is

$$y_{ijk} = \mu + \alpha_i + \beta_j + \alpha\beta_{ij} + \varepsilon_{ijk}$$

where

i equals 1, 2.

j equals 1, 2, 3.

i and j have elements as defined in Section 4.3.1, "General Considerations," earlier in this chapter. The model contains twelve parameters, which are more than can be estimated uniquely by the six cell means that are the basis for estimating parameters. The analysis is implemented with the following SAS statements:

```
proc glm;
   class a b;
   model y=a b a*b / ss1 ss2 ss3 ss4 solution;
```

The statements above cause PROC GLM to create the following 12 dummy variables:

□   1 dummy variable for the mean (or intercept)

□   2 dummy variables for factor A (ration)

□   3 dummy variables for factor B (sire)

□   6 dummy variables for the interaction A*B (all six possible pairwise products of the variables from factor A with those from factor B).

The options requested are SOLUTION, and, for purposes of illustration, all four types of sums of squares. The results appear in Output 4.8.

Output 4.8
Sums of Squares
for Unbalanced
Two-Way
Classification

```
                              The SAS System                              1
                      General Linear Models Procedure
Dependent Variable: Y
                                Sum of           Mean
Source               DF        Squares         Square    F Value    Pr > F
Model                 5     51.04444444    10.20888889       4.70    0.0131
Error                12     26.06666667     2.17222222
Corrected Total      17     77.11111111
                 R-Square           C.V.        Root MSE              Y Mean
                 0.661960       28.22258       1.4738461           5.2222222
Source               DF      Type I SS    Mean Square    F Value    Pr > F
A                     1     5.13611111     5.13611111       2.36    0.1501
B                     2    15.68286517     7.84143258       3.61    0.0592
A*B                   2    30.22546816    15.11273408       6.96    0.0099
Source               DF     Type II SS    Mean Square    F Value    Pr > F
A                     1     9.70786517     9.70786517       4.47    0.0561
B                     2    15.68286517     7.84143258       3.61    0.0592
A*B                   2    30.22546816    15.11273408       6.96    0.0099
Source               DF    Type III SS    Mean Square    F Value    Pr > F
A                     1     3.59186992     3.59186992       1.65    0.2227
B                     2    21.00074906    10.50037453       4.83    0.0289
A*B                   2    30.22546816    15.11273408       6.96    0.0099
Source               DF     Type IV SS    Mean Square    F Value    Pr > F
A                     1     3.59186992     3.59186992       1.65    0.2227
B                     2    21.00074906    10.50037453       4.83    0.0289
A*B                   2    30.22546816    15.11273408       6.96    0.0099

                                      T for H0:    Pr > |T|    Std Error of
Parameter                Estimate   Parameter=0                  Estimate
INTERCEPT             5.400000000 B        8.19      0.0001      0.65912400
A          1         -2.400000000 B       -1.49      0.1629      1.61451747
           2          0.000000000 B          .          .           .
B          1         -2.900000000 B       -2.35      0.0366      1.23310809
           2          2.933333333 B        2.73      0.0184      1.07634498
           3          0.000000000 B          .          .           .
A*B        1 1        5.400000000 B        2.47      0.0295      2.18606699
           1 2       -1.333333333 B       -0.69      0.5051      1.94040851
           1 3        0.000000000 B          .          .           .
           2 1        0.000000000 B          .          .           .
           2 2        0.000000000 B          .          .           .
           2 3        0.000000000 B          .          .           .
```

```
                                                                          2

                      General Linear Models Procedure

NOTE: The X'X matrix has been found to be singular and a generalized inverse
      was used to solve the normal equations.  Estimates followed by the
      letter 'B' are biased, and are not unique estimators of the parameters.
```

The first portion shows the statistics for the overall model. The overspecification of the model is obvious: the twelve dummy variables generate only six degrees of freedom (five for the terms listed in the MODEL statement plus one for the intercept).

The next portion of the output shows the four types of sums of squares. Note that Types III and IV give identical results. This is because $n_{ij} > 0$ for all i,j.

As noted in Section 4.3.3, "Interpreting Sums of Squares in Reduction Notation," the parameter estimates printed by PROC GLM are a solution to the normal equations corresponding to the restriction in equation 4.2. The same condition applies to the parameter estimates

$$\hat{\alpha}_2 = \hat{\beta}_3 = \widehat{\alpha\beta}_{13} = \widehat{\alpha\beta}_{21} = \widehat{\alpha\beta}_{22} = \widehat{\alpha\beta}_{23} = 0 \quad . \tag{4.4}$$

These values, which now equal 0, appear in Output 4.8.

Section 4.3.4, "Interpreting Sums of Squares in μ-Model Notation," also shows that the parameters of the μ model relate to the parameters of the standard analysis-of-variance model (see equation 4.3). A corresponding relation holds between the respective parameter estimates, namely

$$\bar{y}_{ij} = \hat{\mu}_{ij} = \hat{\mu} + \hat{\alpha}_i + \hat{\beta}_j + \widehat{\alpha\beta}_{ij} \quad . \tag{4.5}$$

Putting equations 4.4 and 4.5 together as shown in the table below gives the interpretation of the parameter estimates printed by PROC GLM. The table below also shows the relationship between means and parameter estimates.

	Sire 1	Sire 2	Sire 3
Ration 1	$\hat{\mu}_{11} = \bar{y}_{11.}$ $= \hat{\mu} + \hat{\alpha}_1 + \hat{\beta}_1 + \widehat{\alpha\beta}_{11}$	$\hat{\mu}_{12} = \bar{y}_{12.}$ $= \hat{\mu} + \hat{\alpha}_1 + \hat{\beta}_2 + \widehat{\alpha\beta}_{12}$	$\hat{\mu}_{13} = \bar{y}_{13.}$ $= \hat{\mu} + \hat{\alpha}_1$
Ration 2	$\hat{\mu}_{21.} = \bar{y}_{21.}$ $= \hat{\mu} + \hat{\beta}_1$	$\hat{\mu}_{22} = \bar{y}_{22.}$ $= \hat{\mu} + \hat{\beta}_2$	$\hat{\mu}_{23} = \bar{y}_{23.}$ $= \hat{\mu}$

Note especially the following items in Output 4.8:

1. The intercept $\hat{\mu}$ printed by PROC GLM is the cell mean $\bar{y}_{23.}$ for the lower right-hand cell (ration 2, sire 3).

2. The estimate $\hat{\alpha}_1 = -2.4$ is the difference between the cell means for the two rations fed to sire 3, $\hat{\alpha}_1 = \bar{y}_{13.} - \bar{y}_{23.}$.

3. The interaction parameter estimate $\widehat{\alpha\beta}_{11} = 5.4$ is the interaction of ration 1 and ration 2 by sire 1 and sire 3, $\widehat{\alpha\beta}_{11} = \bar{y}_{11.} - \bar{y}_{13.} - \bar{y}_{21.} + \bar{y}_{23.}$. Generally, in a two-way layout with a rows and b columns, the interaction parameter estimates $\alpha\beta_{ij}$ and measures the interaction of rows i and a by columns j and b.

4.3.6 MEANS, LSMEANS, CONTRAST, and ESTIMATE Statements in the Two-Way Layout

The parameter estimates printed by PROC GLM are the result of a computational algorithm and may or may not be the estimates with the greatest practical value. However, there is no single choice of estimates (corresponding to a particular generalized inverse or set of restrictions) that satisfies the requirements of all applications. In most instances, specific estimable functions of these parameter estimates, like the estimates obtained with the LSMEANS, CONTRAST, and ESTIMATE statements, can be used to provide more useful estimates. The

CONTRAST and ESTIMATE statements for balanced data applications are discussed in Chapter 2.

CONTRAST, LSMEANS, and ESTIMATE statements are similar for one- and two-way models, but principles and interpretations become more complex. Consider the results from the following SAS statements:

```
proc glm;
   class a b;
   model y=a b a*b;
   means a b;
   lsmeans a b / stderr;
   contrast 'A EFFECT' a -1 1;
   contrast 'B 1 vs 2 & 3' b -2 1 1;
   contrast 'B 2 vs 3' b 0 -1 1;
   contrast 'ALL B' b -2 1 1, b 0 -1 1;
   contrast 'A*B 2 vs 3' a*b 0 1 -1 0 -1 1;
   estimate 'B2, B3 MEAN' intercept 1 a .5 .5 b 0 .5 .5
                                    a*b 0 .25 .25 0 .25 .25;
   estimate 'A in B1' a -1 1 a*b -1 0 0 1;
```

The MEANS statement provides the raw or unadjusted main-effect and interaction means. The LSMEANS statement produces least-squares (adjusted) means for main effects together with their standard errors. The results of these two statements are combined in Output 4.9. (PROC GLM prints these results on separate pages.)

Output 4.9
Results of the MEANS and LSMEANS Statements for Two-Way Classification

```
                          The SAS System                        1

                  General Linear Models Procedure
                     Class Level Information

                  Class     Levels     Values

                    A          2        1 2

                    B          3        1 2 3


          Number of observations in data set = 18
```

```
                                                                2

                  General Linear Models Procedure

          Level of        --------------Y--------------
          A          N       Mean            SD

          1          8    4.62500000      1.76776695
          2         10    5.70000000      2.35937845

          Level of        --------------Y--------------
          B          N       Mean            SD

          1          4    4.00000000      1.82574186
          2          8    6.00000000      2.50713268
          3          6    5.00000000      1.54919334
```

(continued on next page)

(continued from previous page)

```
                                                                    3

                     General Linear Models Procedure
                          Least Squares Means

           A          Y          Std Err      Pr > |T|
                    LSMEAN       LSMEAN      H0:LSMEAN=0

           1      4.36666667    0.64055339     0.0001
           2      5.41111111    0.49940294     0.0001




           B          Y          Std Err      Pr > |T|
                    LSMEAN       LSMEAN      H0:LSMEAN=0

           1      4.00000000    0.73692303     0.0002
           2      6.46666667    0.53817249     0.0001
           3      4.20000000    0.80725874     0.0002
```

The raw and least-squares means are different for all levels except B1, which is balanced with respect to factor A.

Quantities estimated by the raw means and least-squares means can be expressed in terms of the μ model. For level 1 of factor A, the raw mean (4.625) is an estimate of $(2\mu_{11}+5\mu_{12}+\mu_{13})/(2+5+1)$, whereas the least-squares mean (4.367) is an estimate of $(\mu_{11}+\mu_{12}+\mu_{13})/3$. The raw means estimate weighted averages of the μ_{ij} whose weights are a function of sample sizes. The least-squares means estimate unweighted averages of the μ_{ij}.

The results of the five CONTRAST statements appear in Output 4.10.

Output 4.10
Contrast in
Two-Way
Classification

```
                                                                    1
                          The SAS System

                   General Linear Models Procedure
                       Class Level Information

              Class      Levels     Values

              A             2       1 2

              B             3       1 2 3


      Number of observations in data set = 18
```

```
                                                                    2

                   General Linear Models Procedure

   Dependent Variable: Y
                                   Sum of        Mean
   Contrast              DF     Contrast SS    Mean Square   F Value   Pr > F

   A EFFECT               1      3.59186992    3.59186992     1.65     0.2227
   B 1 vs 2 & 3           1      4.96124031    4.96124031     2.28     0.1566
   B 2 vs 3               1     11.85641026   11.85641026     5.46     0.0376
   ALL B                  2     21.00074906   10.50037453     4.83     0.0289
   A*B 2 vs 3             1      1.02564103    1.02564103     0.47     0.5051
```

The first four CONTRAST statements are similar to those presented for the one-way structure. Note that when a contrast uses all available degrees of freedom for the factor (such as the ALL B contrast), the sums of squares are the same as the Type III sums of squares for the factor.

The fifth CONTRAST statement requests the interaction between the factor A contrast and the B2 vs 3 contrast. It is constructed by computing the product of corresponding main-effect contrasts for each AB treatment combination. The procedure is illustrated in the table below:

Construction of Interaction Contrast

Level of Factor A	Factor A Contrast	Level of Factor B		
		1	2	3
		Factor B Contrast		
		0	1	−1
1	1	0	1	−1
2	−1	0	−1	1

Main-effect contrasts are given on the top and left, and interaction contrasts (products of marginal entries) are given in the body of the table. These are inserted into the CONTRAST statement in the same order of interaction cells as indicated by the CLASS statement (levels of B within levels of A).

In terms of the μ model, the hypothesis tested by the F statistic for this interaction contrast is

$$H_0: \mu_{12} - \mu_{13} - \mu_{22} + \mu_{23} = 0 \quad .$$

The two ESTIMATE statements request estimates of linear functions of the model parameters. The first function to be estimated is the average of the cell means for levels 2 and 3 of factor B. The other statement requests an estimate of the effect of factor A within level 1 of factor B, or an estimate of $\mu_{21} - \mu_{11}$. Output 4.11 summarizes results from the ESTIMATE statements.

Output 4.11
Parameter
Estimates in
Two-Way
Classification

```
                        The SAS System                        1

                 General Linear Models Procedure
                    Class Level Information

                  Class    Levels    Values

                   A          2      1 2

                   B          3      1 2 3

           Number of observations in data set = 18
```

(continued on next page)

(continued from previous page)

```
                                            T for H0:    Pr > |T|    Std Error of      2
   Parameter               Estimate       Parameter=0                 Estimate

   B2, B3 MEAN            5.33333333          10.99       0.0001      0.48510213
   A in B1              -3.00000000          -2.04       0.0645      1.47384606
```

Expressing each comparison in terms of model parameters α_i, β_j, $\alpha\beta_{ij}$ is the key to filling in the coefficients of the CONTRAST and ESTIMATE statements. Consider the ESTIMATE 'A in B1' statement, which is used to estimate $\mu_{21} - \mu_{11}$. Writing this expression as a function of the model parameters by substituting

$$\mu_{ij} = \alpha_i + \beta_j + \alpha\beta_{ij}$$

yields

$$\mu_{21} - \mu_{11} = -\alpha_1 + \alpha_2 - \alpha\beta_{11} + \alpha\beta_{21} \quad .$$

The $-\alpha_1 + \alpha_2$ term tells you to insert A -1 1 into the ESTIMATE statement. There are no βs in the function, so no B expression appears in the ESTIMATE statement. The $-\alpha\beta_{11} + \alpha\beta_{21}$ term tells you to insert A*B -1 0 0 1 0 0, or, equivalently, A*B -1 0 0 1 into the ESTIMATE statement. The ordering in the statement

```
   class a b;
```

specifies that the ordering of the coefficients following A*B corresponds to $\alpha\beta_{11}$ $\alpha\beta_{12}$ $\alpha\beta_{13}$ $\alpha\beta_{21}$ $\alpha\beta_{22}$ $\alpha\beta_{23}$. The SAS statement

```
   class b a;
```

would indicate an ordering that corresponds to $\alpha\beta_{11}$ $\alpha\beta_{21}$ $\alpha\beta_{12}$ $\alpha\beta_{22}$ $\alpha\beta_{13}$ $\alpha\beta_{23}$.

Now consider the CONTRAST 'A' statement. The hypothesis to be tested is

$$H_0: -(\mu_{11} + \mu_{12} + \mu_{13})/3 + (\mu_{21} + \mu_{22} + \mu_{23})/3 = 0 \quad .$$

Substituting $\mu_{ij} + \alpha_i + \beta_j + \alpha\beta_{ij}$ gives the equivalent hypothesis:

$$H_0: -\alpha_1 + \alpha_2 - (\alpha\beta_{11} + \alpha\beta_{12} + \alpha\beta_{13})/3$$
$$+ (\alpha\beta_{21} + \alpha\beta_{22} + \alpha\beta_{23})/3 = 0 \quad .$$

Again the $-\alpha_1 + \alpha_2$ term in the function tells you to insert A -1 1. This brings up an important usage note: specifying A -1 1 causes the coefficients of the A*B interaction term to be automatically included by PROC GLM. That is, the SAS statement

```
   contrast 'A' a -1 1;
```

is equivalent to the statement

```
contrast 'A' a -1 1 a*b -.333333 -.333333 -.333333
                       .333333 .333333 .333333;
```

Similarly, the SAS statement

```
estimate 'A EFFECT' a -1 1;
```

provides an estimate of

$$-(\mu_{11} + \mu_{12} + \mu_{13}) / 3 + (\mu_{21} + \mu_{22} + \mu_{23}) / 3$$

without explicitly specifying the coefficients of the $\alpha\beta_{ij}$ terms. However, you should note that specifying the $\alpha\beta_{ij}$ coefficients does not cause PROC GLM to automatically include coefficients for the α_is or β_js. For example, the term A$-$1 1 must appear in the ESTIMATE 'A in B1' statement. Similarly, a contrast to test H$_0$: $-\mu_{11}+\mu_{21}=0$ requires the following statement:

```
contrast 'A in B1' a -1 1 a*b -1 0 0 1;
```

The A $-$1 1 term must be included.

4.3.7 Estimable Functions for Two-Way Classification

The previous section discusses the application of the CONTRAST statement, which employs the concept of estimable functions. PROC GLM can display the construction of estimable functions as an optional request in MODEL, LSMEANS, CONTRAST, and ESTIMATE statements. This section discusses the construction of estimable functions and their relation to the sums of squares and associated hypotheses available in the GLM procedure, and to CONTRAST, ESTIMATE, and LSMEANS statements. The presentation of estimable functions consists of results obtained using the unbalanced factorial data given in Output 4.7. For more thorough discussions of these principles, see Graybill (1976) and Searle (1971).

General Form of Estimable Functions

The general form of estimable functions is a vector of elements that are the building blocks for generating specific estimable functions. The number of unique symbols in the vector represents the maximum number of linearly independent coefficients estimated by the model, which is equal to the rank of the $X'X$ matrix. In the GLM procedure this is obtained by the E option in the MODEL statement:

```
proc glm;
   class a b;
   model y=a b a*b / e solution;
```

Table 4.2 gives the vector of coefficients of the general form of estimable functions for our example. There are only six elements (L1, L2, L4, L5, L7, L8), which correspond to the number of degrees of freedom in the model (including the intercept). The number of elements for an effect corresponds to the degrees of freedom for that effect; for example, L4 and L5 are introduced opposite the effect B, indicating B has 2 degrees of freedom.

Table 4.2
General Form of
Estimable
Functions

Effect			Parameters *	Coefficients
Intercept			μ	L1
A	1		α_1	L2
	2		α_2	L1 − L2
B	1		β_1	L4
	2		β_2	L5
	3		β_3	L1 − L4 − L5
A*B	1	1	$\alpha\beta_{11}$	L7
	1	2	$\alpha\beta_{12}$	L8
	1	3	$\alpha\beta_{13}$	L2 − L7 − L8
	2	1	$\alpha\beta_{21}$	L4 − L7
	2	2	$\alpha\beta_{22}$	L5 − L8
	2	3	$\alpha\beta_{23}$	L1 − L2 − L4 − L5 + L7 + L8

* These are implied by the output but not printed in this manner.

According to Table 4.2, any estimable function **Lβ** must be of the form

$$\begin{aligned}
\mathbf{L\beta} = {}& L1\mu + L2\alpha_1 + (L1-L2)\alpha_2 + L4\alpha\beta_1 + L5\beta_2 + (L1 - L_4-L5)\beta_3 \\
& + L7\alpha\beta_{11} + L8\alpha\beta_{12} + (L2-L7-L8)\alpha\beta_{13} + (L4-L7)\alpha\beta_{21} \\
& + (L5-L8)\alpha\beta_{22} + (L1-L2-L4-L5 + L7 + L8)\alpha\beta_{23}
\end{aligned} \tag{4.6}$$

for some specific values of L1 through L8. The various tests in PROC GLM test hypotheses of the form H_0: **Lβ**=0.

Coefficients for any specific estimable function are constructed by assigning values to the individual Ls. For example, setting L2=1 and all others equal to 0 provides the estimable function $\alpha_1 - \alpha_2 + \alpha\beta_{13} - \alpha\beta_{23}$. It is clear, however, that no estimable function can be constructed in this manner to equal α_1 or α_2 individually. That is, no matter what values you choose for L1 through L8, you cannot make **Lβ**=α_1 or **Lβ**=α_2. This is because α_1 and α_2 are nonestimable functions; without additional restrictions there is no linear function of the data whose expected value is α_1 or α_2.

Interpreting Sums of Squares Using Estimable Functions

The coefficients required to construct estimable functions for each effect in the MODEL statement are available for any type of sum of squares requested as an option in the MODEL statement. For example,

```
model y = a b a*b / e e1 e2 e3;
```

will provide the general form, the coefficients of estimable functions for Types I, II, and III, and the corresponding sums of squares for each effect listed in the MODEL statement.

Table 4.3 gives the coefficients of the Type I, Type II, and Type III estimable functions associated with factor A. Types III and IV are identical for this example because all $n_{ij} > 0$.

Table 4.3
Estimable Functions for Factor A

Effect			Type I Parameters	Type II Coefficients	Type III Coefficients
Intercept			0	0	0
A	1		L2	L2	L2
	2		−L2	−L2	−L2
B	1		0.05*L2	0	0
	2		0.325*L2	0	0
	3		−0.375*L2	0	0
A*B	1	1	0.25*L2	0.2697*L2	0.3333*L2
	1	2	0.625*L2	0.5056*L2	0.3333*L2
	1	3	0.125*L2	0.2247*L2	0.3333*L2
	2	1	−0.2*L2	−0.2697*L2	−0.3333*L2
	2	2	−0.3*L2	−0.5056*L2	−0.3333*L2
	2	3	−0.5*L2	−0.2247*L2	−0.3333*L2

All coefficients involve only one element (L2), since the A effect has only 1 degree of freedom. Estimable functions are constructed by assigning specific values to the elements. For factor A, with only one variable, the best choice is $L2 = 1$. Application to the Type I coefficients generates the estimable function

$$\mathbf{L\beta} = \alpha_1 - \alpha_2$$
$$+ 0.05\beta_1 + 0.325\beta_2 - 0.375\beta_2$$
$$+ 0.25\alpha\beta_{11} + 0.625 \, \alpha\beta_{12} + 0.125\alpha\beta_{13}$$
$$- 0.2\alpha\beta_{21} - 0.3\alpha\beta_{22} - 0.5\alpha\beta_{23} \quad .$$

Thus, using the Type I sum of squares in the numerator of an F statistic tests the hypothesis $\mathbf{L\beta} = 0$ for this particular $\mathbf{L\beta}$. In addition to $\alpha_1 - \alpha_2$, this $\mathbf{L\beta}$ also involves the function of coefficients of factor B

$$0.05\beta_1 + 0.325\beta_2 - 0.375\beta_3$$

as well as a function of the interaction parameters. Actually, this is to be expected, since the Type I function for A is unadjusted: it is based on the difference between the two A factor means $(\bar{y}_{1..} - \bar{y}_{2..})$.

As explained in Section 4.3.1, the mean for A is

$$\bar{y}_{1..} = 1/8[(2\bar{y}_{11.} + 5 \, \bar{y}_{12.} + \bar{y}_{13.})] \quad .$$

Each cell mean $\bar{y}_{ij.}$ is an estimate of the function $\mu + \alpha_{ii} + \beta_j + \alpha\beta_{ij}$. Omitting for this discussion the interaction parameters, $\bar{y}_{1..}$ is an estimate of

$$1/8\ [2(\mu + \alpha_1 + \beta_1)\ +\ 5\ (\mu + \alpha_1 + \beta_2)\ +\ (\mu + \alpha_1 + \beta_3)]$$
$$=\ \mu\ +\ \alpha_1\ +\ (0.25\beta_1\ +\ 0.625\beta_2\ +\ 0.125\beta_3)\quad.$$

Likewise $\bar{y}_{2..}$ is an estimate of

$$\mu\ +\ \alpha_2\ +\ (0.2\beta_1\ +\ 0.3\beta_2\ +\ 0.5\beta_3)\quad.$$

Hence, $(\bar{y}_{1..} - \bar{y}_{2..})$ is an estimate of

$$\alpha_1\ -\ \alpha_2\ +\ 0.05\beta_1\ +\ 0.325\beta_2\ -\ 0.375\beta_3$$

which is the function provided by Type I.

The coefficients associated with A*B provide the coefficients of the interaction terms in the Type I estimable functions. The coefficients associated with A*B are useful for expressing the estimable functions and interpreting the tests in terms of the μ model. Recall that

$$\mu_{ij}\ =\ \mu\ +\ \alpha_i\ +\ \beta_j\ +\ \alpha\beta_{ij}\quad.$$

A little algebra shows that any estimable $\mathbf{L\beta}$ with coefficients as given in Table 4.3 can also be written as

$$\mathbf{L\beta} = L7\mu_{11} + L8\mu_{12} + (L2 - L7 - L8)\mu_{13} + (L4 - L7)\mu_{21}$$
$$+\ (L5 - L8)\mu_{22} + (L1 - L2 - L4 - L5 + L8)\mu_{23}\quad. \tag{4.7}$$

This is easily verified by starting with $\mathbf{L\beta}$ in equation 4.7 above, replacing each μ_{ij} with $\mu + \alpha_i + \beta_j + \alpha\beta_{ij}$, and combining terms to end up with the original expression for $\mathbf{L\beta}$ in equation 4.6. For example, after factoring out L2, we see that the Type I estimable function for A is

$$\mathbf{L\beta} = L2(0.25\mu_{11} + 0.625\mu_{12} + 0.125\mu_{13} - 0.2\mu_{21} - 0.3\mu_{22} - 0.5\mu_{23})\quad.$$

Thus the Type I F test for A tests the hypothesis H_0: $\mathbf{L\beta}=0$, or equivalently,

$$H_0\text{: } 0.25\ \mu_{11} + 0.625\mu_{12} + 0.125\mu_{12} = 0.2\mu_{21} + 0.3\mu_{22} + 0.5\mu_{23}\quad.$$

This is the hypothesis that is tested in Table 4.1. Since the coefficients are functions of the frequencies of the cells, the hypothesis might not be particularly useful.

Applying the same method to the Type II coefficients for A, we have, after setting L2=1,

$$\mathbf{L\beta} = .2697\mu_{11} + .5056\mu_{12} + .2247\mu_{13} - .2697\mu_{21} - .5056\mu_{22} - .2247\mu_{23}$$
$$=\ .2697(\mu_{11} - \mu_{21})\ +\ .5056(\mu_{12} - \mu_{22})\ +\ .2247(\mu_{13} - \mu_{23})\quad.$$

This expression sheds some light on the meaning of the Type II coefficients. Recall that the Type II SS are based on a main-effects model. With no interaction we have, for example, $\mu_{11}-\mu_{21}=\mu_{12}-\mu_{22}=\mu_{13}-\mu_{23}$. Let Δ denote the common value of these differences. The Type II coefficients are the coefficients of the best linear unbiased estimate $\hat{\Delta}$ of Δ given by

$$\hat{\Delta} = \Sigma w_j \, (\bar{y}_{1j.} - \bar{y}_{2j.})$$

where

$$w_j = \frac{n_{1j}n_{2j} / (n_{1j} + n_{2j})}{\Sigma_k(n_{1k}n_{2k} / (n_{1k} + n_{2k}))} \quad .$$

For example,

$$.2697 = \frac{(2)(2) / (2 + 2)}{(2)(2) / (2 + 2) \; + (5)(3) / (5 + 3) + (1)(5) / (1 + 5)}$$

Note that these are functions of cell frequencies and thus do not necessarily generate meaningful hypotheses.

Type III (and Type IV) estimable functions for A likewise (Table 4.2) do not involve the parameters of the B factor. Further, in terms of the parameters of the cell means (μ model)

$$\mathbf{L}\boldsymbol{\beta} = 1/3(\mu_{11} + \mu_{12} + \mu_{13}) - 1/3(\mu_{21} + \mu_{22} + \mu_{23}) \quad .$$

Thus the Type III F statistic tests $H_0: \bar{\mu}_{1.} = \bar{\mu}_{2.}$ as stated in Table 4.1. Note again that this hypothesis does not involve the cell frequencies, n_{1j}.

Table 4.3 gives the coefficients of estimable functions for factor B. There are 2 degrees of freedom for factor B, thus two elements, L4 and L5. Consider first the Type III coefficients because they are more straightforward. The Type III F test for factor B is testing simultaneously that any two linearly independent functions are equal to 0; functions are obtained by selecting two choices of values for L4 and L5.

The simplest choices are to take L4=1, L5=0 and L4=0, L5=1. This gives the estimable functions

$$\mathbf{L}_1\boldsymbol{\beta} = \beta_1 - \beta_3 + (\alpha\beta_{11} - \alpha\beta_{13} + \alpha\beta_{21} - \alpha\beta_{23}) \, / \, 2$$

and

$$\mathbf{L}_2\boldsymbol{\beta} = \beta_2 - \beta_3 + (\alpha\beta_{12} - \alpha\beta_{13} + \alpha\beta_{22} - \alpha\beta_{23}) \, / \, 2 \quad .$$

In terms of the μ model, this gives

$$\mathbf{L}_1\boldsymbol{\beta} = (\mu_{11} - \mu_{13} + \mu_{21} - \mu_{23}) \, / \, 2$$

and

$$\mathbf{L}_2\boldsymbol{\beta} = (\mu_{12} - \mu_{13} + \mu_{22} - \mu_{23}) \, / \, 2 \quad .$$

Thus, the Type III F statistic tests

$$H_0: \bar{\mu}_{.1} = \bar{\mu}_{.3} \quad \text{and} \quad \bar{\mu}_{.2} = \bar{\mu}_{.3}$$

or, in equivalent form

$$H_0: \overline{\mu}_{.1} = \overline{\mu}_{.2} = \overline{\mu}_{.3} \quad . \tag{4.8}$$

Another set of choices is L4=1, L5=−1 and L4=L5=1. These lead to

$$H_0: \overline{\mu}_{.1} = \overline{\mu}_{.2} \text{ and } (\overline{\mu}_{.1} + \overline{\mu}_{.2}) / 2 = \overline{\mu}_{.3}$$

which is also equivalent to equation 4.8 above. Therefore, both sets of choices lead to the same H_0. It is significant that the H_0 in equation 4.8 is independent of cell frequencies and, thus, is desirable for the usual case where cell frequencies are unrelated to the effects of the factors. Table 4.4 gives the coefficients of the Type I & Type II and Type III & Type IV estimable functions associated with factor B.

Table 4.4
Estimable
Functions for
Factor B

Effect			Type I & Type II Coefficients	Type III & Type IV Coefficients
Intercept			0	0
A	1		0	0
	2		0	0
B	1		L4	L4
	2		L5	L5
	3		−L4 − L5	−L4 − L5
A*B	1	1	0.401*L4 − 0.1236*L5	0.5*L4
	1	2	−0.1685*L4 + 0.3933*L5	0.5*L5
	1	3	−0.2416*L4 − 0.2697*L5	−0.5*L4 − 0.5*L5
	2	1	0.5899*L4 + 0.1236*L5	0.5*L4
	2	2	0.1685*L4 + 0.6067*L5	0.5*L5
	2	3	−0.7584*L4 − 0.7303*L5	−0.5*L4 − 0.5*L5

Recall that since B followed A in the MODEL statement, the Type I SS for B is the same as the Type II SS for B. The coefficients are again a function of the cell frequencies. The nature of the function is not easy to determine but is similar to the Type II coefficients for factor A (see Table 4.1).

As a matter of computational interest, the Type II estimable functions for B are equal to the Type III estimable functions if there is no interaction. For then $\alpha\beta_{ij}=0$, and Table 4.4 shows that the coefficients for α_i and β_j are the same for Types II and III. This is not to say that the Type II SS and Type III SS will be equal, but rather that they give tests of the same hypothesis when there is no interaction. If, indeed, there is no interaction, then the Type II F test is more powerful than the Type III F test. The assumption of no interaction is, however, probably rarely satisfied in nature.

Table 4.5
Estimable Functions for A*B

Effect		Coefficients for All Types
Intercept		0
A	1	0
	2	0
B	1	0
	2	0
	3	0
A*B	1	L7
	1	L8
	1	−L7−L8
	2	−L7
	2	−L8
	2	L7 + L8

Table 4.5 gives the coefficients of the estimable function for the A*B interaction and, again, two elements are available. In this case all types of effects give the same results, since for each type the interaction effects are adjusted for all other effects. The estimable functions can be readily interpreted if the coefficients are recorded in the 2×3 cell format implied by the factorial array. For example, let L7=−1 and L8=0; the resulting function can be illustrated as follows:

		B		
		1	2	3
A	1	−1	0	+1
	2	+1	0	−1

This is the interaction in the 2×2 subtable consisting of the columns for B1 and B3, or the interaction of the contrast $(\alpha_1 - \alpha_2)$ with the contrast $(\beta_1 - \beta_2)$.

Estimating Estimable Functions

Estimates of estimable functions can be obtained by multiplying the vector of coefficients by the vector of parameter estimates using the SOLUTION option. For example, letting L2=1 in Table 4.3 for Type I results in the vector

$$\mathbf{L} = (0 \ 1 \ -1 \ .05 \ .325 \ -.375 \ .25 \ .625 \ .125 \ -.2 \ -.3 \ -.5) \ .$$

The vector of parameter estimates (see Output 4.7) is

$$\hat{\boldsymbol{\beta}} = (5.4 \ -2.4 \ .0 \ -2.9 \ 2.933 \ .0 \ 5.4 \ -1.333 \ .0 \ .0 \ .0 \ .0) \ .$$

The estimate $\mathbf{L}\hat{\boldsymbol{\beta}} = -1.075$ is equal to $\bar{y}_{1..} - \bar{y}_{2..}$, the unadjusted treatment difference. Likewise, using the Type III coefficients gives an estimate of -1.044, which is the difference between the two least-squares means of the A factor (see Table 4.8).

Variances of these estimates can be obtained by the standard formula for the variance of a linear function. The estimated variance of the estimates is $s^2(\mathbf{L}\,(\mathbf{X'X})^{-}\mathbf{L'})$, where s^2, the estimated error variance, is the residual mean square from the overall analysis of variance, and $(\mathbf{X'X})^{-}$ is the generalized inverse of the $\mathbf{X'X}$ matrix generated by the dummy variables. The square root of this variance provides the standard error of the estimated function; hence, a t test is readily constructed.

Since LSMEANS, CONTRAST, and ESTIMATE statements offer methods of estimating and testing most desired functions, the preceding technique is seldom employed. However, if these statements produce functions that are nonestimable, the generation of estimates from scratch may provide otherwise unobtainable estimates.

Interpreting LSMEANS, CONTRAST, and ESTIMATE Results Using Estimable Functions

Sometimes it may be useful to examine the construction of estimable functions associated with the LSMEANS, CONTRAST, and ESTIMATE statements. Information on the construction of these functions is available by specifying E as one of the options in the statement. (Don't confuse this with the E=*effect* option, which specifies an alternate error term.) Output 4.12 shows the results from the E option:

```
proc glm;
   class a b;
   model y=a b a*b / solution;
   contrast 'B 2 vs 3' b 0 -1 1 / e;
   estimate 'A in B1' a -1 1 a*b -1 0 0 1 / e;
   lsmeans a / stderr e;
```

Output 4.12
Estimable
Functions for
LSMEANS,
CONTRAST, and
ESTIMATE
Statements

```
                        The SAS System                        1

                  General Linear Models Procedure

    Coefficients for contrast B 2 vs 3


                                            Row  1

    INTERCEPT                                  0

    A        1                                 0
             2                                 0

    B        1                                 0
             2                                -1
             3                                 1

    A*B      1 1                               0
             1 2                              -0.5
             1 3                               0.5
             2 1                               0
             2 2                              -0.5
             2 3                               0.5
```

The hypothesis tested by the CONTRAST statement is

$$H_0: -\beta_2 + \beta_3 - .5\alpha\beta_{12} + .5\alpha\beta_{13} - .5\alpha\beta_{22} + .5\alpha\beta_{23} = 0$$

or in the μ-model notation

$$-.5\mu_{12} + .5\mu_{13} - .5\mu_{22} + .5\mu_{23} \quad .$$

Note that the coefficients of the interaction effects are supplied by the procedure.

```
                                                                2
                        General Linear Models Procedure

        Coefficients for estimate A in B1


                                                     Row   1

        INTERCEPT                                         0

        A         1                                      -1
                  2                                       1

        B         1                                       0
                  2                                       0
                  3                                       0

        A*B       1 1                                    -1
                  1 2                                     0
                  1 3                                     0
                  2 1                                     1
                  2 2                                     0
                  2 3                                     0
```

The function estimated by the ESTIMATE statement is

$$\mathbf{L\beta} = -\alpha_1 + \alpha_2 - \alpha\beta_{11} + \alpha\beta_{21}$$

or in μ-model notation

$$\mathbf{L\beta} = -\mu_{11} + \mu_{21} \quad .$$

```
                                                                    3

                        General Linear Models Procedure
                             Least Squares Means
                     Coefficients for A Least Square Means


  A                                          1            2

  Effect                              Coefficients

  INTERCEPT                                  1            1

  A        1                                 1            0
           2                                 0            1

  B        1                         0.3333333333  0.3333333333
           2                         0.3333333333  0.3333333333
           3                         0.3333333333  0.3333333333

  A*B      1 1                       0.3333333333            0
           1 2                       0.3333333333            0
           1 3                       0.3333333333            0
           2 1                                 0  0.3333333333
           2 2                                 0  0.3333333333
           2 3                                 0  0.3333333333
```

The least-squares means for A1 estimates is

$$\mu + \alpha_1 + (\beta_1 + \beta_2 + \beta_3 + \alpha\beta_{11} + \alpha\beta_{12} + \alpha\beta_{13}) / 3$$

or, in μ-model notation

$$(\mu_{11} + \mu_{12} + \mu_{13}) / 3 \quad .$$

4.3.8 Empty Cells

Analyzing multifactor data with empty (or missing) cells often gives results of questionable value, since the data contain insufficient information to estimate the parameters of the model. (See Freund (1980) for a discussion of this problem.) The absence of data in one or more cells makes it very difficult to establish guidelines for imposing restrictions or generating appropriate estimable functions. PROC GLM helps investigate alternate estimable functions for such analyses, but no packaged program, including PROC GLM, provides a single best solution for all situations.

The problem of empty cells is illustrated by deleting the A=1, B=3 cell from the 2×3 factorial data in Output 4.7.

Table 4.6 gives the general form of estimable functions, showing that the data with the empty cells generate only five parameters. This is because there are only five cells with data, so that only five (linearly independent) parameters are estimable.

For this example, only the Type III and Type IV estimable functions will be discussed. The following statements are used:

```
proc glm;
  class a b;
  model y=a b a*b / e3 e4 solution;
  lsmeans a b / e stderr;
```

Table 4.6
General Form of Estimable Functions

Effect			Coefficients
Intercept			L1
A	1		L2
	2		L1 − L2
B	1		L4
	2		L5
	3		L1 − L4 − L5
A*B	1	1	L7
	1	2	L2 − L7
	2	1	L4 − L7
	2	2	−L2 + L5 + L7
	2	3	L1 − L4 − L5

The coefficients of the functions for the A effect appear in Table 4.7. Type III and Type IV are identical for A, since A has only two levels.

Table 4.7
Estimable Functions for Factor A

Effect			Type III & Type IV Coefficients
Intercept	1		0
A	1		L2
	2		−L2
B	1		0
	2		0
	3		0
A*B	1	1	0.5*L2
	1	2	0.5*L2
	2	1	−0.5*L2
	2	2	−0.5*L2
	2	3	0

As in a classification with complete data, Type III and Type IV functions for A do not involve the parameters of factor B. Setting L2=1 shows that the A effect is equal to

$$\mathbf{L\beta} = .5(\mu_{11} + \mu_{12}) - .5(\mu_{21} + \mu_{22}) \quad .$$

This is shown in this two-way, μ-model diagram:

$$
\begin{array}{c c c c c}
 & & \multicolumn{3}{c}{B} \\
 & & 1 & 2 & 3 \\
\hline
 & 1 & .5 & .5 & . \\
A & & \multicolumn{3}{c}{\rule{3cm}{0.4pt}} \\
 & 2 & -.5 & -.5 & 0 \\
\end{array}
$$

No information from the A_2B_3 cell is used, since there is no matching data from the A_1B_3 cell.

Table 4.8 gives the Type III and Type IV coefficients associated with the B factor. (Notice that there are no coefficients for μ, α_1, and α_2.)

Table 4.8
Estimable Functions for Factor B

Effect			Type III Coefficients	Type IV Coefficients
Intercept			0	0
A	1		0	0
	2		0	0
B	1		L4	L4
	2		L5	L5
	3		−L4 − L5	−L4 − L5
A*B	1	1	0.25*L4 − 0.25*L5	0
	1	2	−0.25*L4 + 0.25*L5	0
	2	1	0.75*L4 + 0.25*L5	L4
	2	2	0.25*L4 + 0.75*L5	L5
	2	3	−L4 − L5	−L4 − L5

First, consider the Type III coefficients. A set of two estimable functions tested with the Type III F statistic for B can be obtained by setting $L4=1$, $L5=0$ and $L4=0$, $L5=1$, which test H_0: $(\beta_1-\beta_3=0)$ and $(\beta_2-\beta_3=0)$, respectively. The coefficients of the cell means in terms of the μ model are shown in the diagram:

$$
\begin{array}{c c c c c c c c}
 & \multicolumn{3}{c}{(L4 = 1,\ L5 = 0)} & & \multicolumn{3}{c}{(L4 = 0,\ L5 = 1)} \\
 & .25 & -.25 & & & -.25 & .25 & \\
\text{Type III}\quad A & \multicolumn{3}{c}{\rule{3cm}{0.4pt}} & A & \multicolumn{3}{c}{\rule{3cm}{0.4pt}} \\
 & .75 & .25 & -1.0 & & .25 & .75 & -1.0 \\
\end{array}
$$

The choices $L4=1$, $L5=0$ and $L4=0$, $L5=1$ did not result in very appealing comparisons, since they involve cell means from levels of B that are not part of the desired hypotheses. Therefore, make another selection. Taking $L4=1$, $L5=1$ and $L4=1$, $L5=-1$, more interesting coefficients result.

	(L4 = 1, L5 = 1)				(L4 = 1, L5 = −1)		
Type III A	0	0		A	.5	−.5	
	1	1	−2		.5	−.5	0

The hypothesis being tested is

$$H_0: \mu_{21} + \mu_{22} - 2\mu_{23} = 0 \quad \text{and} \quad .5(\mu_{11} + \mu_{21} - \mu_{12} - \mu_{22}) = 0$$

or equivalently

$$H_0: .5(\mu_{21} + \mu_{22}) = \mu_{23} \quad \text{and} \quad \bar{\mu}_{.1} = \bar{\mu}_{.2} \ .$$

Thus, the Type III F test for B simultaneously compares B3 with the average of B1 and B2 within the level of A that has complete data and compares B1 with B2 averaged across the levels of A. Remember that the first selection of coefficients ($L4=1$, $L5=0$ and $L4=0$, $L5=1$) provides an equivalent H_0; it is just more difficult to understand.

For the same Type III test with no missing cells, the Type III hypothesis for B is

$$H_0: \bar{\mu}_{.1} = \bar{\mu}_{.2} = \bar{\mu}_{.3}$$

or equivalently

$$H_0: \bar{\mu}_{.1} = \bar{\mu}_{..}, \quad \bar{\mu}_{.2} = \bar{\mu}_{..}, \quad \bar{\mu}_{.3} = \bar{\mu}_{..} \ .$$

For the example with the empty A_1B_3 cell, the parameter μ_{13} is not estimable unless further conditions are imposed. (If there are no data from a population, the mean of that population cannot be estimated unless some relationship between this mean and other means is established.) The Type III hypothesis is equivalent to

$$H_0: \mu_{.1} = \mu_{.2} = \mu_{.3}$$

subject to $\mu_{13} = .5(\mu_{11} + \mu_{12})$.

Now consider the Type IV coefficients. Taking $L4=1$, $L5=0$ and $L4=0$, $L5=1$ results in the diagram

	(L4 = 1, L5 = 0)				(L4 = 0, L5 = 1)		
Type IV A	0	0		A	0	0	
	1	0	−1		0	1	−1

Thus, the Type IV H_0 is clearly different from the Type III H_0, because the Type IV H_0 does not involve the means in level 1 of A, namely μ_{11} and μ_{12}, even though there are data in these cells.

Output 4.13 shows that Type III and Type IV sums of squares are indeed different (Type III SS = 16.073, Type IV SS = 41.733).

Output 4.13
Comparison of the Type III and Type IV Sums of Squares with Empty Cells

```
                        The SAS System                          1

                 General Linear Models Procedure
                    Class Level Information

                 Class     Levels    Values

                 A            2       1 2

                 B            3       1 2 3


            Number of observations in data set = 17
```

```
                                                                2
                  General Linear Models Procedure

  Dependent Variable: Y
                               Sum of          Mean
  Source            DF         Squares        Square    F Value   Pr > F

  Model              4       45.81568627   11.45392157    5.27    0.0110

  Error             12       26.06666667    2.17222222

  Corrected Total   16       71.88235294

               R-Square          C.V.        Root MSE          Y Mean

               0.637370       27.53339      1.4738461        5.3529412


  Source            DF      Type III SS    Mean Square   F Value   Pr > F

  A                  1       0.35072464     0.35072464     0.16    0.6949
  B                  2      16.07330642     8.03665321     3.70    0.0560
  A*B                1      29.56811594    29.56811594    13.61    0.0031

  Source            DF      Type IV SS     Mean Square   F Value   Pr > F

  A                 1*       0.35072464     0.35072464     0.16    0.6949
  B                 2*      41.73333333    20.86666667     9.61    0.0032
  A*B                1      29.56811594    29.56811594    13.61    0.0031

  * NOTE: Other Type IV Testable Hypotheses exist which may yield different SS.



                                        T for H0:   Pr > |T|   Std Error of
  Parameter               Estimate    Parameter=0              Estimate

  INTERCEPT            5.400000000 B      8.19      0.0001      0.65912400
  A         1         -3.733333333 B     -3.47      0.0046      1.07634498
            2          0.000000000 B        .          .           .
  B         1         -2.900000000 B     -2.35      0.0366      1.23310809
            2          2.933333333 B      2.73      0.0184      1.07634498
            3          0.000000000 B        .          .           .
  A*B      1 1         6.733333333 B      3.69      0.0031      1.82503171
           1 2         0.000000000 B        .          .           .
           2 1         0.000000000 B        .          .           .
           2 2         0.000000000 B        .          .           .
           2 3         0.000000000 B        .          .           .

  NOTE: The X'X matrix has been found to be singular and a generalized inverse
        was used to solve the normal equations.  Estimates followed by the
        letter 'B' are biased, and are not unique estimators of the parameters.
```

The message in Output 4.13,

```
*NOTE: Other Type IV Testable Hypotheses exist which may yield different SS.
```

is a warning that the Type IV estimable functions (and consequently the associated hypotheses and sums of squares) are not unique. This refers to the phenomenon that Type IV estimable functions depend on the location of the empty cell.

Suppose, for example, that the values of the levels of B are changed, say, from B=1 to B=9, B=2 to B=8, and B=3 to B=7. Since PROC GLM sorts on the levels, the first and third columns are interchanged, placing the empty cell in the upper-left-hand corner. An examination of the estimable functions (which involve all cells that contain data) reveals these coefficients:

		B					B	
	7	8	9			7	8	9
Type IV A		0	0		A		.5	−.5
	1	0	−1			0	.5	−.5
	old	old	old			old	old	old
	B=3	B=2	B=1			B=3	B=2	B=1

Now we repeat the analysis with the missing cells placed in all possible locations. Note that the data are not changed. The same data are missing, only subscripts are changed to locate the missing cell in a different position.

The partitioning of the sums of squares from these analyses is given in the first two columns of Table 4.8. Two items are of interest:

□ the Type III and Type IV sums of squares always give identical results for the sum of squares due to the A factor

□ the Type IV sums of squares due to B depend on the location of the missing cell with respect to the B factor and are never the same as the Type III sums of squares.

The right-hand portion of Table 4.8 gives estimates of functions whose analogs with no missing data would be B1 vs B3 and B2 vs B3, obtained by taking L4=1, L5=0 and L4=0, L5=1 from the table. Estimates of the A effects are not given since they are not affected by changing the location of the missing cell. Note that the Type III and Type IV estimates disagree even in some cases when the function does not involve the missing cell. When the missing cell is in the last level of B, they always differ, in which case the Type IV function uses only information in rows not containing the empty cell.

Table 4.9 gives the estimable function for the interaction effect. Since there is only one degree of freedom, there is one function, involving only the complete portion of the factorial structure.

Table 4.9   Sums of Squares and Estimates for B Effect

Location of Missing Cell	Sums of Squares Type IV		B1 vs B3 (L4=1, L5=0) Type IV				B2 vs B3 (L4=0, L5=1) Type IV			
	A	B	Basis			Estimate	Basis			Estimate
1,3	.351	41.733	0	0		−2.900	0	0		2.933
			1	0	−1		1	0	−1	
2,3	.351	41.733	0	0		−2900	0	0		2.933
			1	0	−1		0	1	−1	
1,1	.351	23.386	.5	−.5		.467	0	0		2.933
			.5	+.5	−1		0	1	−1	
2,1	.351	23.386	.5	−.5		.467	0	0		2.933
			.5	.5	−1		0	1	−1	
1,2	.351	18.978	0	0		−2.900	−.5	.5		−4.33
			1	0	−1		.5	.5	−1	
2,2	.351	23.286	.5	−.5		.467	0	0		2.933
			.5	.5	−1		0	1	−1	
All Type III	.351	16.073	.25	−.25	x	−1.217	−.25	.25	x	1.250
			.75	.25	−1		.25	.75	−1	

Table 4.10
Estimable Functions for A*B

Effect			All Types Coefficients
Intercept			0
A	1		0
	2		0
B	1		0
	2		0
	3		0
A*B	1	1	L7
	1	2	−L7
	2	1	−L7
	2	2	L7
	2	3	0

Now consider these CONTRAST, ESTIMATE, and LSMEANS statements used on the data with an empty A_1B_3 cell:

```
proc glm;
  class a b;
  model y=a b a*b;
  contrast 'B 2 vs 3' b 0 -1 1 / e;
  estimate 'A in B1' a -1 1 a*b -1 0 1 / e;
  lsmeans a / stderr e;
```

The estimable functions resulting from the E option appear in Output 4.14.

Output 4.14
Estimable Functions for CONTRAST, ESTIMATE, and LSMEANS Statements

```
                              The SAS System                              1

                     General Linear Models Procedure
                        Class Level Information

             Class     Levels     Values

             A              2     1 2

             B              3     1 2 3


        Number of observations in data set = 17
```

```
                                                                          2

                     General Linear Models Procedure

        Coefficients for contrast B 2 vs 3


                                          Row   1

        INTERCEPT                                0

        A         1                              0
                  2                              0

        B         1                              0
                  2                             -1
                  3                              1

        A*B       1 1                            0
                  1 2                           -0.5
                  2 1                            0
                  2 2                           -0.5
                  2 3                            1
```

(continued on next page)

(continued from previous page)

```
                                                                           3

                        General Linear Models Procedure

Coefficients for estimate A in B1


                                                    Row  1

INTERCEPT                                             0

A          1                                         -1
           2                                          1

B          1                                          0
           2                                          0
           3                                          0

A*B        1 1                                       -1
           1 2                                        0
           2 1                                        1
           2 2                                        0
           2 3                                        0
```

```
                                                                           4

                        General Linear Models Procedure
                             Least Squares Means
                      Coefficients for A Least Square Means


A                                              1              2

Effect                                  Coefficients

INTERCEPT                                       1              1

A          1                                    1              0
           2                                    0              1

B          1                           0.3333333333   0.3333333333
           2                           0.3333333333   0.3333333333
           3                           0.3333333333   0.3333333333

A*B        1 1                                0.5              0
           1 2                                0.5              0
           2 1                                  0    0.3333333333
           2 2                                  0    0.3333333333
           2 3                                  0    0.3333333333
```

Output 4.15
Output from
ESTIMATE and
LSMEANS
Statements

```
                            The SAS System                                 1

                     General Linear Models Procedure
                          Least Squares Means

            A          Y          Std Err      Pr > |T|
                     LSMEAN       LSMEAN     H0:LSMEAN=0

            1       Non-est
            2     5.41111111    0.49940294      0.0001


                                       T for H0:    Pr > |T|    Std Error of
Parameter                  Estimate   Parameter=0               Estimate

A in B1                  -3.00000000      -2.04      0.0645     1.47384606
```

The function specified by the CONTRAST statement 'B2 vs 3' is designated nonestimable in the SAS log (not shown) because it involves level 3 of B, which contained the empty cell. Therefore, no statistical computation is printed. A more technical reason for the nonestimable CONTRAST function is ascertainable from the coefficients printed in Output 4.14. They show that the function is

$$\mathbf{L\beta} = -\beta_2 + \beta_3 - .5\alpha\beta_{12} - .5\alpha\beta_{22} + \alpha\beta_{23} \quad .$$

In order for a function $\mathbf{L\beta}$ to be estimable, it must be equal to a linear function of the μ_{ij}. This is equivalent to the condition that the coefficients of the μ_{ij} are equal to the corresponding coefficients of $\alpha\beta_{ij}$ in $\mathbf{L\beta}$. Thus, the condition for the $\mathbf{L\beta}$ in the CONTRAST statement to be estimable is that $\mathbf{L\beta}$ is equal to

$$-.5\mu_{12} - .5\mu_{22} + \mu_{23} \quad .$$

But

$$-.5\mu_{12} - .5\mu_{22} + \mu_{23} = -.5\alpha_1 + .5\alpha_2 +$$
$$[-\beta_2 + \beta_3 - .5\alpha\beta_{12} - .5\alpha\beta_{22} + \alpha\beta_{23}]$$

which contains α_2 and is thus not the same function as $\mathbf{L\beta}$.

Compare the estimable functions in Output 4.14 with those in Output 4.12 to see further effects of the empty cell. Later in this section, you see that this CONTRAST statement does produce an estimable function if no interaction is specified in the model.

The function specified in the ESTIMATE statement is estimable because it involves only cells that contain data; namely A_1B_1 and A_2B_1 (see Output 4.14). From the printed coefficients in Output 4.14, the function is evidently

$$-\alpha_1 + \alpha_2 - \alpha\beta_{11} + \alpha\beta_{21} \quad .$$

In terms of the μ model the function is

$$-\mu_{11} + \mu_{21}$$

and is therefore estimable because it is expressible as a linear function of the μ_{ij} for cells containing data.

Caution is required in using the ESTIMATE or CONTRAST statements with empty cells. Compare the ESTIMATE statements that produced Output 4.12 and Output 4.14. If we used the ESTIMATE statement that produced Output 4.12 with a data set that had the A_1B_3 cell empty, the following nonestimable function would result:

Table 4.11
Coefficients
Produced by the
ESTIMATE
Statement

Effect			Coefficients
Intercept			0
A	1		−1
	2		1
B	1		0
	2		0
	3		0
A*B	1	1	−1
	1	2	0
	2	1	0
	2	2	1
	2	3	0

That is, specifying A*B −1 0 0 1 places the −1 as a coefficient on $\alpha\beta_{22}$ instead of $\alpha\beta_{21}$ as desired. When interaction parameters are involved, it is necessary to know the location of the empty cells if you are using the ESTIMATE statement.

The estimable functions from the LSMEANS statement show the least-squares mean for A1 to be nonestimable and the least-squares mean for A2 to be estimable. The principles involved are the same as those already discussed with respect to the CONTRAST and ESTIMATE statements.

To illustrate the computations, consider the estimability of functions produced by CONTRAST, ESTIMATE, and LSMEANS statements in the context of a MODEL statement that contains no interaction:

```
proc glm;
   class a b;
   model y=a b / solution ss1 ss2 ss3 ss4;
   contrast 'B 2 vs 3' b 0 -1 1 / e;
   estimate 'A EFFECT' a -1 1 / e;
   lsmeans a / e;
```

Partial results appear in Output 4.16. None of the functions are nonestimable even though the A_1B_3 cell has no data. This is because the functions involve only the parameters in the model

$$Y_{ijk} = \mu + \alpha_i + \beta_j + \varepsilon_{ijk}$$

under which the means ($\mu_{ij}=\mu+\alpha_i+\beta_j$) are all estimable, even μ_{13}. Any linear function of the μ_{ij} is estimable, and all the functions in Output 4.16 are linear functions of the μ_{ij}. For example, the A1 least-squares mean is

$$\mathbf{L\beta} = \mu + \alpha_1 + .3333(\beta_1 + \beta_2 + \beta_3)$$
$$= .3333(3\mu + 3\alpha_1 + \beta_1 + \beta_2 + \beta_3)$$
$$= .3333(\mu_{11} + \mu_{12} + \mu_{13}) \quad .$$

Output 4.16
Coefficients with Empty Cell and No Interaction

```
                              The SAS System                          1

                       General Linear Models Procedure
                          Class Level Information

                      Class    Levels    Values

                      A           2      1 2

                      B           3      1 2 3


                  Number of observations in data set = 17
```

```
                                                                      2



                       General Linear Models Procedure

        Coefficients for contrast B 2 vs 3


                                                     Row   1

        INTERCEPT                                       0

        A        1                                      0
                 2                                      0

        B        1                                      0
                 2                                     -1
                 3                                      1
```

```
                                                                      3



                       General Linear Models Procedure

        Coefficients for estimate A EFFECT


                                                     Row   1

        INTERCEPT                                       0

        A        1                                     -1
                 2                                      1

        B        1                                      0
                 2                                      0
                 3                                      0
```

(continued on next page)

(continued from previous page)

```
                                                                        4

                        General Linear Models Procedure
                             Least Squares Means
                      Coefficients for A Least Square Means


   A                                            1           2

   Effect                            Coefficients

   INTERCEPT                                     1           1

   A          1                                  1           0
              2                                  0           1

   B          1                     0.3333333333  0.3333333333
              2                     0.3333333333  0.3333333333
              3                     0.3333333333  0.3333333333
```

Table 4.12 summarizes results of the CONTRAST, ESTIMATE, and LSMEANS statements.

Table 4.12
Summary of
Results from
CONTRAST,
ESTIMATE, and
LSMEANS Output
for Two-Way
Layout with Empty
Cell and No
Interaction

Contrast	DF	SS	F	Pr>F
B2 vs 3	1	4.68597211	1.09	0.3144

Parameter	Estimate	T for H_0 Parameter$=0$	Pr> | T |	STD Error of Estimate
A	-1.39130435	-1.14	0.2747	1.22006396

Least-Squares Means

A	Y LSMEAN	Std Err LSMEAN	Pr > | T | H_0: LSMEAN$=0$
1	4.26376812	0.92460046	0.0005
2	5.65507246	0.69479997	0.0001

Understanding the results from an analysis with empty cells is admittedly difficult, another reminder that the existence of empty cells precludes a universally correct analysis. The problem is that empty cells leave a gap in the data and make it difficult to estimate interactions and to adjust for interaction effects. If the interaction is not requested, the empty cell causes fewer problems. Of course, the analysis is incorrect if the interaction is present in the data.

For situations that require analyses including interaction effects, the GLM procedure does not claim to always have the *correct* answer, but it does provide information about the nature of the estimates and allows the experimenter to decide whether these results have any real meaning.

4.4 Proper Error Terms

Previous sections in this chapter have been concerned with fixed-effect models, in which all parameters are measures of the effects of given levels of the factors. For such models, *F* tests of hypotheses on those parameters use the residual mean square in the denominator. In some models, however, one or more terms represent a random variable that measures the effect of a random sample of levels of the corresponding factor. Such terms are called random effects; models containing random effects only are called *random models*, whereas models containing both random and fixed effects are called *mixed models*. (See Steel and Torrie (1980), especially Sections 7.5 and 16.6.)

For situations in which the proper error term is known by the construction of the design, PROC GLM provides the TEST statement, which is identical to the TEST statement available in PROC ANOVA (see Section 3.5.1, "A Standard Split-Plot Experiment"). PROC GLM also allows specification of appropriate error terms in MEANS, LSMEANS, and CONTRAST statements. For situations that are not clear-cut (such as unbalanced data), PROC GLM gives a set of expected mean squares that can be used to indicate proper error variances for tests that must usually be computed by hand. A different error term can be specified with the DUNCAN option and other multiple comparison options in the MEANS statement and in the CONTRAST statement. To illustrate the use of these specifications, consider a variation of the split-plot design (see Section 3.5, "Split-Plot Experiments") involving the effect on yield of different irrigation treatments and cultivars.

Irrigation treatments are more easily applied to larger areas (main plots), whereas different cultivars may be planted in smaller areas (subplots). In this example, consider three irrigation treatments (IRRIG) assigned in a completely random manner to nine main-plot units (REPS). REPS are each split into two subplots, and two cultivars (CULT), **A** and **B**, are randomly assigned to the subplots.

The appropriate partitioning of sums of squares is

Source	DF
IRRIG	2
REPS in IRRIG	6
CULT	1
IRRIG*CULT	2
ERROR	6
TOTAL	17

The proper error term for irrigation is REPS within IRRIG because the REPS are the experimental units for the IRRIG factor. The other effects are tested by ERROR (which is actually CULT*REPS in IRRIG). Data for the irrigation experiment appear in Output 4.17.

Output 4.17
Data for Split-Plot Experiment

```
                       The SAS System                          1

           OBS    IRRIG    REPS    CULT    YIELD

            1       1       1       A       1.6
            2       1       1       B       3.3
            3       1       2       A       3.4
            4       1       2       B       4.7
            5       1       3       A       3.2
            6       1       3       B       5.6
            7       2       1       A       2.6
            8       2       1       B       5.1
            9       2       2       A       4.6
           10       2       2       B       1.1
           11       2       3       A       5.1
           12       2       3       B       6.2
           13       3       1       A       4.7
           14       3       1       B       6.8
           15       3       2       A       5.5
           16       3       2       B       6.6
           17       3       3       A       5.7
           18       3       3       B       4.5
```

The analysis is implemented as follows:

```
proc glm;
   class irrig reps cult;
   model yield=irrig reps(irrig)
         cult irrig*cult;
   test h=irrig e=reps(irrig);
   contrast 'IRRIG 1 vs IRRIG 2' irrig 1 -1 / e=reps(irrig);
```

Note the use of the nested effect in the MODEL statement (See Section 3.2, "Nested Classifications").

The TEST statement requests that the IRRIG effect be tested against the REP within the IRRIG mean square.

The CONTRAST statement requests a comparison of the means for irrigation methods 1 and 2. The appropriate error mean square for testing the contrast is REPS(IRRIG) for the same reason that this was the appropriate error term for testing the IRRIG factor. The results appear in Output 4.18.

Output 4.18
F Tests with Correct Denominators

```
                       The SAS System                          1

                General Linear Models Procedure
                   Class Level Information

            Class    Levels    Values

            IRRIG       3       1 2 3

            REPS        3       1 2 3

            CULT        2       A B

         Number of observations in data set = 18
```

```
                                                                    2
                         General Linear Models Procedure

Dependent Variable: YIELD
                                      Sum of            Mean
Source                    DF         Squares          Square    F Value    Pr > F

Model                     11      31.91611111      2.90146465      1.34    0.3766

Error                      6      13.02666667      2.17111111

Corrected Total           17      44.94277778

                 R-Square              C.V.        Root MSE           YIELD Mean

                 0.710150          33.02919       1.4734691           4.4611111


Source                    DF      Type III SS    Mean Square    F Value    Pr > F

IRRIG                      2      13.06777778     6.53388889       3.01    0.1244
REPS(IRRIG)               6      13.32000000     2.22000000       1.02    0.4896
CULT                      1       3.12500000     3.12500000       1.44    0.2755
IRRIG*CULT                2       2.40333333     1.20166667       0.55    0.6017

Tests of Hypotheses using the Type III MS for REPS(IRRIG) as an error term

Source                    DF      Type III SS    Mean Square    F Value    Pr > F

IRRIG                     2      13.06777778     6.53388889       2.94    0.1286

Tests of Hypotheses using the Type III MS for REPS(IRRIG) as an error term

Contrast                  DF      Contrast SS    Mean Square    F Value    Pr > F

IRRIG 1 vs IRRIG 2         1       0.70083333     0.70083333       0.32    0.5946
```

4.4.1 More On Expected Mean Squares

In all of the examples of fixed models in previous sections, the error term is always the last line of the partitioning of sums of squares. The proper tool for determining appropriate error variances for more complex situations is the set of expected mean squares. Expected mean squares are algebraic expressions specifying the functions of the model parameters that are estimated by the mean squares resulting from partitioning the sums of squares. Generally, these expected mean squares are linear functions of elements that represent

□ the error variance

□ functions of variances of random effects

□ functions of sums of squares and products (quadratic forms) of fixed effects.

The underlying principle of an *F* test on a set of fixed-effect parameters is that the expected mean square for the denominator contains a linear function of variances of random effects, whereas the expected mean square for the numerator contains the same function of these variances plus a quadratic form of the parameters being tested. If no such matching pair of variance functions is available, no proper test exists; however, approximate tests are available.

For fixed models, all mean squares estimate the residual error variance plus a quadratic form (variance) of the parameters in question. Hence, the proper denominator for all tests is the error term. Expected mean squares are usually not required for fixed models.

For a mixed model, the expected mean squares are requested by a RANDOM statement in PROC GLM, specifying the model effects that are random.

For the irrigation example, REPS within IRRIG is random. Regarding IRRIG and CULT as fixed effects in the example, a model is

$$y_{ijk} = \mu + \alpha_i + \delta_{ij} + \beta_k + \alpha\beta_{ik} + \varepsilon_{ijk} \tag{4.9}$$

where α_i, β_k, and $\alpha\beta_{ik}$ are the main effect of IRRIG, main effect of CULT, and interaction effect of IRRIG*CULT. The δ_{ij} term is the random effect of REPS within IRRIG.

Use the following SAS statements to obtain an analysis for this model:

```
proc glm;
   class irrig reps cult;
   model yield=irrig reps(irrig) cult cult*irrig / ss3;
   contrast 'IRRIG 1 vs IRRIG 2' irrig 1-1 / e=reps(irrig);
   random reps(irrig) / q;
```

The RANDOM statement specifies that REPS(IRRIG) is a random effect. The Q option requests that the coefficients of the quadratic form in the expected mean squares (EMS) are printed. The analysis of variance is the same as in Output 4.18.

The expected mean squares appear in Output 4.19.

Output 4.19
Expected Mean
Squares and
Quadratic Forms

```
                              The SAS System                              1

                      General Linear Models Procedure
            Quadratic Forms of Fixed Effects in the Expected Mean Squares

    Source: Type III Mean Square for IRRIG

                        IRRIG 1        IRRIG 2        IRRIG 3       DUMMY010

    IRRIG 1          4.00000000    -2.00000000    -2.00000000     2.00000000
    IRRIG 2         -2.00000000     4.00000000    -2.00000000    -1.00000000
    IRRIG 3         -2.00000000    -2.00000000     4.00000000    -1.00000000
    DUMMY010         2.00000000    -1.00000000    -1.00000000     1.00000000
    DUMMY011         2.00000000    -1.00000000    -1.00000000     1.00000000
    DUMMY012        -1.00000000     2.00000000    -1.00000000    -0.50000000
    DUMMY013        -1.00000000     2.00000000    -1.00000000    -0.50000000
    DUMMY014        -1.00000000    -1.00000000     2.00000000    -0.50000000
    DUMMY015        -1.00000000    -1.00000000     2.00000000    -0.50000000


                        DUMMY011       DUMMY012       DUMMY013       DUMMY014

    IRRIG 1          2.00000000    -1.00000000    -1.00000000    -1.00000000
    IRRIG 2         -1.00000000     2.00000000     2.00000000    -1.00000000
    IRRIG 3         -1.00000000    -1.00000000    -1.00000000     2.00000000
    DUMMY010         1.00000000    -0.50000000    -0.50000000    -0.50000000
    DUMMY011         1.00000000    -0.50000000    -0.50000000    -0.50000000
    DUMMY012        -0.50000000     1.00000000     1.00000000    -0.50000000
    DUMMY013        -0.50000000     1.00000000     1.00000000    -0.50000000
    DUMMY014        -0.50000000    -0.50000000    -0.50000000     1.00000000
    DUMMY015        -0.50000000    -0.50000000    -0.50000000     1.00000000


                        DUMMY015

    IRRIG 1         -1.00000000
    IRRIG 2         -1.00000000
    IRRIG 3          2.00000000
    DUMMY010        -0.50000000
    DUMMY011        -0.50000000
    DUMMY012        -0.50000000
    DUMMY013        -0.50000000
    DUMMY014         1.00000000
    DUMMY015         1.00000000
```

```
                                                                      2
                        General Linear Models Procedure

   Source          Type III Expected Mean Square

   IRRIG           Var(Error) + 2 Var(REPS(IRRIG)) + Q(IRRIG,IRRIG*CULT)

   REPS(IRRIG)     Var(Error) + 2 Var(REPS(IRRIG))

   CULT            Var(Error) + Q(CULT,IRRIG*CULT)

   IRRIG*CULT      Var(Error) + Q(IRRIG*CULT)



   Contrast                 Contrast Expected Mean Square

   IRRIG 1 vs IRRIG 2       Var(Error) + 2 Var(REPS(IRRIG)) + Q(IRRIG,IRRIG*CULT)
```

Because this experiment is completely balanced, all four types of expected mean squares are identical. To illustrate, consider the EMSs for IRRIG. The results in Output 4.19 translate into

$$\sigma_\varepsilon^2 + 2\sigma_\delta^2 + (\text{quadratic form in } \alpha\text{'s and } \alpha\beta\text{s}) / (a - 1)$$

where $\sigma_\varepsilon^2 = V(\varepsilon)$, $\sigma_\delta^2 = V(\delta)$, and $a = $ number of levels of IRRIG. (The $a - 1$ term is not explicitly indicated by PROC GLM.) The quadratic form is a measure of differences among the irrigation means

$$\mu_{i..} = E(\bar{y}_{i..}) = \mu + \alpha_i + \beta_k + \alpha\beta_{ik} .$$

The coefficients appear in Output 4.19. (Although not shown here, the labels DUMMY010-DUMMY015 would be previously indicated in the output to correspond to $\alpha\beta_{11}$, $\alpha\beta_{12}$, $\alpha\beta_{21}$, $\alpha\beta_{22}$, $\alpha\beta_{31}$, and $\alpha\beta_{32}$.) In matrix notation, the quadratic form is $\alpha'A\alpha$, where

$$\mathbf{A} = \begin{bmatrix}
4 & -2 & -2 & 2 & 2 & -1 & -1 & -1 & -1 \\
-2 & 4 & -2 & -1 & -1 & 2 & 2 & -1 & -1 \\
-2 & -2 & 4 & -1 & -1 & -1 & -1 & 2 & 2 \\
2 & -1 & -1 & 1 & 1 & -.5 & -.5 & -.5 & -.5 \\
2 & -1 & -1 & 1 & 1 & -.5 & -.5 & -.5 & -.5 \\
-1 & 2 & -1 & -.5 & -.5 & 1 & 1 & -.5 & -.5 \\
-1 & 2 & -1 & -.5 & -.5 & 1 & 1 & -.5 & -.5 \\
-1 & -1 & 2 & -.5 & -.5 & -.5 & -.5 & 1 & 1 \\
-1 & -1 & 2 & -.5 & -.5 & -.5 & -.5 & 1 & 1
\end{bmatrix}$$

and

$$\alpha' = \alpha_1 \; \alpha_2 \; \alpha_3 \; \alpha\beta_{11} \; \alpha\beta_{12} \; \alpha\beta_{21} \; \alpha\beta_{22} \; \alpha\beta_{31} \; \alpha\beta_{32} \quad .$$

This is the general expression for the quadratic form in which no constraints are assumed on the parameters. In this representation, irrigation mean differences are functions not only of the α_i but also of the $\alpha\beta_{ij}$, that is,

$$\mu_{1..} - \mu_{2..} = \alpha_1 - \alpha_2 + \alpha\beta_{1.} - \alpha\beta_{2.} \quad .$$

Thus, the quadratic form measuring these combined differences involves the $\alpha\beta_{ij}$s. In most texts, these expected mean squares are presented with the constraints $\alpha_1 + \alpha_2 + \alpha_3 = 0$ and $\alpha\beta_{1.} = \alpha\beta_{2.} = \alpha\beta_{3.} = 0$. When these constraints are imposed, the quadratic form reduces to

$$\boldsymbol{\alpha'A\alpha} = 6\alpha_1^2 + 6\alpha_2^2 + 6\alpha_3^2 \quad .$$

To see this, note that the contribution from the first row of $\mathbf{A}$ is

$$\alpha_1(4\alpha_1 - 2\alpha_2 - 2\alpha_3 + 2\alpha\beta_{11} + 2\alpha\beta_{12} - \alpha\beta_{21} - \alpha\beta_{22} - \alpha\beta_{31} - \alpha\beta_{32})$$

$$= \alpha_1(4\alpha_1 + 2(-\alpha_2 - \alpha_3 + 2\alpha\beta_{1.} - \alpha\beta_{2.} - \alpha\beta_{3.})$$

$$= \alpha_1(4\alpha_1 + 2\alpha_1 - 0 - 0 - 0)$$

$$= 6\alpha_1^2 \quad .$$

Similarly, row 2 and row 3 yield $6\alpha_2^2$ and $6\alpha_3^2$, respectively. Row 4 gives

$$\alpha\beta_{11}(2\alpha_1 - \alpha_2 - \alpha_3 + \alpha\beta_{11} + \alpha\beta_{12} - .5\alpha\beta_{21} - .5\alpha\beta_{22} - .5\alpha\beta_{31} - .5\alpha\beta_{32})$$
$$= \alpha\beta_{11}(3\alpha_1)$$

and row 5 gives $\alpha\beta_{12}(3\alpha_1)$. Thus, the sum of rows 4 and 5 is 0. Similarly, the net contribution from rows 6 through 9 is 0.

Under the null hypothesis of no difference between irrigation methods, the expected mean squares for IRRIG becomes $\sigma_\varepsilon^2 + 4\sigma_\delta^2$. But this is the same as the expected mean squares for REPS(IRRIG). Therefore, REPS(IRRIG) is, in fact, the correct denominator in the F test for IRRIG.

Now, view this example as if the irrigation treatments are in a randomized-blocks design instead of a completely random design; that is, assume REPS is crossed with IRRIG rather than nested in IRRIG. If both IRRIG and CULT are fixed effects, then a model is

$$y_{ijk} = \mu + \varphi_j + \alpha_i + \delta_{ij} + \beta_k + \alpha\beta_{ik} + \varepsilon_{ijk} \tag{4.10}$$

where α_i, β_k, $\alpha\beta_{ik}$, and ε_{ijk} have the same meaning as in the model shown in equation 4.9 earlier in this section. The φ_j term is the random block (REPS) effect, with $V(\varphi_j) = \sigma_\rho^2$, and δ_{ij} is the random main-plot error, that is, the random block by irrigation (REP*IRRIG) effect. The model in equation 4.10 is equivalent to model 12.3 of Steel and Torrie (1980, p. 245) with their A=IRRIG and B=CULT. Now it is commonly presumed that any interaction effect must be a random effect if it involves a random main effect. In terms of equation 4.10, this presumption implies that if φ_j is random, then δ_{ij} must be random. However, PROC GLM does not operate under this presumption, and, therefore, both REPS and REPS*IRRIG must be explicitly designated as random in the RANDOM statement in order to obtain expected mean squares corresponding to φ_j and δ_{ij} both as random. In other words, if only REPS appears in the RANDOM statement, then the expected mean squares printed by PROC GLM would correspond to δ_{ij} as a fixed effect.

Output 4.20 contains the expected mean squares resulting from the following statements:

```
proc glm;
   class reps irrig cult;
   model yield=reps irrig reps*irrig cult cult*irrig / ss1;
   random reps reps*irrig;
```

Output 4.20
Expected Mean
Squares for Split
Plot: Fixed
Main-Plot and
Subplot Factors

```
                              The SAS System                          1
                       General Linear Models Procedure

  Source        Type III Expected Mean Square

  REPS          Var(Error) + 2 Var(IRRIG*REPS) + 6 Var(REPS)

  IRRIG         Var(Error) + 2 Var(IRRIG*REPS) + Q(IRRIG,IRRIG*CULT)

  IRRIG*REPS    Var(Error) + 2 Var(IRRIG*REPS)

  CULT          Var(Error) + Q(CULT,IRRIG*CULT)

  IRRIG*CULT    Var(Error) + Q(IRRIG*CULT)
```

The line for IRRIG in the output translates to

$$\delta_\varepsilon^2 + 2\delta_\delta^2 + (\text{quadratic form in } \alpha\text{'s and } \alpha\beta\text{s}) \, / \, 2$$

and, as discussed above, the quadratic form reduces to $6\Sigma_i \alpha_i^2$ if $\Sigma_i \, \alpha_i = \Sigma_i \, \alpha\beta_{ij} = 0$. This matches the expected mean squares given in Steel and Torrie (1980, p. 394) for this design.

Before leaving this example, you should understand one more point concerning the expected mean squares in mixed models. Suppose that CULT is a random effect, but IRRIG remains fixed. Following Steel and Torrie (1980), the table below shows the expected mean squares:

Source	Expected Mean Squares
REPS	$\sigma_\varepsilon^2 + 2\sigma_\gamma^2 + 6\sigma_\rho^2$
IRRIG	$\sigma_\varepsilon^2 + 2\sigma_\gamma^2 + 3(3/2)\sigma_{\alpha\beta}^2 + 6\,\Sigma_i\,\alpha_i^2/2$
Error(A) = REPS*IRRIG	$\sigma_\varepsilon^2 + 2\sigma_\gamma^2$
CULT	$\sigma_\varepsilon^2 + 9\sigma_\beta^2$
CULT*IRRIG	$\sigma_\varepsilon^2 + 3(3/2)\,\sigma_{\alpha\beta}^2$
Error(B)	σ_ε^2

Output 4.21 contains the expected mean squares output from the following statements:

```
proc glm;
    class reps irrig cult;
    model yield=reps irrig reps*irrig cult
                irrig*cult / ss3;
    random reps reps*irrig cult cult*irrig;
```

Output 4.21
Expected Mean
Squares for Split
Plot Design: Fixed
Main-Plot and
Random Subplot
Factors

```
                        The SAS System                        1
                  General Linear Models Procedure

    Source      Type III Expected Mean Square

    REPS        Var(Error) + 2 Var(IRRIG*REPS) + 6 Var(REPS)

    IRRIG       Var(Error) + 3 Var(IRRIG*CULT) + 2 Var(IRRIG*REPS) + Q(IRRIG)

    IRRIG*REPS  Var(Error) + 2 Var(IRRIG*REPS)

    CULT        Var(Error) + 3 Var(IRRIG*CULT) + 9 Var(CULT)

    IRRIG*CULT  Var(Error) + 3 Var(IRRIG*CULT)
```

The only quadratic form for fixed effects is Q(IRRIG) in the IRRIG line, which corresponds to $6\Sigma\alpha_i^2$, assuming $\Sigma\alpha_i=0$. The IRRIG line also contains Var(IRRIG*CULT) and Var(IRRIG*REPS), in agreement with the expected mean squares of Steel and Torrie given above. The lines in the output for REPS, IRRIG*REPS, and IRRIG*CULT also agree with these expected mean squares. However, although the line for CULT in Output 4.21 contains Var(IRRIG*CULT), the expected mean squares given by Steel and Torrie for CULT **B** does not contain $\sigma_{\alpha\beta}^2$. The exclusion by Steel and Torrie is in agreement with the general principle that if U is a fixed effect and V is a random effect, then the expected mean squares for U contains σ_{U*V}^2, but the expected mean squares for V does not contain σ_{U*V}^2.

This principle is an item of controversy among statisticians and relates to formulation and parameterization of the model. Basically, exclusion or inclusion of $\sigma_{\alpha\beta}^2$ in the line for CULT depends on variance and covariance definitions in the model. See Hocking (1973) for a detailed account of modeling ramifications for the two-way mixed model, and refer to Hartley and Searle (1969), who point out that exclusion of $\sigma_{\alpha\beta}^2$ is inconsistent with results commonly reported for the unbalanced case. The PROC GLM output for a two-way mixed model corresponds to the results shown by Hocking for Model III in his Table 2.

Chapter 5 Examples of Special Applications

5.1 *Introduction 199*

5.2 *Confounding in a Factorial Experiment 199*

5.3 *A Balanced Incomplete Blocks Design 203*

5.4 *A Crossover Design to Estimate Residual Effects 205*

5.5 *Experiments with Qualitative and Quantitative Variables 209*

5.6 *Lack-of-Fit Analysis 214*

5.7 *Unbalanced Nested Structure 216*

5.8 *Absorbing Nesting Effects 220*

5.1 Introduction

As already noted, the GLM procedure can be used to analyze a multitude of data structures. In this chapter several applications are presented that utilize tools discussed in the previous chapters. Some of these applications involve statistical topics that are not discussed in great detail in this book. References are given to provide the necessary background information.

5.2 Confounding in a Factorial Experiment

The example for this topic is a 2^3 factorial with factors labeled A, B, and C in blocks of size four. There are three replications with interactions ABC, AC, and BC, confounded with blocks in replications: 1, 2, and 3, respectively.* These factors are thus partially confounded with blocks. The data appear in Output 5.1.

Output 5.1
Data for Two-Cube Factorial in Blocks of Size Four

```
                          The SAS System                                1

      OBS   REP   BLK   A   B   C     Y      CA    CB    CC

       1     1     1    1   1   1    3.99     1     1     1
       2     1     1    1   0   0    1.14     1    -1    -1
       3     1     1    0   1   0    1.52    -1     1    -1
       4     1     1    0   0   1    3.33    -1    -1     1
       5     1     2    1   1   0    2.06     1     1    -1
       6     1     2    1   0   1    5.58     1    -1     1
       7     1     2    0   1   1    2.06    -1     1     1
       8     1     2    0   0   0   -0.17    -1    -1    -1
       9     2     1    1   1   1    3.77     1     1     1
      10     2     1    1   0   1    6.69     1    -1     1

                                        (continued on next page)
```

---

*   Confounding is covered in most textbooks on experimental design (Hicks 1973).

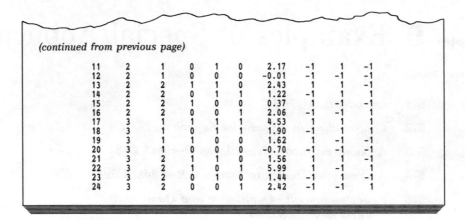

11	2	1	0	1	0	2.17	-1	1	-1
12	2	1	0	0	0	-0.01	-1	-1	-1
13	2	2	1	1	0	2.43	1	1	-1
14	2	2	0	1	1	1.22	-1	1	1
15	2	2	1	0	0	0.37	1	-1	-1
16	2	2	0	0	1	2.06	-1	-1	1
17	3	1	1	1	1	4.53	1	1	1
18	3	1	0	1	1	1.90	-1	1	1
19	3	1	1	0	0	1.62	1	-1	-1
20	3	1	0	0	0	-0.70	-1	-1	-1
21	3	2	1	1	0	1.56	1	1	-1
22	3	2	1	0	1	5.99	1	-1	1
23	3	2	0	1	0	1.44	-1	1	-1
24	3	2	0	0	1	2.42	-1	-1	1

(continued from previous page)

Contrasts corresponding to confounded effects can only be estimated from those replications in which they are not confounded. In this example, they are estimated from only two-thirds of the data; thus their standard errors should be larger by a factor of $\sqrt{3/2}$.

The analysis using PROC GLM is straightforward. You can generate contrasts in the DATA step instead of specifying classes for treatments and using CONTRAST statements, as the following code shows:

```
data confound;
 input rep blk a b c y;
ca= -(a=0) + (a=1);
cb= -(b=0) + (b=1);
cc= -(c=0) + (c=1);
cards;
.
data
.
proc glm;
 classes rep blk;
 model y=rep blk(rep) ca|cb|cc/ solution;
```

The results appear in Output 5.2.

Output 5.2
ANOVA for
Two-Cube
Factorial in Blocks
of Size 4

```
                    The SAS System                        1

              General Linear Models Procedure
                  Class Level Information

          Class     Levels    Values

          REP          3      1 2 3

          BLK          2      1 2


        Number of observations in data set = 24
```

```
                                                                          2

                        General Linear Models Procedure

Dependent Variable: Y
                                   Sum of           Mean
Source                  DF         Squares         Square   F Value   Pr > F

Model                   12     81.74957500     6.81246458     33.60   0.0001

Error                   11      2.23018750     0.20274432

Corrected Total         23     83.97976250

               R-Square            C.V.        Root MSE            Y Mean

               0.973444        18.96878       0.4502714         2.3737500


Source          DF         Type I SS     Mean Square    F Value     Pr > F

REP              2        0.05092500      0.02546250       0.13     0.8832
BLK(REP)         3        7.43221250      2.47740417      12.22     0.0008
CA               1       21.07500417     21.07500417     103.95     0.0001
CB               1        0.00453750      0.00453750       0.02     0.8838
CA*CB            1        1.72270417      1.72270417       8.50     0.0141
CC               1       37.77550417     37.77550417     186.32     0.0001
CA*CC            1        2.31800625      2.31800625      11.43     0.0061
CB*CC            1       11.34005625     11.34005625      55.93     0.0001
CA*CB*CC         1        0.03062500      0.03062500       0.15     0.7049

Source          DF        Type III SS    Mean Square    F Value     Pr > F

REP              2        0.05092500      0.02546250       0.13     0.8832
BLK(REP)         3        1.66755417      0.55585139       2.74     0.0938
CA               1       21.07500417     21.07500417     103.95     0.0001
CB               1        0.00453750      0.00453750       0.02     0.8838
CA*CB            1        1.72270417      1.72270417       8.50     0.0141
CC               1       37.77550417     37.77550417     186.32     0.0001
CA*CC            1        2.31800625      2.31800625      11.43     0.0061
CB*CC            1       11.34005625     11.34005625      55.93     0.0001
CA*CB*CC         1        0.03062500      0.03062500       0.15     0.7049


                                         T for H0:    Pr > |T|   Std Error of
Parameter                  Estimate     Parameter=0                Estimate

INTERCEPT               2.010625000 B       7.99       0.0001      0.25170936
REP         1           0.328125000 B       0.92       0.3764      0.35597078
            2          -0.110000000 B      -0.31       0.7631      0.35597078
            3           0.000000000 B         .          .            .
BLK(REP)  1 1           0.200000000 B       0.51       0.6182      0.38994646
          2 1           0.000000000 B         .          .            .
          1 2           0.873750000 B       2.24       0.0466      0.38994646
          2 2           0.000000000 B         .          .            .
          1 3           0.668750000 B       1.71       0.1143      0.38994646
          2 3           0.000000000 B         .          .            .
CA                      0.937083333        10.20       0.0001      0.09191126
CB                      0.013750000         0.15       0.8838      0.09191126
```

```
                                                                          3

                        General Linear Models Procedure

Dependent Variable: Y

                                         T for H0:    Pr > |T|   Std Error of
Parameter                  Estimate     Parameter=0                Estimate

CA*CB                  -0.267916667        -2.91       0.0141      0.09191126
CC                      1.254583333        13.65       0.0001      0.09191126
CA*CC                   0.380625000         3.38       0.0061      0.11256785
CB*CC                  -0.841875000        -7.48       0.0001      0.11256785
CA*CB*CC               -0.043750000        -0.39       0.7049      0.11256785

NOTE: The X'X matrix has been found to be singular and a generalized inverse
      was used to solve the normal equations.  Estimates followed by the
      letter 'B' are biased, and are not unique estimators of the parameters.
```

Note that the standard errors of the coefficients of the confounded effects (ABC, AC, BC) are indeed larger by $\sqrt{3/2}$ than the coefficients of the effects not confounded. You can verify that the sums of squares of the confounded effects, based on data from the replications in which they are not confounded, are identical to the sums of squares in Output 5.2.

The estimable functions option can be used to indicate the nature of the confounding. Requesting the Type I functions for effects in the same order as in the MODEL statement above gives the effects for BLK(REP) unadjusted for the factorial effects and reveals how the blocks are related to the factorial effects.

Output 5.3
Estimable
Functions for
Two-Cube
Factorial in Blocks
of Size 4

```
                          The SAS System                         1

                  General Linear Models Procedure
                      Class Level Information

                 Class      Levels      Values

                 REP           3        1 2 3

                 BLK           2        1 2


            Number of observations in data set = 24
```

```
                                                                 2

                  General Linear Models Procedure
                Type I Estimable Functions for: BLK(REP)

       Effect             Coefficients

       INTERCEPT          0

       REP        1       0
                  2       0
                  3       0

       BLK(REP)   1 1     L5
                  2 1     -L5
                  1 2     L7
                  2 2     -L7
                  1 3     L9
                  2 3     -L9

       CA                 0

       CB                 0

       CA*CB              0

       CC                 0

       CA*CC              2L7

       CB*CC              2L9

       CA*CB*CC           2L5
```

Output 5.3 gives the non-zero coefficients of BLK(REP). The coefficient L5 appears on the terms for BLKs in REP 1 and also the CA*CB*CC interaction term. This happens because CA*CB*CC is confounded with BLKs in REP 1. This is apparent from the data set shown in Output 5.1. The product CA*CB*CC is equal to 1 for all observations in REP 1 of BLK 1 and CA*CB*CC= −.1 for REP 2 of BLK 1. In some data sets, the confounding pattern is not so obvious. You can discover the confounding pattern from the coefficients for estimable functions.

5.3 A Balanced Incomplete Blocks Design

For the balanced incomplete blocks (BIB) design with four treatments in blocks of size two, six blocks (three replications) are required (Cochran and Cox 1957). The data appear in Output 5.4. The design is shown below:

BIB Design Example Data
(Numbers in parenthesis indicate treatment number)

Block

1	2	3	4	5	6
2.7(1)	7.1(3)	7.1(1)	8.8(2)	9.7(1)	13.0(2)
2.7(2)	8.6(4)	9.7(3)	15.1(4)	17.4(4)	16.6(3)

Output 5.4
Data for Balanced Incomplete Block Design

```
                        The SAS System                        1

              OBS     BLK     TRT       Y

               1       1       1       1.2
               2       1       2       2.7
               3       2       3       7.1
               4       2       4       8.6
               5       3       1       7.1
               6       3       3       9.7
               7       4       2       8.8
               8       4       4      15.1
               9       5       1       9.7
              10       5       4      17.4
              11       6       2      13.0
              12       6       3      16.6
```

Consider the following statements:

```
proc glm;
 class blk trt;
 model y=trt blk / e1 ss3;
 means trt blk;
 lsmeans trt / stderr;
```

The analysis-of-variance portion appears in Output 5.5. The Type I sum of squares is easily seen to be the *unadjusted* treatment sum of squares; Type III is the *adjusted* treatment sum of squares. Table 5.1 shows the estimable functions.

Output 5.5
Analysis of Variance for Balanced Incomplete Block Design

```
                             The SAS System                              1

                      General Linear Models Procedure

Dependent Variable: Y
                                   Sum of         Mean
Source                  DF        Squares       Square    F Value    Pr > F

Model                    8    281.12750000   35.14093750     40.82    0.0056

Error                    3      2.58250000    0.86083333

Corrected Total         11    283.71000000

                 R-Square          C.V.       Root MSE              Y Mean

                 0.990897      9.516011      0.9278110           9.7500000


Source                  DF       Type I SS   Mean Square  F Value    Pr > F

BLK                      5    222.11000000   44.42200000     51.60    0.0041
TRT                      3     59.01750000   19.67250000     22.85    0.0144

Source                  DF     Type III SS   Mean Square  F Value    Pr > F

BLK                      5    178.87083333   35.77416667     41.56    0.0057
TRT                      3     59.01750000   19.67250000     22.85    0.0144
```

Table 5.1
Type I Estimable Functions for Treatments

Effect		Symbolic Expression	Coefficients For TRT1 Effect
TRT	1	L2	+.75
	2	L3	−.25
	3	L4	−.25
	4	−L2 − L3 − L4	−.25
BLK	1	.333L2 + .333L3	.167
	2	−.333L2 − .333L3	−.167
	3	.333L2 + .333L4	.167
	4	−.333L2 − .333L4	−.167
	5	−.333L3 − .333L4	.167
	6	.333L3 + .333L4	−.167

The Type I estimable function for treatments (TRT) is of some interest. Consider the comparison

$$TRT1 - 1/4(TRT1 + TRT2 + TRT3 + TRT4) \quad .$$

This is often called the *effect* of treatment 1, or the difference between the treatment 1 mean from the mean of *all* treatments. Simplification gives

$$3/4(TRT1) - 1/4(TRT2) - 1/4(TRT3) - 1/4(TRT4) \quad .$$

This expression is obtained by defining

$$L2 = 3/4$$

$$L3 = -1/4$$

$$L4 = -1/4$$

and results in the coefficients that appear in the right-hand column of Table 5.1. You can see that the Type I (unadjusted) estimate of the TRT 1 effect is also a contrast between blocks 1, 3 and 5, which contain treatment 1, and blocks 2, 4, and 6, which do not.

The least-squares means (see Output 5.6) are means which have been adjusted for block effects. The corresponding estimable functions (not reproduced here) show that the LSMEANs contain equal representation of block parameters even though individual treatments do not appear in all the blocks.

Output 5.6
Least-Squares
Means for
Balanced
Incomplete Block
Design

```
                         The SAS System                          1

                   General Linear Models Procedure
                        Least Squares Means

            TRT          Y          Std Err      Pr > |T|
                       LSMEAN       LSMEAN      H0:LSMEAN=0

             1       6.8000000     0.6281310      0.0017
             2       7.6500000     0.6281310      0.0012
             3      10.9250000     0.6281310      0.0004
             4      13.6250000     0.6281310      0.0002
```

5.4 A Crossover Design to Estimate Residual Effects

Cochran and Cox (1957) present two 3×3 Latin squares as a design for estimating the residual effects on milk yields of treatment from the preceding period. The treatment allocation is shown in the table below.

Square		1			2	
Cow		I	II	III	IV	V	VI
	1	A	B	C	A	B	C
Period	2	B	C	A	C	A	B
	3	C	A	B	B	C	A

Construct variables are named RESIDA and RESIDB, whose values in periods 2 and 3 are ±1 depending on the treatment in the preceding period and whose value in period 1 is 0. The data for the crossover design appear in Output 5.7.

Output 5.7
Data for Crossover Design to Estimate Residual Effects

```
                                  The SAS System                              1

   OBS    COW    PERIOD    TRTMENT    SQUARE    MILK    RESID    RESIDA    RESIDB

    1      1        1         A          1        38      0        0         0
    2      1        2         B          1        25      A        1         0
    3      1        3         C          1        15      B        0         1
    4      2        1         B          1       109      0        0         0
    5      2        2         C          1        86      B        0         1
    6      2        3         A          1        39      C       -1        -1
    7      3        1         C          1       124      0        0         0
    8      3        2         A          1        72      C       -1        -1
    9      3        3         B          1        27      A        1         0
   10      4        1         A          2        86      0        0         0
   11      4        2         C          2        76      A        1         0
   12      4        3         B          2        46      C       -1        -1
   13      5        1         B          2        75      0        0         0
   14      5        2         A          2        35      B        0         1
   15      5        3         C          2        34      A        1         0
   16      6        1         C          2       101      0        0         0
   17      6        2         B          2        63      C       -1        -1
   18      6        3         A          2         1      B        0         1
```

The following statements produce the ANOVA table in Output 5.8.

```
proc glm;
   class cow period trtment resid square;
   model milk = cow period(square) trtment resida residb/
              solution;
```

Output 5.8
Analysis of Variance for Crossover Design to Estimate Residual Effects

```
                          The SAS System                              1

                  General Linear Models Procedure
                       Class Level Information

          Class     Levels     Values

          COW          6       1 2 3 4 5 6

          PERIOD       3       1 2 3

          TRTMENT      3       A B C

          SQUARE       2       1 2


          Number of observations in data set = 18
```

```
                                                                          2

                        General Linear Models Procedure

Dependent Variable: MILK
                                    Sum of            Mean
Source                  DF          Squares          Square    F Value    Pr > F

Model                   13      20163.194444      1551.014957    31.14    0.0023

Error                    4        199.250000        49.812500

Corrected Total         17      20362.444444

                R-Square            C.V.          Root MSE          MILK Mean

                0.990215         12.07608        7.0577971         58.444444


Source                  DF        Type I SS     Mean Square    F Value    Pr > F

COW                      5      5781.111111     1156.222222     23.21     0.0047
PERIOD(SQUARE)           4     11489.111111     2872.277778     57.66     0.0009
TRTMENT                  2      2276.777778     1138.388889     22.85     0.0065
RESIDA                   1       546.750000      546.750000     10.98     0.0296
RESIDB                   1        69.444444       69.444444      1.39     0.3031

Source                  DF       Type III SS    Mean Square    F Value    Pr > F

COW                      4      3817.950000      954.487500     19.16     0.0071
PERIOD(SQUARE)           4     11489.111111     2872.277778     57.66     0.0009
TRTMENT                  2      2854.550000     1427.275000     28.65     0.0043
RESIDA                   1       258.673611      258.673611      5.19     0.0849
RESIDB                   1        69.444444       69.444444      1.39     0.3031


                                      T for H0:    Pr > |T|    Std Error of
Parameter                 Estimate   Parameter=0                 Estimate

INTERCEPT               40.16666667 B     6.83      0.0024      5.88149759
COW            1       -24.25000000 B    -3.14      0.0347      7.71351177
               2        21.00000000 B     2.82      0.0477      7.43957137
               3        18.62500000 B     2.41      0.0732      7.71351177
               4        15.62500000 B     2.56      0.0629      6.11223159
               5        -0.25000000 B    -0.04      0.9693      6.11223159
               6         0.00000000 B      .          .            .
PERIOD(SQUARE) 1 1      63.33333333 B    10.99      0.0004      5.76266721
               2 1      34.00000000 B     5.90      0.0041      5.76266721
               3 1       0.00000000 B      .          .            .
               1 2      60.33333333 B    10.47      0.0005      5.76266721
               2 2      31.00000000 B     5.38      0.0058      5.76266721
               3 2       0.00000000 B      .          .            .
TRTMENT        A       -34.25000000 B    -7.52      0.0017      4.55578844
               B       -20.62500000 B    -4.53      0.0106      4.55578844
               C         0.00000000 B      .          .            .
RESIDA                  -8.04166667      -2.28      0.0849      3.52889855
RESIDB                  -4.16666667      -1.18      0.3031      3.52889855
```

```
                                                                          3



                        General Linear Models Procedure

NOTE: The X'X matrix has been found to be singular and a generalized inverse
      was used to solve the normal equations.  Estimates followed by the
      letter 'B' are biased, and are not unique estimators of the parameters.
```

The desired ANOVA table, as shown by Cochran and Cox (1957), is constructed as follows:

Source	DF	SS	
Cow	5	5781.1	(Type I)
Period(Square)	4	11489.1	(Type I)
Direct effects(adjusted)	2	2854.6	(Type III)
Residual effects(adjusted)	2	616.2	(Type I SS RESIDA+Type I SS RESIDB)

The direct treatment effects reported by Cochran and Cox (1957) can be obtained from the TRTMENT parameters according to

$$-15.958 = -34.250 - (^1/_3)(-34.250 - 20.625 + 0.000)$$
$$- \ 2.333 = -20.625 - (^1/_3)(-34.250 - 20.625 + 0.000)$$
$$18.292 = \ \ \ \ 0.000 - (^1/_3)(-34.250 - 20.625 + 0.000) \ \ .$$

Thus, the direct effects can be obtained from the following ESTIMATE statements:

```
estimate 'DIRECT EFFECT OF A'
        trtment .666667 - .333333 - .333333;
estimate 'DIRECT EFFECT OF B'
        trtment - .333333 .666667 - .333333;
estimate 'DIRECT EFFECT OF C'
        trtment - .333333 - .333333 .666667;
```

The residual effects presented by Cochran and Cox (1957) are obtained from the parameter estimates for RESIDA and RESIDB. The values are:

A:-8.042
B:-4.167
C:$-(-8.042 - 4.167) = 12.2$

The direct effect means reported by Cochran and Cox (1957) are equal to the overall mean 58.4444 added to the direct effects. They are equal to the GLM least-squares means, obtained from the following statement:

```
lsmeans trtment;
```

The results appear in Output 5.9.

Output 5.9
Adjusted
Treatment Means
for Crossover
Design to Estimate
Residual Effects

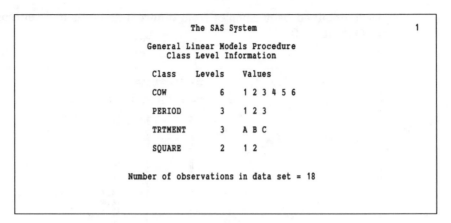

```
                        The SAS System                        1

                General Linear Models Procedure
                    Class Level Information

            Class    Levels    Values

            COW         6       1 2 3 4 5 6

            PERIOD      3       1 2 3

            TRTMENT     3       A B C

            SQUARE      2       1 2


        Number of observations in data set = 18
```

```
                                                              2

                General Linear Models Procedure
                    Least Squares Means

            TRTMENT            MILK
                               LSMEAN

            A               42.4861111
            B               56.1111111
            C               76.7361111
```

5.5 Experiments with Qualitative and Quantitative Variables

The material in this section is related to the discussion of regression analysis in Chapter 1, "Regression," and to the analysis of covariance in Chapter 6, "Covariance and the Heterogeneity of Slopes." This section concerns details of models with dummy variables generated from the CLASS statement.

Many experiments involve both qualitative and quantitative factors. For example, the tensile strength (TS) of a monofilament fiber depends on the amount (AMT) of a chemical used in the manufacturing process. This chemical can be obtained from three different sources (SOURCE), with values **A**, **B**, or **C**. SOURCE is a qualitative variable and AMT is a quantitative variable. Measurements of TS were obtained from samples from different amounts and sources. The data appear in Output 5.10.

Output 5.10
Data for
Experiment with
Qualitative and
Quantitative
Variables

```
                        The SAS System                              1

             OBS      SOURCE      AMT      TS

              1          A         1      11.5
              2          A         2      13.8
              3          A         3      14.4
              4          A         4      16.8
              5          A         5      18.7
              6          B         1      10.8
              7          B         2      12.3
              8          B         3      13.7
              9          B         4      14.2
             10          B         5      16.6
             11          C         1      13.1
             12          C         2      16.2
             13          C         3      19.0
             14          C         4      22.9
             15          C         5      26.5
```

A simple linear regression model for each source relates TS to AMT.

$$TS = \alpha_A + \beta_A AMT + \varepsilon \qquad (\text{SOURCE } \mathbf{A})$$

$$TS = \alpha_B + \beta_B AMT + \varepsilon \qquad (\text{SOURCE } \mathbf{B})$$

$$TS = \alpha_C + \beta_C AMT + \varepsilon \qquad (\text{SOURCE } \mathbf{C})$$

The parameters α_A and β_A are the intercept and slope, respectively, for SOURCE=**A**.

The following statements produce the analysis of variance and parameter estimates in Output 5.11.

```
proc glm;
   class source;
   model ts=source amt source*amt / solution;
```

Output 5.11
Analysis of
Variance and
Parameter
Estimates for an
Experiment with
Qualitative and
Quantitative
Variables

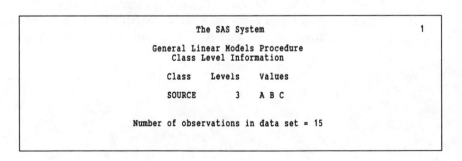

```
                        The SAS System                              1

                General Linear Models Procedure
                    Class Level Information

            Class      Levels      Values

            SOURCE        3        A B C


       Number of observations in data set = 15
```

```
                                                                         2
                        General Linear Models Procedure
Dependent Variable: TS
                                    Sum of              Mean
Source                 DF          Squares            Square   F Value   Pr > F

Model                   5     258.72733333       51.74546667    263.71   0.0001

Error                   9       1.76600000        0.19622222

Corrected Total        14     260.49333333

                 R-Square              C.V.         Root MSE            TS Mean

                 0.993221          2.762805        0.4429698          16.033333


Source                 DF        Type I SS    Mean Square   F Value   Pr > F

SOURCE                  2      98.00133333    49.00066667    249.72   0.0001
AMT                     1     138.24533333   138.24533333    704.53   0.0001
AMT*SOURCE              2      22.48066667    11.24033333     57.28   0.0001

Source                 DF      Type III SS    Mean Square   F Value   Pr > F

SOURCE                  2       0.07024242     0.03512121      0.18   0.8390
AMT                     1     138.24533333   138.24533333    704.53   0.0001
AMT*SOURCE              2      22.48066667    11.24033333     57.28   0.0001


                                         T for H0:   Pr > |T|   Std Error of
Parameter              Estimate        Parameter=0               Estimate

INTERCEPT           9.490000000 B           20.43     0.0001     0.46459062
SOURCE    A         0.330000000 B            0.50     0.6275     0.65703036
          B        -0.020000000 B           -0.03     0.9764     0.65703036
          C         0.000000000 B            .          .          .
AMT                 3.350000000 B           23.92     0.0001     0.14007934
AMT*SOURCE A       -1.610000000 B           -8.13     0.0001     0.19810211
           B       -2.000000000 B          -10.10     0.0001     0.19810211
           C        0.000000000 B            .          .          .

NOTE: The X'X matrix has been found to be singular and a generalized inverse
      was used to solve the normal equations.  Estimates followed by the
      letter 'B' are biased, and are not unique estimators of the parameters.
```

These parameter estimates pertain to the integrated model

$$TS = \alpha_C + \alpha'_A D_A + \alpha'_B D_B + \beta_C AMT + \beta'_A D_A AMT + \beta'_B D_B AMT + \varepsilon \quad .$$

The parameters α' and β' are further defined as

$$\alpha'_A = \alpha_A - \alpha_C \qquad \alpha'_B = \alpha_B - \alpha_C$$

$$\beta'_A = \beta_A - \beta_C \qquad \beta'_B = \beta_B - \beta_C \quad .$$

The variable D_A is a dummy variable equal to 1 for SOURCE=**A** and equal to 0 otherwise, and D_B has a corresponding definition with respect to SOURCE=**B**. Thus, the regression models for the three nitrogen sources are

$$TS = (\alpha_C + \alpha'_A) + (\beta_C + \beta'_A)AMT + \varepsilon \qquad (\text{SOURCE } \mathbf{A})$$
$$TS = (\alpha_C + \alpha'_B) + (\beta_C + \beta'_B)AMT + \varepsilon \qquad (\text{SOURCE } \mathbf{B})$$
$$TS = \alpha_C + \beta_C AMT + \varepsilon \qquad\qquad\qquad (\text{SOURCE } \mathbf{C})$$

Therefore, the fitted equations are

$$TS = 9.49 + 0.33 + (3.35 - 1.61)AMT \qquad \text{(SOURCE A)}$$
$$= 9.82 + 1.74\ AMT$$
$$TS = 9.49 - 0.02 + (3.35 - 2.00)AMT \qquad \text{(SOURCE B)}$$
$$= 9.47 + 1.35\ AMT$$
$$TS = 9.49 + 3.35\ AMT \qquad \text{(SOURCE C)}$$

The GLM parameter estimates, in effect, treat the regression line for SOURCE=C as a reference line, and the parameters α'_A, α'_B, β'_A, and β'_B are parameters for lines A and B minus parameters for line C. The AMT source parameters β'_A and β'_B measure differences between the slopes for regression lines A and B, and line C, respectively. Thus, a test that these parameters are 0 is testing that the lines are parallel, that is, have equal slopes. The appropriate statistic is the $F=57.28$ for the AMT*SOURCE effect, which has significant probability $p=0.0001$.

Caution is advised in using the Type III F test for SOURCE. It is a test of the equality of the intercepts (H_0: $\alpha_A=\alpha_B=\alpha_C$), which probably has no practical interpretation because the intercepts are simply extrapolations of the lines to L=0. The Type I F test, on the other hand, tests equality of the midpoints of the regression lines (H_0: $\alpha_A+\beta_A(2)=\alpha_B+\beta_B(2)=\alpha_C+\beta_C(2)$).

You can compare two sources at a given amount with an ESTIMATE statement. Suppose you want to compare SOURCE=A with SOURCE=B using AMT=3.5. This difference is

$$(\alpha_A + \beta_A(3.5)) - (\alpha_B + \beta_B(3.5))$$
$$= ((\alpha_C + \alpha'_A) + (\beta_C + \beta'_C)3.5)$$
$$= ((\alpha_C + \alpha'_B) + (\beta_C + \beta'_C)3.5)$$
$$= \alpha'_A - \alpha'_B + (\beta'_A - \beta'_B)3.5 \quad .$$

So the appropriate ESTIMATE statement is

```
estimate 'A vs B at AMT=3.5'
source 1 -1 0
source*amt 3.5 -3.5 0;
```

The results appear in Output 5.12.

Output 5.12
Difference Between
SOURCE=A and
SOURCE=B at
AMT=3.5

```
                        The SAS System                          1

                    General Linear Models Procedure
                        Class Level Information

                    Class     Levels     Values

                    SOURCE       3        A B C

              Number of observations in data set = 15
```

```
                                                                        2

                        General Linear Models Procedure

Dependent Variable: TS
                                       Sum of          Mean
                                     T for H0:      Pr > |T|    Std Error of
Parameter                 Estimate   Parameter=0                 Estimate

A vs B at AMT=3.5       1.71500000          5.77     0.0003     0.29715316
```

Suppose TS also is measured for AMT=0. This variation of the experiment is commonly mishandled by data analysts. Since AMT=0 means there is no chemical, the intercepts for the models are all equal, $\alpha_A = \alpha_B = \alpha_C$. Thus, a correct analysis should provide equal estimates of the intercepts. The regressions can be written simultaneously as

$$TS = \alpha + \gamma_A D_A AMT + \gamma_B D_B AMT + \gamma_C D_C AMT + \varepsilon$$

where D_A is a dummy variable equal to 1 for SOURCE=**A** and equal to 0 otherwise, and D_B and D_C have corresponding definitions with respect to SOURCE=**B** and SOURCE=**C**. Use PROC GLM to create D_A, D_B, and D_C by including the SOURCE variable in a CLASS statement.

Look at the data set in Output 5.13. The value **C** is arbitrarily assigned to SOURCE when AMT=0. The following statements produce Output 5.14.

```
proc glm;
  class source;
  model ts=amt*source / solution;
```

Output 5.13
Data with AMT=0

```
                          The SAS System                         1

            OBS    SOURCE    AMT      TS

              1      A        1      11.5
              2      A        2      13.8
              3      A        3      14.4
              4      A        4      16.8
              5      A        5      18.7
              6      B        1      10.8
              7      B        2      12.3
              8      B        3      13.7
              9      B        4      14.2
             10      B        5      16.6
             11      C        1      13.1
             12      C        2      16.2
             13      C        3      19.0
             14      C        4      22.9
             15      C        5      26.5
             16      C        0      10.1
             17      C        0      10.2
             18      C        0       9.8
             19      C        0       9.9
             20      C        0      10.2
```

Parameter estimates in Output 5.14 yield the three prediction equations

$$TS = 9.88 + 1.72 \text{ AMT} \qquad \text{(SOURCE A)}$$
$$TS = 9.88 + 1.24 \text{ AMT} \qquad \text{(SOURCE B)}$$
$$TS = 9.88 + 3.24 \text{ AMT} \qquad \text{(SOURCE C)}$$

Output 5.14
Parameter
Estimates AMT=0

```
                              The SAS System                        1

                       General Linear Models Procedure
                          Class Level Information

                       Class     Levels     Values
                       SOURCE       3        A B C

                 Number of observations in data set = 20
```

```
                                                                    2

                       General Linear Models Procedure

Dependent Variable: TS
                                  Sum of          Mean
Source              DF          Squares         Square    F Value    Pr > F

Model                3      393.00517914   131.00172638    903.34    0.0001

Error               16        2.32032086     0.14502005

Corrected Total     19      395.32550000

                R-Square           C.V.        Root MSE              TS Mean

                0.994131       2.619986       0.3808150             14.535000


Source              DF        Type I SS    Mean Square    F Value    Pr > F

AMT*SOURCE           3      393.00517914   131.00172638    903.34    0.0001

Source              DF      Type III SS    Mean Square    F Value    Pr > F

AMT*SOURCE           3      393.00517914   131.00172638    903.34    0.0001


                                     T for H0:    Pr > |T|    Std Error of
Parameter              Estimate     Parameter=0                 Estimate

INTERCEPT            9.882352941        72.14      0.0001       0.13699380
AMT*SOURCE A         1.722994652        27.13      0.0001       0.06350310
           B         1.237540107        19.49      0.0001       0.06350310
           C         3.242994652        51.07      0.0001       0.06350310
```

5.6 Lack-of-Fit Analysis

When estimating and testing an incomplete model (one that does not include all main effects and interactions), a lack-of-fit analysis can provide information on the adequacy of a model that does not include all possible terms. The sums of squares for the full model can be obtained by analyzing the data as a one-way analysis of variance that computes the sums of squares among all unique treatment combinations (cells). The error sums of squares for the full model is subtracted from the error sum of squares for the incompletely specified model to obtain the sum of squares for all terms not specified. Of course, if there is more than one unspecified term, the resulting test provides no information about individual terms.

This procedure is actually an extension of the most common application of testing for lack of fit, which is testing the adequacy of a regression model. In this procedure, you want to determine if a fitted model accounts for essentially all of the variation in a response variable due to differences between the levels of a quantitative independent variable. For example, suppose an experiment provides responses Y corresponding to five values of an independent variable X, and suppose three Ys are measured at each X, giving fifteen measurements in all. The data for this experiment are represented in the table below:

X	Y	LACKOFIT
1	5.7	1
1	6.3	1
1	6.1	1
2	7.4	2
2	7.8	2
.	.	.
.	.	.
.	.	.
5	15.6	5

The variable LACKOFIT is defined to be equal to X in the DATA step. You want to fit a quadratic regression of Y on X and to determine if the quadratic equation adequately models the response of Y to X. The Type I breakdown is as follows:

Source	DF
X	1
X*X	1
LACKOFIT	2

The Type I sums of squares are provided by the following statements:

```
proc glm;
   class lackofit;
   model y=x x*x lackofit;
```

The terms X and X*X are the usual linear and quadratic effects of X. The LACKOFIT variable measures the variation in Y due to X that is not accounted for by the quadratic polynomial. Specifying the variable LACKOFIT, which has five levels, in the CLASS statement causes the generation of five dummy variables. If LACKOFIT were the only variable in the MODEL statement, then it would account for 4 DF, 2 of which are confounded with the linear and quadratic effects. Preceding LACKOFIT by X and X*X leaves only 2 DF for LACKOFIT in the Type I sums of squares. It is important to precede LACKOFIT by X and X*X, for if

LACKOFIT preceded X and X*X, all 4 degrees of freedom would go to LACKOFIT and 0 degrees of freedom would go to X and X*X. Note, however, that all other types of sums of squares are 0 for X and X*X.

Now consider a three-factor factorial experiment with factors A, B, and C. Suppose you specify an incomplete model that omits the B*C and A*B*C interactions, and you want to test for lack of fit of this model. Run the following statements:

```
proc glm;
   class a b c;
   model y=a b a*b c a*c;
```

The difference between the error sum of squares that you obtain and the error sum of squares from a between-cell analysis of variance provides the additional sum of squares due to both B*C and A*B*C.

You can get the between-cell analysis of variance from PROC ANOVA. If the CLASS variables are integers, a single variable can be generated to represent all cell combinations. Assume, for example, that the values of three CLASS variables (A, B, C) consist of integers between 1 and 10. The following assignment statement placed in the DATA step provides the subscript:

```
group=100*a+10*b+c;
```

The following SAS statements provide the desired error sums of squares.

```
proc anova;
   class group;
   model y=group;
```

The CLASS variables may not conform to these specifications. Character values can be concatenated, but the resulting single classification variable may exceed eight characters. Alternately, the following statements can be used to compute the sum of squares for differences between the cells:

```
proc anova;
   class a b c;
   model y=a*b*c;
```

5.7 Unbalanced Nested Structure

Nested structure concerns samples within samples, as discussed in Section 3.2, "Nested Classifications." An example is treatments applied to plants in pots. There are several pots per treatment and several plants per pot. The pots do not necessarily have the same number of plants, and there may be different numbers of pots per treatment. Another example of nested structure occurs in sample surveys in which households are sampled within blocks, blocks are sampled within precincts, precincts are sampled within cities, and so on. Normally, the most appropriate procedure to analyze such data is PROC NESTED. Some applications, however, require PROC GLM.

Data containing a nested structure often have both fixed and random components, which raises questions about proper error terms. Consider an experiment with t treatments (TRT) applied randomly to a number of pots (POT), each containing several plants (PLANT). The data appear in Output 5.15.

Output 5.15
Data for
Unbalanced Nested
Experiment

```
                          The SAS System                           1

          OBS     TRT     POT     PLANT      Y

            1      1       1        1       15
            2      1       1        2       13
            3      1       1        3       16
            4      1       2        1       17
            5      1       2        2       19
            6      1       3        1       12
            7      2       1        1       20
            8      2       1        2       21
            9      2       2        1       20
           10      2       2        2       23
           11      2       2        3       19
           12      2       2        4       19
           13      3       1        1       12
           14      3       1        2       13
           15      3       1        3       14
           16      3       2        1       11
           17      3       3        1       12
           18      3       3        2       13
           19      3       3        3       15
           20      3       3        4       11
           21      3       3        5        9
```

The model is

$$y_{ijk} = \mu + \lambda_i + \rho_{ij} + \varepsilon_{ijk}$$

where

y_{ijk} is the observed response in the kth PLANT of the jth POT in the ith TREATMENT.

μ is the overall mean response.

λ_i is the effect of the ith TREATMENT.

ρ_{ij} is the effect of the jth POT within the ith TREATMENT.

ε_{ijk} is the effect of the kth individual PLANT in the jth POT of the ith TREATMENT. This effect is usually considered to be the random error.

You are primarily interested in tests and estimates related to the TREATMENTS as well as the variation among POTS and PLANTS. The analysis is implemented by the following SAS statements:

```
proc glm;
   class trt pot;
   model y=trt pot(trt) / ss1 ss3;
   means trt pot(trt);
   lsmeans trt pot(trt);
```

Most items in these statements are similar to those from previous examples. The analysis of variance appears in Output 5.16. The means and least-squares means are shown in Output 5.17.

Output 5.16
Analysis of
Variance for
Unbalanced Nested
Experiment

```
                          The SAS System                          1

                   General Linear Models Procedure
                       Class Level Information

                   Class    Levels    Values

                   TRT         3      1 2 3

                   POT         3      1 2 3


              Number of observations in data set = 21
```

```
                                                                  2

                   General Linear Models Procedure

Dependent Variable: Y
                                Sum of           Mean
Source                 DF       Squares         Square     F Value    Pr > F

Model                   7    267.22619048    38.17517007    12.43     0.0001

Error                  13     39.91666667     3.07051282

Corrected Total        20    307.14285714

                 R-Square          C.V.        Root MSE              Y Mean

                 0.870039       11.35742      1.7522879           15.428571


Source                 DF      Type I SS     Mean Square   F Value    Pr > F

TRT                     2    236.92063492   118.46031746    38.58     0.0001
POT(TRT)                5     30.30555556     6.06111111     1.97     0.1499

Source                 DF     Type III SS    Mean Square   F Value    Pr > F

TRT                     2    200.11097255   100.05548628    32.59     0.0001
POT(TRT)                5     30.30555556     6.06111111     1.97     0.1499
```

Output 5.17
Mean and
LSMEAN for an
Unbalanced Nested
Experiment

```
                              The SAS System                          1

                      General Linear Models Procedure

              Level of      --------------Y--------------
              TRT      N       Mean              SD

               1       6     15.3333333      2.58198890
               2       6     20.3333333      1.50554531
               3       9     12.2222222      1.78730088

       Level of   Level of           --------------Y--------------
       POT        TRT        N          Mean              SD

         1          1        3        14.6666667      1.52752523
         2          1        2        18.0000000      1.41421356
         3          1        1        12.0000000          .
         1          2        2        20.5000000      0.70710678
         2          2        4        20.2500000      1.89296945
         1          3        3        13.0000000      1.00000000
         2          3        1        11.0000000          .
         3          3        5        12.0000000      2.23606798
```

```
                                                                     2

                      General Linear Models Procedure
                             Least Squares Means

                        TRT              Y
                                       LSMEAN

                         1          14.8888889
                         2          20.3750000
                         3          12.0000000



                   POT    TRT              Y
                                         LSMEAN

                    1      1          14.6666667
                    2      1          18.0000000
                    3      1          12.0000000
                    1      2          20.5000000
                    2      2          20.2500000
                    1      3          13.0000000
                    2      3          11.0000000
                    3      3          12.0000000
```

The analysis of variance has the same form as given in Output 3.5. Note, however, that there is a slight difference in the Type I and Type III sums of squares of TRT in Output 5.17. This difference is made clearer by noting the differences between the unadjusted means from the MEANS statement and the adjusted or least-squares means from the LSMEANS statement. Table 5.2 shows the differences.

Table 5.2
Means and
Least-Squares
Means

TRT	POT	N	Means	Least-Squares Means
1		6	15.333	14.889
2		6	20.333	20.375
3		9	12.222	12.000
1	1	3	14.667	14.667
	2	2	18.000	18.000
	3	1	12.000	12.000
2	1	2	20.500	20.500
	2	4	20.250	20.250
3	1	3	13.000	13.000
	2	1	11.000	11.000
	3	5	12.000	12.000

The values produced by the MEANS statement are the means of all observations in a TREATMENT. These are the weighted POT means, as shown in the following equation:

$$\text{mean}(i) = \bar{y}_{i..} = (1 / n_{i.}) \, \Sigma_j \, n_{ij}\bar{y}_{ij.}$$

n_{ij} is the number of plants in POT j of TREATMENT i. On the other hand, the least-squares means are the unweighted POT means, as shown in the following equation:

$$\text{least-squares mean}(i) = (1 / k_i) \, \Sigma_j \, \bar{y}_{ij.}$$

k_i is the number of pots in TREATMENT i.

Both of these types of means have specific uses. In sample surveys, particularly self-weighting samples, it is usually appropriate to use the ordinary means. For the present case, POTS would probably be considered a random effect (see Section 3.2.4, "Analysis of Variance for Nested Classification: Using the GLM Procedure to Compute Expected Mean Squares"). In this event, the variance of least-squares mean(i) is less than the variance of mean(i) if σ_ρ^2 is large relative to σ^2 and conversely, where $\sigma_\rho^2 = V(\rho_{ij})$ and $\sigma^2 = V(\varepsilon_{ijk})$.

5.8 Absorbing Nesting Effects

Nested structures can easily produce a very large number of dummy variables and exceed memory capacity. For strictly nested structures, PROC NESTED is less demanding, but this procedure is not useful for mixed structures. For such situations, a methodology called *absorption* greatly reduces the size of the problem by eliminating the need to obtain an explicit solution to the complete set of normal equations.

Absorption can be thought of as reducing the number of normal equations by eliminating the parameters for one factor from the system before a solution is obtained. This is analogous to the method of solving a set of three equations in three unknowns, x_1, x_2, and x_3. Suppose you combine the first and second equations and eliminate x_3. Next, combine the first and third equations and eliminate x_3. Then, with two equations left involving x_1 and x_2 (the variable x_3 having been absorbed), solve the reduced set for x_1 and x_2.

The use of the ABSORB statement is illustrated with data on 65 steers from Harvey (1975). Several values are recorded for each steer, including line number (LINE), sire number (SIRE), age of dam (AGEDAM), steer age (AGE), initial weight (INTLWT), and the dependent variable, average daily gain (AVDLYGN). Output 5.18 shows the data.

Output 5.18
Data for
Absorption
Example

```
                              The SAS System                              1

  OBS    LINE    SIRE    AGEDAM    STEERNO    AGE    INTLWT    AVDLYGN

    1      1       1        3          1       192     390       2.24
    2      1       1        3          2       154     403       2.65
    3      1       1        4          3       185     432       2.41
    4      1       1        4          4       193     457       2.25
    5      1       1        5          5       186     483       2.58
    6      1       1        5          6       177     469       2.67
    7      1       1        5          7       177     428       2.71
    8      1       1        5          8       163     439       2.47
    9      1       2        4          9       188     439       2.29
   10      1       2        4         10       178     407       2.26
   11      1       2        5         11       198     498       1.97
   12      1       2        5         12       193     459       2.14
   13      1       2        5         13       186     459       2.44
   14      1       2        5         14       175     375       2.52
   15      1       2        5         15       171     382       1.72
   16      1       2        5         16       168     417       2.75
   17      1       3        3         17       154     389       2.38
   18      1       3        4         18       184     414       2.46
   19      1       3        5         19       174     483       2.29
   20      1       3        5         20       170     430       2.30
   21      1       3        5         21       169     443       2.94
   22      2       4        3         22       158     381       2.50
   23      2       4        3         23       158     365       2.44
   24      2       4        4         24       169     386       2.44
   25      2       4        4         25       144     339       2.15
   26      2       4        5         26       159     419       2.54
   27      2       4        5         27       152     469       2.74
   28      2       4        5         28       149     379       2.50
   29      2       4        5         29       149     375       2.54
   30      2       5        3         30       189     395       2.65
   31      2       5        4         31       187     447       2.52
   32      2       5        4         32       165     430       2.67
   33      2       5        5         33       181     453       2.79
   34      2       5        5         34       177     385       2.33
   35      2       5        5         35       151     414       2.67
   36      2       5        5         36       147     353       2.69
   37      3       6        4         37       184     411       3.00
   38      3       6        4         38       184     420       2.49
   39      3       6        5         39       187     427       2.25
   40      3       6        5         40       184     409       2.49
   41      3       6        5         41       183     337       2.02
   42      3       6        5         42       177     352       2.31
   43      3       7        3         43       205     472       2.57
   44      3       7        3         44       193     340       2.37
   45      3       7        4         45       162     375       2.64
   46      3       7        5         46       206     451       2.37
   47      3       7        5         47       205     472       2.22
   48      3       7        5         48       187     402       1.90
   49      3       7        5         49       178     464       2.61
   50      3       7        5         50       175     414       2.13
   51      3       8        3         51       200     466       2.16
   52      3       8        3         52       184     356       2.33
   53      3       8        3         53       175     449       2.52
   54      3       8        4         54       178     360       2.45
   55      3       8        5         55       189     385       1.44
   56      3       8        5         56       184     431       1.72
```

(continued on next page)

(continued from previous page)

57	3	8	5	57	183	401	2.17
58	3	9	3	58	166	404	2.68
59	3	9	4	59	187	482	2.43
60	3	9	4	60	186	350	2.36
61	3	9	4	61	184	483	2.44
62	3	9	5	62	180	425	2.66
63	3	9	5	63	177	420	2.46
64	3	9	5	64	175	440	2.52
65	3	9	5	65	164	405	2.42

The analysis, as performed by Harvey, can be obtained directly by PROC GLM with the following SAS statements:

```
proc glm;
    class line sire agedam;
    model avdlygn=line sire(line) agedam
            line*agedam age intlwt / solution ss3;
    test h=line e=sire(line);
```

The results appear in Output 5.19.

Output 5.19
Complete
Least-Squares
Analysis of
Variance

```
                            The SAS System                            1

                    General Linear Models Procedure
                       Class Level Information

            Class    Levels    Values

            LINE        3      1 2 3

            SIRE        9      1 2 3 4 5 6 7 8 9

            AGEDAM      3      3 4 5


        Number of observations in data set = 65
```

```
                                                                      2

                    General Linear Models Procedure

Dependent Variable: AVDLYGN
                               Sum of           Mean
Source                 DF     Squares         Square   F Value    Pr > F

Model                  16    2.52745871     0.15796617     3.14    0.0011

Error                  48    2.41191667     0.05024826

Corrected Total        64    4.93937538

             R-Square         C.V.      Root MSE         AVDLYGN Mean

             0.511696      9.295956     0.2241612           2.4113846


Source                 DF    Type III SS   Mean Square   F Value    Pr > F

LINE                    2    0.13620255    0.06810128      1.36     0.2676
SIRE(LINE)              6    0.97388905    0.16231484      3.23     0.0095
AGEDAM                  2    0.13010623    0.06505311      1.29     0.2834
```

```
LINE*AGEDAM              4        0.45343434     0.11335859      2.26     0.0768
AGE                     1        0.38127612     0.38127612      7.59     0.0083
INTLWT                  1        0.26970425     0.26970425      5.37     0.0248


                                              T for H0:    Pr > |T|   Std Error of
Parameter                      Estimate     Parameter=0               Estimate

INTERCEPT                     2.996269167 B       5.84       0.0001     0.51285394
LINE            1             0.071824656 B       0.49       0.6238     0.14550628
                2             0.252468579 B       1.84       0.0719     0.13716655
                3             0.000000000 B        .          .           .
SIRE(LINE)    1 1             0.085729012 B       0.66       0.5137     0.13027803
              2 1            -0.121705157 B      -0.89       0.3761     0.13622078
              3 1             0.000000000 B        .          .           .
              4 2            -0.244601122 B      -1.93       0.0594     0.12669287
              5 2             0.000000000 B        .          .           .
              6 3             0.105395737 B       0.82       0.4183     0.12908764
              7 3            -0.019520926 B      -0.16       0.8719     0.12037674
              8 3            -0.330235387 B      -2.63       0.0115     0.12566795
              9 3             0.000000000 B        .          .           .
AGEDAM          3             0.370387027 B       3.23       0.0022     0.11455814
                4             0.275459487 B       2.65       0.0107     0.10377628
                5             0.000000000 B        .          .           .
LINE*AGEDAM   1 3            -0.448936131 B      -2.29       0.0263     0.19581259
              1 4            -0.282831924 B      -1.76       0.0851     0.16085047
              1 5             0.000000000 B        .          .           .
              2 3            -0.260782670 B      -1.34       0.1880     0.19528690
              2 4            -0.350258133 B      -2.01       0.0502     0.17438656
              2 5             0.000000000 B        .          .           .
              3 3             0.000000000 B        .          .           .
              3 4             0.000000000 B        .          .           .
              3 5             0.000000000 B        .          .           .
AGE                          -0.008530438        -2.75       0.0083     0.00309679
INTLWT                        0.002026334         2.32       0.0248     0.00087464
```

```
                                                                              3



                        General Linear Models Procedure

NOTE: The X'X matrix has been found to be singular and a generalized inverse
      was used to solve the normal equations.   Estimates followed by the
      letter 'B' are biased, and are not unique estimators of the parameters.
```

The factor AGEDAM is treated as a discrete variable with levels (3, 4, and ≥ 5). The denominator for the *F* test for testing LINE is SIRE(LINE).

To introduce the ABSORB statement, Harvey's model has been simplified. All sources of variation except the main effects of SIRE and AGEDAM have been disregarded. For the abbreviated model, the following SAS statements give the desired analysis:

```
proc glm;
    class sire agedam;
    model avdlygn=sire agedam / solution ss1 ss2 ss3;
```

The output appears in Output 5.20.

Output 5.20
Abbreviated
Least-Squares
Analysis of
Variance

```
                          The SAS System                            1

                   General Linear Models Procedure

Dependent Variable: AVDLYGN
                                 Sum of            Mean
Source              DF          Squares           Square    F Value   Pr > F

Model               10       1.42537863       0.14253786      2.19    0.0324

Error               54       3.51399676       0.06507401

Corrected Total     64       4.93937538

               R-Square            C.V.        Root MSE         AVDLYGN Mean

               0.288575         10.57882       0.2550961          2.4113846


Source              DF        Type I SS     Mean Square    F Value    Pr > F

SIRE                 8       1.30643634      0.16330454       2.51     0.0214
AGEDAM               2       0.11894229      0.05947115       0.91     0.4071

Source              DF       Type II SS     Mean Square    F Value    Pr > F

SIRE                 8       1.33017081      0.16627135       2.56     0.0194
AGEDAM               2       0.11894229      0.05947115       0.91     0.4071

Source              DF      Type III SS     Mean Square    F Value    Pr > F

SIRE                 8       1.33017081      0.16627135       2.56     0.0194
AGEDAM               2       0.11894229      0.05947115       0.91     0.4071

Contrast            DF      Contrast SS     Mean Square    F Value    Pr > F

young vs old         1       0.10295042      0.10295042       1.58     0.2139

                                        T for H0:   Pr > |T|   Std Error of
Parameter               Estimate      Parameter=0              Estimate

young vs old          0.08284028           1.26     0.2139     0.06586145


                                        T for H0:   Pr > |T|   Std Error of
Parameter               Estimate      Parameter=0              Estimate

INTERCEPT             2.463465431 B       25.60     0.0001     0.09621570
SIRE        1        -0.007385569 B       -0.06     0.9543     0.12818580
            2        -0.214289931 B       -1.67     0.1015     0.12860642
            3        -0.022601542 B       -0.15     0.8776     0.14605021
            4        -0.023635569 B       -0.18     0.8544     0.12818580
            5         0.123109061 B        0.93     0.3559     0.13219310
            6        -0.052898097 B       -0.38     0.7036     0.13831973
            7        -0.147598320 B       -1.14     0.2578     0.12906055
            8        -0.407814812 B       -3.02     0.0039     0.13505419
            9         0.000000000 B         .         .           .
AGEDAM      3         0.117382555 B        1.32     0.1933     0.08911680
            4         0.048297999 B        0.63     0.5340     0.07715379
AGEDAM      5         0.000000000 B         .         .           .

NOTE: The X'X matrix has been found to be singular and a generalized inverse
      was used to solve the normal equations.  Estimates followed by the
      letter 'B' are biased, and are not unique estimators of the parameters.
```

If the number of sires were large, then this analysis would be expensive. However, because there is little concern for the actual estimates of the effects of SIRE, considerable expense can be avoided by using the ABSORB statement:

```
proc glm;
   absorb sire;
   class agedam;
   model avdlygn=agedam / solution ss1 ss2 ss3;
```

The results appear in Output 5.21.

Output 5.21
Abbreviated Least-Squares Analysis of Variance Using the ABSORB Statement

```
                              The SAS System                          1

                      General Linear Models Procedure
                        Class Level Information

                      Class    Levels    Values

                      AGEDAM      3       3 4 5


                 Number of observations in data set = 65
```

```
                                                                      2

                       General Linear Models Procedure

Dependent Variable: AVDLYGN
                                    Sum of            Mean
Source                  DF         Squares          Square   F Value   Pr > F

Model                   10      1.42537863      0.14253786      2.19   0.0324

Error                   54      3.51399676      0.06507401

Corrected Total         64      4.93937538

                R-Square           C.V.        Root MSE        AVDLYGN Mean

                0.288575        10.57882       0.2550961          2.4113846


Source                  DF      Type I SS    Mean Square   F Value   Pr > F

SIRE                     8     1.30643634     0.16330454      2.51   0.0214
AGEDAM                   2     0.11894229     0.05947115      0.91   0.4071

Source                  DF     Type II SS    Mean Square   F Value   Pr > F

AGEDAM                   2     0.11894229     0.05947115      0.91   0.4071

Source                  DF    Type III SS    Mean Square   F Value   Pr > F

AGEDAM                   2     0.11894229     0.05947115      0.91   0.4071

Contrast                DF    Contrast SS    Mean Square   F Value   Pr > F

young vs old             1     0.10295042     0.10295042      1.58   0.2139


                                    T for H0:     Pr > |T|   Std Error of
Parameter               Estimate   Parameter=0               Estimate

young vs old          0.08284028          1.26     0.2139    0.06586145


                                    T for H0:     Pr > |T|   Std Error of
Parameter               Estimate   Parameter=0               Estimate

AGEDAM     3      0.1173825552 B          1.32     0.1933    0.08911680
           4      0.0482979994 B          0.63     0.5340    0.07715379
           5      0.0000000000 B             .        .           .

NOTE: The X'X matrix has been found to be singular and a generalized inverse
      was used to solve the normal equations.  Estimates followed by the
      letter 'B' are biased, and are not unique estimators of the parameters.
```

The results in Output 5.20 and Output 5.21 are the same except that the SIRE sums of squares and the SIRE parameter estimates are not printed when SIRE is absorbed. (Note: Type I sums of squares for absorbed effects are computed as nested effects.)

Both Output 5.20 and Output 5.21 include results for the following statements:

```
contrast 'young vs old' agedam .5 .5 -1;
estimate 'young vs old' agedam .5 .5 -1;
```

The output illustrates that the CONTRAST and ESTIMATE statements are legitimate with the ABSORB statement as long as the coefficients of the linear function do not involve absorbed effects, that is, parameter estimates that are not printed (in this case the SIRE parameter estimates). The following ESTIMATE statement would not be legitimate when SIRE is absorbed because it involves the SIRE parameters:

```
estimate 'oldmean' sire .111111 ... .111111 agedam 1;
```

For the same reason, the LSMEANS statement for SIRE is not legitimate with the ABSORB statement.

The ABSORB statement is now applied to the full analysis as given by Harvey (see Output 5.19). If the sums of squares for LINE and SIRE(LINE) are not required, the remaining sums of squares can be obtained with the following statements:

```
proc glm;
    absorb line sire;
    class line agedam;
    model avdlygn=agedam line*agedam age
        intlwt / solution ss3;
```

Output 5.22 contains the output, which is identical to Harvey's output (see Output 5.19) except that neither the sums of squares nor the parameter estimates for LINE and SIRE(LINE) are computed when LINE and SIRE are absorbed.

Output 5.22
Complete
Least-Squares
Analysis of
Variance Using the
ABSORB Statement

```
                          The SAS System                              1

                  General Linear Models Procedure
                     Class Level Information

              Class     Levels     Values

              LINE          3      1 2 3

              AGEDAM        3      3 4 5


        Number of observations in data set = 65
```

```
                                                                        2

                        General Linear Models Procedure

Dependent Variable: AVDLYGN
                                     Sum of              Mean
Source                    DF         Squares            Square    F Value    Pr > F

Model                     16        2.52745871        0.15796617     3.14     0.0011

Error                     48        2.41191667        0.05024826

Corrected Total           64        4.93937538

               R-Square             C.V.          Root MSE          AVDLYGN Mean

               0.511696           9.295956        0.2241612           2.4113846


Source                    DF      Type III SS      Mean Square    F Value    Pr > F

AGEDAM                     2       0.13010623       0.06505311       1.29     0.2834
LINE*AGEDAM                4       0.45343434       0.11335859       2.26     0.0768
AGE                       1       0.38127612       0.38127612       7.59     0.0083
INTLWT                    1       0.26970425       0.26970425       5.37     0.0248


                                              T for H0:     Pr > |T|    Std Error of
Parameter                       Estimate    Parameter=0                   Estimate

AGEDAM        3             0.3703870271 B       3.23        0.0022      0.11455814
              4             0.2754594872 B       2.65        0.0107      0.10377628
              5             0.0000000000 B        .            .             .
LINE*AGEDAM  1 3           -.4489361310 B       -2.29        0.0263      0.19581259
             1 4           -.2828319237 B       -1.76        0.0851      0.16085047
             1 5            0.0000000000 B        .            .             .
             2 3           -.2607826701 B       -1.34        0.1880      0.19528690
             2 4           -.3502581329 B       -2.01        0.0502      0.17438656
             2 5            0.0000000000 B        .            .             .
             3 3            0.0000000000 B        .            .             .
             3 4            0.0000000000 B        .            .             .
             3 5            0.0000000000 B        .            .             .
AGE                        -.0085304380         -2.75        0.0083      0.00309679
INTLWT                      0.0020263340          2.32        0.0248      0.00087464

NOTE: The X'X matrix has been found to be singular and a generalized inverse
      was used to solve the normal equations.   Estimates followed by the
      letter 'B' are biased, and are not unique estimators of the parameters.
```

Chapter **6** Covariance and the Heterogeneity of Slopes

6.1   *Introduction*   *229*

6.2   *A One-Way Structure*   *230*
   6.2.1   *Covariance Model*   *230*
   6.2.2   *Means and Least-Squares Means*   *233*
   6.2.3   *Contrasts*   *234*
   6.2.4   *Multiple Covariates*   *235*

6.3   *Two-Way Structure without Interaction*   *235*

6.4   *Two-Way Structure with Interaction*   *238*

6.5   *Heterogeneity of Slopes*   *243*

6.1   Introduction

Analysis of covariance can be described as a combination of the methods of regression and analysis of variance. The basic objective is to make inferences about treatment means of a response variable y that is measured on each unit. Another variable x, called a covariable, is also measured on each unit. Analysis of covariance uses information about y that is contained in x. This is done primarily in two ways:

☐   Variation in y that is associated with x is removed from the error variance, resulting in more precise estimates and more powerful tests.

☐   Group means of the y variable are adjusted to correspond to a common value of x, thereby producing an equitable comparison of the groups.

Textbook discussions of covariance analysis focus on establishing differences between the adjusted treatment means. By explicitly bringing into the model a concomitant variable of the dependent variable of interest, you can reduce error variance. This increases the precision of the model parameter estimates. Broader uses of the covariance model are possible, such as the study of partial regression coefficients adjusted for treatment effects. Associated with the analysis of covariance is the test for differences in regression relationships among the treatments. In most cases, this test should be conducted as a preliminary step before an analysis of covariance, because the validity of the analysis of covariance requires that the slopes be homogeneous.

To give a practical definition, analysis of covariance is a model containing both continuous variables and group indicators (CLASS variables in the GLM procedure). Because the existence of CLASS variables creates less-than-full-rank models, the increased complexity can make the resulting models more difficult to interpret.

6.2   A One-Way Structure

Analysis of covariance can be applied in any data classification whenever covariables are measured. This section deals with the simplest type of classification, the one-way structure.

6.2.1   Covariance Model

The simplest covariance model is written

$$y_{ij} = \mu + \tau_i + \beta(x_{ij} - \bar{x}_{..}) + \varepsilon_{ij}$$

and combines a one-way treatment structure with parameters τ_i, one independent covariate x_{ij}, and associated regression parameter β.

An equivalent model is

$$y_{ij} = \beta_0 + \tau_i + \beta x_{ij} + \varepsilon_{ij}$$

where $\beta_0 = (\mu - \beta\bar{x}_{..})$. This expression reveals a model that represents a set of parallel lines; the common slope of the lines is β, and the intercepts are $(\beta_0 + \tau_i)$. The model contains all the elements of an analysis-of-variance model of less-than-full rank, requiring restrictions on the τ_i or the use of generalized inverses and estimable functions. Note, however, that the regression coefficient β is not affected by the singularity of the $\mathbf{X'X}$ matrix; hence, the estimate of β is unique.

The analysis of covariance is illustrated below by data on the growth of oysters. The goal is to determine

□   if exposure to water heated artificially affects growth

□   if the position in the water column (surface or bottom) affects growth.

Four bags with ten oysters in each bag are randomly placed at each of five stations in the cooling water canal of a power-generating plant. Each location, or station, is considered a treatment and is represented by the variable TRT. Each bag is considered to be one experimental unit. Two stations are located in the intake canal, and two stations are located in the discharge canal, one at the surface (TOP), the other at the bottom (BOTTOM) of each location. A single mid-depth station is located in a shallow portion of the bay near the power plant. The treatments are described below:

Treatment (TRT)	Station
1	INTAKE-BOTTOM
2	INTAKE-SURFACE
3	DISCHARGE-BOTTOM
4	DISCHARGE-SURFACE
5	BAY

Stations in the intake canal act as controls for those in the discharge canal, which has a higher temperature. The station in the bay is an overall control in case some factor other than the heat difference due to water depth or location is responsible for an observed change in growth rate.

The oysters are cleaned and measured at the beginning of the experiment and then again about one month later. The initial weight and the final weight are recorded for each bag. The data appear in Output 6.1.

Output 6.1
Data for Analysis of Covariance

```
                          The SAS System                        1

        OBS    TRT    REP    INITIAL    FINAL

         1      1      1      27.2      32.6
         2      1      2      32.0      36.6
         3      1      3      33.0      37.7
         4      1      4      26.8      31.0
         5      2      1      28.6      33.8
         6      2      2      26.8      31.7
         7      2      3      26.5      30.7
         8      2      4      26.8      30.4
         9      3      1      28.6      35.2
        10      3      2      22.4      29.1
        11      3      3      23.2      28.9
        12      3      4      24.4      30.2
        13      4      1      29.3      35.0
        14      4      2      21.8      27.0
        15      4      3      30.3      36.4
        16      4      4      24.3      30.5
        17      5      1      20.4      24.6
        18      5      2      19.6      23.4
        19      5      3      25.1      30.3
        20      5      4      18.1      21.8
```

The following SAS statements are required for the analysis:

```
proc glm;
   class trt;
   model final=trt initial / solution;
```

The CLASS statement specifies that TRT is a classification variable. The variable INITIAL is the covariate. Specifying the SOLUTION option requests printing of the coefficient vector.

Results of these statements appear in Output 6.2.

Output 6.2
Results of Analysis of Covariance

```
                          The SAS System                        1

                  General Linear Models Procedure

Dependent Variable: FINAL
                               Sum of          Mean
Source            DF           Squares         Square     F Value    Pr > F

Model              5        354.44717675    70.88943535    235.05    0.0001

Error             14          4.22232325     0.30159452

Corrected Total   19        358.66950000

             R-Square          C.V.         Root MSE           FINAL Mean

             0.988228        1.780438      0.5491762           30.845000
```

(continued on next page)

(continued from previous page)

Source	DF	Type I SS	Mean Square	F Value	Pr > F
TRT	4	198.40700000	49.60175000	164.47	0.0001
INITIAL	1	156.04017675	156.04017675	517.38	0.0001

Source	DF	Type III SS	Mean Square	F Value	Pr > F
TRT	4	12.08935928	3.02233982	10.02	0.0005
INITIAL	1	156.04017675	156.04017675	517.38	0.0001

Parameter		Estimate	T for H0: Parameter=0	Pr > |T|	Std Error of Estimate
INTERCEPT		2.494859769 B	2.43	0.0293	1.02786287
TRT	1	-0.244459378 B	-0.42	0.6780	0.57658196
	2	-0.280271345 B	-0.57	0.5786	0.49290825
	3	1.654757698 B	3.85	0.0018	0.42943036
	4	1.107113519 B	2.35	0.0342	0.47175112
	5	0.000000000 B	.	.	.
INITIAL		1.083179819	22.75	0.0001	0.04762051

NOTE: The X'X matrix has been found to be singular and a generalized inverse was used to solve the normal equations. Estimates followed by the letter 'B' are biased, and are not unique estimators of the parameters.

Consider the Type I and Type III SS (Type II and Type IV would be the same as Type III here). The Type I SS for TRT is the unadjusted treatment sum of squares. The ERROR SS for a simple analysis of variance can be reconstructed by subtracting the Type I SS from the TOTAL SS, for example,

Source	DF	SS	MS	F
TRT	4	198.407	49.602	4.642
ERROR	15	160.263	10.684	
TOTAL	19	358.670		

The resulting F value indicates that p is less than .01. Thus, a simple analysis of variance discovers treatment differences in final weight even when initial weights are not considered.

Now compare these results with the analysis of covariance. The Type III TRT SS (12.089) is the *adjusted* treatment sum of squares. The unadjusted TRT SS (198.407) is much larger than the adjusted one (12.089); however, the reduction in error mean squares from 10.684 to 0.302 allows an increase in the F statistic from 4.642 in the simple analysis of variance to 10.02 in Output 6.2. The power of the test for treatment differences increases when the covariate is included because most of the error in the simple analysis of variance is due to variation in INITIAL values.

The last part of Output 6.2 contains the SOLUTION vector. In this one-factor case, the TRT estimates are obtained by setting the estimates for the last treatment (TRT 5) to 0. Therefore, the INTERCEPT estimate is the intercept for TRT 5, and the other four treatment effects are differences between each TRT and TRT 5. Because TRT 5 is the control, the output estimates, standard errors, and t tests are for treatment versus control. Note that the means of TRT 3 and TRT 4 in the discharge canal differ from TRT 5.

The coefficient associated with INITIAL is the pooled within-groups regression coefficient relating FINAL to INITIAL. The coefficient estimate is a weighted average of the regression coefficients of FINAL on INITIAL, estimated separately for each of the five treatment groups. This coefficient estimates that a difference of 1.083 units in FINAL is associated with a one-unit difference in INITIAL.

6.2.2 Means and Least-Squares Means

A MEANS statement requests the unadjusted treatment means of all continuous (non-CLASS) variables in the model. The DEPONLY option prints only means for the dependent variable. These means are not strictly relevant to an analysis of covariance unless they are used to determine the effect of the covariance adjustment. The DUNCAN and WALLER options, among others, for multiple-comparisons tests are also available, but they are not useful here.

The LSMEANS (least-squares means) statement produces the estimates that are usually called adjusted treatment means:

$$\bar{y}_i - \hat{\beta}(\bar{x}_{i.} - \bar{x}_{..}) \quad .$$

This statement is the same one used to obtain adjusted means for the unbalanced two-way classification. Use the following SAS statement:

```
lsmeans trt / stderr pdiff;
```

The results appear in Output 6.3.

Output 6.3
Results of Analysis of Covariance: Adjusted Treatment Means (Least-Squares Means)

```
                          The SAS System                            1

                   General Linear Models Procedure
                        Least Squares Means

        TRT        FINAL       Std Err      Pr > |T|    LSMEAN
                   LSMEAN       LSMEAN     H0:LSMEAN=0   Number

         1       30.1531125    0.3339174     0.0001       1
         2       30.1173006    0.2827350     0.0001       2
         3       32.0523296    0.2796295     0.0001       3
         4       31.5046854    0.2764082     0.0001       4
         5       30.3975719    0.3621988     0.0001       5

              Pr > |T|  H0: LSMEAN(i)=LSMEAN(j)

          i/j     1        2        3        4        5
          1       .      0.9312   0.0010   0.0061   0.6780
          2     0.9312     .      0.0003   0.0032   0.5786
          3     0.0010   0.0003     .      0.1898   0.0018
          4     0.0061   0.0032   0.1898     .      0.0342
          5     0.6780   0.5786   0.0018   0.0342     .

NOTE: To ensure overall protection level, only probabilities associated with
      pre-planned comparisons should be used.
```

The estimated least-squares means are followed by their standard errors, which are printed because of the STDERR option. Significance probabilities for all pairwise tests of treatment differences are printed because of the PDIFF option.

Note the large changes in going from the unadjusted to adjusted treatment means for the variable FINAL in the table below:

TRT	Unadjusted Means	Adjusted Least-Squares Means
1	34.475	30.153
2	31.650	30.117
3	30.850	32.052
4	32.225	31.504
5	25.025	30.398

These changes are due to the large treatment differences for the variable INITIAL. Apparently, the assignment of oysters to treatments was not truly random. Some treatments, particularly TRT 5, received smaller oysters than other treatments. This biases the unadjusted treatment means. Computation of the adjusted treatment means is intended to remove the bias.

6.2.3 Contrasts

This section illustrates comparing means with contrasts, using the oyster growth example discussed in Section 6.2.1, "Covariance Model." The five treatments can also be looked upon as a 2×2 factorial (BOTTOM/TOP $\times$ INTAKE/DISCHARGE) plus a CONTROL. The adjusted treatment means from the analysis of covariance can be analyzed further with four orthogonal contrasts implemented by the following CONTRAST statements:

```
contrast  'CONTROL VS. TREATMENT'  TRT  -1  -1  -1  -1   4 ;
contrast  'BOTTOM VS. TOP'         TRT  -1   1  -1   1     ;
contrast  'INTAKE VS. DISCHARGE'   TRT  -1  -1   1   1     ;
contrast  'BOT/TOP*INT/DIS'        TRT   1  -1  -1   1     ;
```

The output that results from these statements follows the partitioning of sums of squares in Output 6.4. Note that the only significant contrast is INTAKE VS. DISCHARGE.

Equivalent results can be obtained with the ESTIMATE statement, which also gives the estimated coefficients for the contrasts. All options for CONTRAST and ESTIMATE statements discussed in Chapter 2, "Analysis of Variance for Balanced Data," and in Chapter 4, "Details of the Linear Model: Understanding GLM Concepts," apply here. Although constructed to be orthogonal, these contrasts are not orthogonal to the covariable; hence, their sums of squares do not add to the adjusted treatment sums of squares.

Output 6.4
Results of Analysis of Covariance: Orthogonal Contrasts

```
                                The SAS System                               1

Contrast                 DF     Contrast SS    Mean Square   F Value   Pr > F

CONTROL VS. TREATMEN      1      0.52000411     0.52000411      1.72    0.2103
BOTTOM VS. TOP           1      0.33879074     0.33879074      1.12    0.3071
INTAKE VS. DISCHARGE     1      8.59108077     8.59108077     28.49    0.0001
BOT/TOP*INT/DIS          1      0.22934155     0.22934155      0.76    0.3979
```

6.2.4 Multiple Covariates

Multiple covariates are specified as continuous (non-CLASS) variables in the MODEL statement. If the CLASS variable is designated as the first independent variable, the Type I sums of squares for individual covariates can be added to get the adjusted sums of squares due to all covariates. The Type III sums of squares are the fully adjusted sums of squares for the individual regression coefficients as well as those for the adjusted treatment means.

6.3 Two-Way Structure without Interaction

Analysis of covariance can be applied to other experimental and treatment structures. This section illustrates covariance analysis of a two-factor factorial experiment with two covariates.

The data for this example are from a study of the relationship between the price of oranges and sales per customer. The hypothesis is that sales vary as a function of price differences (PRICE), different stores (STORE), and days of the week (DAY). PRICE is varied daily for two comparable varieties of oranges, and the per-customer sales of each variety are recorded. Output 6.5 shows the data. It is expected that a price increase in one of the varieties will produce a decrease in sales of that variety and an increase in sales of the other variety.

Output 6.5
Data for Analysis of Covariance: Two-Way Structure without Interaction

```
                                The SAS System                               1

       OBS    STORE    WEEK    DAY    P1    P2       Q1         Q2

        1       1       1       1     37    61    11.3208      0.0047
        2       1       1       2     37    37    12.9151      0.0037
        3       1       1       3     45    53    18.8947      7.5429
        4       1       1       4     41    41    14.6739      7.0652
        5       1       1       5     57    41     8.6493     21.2085
        6       1       1       6     49    33     9.5238     16.6667
        7       2       1       1     49    49     7.6923      7.1154
        8       2       1       2     53    53     0.0017      1.0000
        9       2       1       3     53    45     8.0477     24.2176
       10       2       1       4     53    53     6.7358      2.9361
       11       2       1       5     61    37     6.1441     40.5720
       12       2       1       6     49    65    21.7939      2.8324
       13       3       1       1     53    45     4.2553      6.0284
       14       3       1       2     57    57     0.0017      2.0906
       15       3       1       3     49    49    11.0196     13.9329
       16       3       1       4     53    53     6.2762      6.5551
       17       3       1       5     53    45    13.2316     10.6870
       18       3       1       6     53    53     5.0676      5.1351
       19       4       1       1     57    57     5.6235      3.9120
       20       4       1       2     49    49    14.9893      7.2805
       21       4       1       3     53    53    13.7233     16.3105
       22       4       1       4     53    45     6.0669     23.8494
       23       4       1       5     53    53     8.1602      4.1543
```

(continued on next page)

(continued from previous page)

24	4	1	6	61	37	1.4423	21.1538
25	5	1	1	45	45	6.9971	6.9971
26	5	1	2	53	45	5.2308	3.6923
27	5	1	3	57	57	8.2560	10.6679
28	5	1	4	49	49	14.5000	16.7500
29	5	1	5	53	53	20.7627	15.2542
30	5	1	6	53	45	3.6115	21.5442
31	6	1	1	53	53	11.3475	4.9645
32	6	1	2	53	45	9.4650	11.7284
33	6	1	3	53	53	22.6103	14.8897
34	6	1	4	61	37	0.0020	19.2000
35	6	1	5	49	65	20.5997	2.3468
36	6	1	6	37	37	28.1828	17.9543

A model for the sales of the two varieties of oranges is

$$Q_1 = \mu_1 + \tau_{1i} + \delta_{1j} + \beta_{11}P_1 + \beta_{12}P_2 + \varepsilon_1$$

$$Q_2 = \mu_2 + \tau_{2i} + \delta_{2j} + \beta_{21}P_1 + \beta_{22}P_2 + \varepsilon_2$$

where, for the two varieties,

Q_1 and Q_2	equal the sales per customer.
τ_{1i} and τ_{2i}	equal the effects of STORE, $i=1, 2, \ldots, 6$.
δ_{1j} and δ_{2j}	equal the effects of DAY, $j=1, 2, \ldots, 6$.
β_{11} and β_{21}	equal the coefficients of the relationship between sales, Q_1 and Q_2, and P_1 (the price of one variety of oranges).
β_{12} and β_{22}	equal the coefficients of the relationship between sales, Q_1 and Q_2, and P_2 (the price of the other variety of oranges).
ε_1 and ε_2	equal the random error terms.

Note that because there is no replication, the interaction between STORE and DAY must be used as the error term. In this example, the primary focus is on the influence of PRICE on sales Q_1 and Q_2; the DAY and STORE differences are of secondary importance.

Because the entire experiment is very large, only data for the first six days for six stores (36 observations) are analyzed. The model is implemented by the following SAS statements:

```
proc glm;
   class store day;
   model q1 q2=store day p1 p2 / solution;
   lsmeans day / stderr;
```

The output for Q1 appears in Output 6.6.

Output 6.6
Results of Analysis of Covariance: Two-Way Structure without Interaction

```
                              The SAS System                            1
                      General Linear Models Procedure

Dependent Variable: Q1
                               Sum of          Mean
Source              DF         Squares         Square    F Value    Pr > F

Model               12      1225.3675481   102.1139623     5.75     0.0002

Error               23       408.3082418    17.7525323

Corrected Total     35      1633.6757899

           R-Square           C.V.          Root MSE            Q1 Mean

           0.750068        41.23842        4.2133754          10.217111


Source              DF       Type I SS    Mean Square   F Value    Pr > F

STORE                5     313.41980708    62.68396142     3.53     0.0163
DAY                  5     250.39727225    50.07945445     2.82     0.0396
P1                   1     622.00821682   622.00821682    35.04     0.0001
P2                   1      39.54225192    39.54225192     2.23     0.1492

Source              DF      Type III SS   Mean Square   F Value    Pr > F

STORE                5     223.83267344    44.76653469     2.52     0.0583
DAY                  5     433.09686996    86.61937399     4.88     0.0035
P1                   1     538.16885116   538.16885116    30.32     0.0001
P2                   1      39.54225192    39.54225192     2.23     0.1492


                                    T for H0:    Pr > |T|   Std Error of
Parameter              Estimate    Parameter=0               Estimate

INTERCEPT            51.69987930 B      5.28      0.0001     9.79103443
STORE       1        -7.64532641 B     -2.84      0.0093     2.69194414
            2        -5.60226472 B     -2.27      0.0327     2.46416942
            3        -7.36284806 B     -2.99      0.0066     2.46416942
            4        -4.36498239 B     -1.75      0.0926     2.48754952
            5        -5.02052157 B     -2.06      0.0508     2.43612208
            6         0.00000000 B       .          .            .
DAY         1        -5.83036664 B     -2.31      0.0299     2.51932754
            2        -4.89997548 B     -2.00      0.0572     2.44708866
            3         2.26978922 B      0.89      0.3808     2.54028189
            4        -2.65249315 B     -1.08      0.2895     2.44667751
            5         4.04702055 B      1.58      0.1271     2.55655852
            6         0.00000000 B       .          .            .
P1                   -0.83036470        -5.51      0.0001     0.15081334
P2                    0.14884706         1.49      0.1492     0.09973319

NOTE: The X'X matrix has been found to be singular and a generalized inverse
      was used to solve the normal equations.  Estimates followed by the
      letter 'B' are biased, and are not unique estimators of the parameters.

                      General Linear Models Procedure
                           Least Squares Means

         DAY         Q1         Std Err    Pr > |T|
                   LSMEAN       LSMEAN    H0:LSMEAN=0

          1       5.5644154    1.7680833    0.0045
          2       6.4948065    1.7289585    0.0010
          3      13.6645712    1.7515046    0.0001
          4       8.7422889    1.7339197    0.0001
          5      15.4418026    1.7858085    0.0001
          6      11.3947820    1.7667260    0.0001


         DAY         Q2         Std Err    Pr > |T|
                   LSMEAN       LSMEAN    H0:LSMEAN=0

          1       7.7156637    2.3264852    0.0030
          2       3.9764457    2.2750039    0.0938
          3      16.5978143    2.3046706    0.0001
          4      11.0445400    2.2815319    0.0001
          5      14.9907861    2.3498084    0.0001
          6      12.0487835    2.3246991    0.0001
```

In addition to the details previously discussed, these also are of interest:

□ The Type I SS for P1 and P2 can be summed to obtain a test for the partial contribution of both prices:

$$F_{2,23} = [(622.01 + 39.54) / 2] / (17.75) = 74.54 \quad .$$

□ The Type III SS show that all effects are highly significant except P2, the price of the competing orange.

□ Each coefficient estimate is the mean difference between each CLASS variable value (STORE, DAY) and the last CLASS variable value, because there is no interaction.

□ The P1 coefficient is negative, indicating the expected negatively sloping price response (demand function). The P2 coefficient, although not significant, has the expected positive sign for the price response of a competing product.

□ Least-squares means are requested only for DAY, which shows the expected higher sales toward the end of the week.

Contrasts and estimates of linear functions could, of course, be requested with this analysis.

6.4 Two-Way Structure with Interaction

The most complex covariance model discussed in this chapter is a two-factor factorial with two stages of subsampling. Using a subset of data from a larger experiment, the objective of the study is to estimate y, the weight of usable lint from x, the total weight of cotton bolls. In addition, it is useful to see if lint estimation is affected by varieties of cotton (VAR) and the distance between planting rows (SPAC), using x, the boll weight, as a covariate in the analysis of y, the lint weight. The study is a factorial experiment with two levels of VAR (37 and 213) and two levels of SPAC (30 and 40). There are two plants for each VAR×SPAC treatment combination, and there are from five to nine bolls per plant (PLT). The model for the analysis is

$$y_{ijkl} = \mu + v_i + \tau_j + (v\tau)_{ij} + \gamma(v\tau)_{ijk} + \beta x_{ijkl} + \varepsilon_{ijkl}$$

where

y_{ijkl}	equals the weight of the lint for the ith VAR, jth SPAC, kth PLT of the (i,j)th cell, and lth boll of each plant.
μ	equals the base or mean intercept.
v_i	equals the effect of the ith VAR.
τ_j	equals the effect of the jth SPAC.
$(v\tau)_{ij}$	equals the VAR×SPAC interaction.
$\gamma(v\tau)_{ijk}$	equals the effect of the kth plant in the (i,j)th VAR and SPAC combination.

β equals the regression effect of the covariate.

x_{ijkl} equals the total weight of each boll, the covariate.

ε_{ijkl} equals the error variation among bolls within plants.

The data appear in Output 6.7.

Output 6.7
Data for Analysis
of Covariance:
Two-Way Structure
with Interaction

```
                         The SAS System                        1

        OBS     VAR    SPAC    PLT    BOLL    LINT

          1      37     30      3     8.4     2.9
          2      37     30      3     8.0     2.5
          3      37     30      3     7.4     2.7
          4      37     30      3     8.9     3.1
          5      37     30      5     5.6     2.1
          6      37     30      5     8.0     2.7
          7      37     30      5     7.6     2.5
          8      37     30      5     5.4     1.5
          9      37     30      5     6.9     2.5
         10      37     40      3     4.5     1.3
         11      37     40      3     9.1     3.1
         12      37     40      3     9.0     3.1
         13      37     40      3     8.0     2.3
         14      37     40      3     7.2     2.2
         15      37     40      3     7.6     2.5
         16      37     40      3     9.0     3.0
         17      37     40      3     2.3     0.6
         18      37     40      3     8.7     3.0
         19      37     40      5     8.0     2.6
         20      37     40      5     7.2     2.5
         21      37     40      5     7.6     2.4
         22      37     40      5     6.9     2.2
         23      37     40      5     6.9     2.5
         24      37     40      5     7.6     2.4
         25      37     40      5     4.7     1.4
         26     213     30      3     4.6     1.7
         27     213     30      3     6.8     1.7
         28     213     30      3     3.5     1.3
         29     213     30      3     2.4     1.0
         30     213     30      3     3.0     1.0
         31     213     30      5     2.8     0.5
         32     213     30      5     3.6     0.9
         33     213     30      5     6.7     1.9
         34     213     40      0     7.4     2.1
         35     213     40      0     4.9     1.0
         36     213     40      0     5.7     1.0
         37     213     40      0     3.0     0.7
         38     213     40      0     4.7     1.5
         39     213     40      0     5.0     1.3
         40     213     40      0     2.8     0.4
         41     213     40      0     5.2     1.2
         42     213     40      0     5.6     1.0
         43     213     40      3     4.5     1.0
         44     213     40      3     5.6     1.2
         45     213     40      3     2.0     0.7
         46     213     40      3     1.2     0.2
         47     213     40      3     4.2     1.2
         48     213     40      3     5.3     1.2
         49     213     40      3     7.0     1.7
```

The primary focus of this study is on estimating lint weight from boll weight (that is, the regression) and only later in determining if this relationship is affected by VAR and SPAC factors. In the SAS program to analyze the data, the order of variables in the MODEL statement is changed so that the Type I sums of squares provide the appropriate information:

```
proc glm;
    class var spac plt;
    model lint=boll var spac var*spac
            plt(var*spac) / solution;
    test h=var spac var*spac e=plt(var*spac);
```

Note that a TEST statement has been added because the plant-to-plant variation provides the appropriate error term. Results of the analysis appear in Output 6.8.

Output 6.8
Results of Analysis
of Covariance:
Two-Way Structure
with Interaction

```
                              The SAS System                       1

                      General Linear Models Procedure

Dependent Variable: LINT
                                      Sum of            Mean
Source                   DF          Squares          Square   F Value   Pr > F

Model                     8      31.16009287      3.89501161     80.70   0.0001

Error                    40       1.93051938      0.04826298

Corrected Total          48      33.09061224

                 R-Square              C.V.        Root MSE          LINT Mean

                 0.941660          12.37325       0.2196884          1.7755102


Source                   DF       Type I SS     Mean Square   F Value   Pr > F

BOLL                      1      29.06931406     29.06931406    602.31   0.0001
VAR                       1       1.26353553      1.26353553     26.18   0.0001
SPAC                      1       0.46664798      0.46664798      9.67   0.0034
VAR*SPAC                  1       0.09326994      0.09326994      1.93   0.1722
PLT(VAR*SPAC)             4       0.26732535      0.06683134      1.38   0.2565

Source                   DF     Type III SS     Mean Square   F Value   Pr > F

BOLL                      1      11.11855999     11.11855999    230.37   0.0001
VAR                       1       0.01420238      0.01420238      0.29   0.5905
SPAC                      1       0.33964071      0.33964071      7.04   0.0114
VAR*SPAC                  1       0.07245571      0.07245571      1.50   0.2276
PLT(VAR*SPAC)             4       0.26732535      0.06683134      1.38   0.2565

Tests of Hypotheses using the Type III MS for PLT(VAR*SPAC) as an error term

Source                   DF     Type III SS     Mean Square   F Value   Pr > F

VAR                       1       0.01420238      0.01420238      0.21   0.6688
SPAC                      1       0.33964071      0.33964071      5.08   0.0872
VAR*SPAC                  1       0.07245571      0.07245571      1.08   0.3566


                                            T for H0:    Pr > |T|   Std Error of
Parameter                    Estimate    Parameter=0                  Estimate

INTERCEPT               -.3709355243 B       -3.01       0.0045      0.12322715
BOLL                     0.3056076686        15.18       0.0001      0.02013479
VAR            37        0.4539343452 B        1.89       0.0656      0.23977703
               213       0.0000000000 B          .           .            .
SPAC           30        0.9707479174 B        3.03       0.0043      0.32030812
               40        0.0000000000 B          .           .            .
VAR*SPAC       37 30    -.6182463958 B        -1.23       0.2276      0.50458273
               37 40     0.0000000000 B          .           .            .
               213 30    0.0000000000 B          .           .            .
               213 40    0.0000000000 B          .           .            .
PLT(VAR*SPAC)  37 30    -.0446143444         -0.59       0.5562      0.07516708
               37 40     0.0135655217          0.24       0.8079      0.05542848
```

```
                                                                              2
                        General Linear Models Procedure

Dependent Variable: LINT

                                       T for H0:   Pr > |T|   Std Error of
Parameter                  Estimate   Parameter=0             Estimate

PLT(VAR*SPAC) 213 30    -.1668598425      -2.08      0.0441     0.08027824
              213 40   0.0328304831       0.88      0.3824     0.03717315

NOTE: The X'X matrix has been found to be singular and a generalized inverse
      was used to solve the normal equations.   Estimates followed by the
      letter 'B' are biased, and are not unique estimators of the parameters.
```

The Type I SS for BOLL is what would be obtained by a simple linear regression of LINT on BOLL. If you ran this simple linear regression, you would get an R^2 value of $(29.069/33.091) = 0.878$, a residual mean square of $(33.091 - 29.069)/47) = 0.08557$, and an F statistic of 339.69, thus indicating a strong relationship of lint weight to boll weight.

However, the complete model fits somewhat better. The Type III SS show significant contributions from VAR and SPAC but not from the VAR*SPAC interaction. Note that the plant-to-plant variation, measured by the mean square of PLT(VAR*SPAC), is not significantly larger than the boll-to-boll variation, measured by the mean square of ERROR.

Given these results, the model has more factors than necessary; hence, the coefficient estimates or other statistics are not needed. Drop VAR*SPAC and PLT(VAR*SPAC), and use the following statements to reestimate:

```
model lint=boll var spac / solution;
lsmeans var spac / stderr;
```

The results in Output 6.9 differ only slightly from those in Output 6.8.

This model specifies a single regression coefficient that relates LINT to BOLL (0.3014), but with different intercepts for the four treatment combinations. These intercepts can be constructed from the SOLUTION vector by summing appropriate component values.

For example, for VAR=37, SPAC=30, the model estimate is

$$y = \mu + \nu_1 + \tau_1 + \beta_x = -.2769 + .4107 + .2052 + .3014x \quad .$$

For the other treatment combinations, the results are

VAR	SPAC	values for model estimate, where x is BOLL, the covariate
37	40	$.1338 + .3014x$
213	30	$-.0715 + .3014x$
213	40	$-.2769 + .3014x$

Note that these results can be obtained with ESTIMATE statements. Least-squares means appear in Output 6.9; other statistics can be obtained but are not necessary in this situation.

Output 6.9
*Results of a
Simplified
Covariance
Analysis: Two-Way
Structure with
Interaction*

```
                             The SAS System                              1

                      General Linear Models Procedure

Dependent Variable: LINT
                                   Sum of            Mean
Source               DF          Squares            Square   F Value   Pr > F

Model                 3       30.79949757      10.26649919    201.65   0.0001

Error                45        2.29111467       0.05091366

Corrected Total      48       33.09061224

             R-Square             C.V.         Root MSE         LINT Mean

             0.930762         12.70849        0.2256406         1.7755102


Source               DF        Type I SS      Mean Square   F Value   Pr > F

BOLL                  1       29.06931406      29.06931406    570.95   0.0001
VAR                   1        1.26353553       1.26353553     24.82   0.0001
SPAC                  1        0.46664798       0.46664798      9.17   0.0041

Source               DF      Type III SS      Mean Square   F Value   Pr > F

BOLL                  1       11.57173388      11.57173388    227.28   0.0001
VAR                   1        1.19732512       1.19732512     23.52   0.0001
SPAC                  1        0.46664798       0.46664798      9.17   0.0041


                                        T for H0:   Pr > |T|   Std Error of
Parameter                 Estimate    Parameter=0                 Estimate

INTERCEPT              -.2769483300 B       -2.67     0.0106     0.10384452
BOLL                   0.3014429094        15.08     0.0001     0.01999507
VAR         37         0.4106564020 B        4.85     0.0001     0.08468173
            213        0.0000000000 B         .          .           .
SPAC        30         0.2052058951 B        3.03     0.0041     0.06778167
            40         0.0000000000 B         .          .           .

NOTE: The X'X matrix has been found to be singular and a generalized inverse
      was used to solve the normal equations.  Estimates followed by the
      letter 'B' are biased, and are not unique estimators of the parameters.
```

```
                  General Linear Models Procedure
                     Least Squares Means

         VAR        LINT        Std Err      Pr > |T|
                    LSMEAN       LSMEAN     HO:LSMEAN=0

         37      2.00805710   0.05320406     0.0001
         213     1.59740070   0.05523778     0.0001



         SPAC       LINT        Std Err      Pr > |T|
                    LSMEAN       LSMEAN     HO:LSMEAN=0

         30      1.90533185   0.05479483     0.0001
         40      1.70012595   0.03988849     0.0001
```

6.5 Heterogeneity of Slopes

Testing for heterogeneity of slopes is a natural extension of covariance analysis. Both types of analyses are usually applied to data characterized by treatment groups and one or more covariates. Covariance analyses test for differences in intercepts assuming a constant regression relationship among groups. The test for heterogeneity of slopes tests the validity of this assumption; that is, it tests whether or not the regression coefficients are constant over groups. For example, consider the model for one independent variable (covariate) and a one-way structure of the form

$$y_{ij} = \beta_{0i} + \beta_{1i}x_{1ij} + \varepsilon$$

where i denotes the treatment group. The hypothesis of interest is

$$H_0: \beta_{1i} = \beta'_{1i} \quad \text{for all } i \neq i' \quad .$$

An alternate formulation of the model is

$$y_{ij} = \bar{\beta}_0 + \beta_{0i} + \bar{\beta}_1 x_{1ij} + \beta_{1i} x_{1ij} + \varepsilon$$

where $\bar{\beta}_0$ and $\bar{\beta}_1$ are average regression coefficients, β_{0i} and β_{1i} are treatment effect coefficients, and the hypothesis is

$$H_0 = \beta_{1i} = 0 \quad i = 1, 2, \ldots, t \quad .$$

Note that any possible intercept differences are irrelevant to both hypotheses.

Regression relationships that differ among treatment groups actually reflect an interaction between the treatment groups and the independent variables or covariates. In fact, the GLM procedure specifies and analyzes this phenomenon as an interaction. Thus, if you use the following statements, the expression X*A produces the appropriate statistics for estimating different regressions of Y on X for the different values, or classes, specified by A:

```
proc glm;
   class a;
   model y=x a x*a / solution;
```

In this application, the Type I sums of squares for this model provide the most useful information:

X   is the sum of squares due to a single regression of Y on X, ignoring the group.

A   is the sum of squares due to different intercepts (adjusted treatment differences), assuming equal slopes.

X*A   is an additional sum of squares due to different regression coefficients for the groups specified by the factor A.

    The associated sequence of tests provides a logical stepwise analysis to determine the most appropriate model. Equivalent results can also be obtained by specifying nested effects. The following statements fit the same model:

```
proc glm;
   class a;
   model y=a x(a) / solution;
```

However, X(A) does not specifically test for heterogeneity of slopes but tests the hypothesis that *all* regression coefficients are 0. For models like this one, the Type III (or Type IV) sums of squares have little meaning; it is not instructive to consider the effect of the CLASS variable over and above the effect of different regressions.

    The orange sales data in Output 6.5 are used here to illustrate the comparison of slopes. For this example, the day-to-day difference in the relationship of orange sales to orange prices for only the first variety of oranges is considered. The desired analysis is implemented by the following statements:

```
proc glm;
   class day;
   model q1=p1 day p1*day / solution;
```

The results of the analysis appear in Output 6.10.

Output 6.10
*Results of Analysis
of Covariance: Test
for Homogeneity
of Regression*

```
                              The SAS System                        1

                      General Linear Models Procedure

Dependent Variable: Q1
                                   Sum of           Mean
Source                DF          Squares          Square   F Value   Pr > F

Model                 11     1111.5225623     101.0475057      4.64   0.0008

Error                 24      522.1532276      21.7563845

Corrected Total       35     1633.6757899

              R-Square           C.V.        Root MSE            Q1 Mean

              0.680381       45.65257       4.6643740          10.217111


Source                DF        Type I SS     Mean Square   F Value   Pr > F

P1                     1    516.59214076    516.59214076     23.74   0.0001
DAY                    5    430.53841746     86.10768349      3.96   0.0093
P1*DAY                 5    164.39200403     32.87840081      1.51   0.2236
```

Source	DF	Type III SS	Mean Square	F Value	Pr > F
P1	1	554.78609850	554.78609850	25.50	0.0001
DAY	5	201.17177008	40.23435402	1.85	0.1412
P1*DAY	5	164.39200403	32.87840081	1.51	0.2236

Parameter		Estimate	T for H0: Parameter=0	Pr > |T|	Std Error of Estimate
INTERCEPT		73.27263578 B	5.43	0.0001	13.48373708
P1		-1.22521164 B	-4.62	0.0001	0.26520396
DAY	1	-54.59714671 B	-2.77	0.0107	19.73545845
	2	-34.78570099 B	-1.72	0.0987	20.25105926
	3	-27.94295765 B	-0.95	0.3518	29.42842946
	4	-24.12342640 B	-1.13	0.2706	21.39334761
	5	4.62631110 B	0.15	0.8812	30.62842608
	6	0.00000000 B	.	.	.
P1*DAY	1	1.00474758 B	2.55	0.0176	0.39410534
	2	0.60164207 B	1.51	0.1444	0.39876566
	3	0.61415851 B	1.08	0.2923	0.57034268
	4	0.42959726 B	1.03	0.3110	0.41510986
	5	0.02936476 B	0.05	0.9594	0.57034268
	6	0.00000000 B	.	.	.

NOTE: The X'X matrix has been found to be singular and a generalized inverse was used to solve the normal equations. Estimates followed by the letter 'B' are biased, and are not unique estimators of the parameters.

The Type I sums of squares show that

□ the PRICE has an effect on SALES

□ the DAY of the week has an effect on SALES at any given PRICE

□ there is no significant difference in the SALES/PRICE relationship for different values of DAY.

Thus, a standard covariance analysis is indicated. The appropriate estimates are obtained by repeating the analysis and by omitting the P1*DAY expression in the MODEL statement.

Although differences in the daily regression coefficients are not statistically significant, it is instructive to look at these estimates. They are obtained with ESTIMATE statements that specify construction of the coefficients. According to the MODEL statement, each daily coefficient is composed of the average price coefficient (labeled P1) and the *i*th daily interaction coefficient (P1*DAY(*i*)). The ESTIMATE statements required to obtain the coefficients appear below:

```
estimate 'P1:DAY1' p1 1  p1*day 1 0 0 0 0 0;
estimate 'P1:DAY2' p1 1  p1*day 0 1 0 0 0 0;
estimate 'P1:DAY3' p1 1  p1*day 0 0 1 0 0 0;
estimate 'P1:DAY4' p1 1  p1*day 0 0 0 1 0 0;
estimate 'P1:DAY5' p1 1  p1*dAy 0 0 0 0 1 0;
estimate 'P1:DAY6' p1 1  p1*day 0 0 0 0 0 1;
```

These statements can be abbreviated by deleting trailing zeros.

The results normally follow the Type III sum of squares, as shown in Output 6.11.

Output 6.11
Estimated Daily
Regression
Coefficients

```
                              The SAS System                              1

                                       T for H0:              Std Error of
          Parameter          Estimate  Parameter=0  Pr > |T|  Estimate

          P1:DAY1          -0.22046406    -0.76       0.4569   0.29152337
          P1:DAY2          -0.62356957    -2.09       0.0470   0.29779341
          P1:DAY3          -0.61105313    -1.21       0.2380   0.50493329
          P1:DAY4          -0.79561438    -2.49       0.0200   0.31934785
          P1:DAY5          -1.19584687    -2.37       0.0263   0.50493329
          P1:DAY6          -1.22521164    -4.62       0.0001   0.26520396
```

Note that these estimated coefficients are larger toward the end of the week. This is quite reasonable given the higher level of overall sales activity near the end of the week, which may result in a proportionately larger response in sales to changes in price. Thus, it is likely that a coefficient specifically testing for a linear trend in price response during the week would be significant.

Using more than one independent variable is straightforward and can determine which variables have a different coefficient for each treatment group. More complex designs are not difficult to implement but may be difficult to interpret.

Chapter **7** Multivariate Linear Models

7.1 *Introduction* *247*

7.2 *Statistical Background* *248*

7.3 *A One-Way Multivariate Analysis of Variance* *249*

7.4 *Hotelling's T^2 Test* *252*

7.5 *A Two-Factor Factorial* *255*

7.6 *Multivariate Analysis of Covariance* *260*

7.7 *Contrasts in Multivariate Analyses* *263*

7.1 Introduction

Although the methods presented in earlier chapters are sufficient for studying one dependent variable at a time, there are many situations in which several dependent variables are studied simultaneously. For example, in monitoring the growth of animals, a researcher might measure the length, weight, and girth of animals receiving different treatments. The goal of the experiment would be to see if the treatments had an effect on the growth of the animals. One way to determine this would be to use analysis of variance or regression methods to analyze the effects of the treatment on the length, weight, and girth of the animals. There are two problems with this approach. First, dealing with the amount of output produced by separate univariate (one variable at a time) analyses of each of the variables can be unwieldy. In the example with three dependent variables, this may not seem like a problem. But if you have ten or twenty dependent variables, the volume of output could be substantial. Second, and more importantly, when many variables are studied simultaneously, they are almost always correlated; that is, the value of each variable may be related to the values of others. This is true for measurements such as height and weight, responses to similar questions on a questionnaire, or measurements made over time. In cases like these, considering the univariate analyses separately would not take into account information contained in the data due to the correlation. Moreover, this approach could mislead a naive researcher into believing that a factor has a very significant effect, when in fact it does not. On the other hand, a significant effect that only becomes apparent when all the dependent variables are studied simultaneously may not be discovered from the univariate analyses alone. When dealing with multivariate data, you should usually examine the results of the multivariate tests first, then examine the univariate analyses only if significant results appear in the multivariate analysis.

Although some of the details of a multivariate analysis differ from those of a univariate analysis, the two are similar in many ways. Experimental factors of interest are related to the dependent variables by a linear model, and functions of sums of squares are computed to test hypotheses about these factors. In general, if you have designed an experiment with only one dependent variable, the extension of the analysis to the multivariate case can be carried out in a very straightforward manner.

7.2 Statistical Background

The multivariate linear model can be written as

$$\mathbf{Y} = \mathbf{XB} + \mathbf{U}$$

where

Y   is an $n \times k$ matrix of observed values of k dependent variables or responses. Each column corresponds to a specific dependent variable and each row to an observation.

X   is an $n \times m$ matrix of n observations on the m independent variables (which may contain dummy variables).

B   is an $m \times k$ matrix of regression coefficients or parameters. Each column of **B** is a vector of coefficients corresponding to each of k dependent variables, and each row contains the coefficients associated with each of m independent variables.

U   is the $n \times k$ matrix of the n random errors, with columns corresponding to the dependent variables.

The matrix of estimated coefficients is

$$\hat{\mathbf{B}} = (\mathbf{X}'\mathbf{X})^{-1}\mathbf{X}'\mathbf{Y} \quad .$$

Each column of $\hat{\mathbf{B}}$ is the vector of estimated coefficients that would be obtained by estimating coefficients for each response variable separately.

The partitioning of sums of squares is parallel to that developed in previous chapters except the partitions consist of $k \times k$ matrices of sums of squares and crossproducts:

Sums of Squares	SSCP Matrix
TOTAL	$\mathbf{Y}'\mathbf{Y}$
MODEL	$\hat{\mathbf{B}}'\mathbf{X}'\mathbf{Y}$
ERROR	$\mathbf{Y}'\mathbf{Y} - \hat{\mathbf{B}}'\mathbf{X}'\mathbf{Y}$

In the univariate analysis of variance, the F statistic is the statistic of choice in most cases for testing hypotheses about the factors being considered. Recall that this statistic is derived by taking the ratio of two sums of squares, one derived from the hypothesis being tested and the other derived from an appropriate error term. In multivariate linear models, these sums of squares are replaced by matrices of sums of squares and crossproducts. These matrices are represented by **H** for the hypothesis, corresponding to the numerator sum of squares, and **E** for the error matrix, corresponding to the denominator sum of squares. Since division of matrices is not possible, $\mathbf{E}^{-1}\mathbf{H}$ is the matrix that is the basis for test statistics for multivariate hypotheses. Four different functions of this matrix are used as test statistics and are available in PROC GLM and PROC ANOVA (as well as many of the other multivariate procedures available with the SAS System). Each of these statistics is a function of the *characteristic roots* (also known as eigenvalues) of the matrix $\mathbf{E}^{-1}\mathbf{H}$. In the formulas below, λ_i represents the characteristic roots.

Corresponding to each characteristic root is a *characteristic vector*, or eigenvector, that represents a linear combination of the dependent variables being analyzed. A function of the characteristic root, $\lambda/(1+\lambda)$, is the value of R^2 that would be obtained if the linear combination of dependent variables represented by the corresponding characteristic vector were used as the dependent variable in a univariate analysis of the same model; for this reason, that function of the characteristic root is sometimes called the *canonical correlation*. In the formulas below, r_i^2 represents the canonical correlations.

Hotelling-Lawley Trace	Pillai's Trace
$= Tr(\mathbf{E}^{-1}\mathbf{H})$	$= Tr(\mathbf{H}(\mathbf{H}+\mathbf{E})^{-1})$
$= \Sigma\, r_i^2 / (1 - r_i^2)$	$= \Sigma\, r_i^2$
$= \Sigma\, \lambda_i$	$= \Sigma\, \lambda_i / (1 + \lambda_i)$

Wilks' Criterion	Roy's Maximum Root
$= \mid \mathbf{E} \mid\, /\, \mid \mathbf{H} + \mathbf{E} \mid$	$= \max \lambda_i$
$= \Pi(1 - r_i^2)$	$= \max r_i^2$
$= \Pi(1 / (1 + \lambda_i))$	

Simulation studies have not been able to identify any one of the criteria as being universally superior to the others, although there are hypothesized situations where one criterion may outperform the others. Because we generally do not know the exact form of the alternative hypotheses being studied, the decision of which test criterion to use often becomes a matter of personal choice. Wilks' criterion is derived from a likelihood-ratio approach and appeals to some statisticians on those grounds.

7.3 A One-Way Multivariate Analysis of Variance

Test scores from two exams taken by students with three different teachers are analyzed in Output 7.1. As shown in Output 7.2, there is no difference among teachers when considering a univariate analysis of SCORE2. The objective now is to see if a model using both scores shows a difference among teachers.

Because this is a one-way structure, it is preferable to use PROC ANOVA. The following SAS statements are used for this analysis:

```
proc anova;
    class teach;
    model score1 score2=teach;
    manova h=teach / printh printe short;
```

The first three statements produce the usual univariate analyses of the two scores shown in Output 7.1. To suppress printing the univariate analyses, use the NOUNI option in the MODEL statement.

Output 7.1
Univariate Results
of One-Way
Multivariate
Analysis

```
                              The SAS System                                    1
                        Analysis of Variance Procedure
Dependent Variable: SCORE1
                                    Sum of             Mean
Source                 DF          Squares           Square    F Value    Pr > F
Model                   2      60.60508309       30.30254154      0.91    0.4143
Error                  28     932.87878788       33.31709957
Corrected Total        30     993.48387097

              R-Square              C.V.          Root MSE         SCORE1 Mean
              0.061003          8.144515         5.7720966           70.870968

Source                 DF         Anova SS      Mean Square    F Value    Pr > F
TEACH                   2      60.60508309       30.30254154      0.91    0.4143
```

```
                                                                                2
                        Analysis of Variance Procedure
Dependent Variable: SCORE2
                                    Sum of             Mean
Source                 DF          Squares           Square    F Value    Pr > F
Model                   2      49.73586091       24.86793046      0.56    0.5776
Error                  28    1243.94155844       44.42648423
Corrected Total        30    1293.67741935

              R-Square              C.V.          Root MSE         SCORE2 Mean
              0.038445          9.062496         6.6653195           73.548387

Source                 DF         Anova SS      Mean Square    F Value    Pr > F
TEACH                   2      49.73586091       24.86793046      0.56    0.5776
```

The results of the multivariate analysis appear in Output 7.2.

Output 7.2
*Results of
One-Way
Multivariate
Analysis:
MANOVA
Statement*

```
                          The SAS System                        1
                   Analysis of Variance Procedure
                     E = Error SS&CP Matrix

       1                    SCORE1              SCORE2

           SCORE1      932.87878788        1018.6818182
           SCORE2     1018.6818182         1243.9415584

                   Analysis of Variance Procedure
                  Multivariate Analysis of Variance

   2 Partial Correlation Coefficients from the Error SS&CP Matrix / Prob > |r|

            DF = 27        SCORE1      SCORE2

            SCORE1       1.000000    0.945640
                         0.0001      0.0001

            SCORE2       0.945640    1.000000
                         0.0001      0.0001




                   Analysis of Variance Procedure
                  Multivariate Analysis of Variance

           3 H = Anova SS&CP Matrix for TEACH

                           SCORE1              SCORE2

           SCORE1      60.605083089        31.511730205
           SCORE2      31.511730205        49.735860913


        Characteristic Roots and Vectors of: E Inverse * H, where
        H = Anova SS&CP Matrix for TEACH   E = Error SS&CP Matrix

    4 Characteristic   Percent      Characteristic Vector  V'EV=1
          Root
                                         SCORE1          SCORE2

       0.4309802669      91.86        -0.10044686      0.08416103
       0.0382119380       8.14         0.00675930      0.02275380


            5 Manova Test Criteria and F Approximations for
               the Hypothesis of no Overall TEACH Effect
         H = Anova SS&CP Matrix for TEACH   E = Error SS&CP Matrix

                   S=2    M=-0.5    N=12.5

   Statistic                 Value          F      Num DF    Den DF    Pr > F

   Wilks' Lambda           0.67310116    2.9548        4        54     0.0279
   Pillai's Trace          0.33798387    2.8470        4        56     0.0322
   Hotelling-Lawley Trace  0.46919220    3.0497        4        52     0.0248
   Roy's Greatest Root     0.43098027    6.0337        2        28     0.0066

       NOTE: F Statistic for Roy's Greatest Root is an upper bound.
             NOTE: F Statistic for Wilks' Lambda is exact.
```

The PRINTH and PRINTE options cause the printing of the hypothesis and
error matrices, respectively. In addition, the PRINTE option produces a matrix of
partial correlation coefficients derived from the error SS&CP matrix. This
correlation matrix represents the correlations of the dependent variables corrected
for all the independent factors in the MODEL statement. The SHORT option prints
the multivariate test statistics and the associated F statistics in a condensed form.

The results in Output 7.2 are described below. The boldface numbers have been added to the output to key the following descriptions:

1. the elements of the error matrix. The diagonal elements of this matrix represent the error sums of squares from the corresponding univariate analyses (see Output 7.1).

2. the associated partial correlation matrix. In this example it appears that SCORE1 and SCORE2 are highly correlated ($r=0.945640$).

3. the elements of the hypothesis matrix, **H**. Again, the diagonal elements correspond to the hypothesis sums of squares from the corresponding univariate analysis.

4. the characteristic roots and vectors of $\mathbf{E^{-1}H}$. The elements of the characteristic vector describe a linear combination of the analysis variables that produces the largest possible univariate F ratio.

5. the four test statistics previously discussed. The values of S, M, and N, printed above the table of statistics, provide information that is used in constructing the F approximations for the criteria. (For more information, see Chapter 13, "The ANOVA Procedure," in the *SAS/STAT User's Guide, Version 6, Fourth Edition, Volume 1*.) All four tests give similar results, although this is not always the case. Note that the probability levels for the Hypothesis of no Overall TEACH Effect are much lower for the multivariate tests than any of the univariate tests would indicate. This is an example of how viewing a set of variables together can help you detect differences that you would not detect by looking at the individual variables.

7.4 Hotelling's T² Test

Consider a common situation in multivariate analysis. You have several different measurements taken on each of several subjects, and you want to know if the means of the different variables are all the same. For example, you may have used different recording devices to measure the same phenomenon, or you may have observed subjects under a variety of conditions and administered a test under each of the conditions. If you had only two means to compare, you could use the familiar t test, but it is important to use an analysis that takes into account the correlations among the dependent variables, just as in the previous examples, even though there are no independent factors in the model, that is, no terms on the right side of the MODEL statement. In this situation you could use Hotelling's T^2 test. As an example, consider the following data taken from Morrison (1976). Weight gains in rats given a special diet were measured at one (GAIN1), two (GAIN2), three (GAIN3), and four (GAIN4) weeks after administration of the diet. The question of interest is whether the rats' weight gains stayed constant over the course of the experiment; in other words, were the mean weight gains of the rats the same at each of the four weeks? Output 7.3 shows the data.

Output 7.3
Data for
Hotelling's T^2 Test

OBS	GAIN1	GAIN2	GAIN3	GAIN4
1	29	28	25	33
2	33	30	23	31
3	25	34	33	41
4	18	33	29	35
5	25	23	17	30
6	24	32	29	22
7	20	23	16	31
8	28	21	18	24
9	18	23	22	28
10	25	28	29	30

Note that the following MODEL statement fits a model with only an intercept:

```
model gain1 gain2 gain3 gain4 = ;
```

Following this statement with a MANOVA statement to test the intercept tests the hypothesis that the means of the four weight gains are all 0; it does not test the hypothesis of interest, that the four means are equal. To test the hypothesis that the four means are equal, the dependent variables must be transformed in such a way that their transformed means being 0 will imply that the original means are equal for all four variables. It turns out that there are many different transformations that have this effect. (This problem is discussed in detail in Chapter 8, "Repeated-Measures Analysis of Variance.") One simple transformation that achieves this goal is subtracting one of the variables from each of the other variables; in this example, the first gain could be subtracted from each of the other gains. You should understand that the only way all the means could be equal to each other is if each of these differences is 0 and that if all the means are equal, then all the differences must be 0. In this way, Hotelling's T^2 test for equality of means can be performed using the MANOVA statement.

One way of producing the transformed variables necessary to perform Hotelling's T^2 test is to produce new variables in a DATA step and to perform an analysis on the new variables. A quicker and more efficient way, however, is to use the M= option in the MANOVA statement. Using the M= option, you can perform an analysis on a set of variables that is a linear transformation of the original variables as listed on the left side of the equal sign in the MODEL statement.

The following SAS statements perform the appropriate analysis:

```
proc anova data=wtgain;
    model gain1 gain2 gain3 gain4 = / nouni;
    manova h=intercept
            m=gain2-gain1, gain3-gain1, gain4-gain1
            mnames=diff2 diff3 diff4 / summary short;
```

The NOUNI option in the MODEL statement suppresses the individual analyses of the gain variables. This is done because the multivariate hypothesis of equality of the four means is the hypothesis of interest. The SUMMARY option in the MANOVA statement produces analysis-of-variance tables of the transformed variables. The MNAMES= option provides labels for these transformed variables;

if omitted, the procedure uses the names MVAR1, MVAR2, and so on. The results appear in Output 7.4.

Output 7.4
Analysis of Transformed Variables: Hotelling's T² Test

```
                              The SAS System                           1
                      Analysis of Variance Procedure
                     Multivariate Analysis of Variance

                 M Matrix Describing Transformed Variables

                   GAIN1          GAIN2          GAIN3          GAIN4

        DIFF2       -1              1             0              0
        DIFF3       -1              0             1              0
        DIFF4       -1              0             0              1


                      Analysis of Variance Procedure
                     Multivariate Analysis of Variance

           Characteristic Roots and Vectors of: E Inverse * H, where
        H = Anova SS&CP Matrix for INTERCEPT   E = Error SS&CP Matrix

                Variables have been transformed by the M Matrix

     Characteristic   Percent            Characteristic Vector  V'EV=1
         Root
                                       DIFF2          DIFF3          DIFF4

       2.9721167579   100.00         -0.11825538     0.11174598    -0.02428445
       0.0000000000     0.00          0.04890337     0.01582539    -0.02339666
       0.0000000000     0.00         -0.10543152     0.06412831     0.05699098


                 Manova Test Criteria and Exact F Statistics for
                  the Hypothesis of no Overall INTERCEPT Effect
             on the variables defined by the M Matrix Transformation
           H = Anova SS&CP Matrix for INTERCEPT   E = Error SS&CP Matrix

                        S=1    M=0.5    N=2.5

     Statistic                 Value         F      Num DF   Den DF   Pr > F

     Wilks' Lambda          0.25175494    6.9349       3        7     0.0167
     Pillai's Trace         0.74824506    6.9349       3        7     0.0167
     Hotelling-Lawley Trace 2.97211676    6.9349       3        7     0.0167
     Roy's Greatest Root    2.97211676    6.9349       3        7     0.0167


                      Analysis of Variance Procedure
                     Multivariate Analysis of Variance

     Dependent Variable: DIFF2

     Source              DF       Anova SS     Mean Square   F Value   Pr > F

     INTERCEPT            1     90.00000000    90.00000000     2.10    0.1814

     Error               9    386.00000000    42.88888889

     Dependent Variable: DIFF3

     Source              DF       Anova SS     Mean Square   F Value   Pr > F

     INTERCEPT            1      1.60000000     1.60000000     0.03    0.8735

     Error               9    536.40000000    59.60000000

     Dependent Variable: DIFF4

     Source              DF       Anova SS     Mean Square   F Value   Pr > F

     INTERCEPT            1    360.00000000   360.00000000     6.53    0.0309

     Error               9    496.00000000    55.11111111
```

Although PROC ANOVA does not produce the Hotelling T^2 statistic, it produces the correct F test and probability level. Note that all the multivariate test statistics result in the same F values and that they are labeled as Exact F Statistics. These tests are always exact when the hypothesis being tested has only 1 degree of freedom, such as the hypothesis of no INTERCEPT effect in this example. In order to calculate the actual value of the T^2 statistic, the following formula can be used:

$$T^2 = (\text{nobs} - 1)((1 / \lambda) - 1) \quad .$$

Nobs is the number of observations in the data set and λ is the value of Wilks' Criterion that is printed by PROC ANOVA. In this case, the calculation leads to $T^2 = (10 - 1)(1/0.2517 - 1) = 26.757$.

7.5 A Two-Factor Factorial

The total weight of a mature cotton boll can be divided into three parts: the weight of the seeds, the weight of the lint, and the weight of the bract. Lint and seed constitute the economic yield of cotton.

In the following data, the differences in the three components of the cotton bolls due to two varieties (VARIETY) and two plant spacings (SPACING) are studied. Five plants are chosen at random from each of the four treatment combinations. Two bolls are picked from each plant, and the weights of the seeds, lint, and bract are recorded. The most appropriate error term for testing VARIETY, SPACING, and the interaction of the two is the variation among plants. In univariate analyses, the TEST statement is used to specify this alternative error term; for multivariate analyses, the error term is specified in the MANOVA statement or statements. (Each MANOVA statement can have, at most, one error term specified.)

Because this is a balanced experiment, the ANOVA procedure is appropriate. The following SAS statements are used:

```
proc anova;
   class variety spacing plant;
   model seed lint bract=variety spacing variety*spacing
                         plant(variety spacing);
   test h=variety|spacing e=plant(variety spacing);
   means variety|spacing;
   manova h=variety|spacing e=plant(variety spacing) / short;
```

The data used in this analysis appear in Output 7.5.

Output 7.5
Data for Two-Way Multivariate Analysis

```
                          The SAS System                            1

   OBS     VARIETY     SPACING     PLANT     SEED     LINT     BRACT

     1       213          30         3       3.1      1.7      2.0
     2       213          30         3       1.5      1.7      1.4
     3       213          30         5       3.0      1.9      1.8
     4       213          30         5       1.4      0.9      1.3
     5       213          30         6       2.3      1.7      1.5
     6       213          30         6       2.2      2.0      1.4
     7       213          30         8       0.4      0.9      1.2
     8       213          30         8       1.7      1.6      1.3
     9       213          30         9       1.8      1.2      1.0
    10       213          30         9       1.2      0.8      1.0
    11       213          40         0       2.0      1.0      1.9
    12       213          40         0       1.5      1.5      1.7
    13       213          40         1       1.8      1.1      2.1
    14       213          40         1       1.0      1.3      1.1
    15       213          40         2       1.3      1.1      1.3
    16       213          40         2       2.9      1.9      1.7
    17       213          40         3       2.8      1.2      1.3
    18       213          40         3       1.8      1.2      1.2
    19       213          40         4       3.2      1.8      2.0
    20       213          40         4       3.2      1.6      1.9
    21        37          30         1       3.2      2.6      1.4
    22        37          30         1       2.8      2.1      1.2
    23        37          30         2       3.6      2.4      1.5
    24        37          30         2       0.9      0.8      0.8
    25        37          30         3       4.0      3.1      1.8
    26        37          30         3       4.0      2.9      1.5
    27        37          30         5       3.7      2.7      1.6
    28        37          30         5       2.6      1.5      1.3
    29        37          30         8       2.8      2.2      1.2
    30        37          30         8       2.9      2.3      1.2
    31        37          40         1       4.1      2.9      2.0
    32        37          40         1       3.4      2.0      1.6
    33        37          40         3       3.7      2.3      2.0
    34        37          40         3       3.2      2.2      1.8
    35        37          40         4       3.4      2.7      1.5
    36        37          40         4       2.9      2.1      1.2
    37        37          40         5       2.5      1.4      0.8
    38        37          40         5       3.6      2.4      1.6
    39        37          40         6       3.1      2.3      1.4
    40        37          40         6       2.5      1.5      1.5
```

Note that the TEST statement is used to obtain the appropriate error terms. The results of the three univariate analyses appear in Output 7.6.

Output 7.6
Results of Two-Way Multivariate Analysis: Univariate Analyses

```
                          The SAS System                            1

                   Analysis of Variance Procedure

Dependent Variable: SEED
                                  Sum of           Mean
Source                DF         Squares          Square     F Value     Pr > F

Model                 19      24.06500000      1.26657895       2.22     0.0425

Error                 20      11.43000000      0.57150000

Corrected Total       39      35.49500000

             R-Square            C.V.         Root MSE          SEED Mean

             0.677983         29.35830        0.7559762         2.5750000
```

Source	DF	Anova SS	Mean Square	F Value	Pr > F
VARIETY	1	12.99600000	12.99600000	22.74	0.0001
SPACING	1	0.57600000	0.57600000	1.01	0.3274
VARIETY*SPACING	1	0.02500000	0.02500000	0.04	0.8364
PLANT(VARIET*SPACIN)	16	10.46800000	0.65425000	1.14	0.3823

Tests of Hypotheses using the Anova MS for PLANT(VARIET*SPACIN) as an error term

Source	DF	Anova SS	Mean Square	F Value	Pr > F
VARIETY	1	12.99600000	12.99600000	19.86	0.0004
SPACING	1	0.57600000	0.57600000	0.88	0.3620
VARIETY*SPACING	1	0.02500000	0.02500000	0.04	0.8475

2

Analysis of Variance Procedure

Dependent Variable: LINT

Source	DF	Sum of Squares	Mean Square	F Value	Pr > F
Model	19	10.62875000	0.55940789	2.28	0.0377
Error	20	4.91500000	0.24575000		
Corrected Total	39	15.54375000			

R-Square	C.V.	Root MSE	LINT Mean
0.683796	27.35072	0.4957318	1.8125000

Source	DF	Anova SS	Mean Square	F Value	Pr > F
VARIETY	1	6.64225000	6.64225000	27.03	0.0001
SPACING	1	0.05625000	0.05625000	0.23	0.6375
VARIETY*SPACING	1	0.00025000	0.00025000	0.00	0.9749
PLANT(VARIET*SPACIN)	16	3.93000000	0.24562500	1.00	0.4934

Tests of Hypotheses using the Anova MS for PLANT(VARIET*SPACIN) as an error term

Source	DF	Anova SS	Mean Square	F Value	Pr > F
VARIETY	1	6.64225000	6.64225000	27.04	0.0001
SPACING	1	0.05625000	0.05625000	0.23	0.6387
VARIETY*SPACING	1	0.00025000	0.00025000	0.00	0.9749

3

Analysis of Variance Procedure

Dependent Variable: BRACT

Source	DF	Sum of Squares	Mean Square	F Value	Pr > F
Model	19	2.70500000	0.14236842	1.63	0.1442
Error	20	1.75000000	0.08750000		
Corrected Total	39	4.45500000			

R-Square	C.V.	Root MSE	BRACT Mean
0.607183	20.05451	0.2958040	1.4750000

(continued on next page)

(continued from previous page)

Source	DF	Anova SS	Mean Square	F Value	Pr > F
VARIETY	1	0.03600000	0.03600000	0.41	0.5285
SPACING	1	0.44100000	0.44100000	5.04	0.0362
VARIETY*SPACING	1	0.00400000	0.00400000	0.05	0.8329
PLANT(VARIET*SPACIN)	16	2.22400000	0.13900000	1.59	0.1626

Tests of Hypotheses using the Anova MS for PLANT(VARIET*SPACIN) as an error term

Source	DF	Anova SS	Mean Square	F Value	Pr > F
VARIETY	1	0.03600000	0.03600000	0.26	0.6178
SPACING	1	0.44100000	0.44100000	3.17	0.0939
VARIETY*SPACING	1	0.00400000	0.00400000	0.03	0.8674

VARIETY has a statistically significant effect on SEED and LINT; no effects are statistically significant for BRACT.

The means for all levels and combinations of levels of VARIETY and SPACING produced by the MEANS statement appear in Output 7.7.

Output 7.7
Results of
Two-Way
Multivariate
Analysis: MEANS
Statement

```
                            The SAS System                              1

                     Analysis of Variance Procedure
```

Level of VARIETY	N	--------------SEED------------- Mean	SD	--------------LINT------------ Mean	SD
37	20	3.14500000	0.72799291	2.22000000	0.57087191
213	20	2.00500000	0.80881655	1.40500000	0.37763112

Level of VARIETY	N	------------BRACT------------ Mean	SD
37	20	1.44500000	0.32843328
213	20	1.50500000	0.35314378

Level of SPACING	N	--------------SEED------------- Mean	SD	--------------LINT------------ Mean	SD
30	20	2.45500000	1.04351380	1.85000000	0.70150215
40	20	2.69500000	0.86540225	1.77500000	0.56835404

Level of SPACING	N	------------BRACT------------ Mean	SD
30	20	1.37000000	0.29037181
40	20	1.58000000	0.35629674

Level of VARIETY	Level of SPACING	N	-----------SEED----------- Mean	SD	-----------LINT----------- Mean	SD
37	30	10	3.05000000	0.91439111	2.26000000	0.68182761
37	40	10	3.24000000	0.51251016	2.18000000	0.46856756
213	30	10	1.86000000	0.82219219	1.44000000	0.44771022
213	40	10	2.15000000	0.81137743	1.37000000	0.31287200

Level of VARIETY	Level of SPACING	N	-----------BRACT----------- Mean	SD
37	30	10	1.35000000	0.27588242
37	40	10	1.54000000	0.36270588
213	30	10	1.39000000	0.31780497
213	40	10	1.62000000	0.36453928

The results of the multivariate analyses appear in Output 7.8.

```
                              The SAS System                           1

                        Analysis of Variance Procedure
                        Multivariate Analysis of Variance

                 Characteristic Roots and Vectors of: E Inverse * H, where
                            H = Anova SS&CP Matrix for VARIETY
                       E = Anova SS&CP Matrix for PLANT(VARIET*SPACIN)

       Characteristic   Percent             Characteristic Vector  V'EV=1
            Root
                                           SEED          LINT          BRACT

          3.4391911613    100.00        0.13061027    0.48969379   -0.64083380
          0.0000000000      0.00       -0.18197166    0.30004546    0.61815600
          0.0000000000      0.00       -0.49168907    0.67719778   -0.14348916


                   Manova Test Criteria and Exact F Statistics for
                    the Hypothesis of no Overall VARIETY Effect
                        H = Anova SS&CP Matrix for VARIETY
                   E = Anova SS&CP Matrix for PLANT(VARIET*SPACIN)

                        S=1    M=0.5    N=6

      Statistic                Value           F      Num DF    Den DF   Pr > F

      Wilks' Lambda          0.22526626    16.0496       3        14     0.0001
      Pillai's Trace         0.77473374    16.0496       3        14     0.0001
      Hotelling-Lawley Trace 3.43919116    16.0496       3        14     0.0001
      Roy's Greatest Root    3.43919116    16.0496       3        14     0.0001
```

```
                                                                       2

                 Characteristic Roots and Vectors of: E Inverse * H, where
                            H = Anova SS&CP Matrix for SPACING
                       E = Anova SS&CP Matrix for PLANT(VARIET*SPACIN)

       Characteristic   Percent             Characteristic Vector  V'EV=1
            Root
                                           SEED          LINT          BRACT

          0.6320947162    100.00        0.27027458   -0.73247531    0.62673044
          0.0000000000      0.00       -0.23860962    0.50168366    0.45186945
          0.0000000000      0.00        0.40242760   -0.01474917   -0.46518481


                   Manova Test Criteria and Exact F Statistics for
                    the Hypothesis of no Overall SPACING Effect
                        H = Anova SS&CP Matrix for SPACING
                   E = Anova SS&CP Matrix for PLANT(VARIET*SPACIN)

                        Analysis of Variance Procedure
                        Multivariate Analysis of Variance

                        S=1    M=0.5    N=6

      Statistic                Value           F      Num DF    Den DF   Pr > F

      Wilks' Lambda          0.61270954     2.9498       3        14     0.0692
      Pillai's Trace         0.38729046     2.9498       3        14     0.0692
      Hotelling-Lawley Trace 0.63209472     2.9498       3        14     0.0692
      Roy's Greatest Root    0.63209472     2.9498       3        14     0.0692


                 Characteristic Roots and Vectors of: E Inverse * H, where
                          H = Anova SS&CP Matrix for VARIETY*SPACING
                       E = Anova SS&CP Matrix for PLANT(VARIET*SPACIN)
```

(continued on next page)

```
(continued from previous page)

Characteristic   Percent              Characteristic Vector   V'EV=1
    Root
                                    SEED          LINT          BRACT

   0.0061671142   100.00           0.42143581   -0.67443149    0.35670210
   0.0000000000     0.00          -0.25533505    0.45881333    0.52358429
   0.0000000000     0.00           0.22166856    0.35079425   -0.64186996


              Manova Test Criteria and Exact F Statistics for
            the Hypothesis of no Overall VARIETY*SPACING Effect
                H = Anova SS&CP Matrix for VARIETY*SPACING
              E = Anova SS&CP Matrix for PLANT(VARIET*SPACIN)

                        S=1      M=0.5     N=6

Statistic                   Value         F      Num DF   Den DF   Pr > F

Wilks' Lambda             0.99387069    0.0288       3       14     0.9931
Pillai's Trace            0.00612931    0.0288       3       14     0.9931
Hotelling-Lawley Trace    0.00616711    0.0288       3       14     0.9931
Roy's Greatest Root       0.00616711    0.0288       3       14     0.9931
```

The only highly significant effect is VARIETY, and all four multivariate statistics are the same because there is only one hypothesis degree of freedom.

7.6 Multivariate Analysis of Covariance

This section illustrates multivariate analysis of covariance using the data on orange sales presented in Output 6.5. Sales of two types of oranges are related to experimentally determined prices (PRICE) as well as stores (STORE) and days of the week (DAY). The analysis is expanded here to consider the simultaneous multivariate relationship of the price to both types of oranges.

The following SAS statements are used for the analysis:

```
proc glm;
    class store day;
    model q1 q2=store day p1 p2 / nouni;
    manova h=store day p1 p2 / printh printe short;
```

Note that PROC ANOVA is not appropriate in this situation because of the presence of the covariates. The NOUNI option in the MODEL statement suppresses printing of the univariate analyses that are already shown in Chapter 6, "Covariance and the Heterogeneity of Slopes." Results of the multivariate analysis appear in Output 7.9.

```
                              The SAS System                        1
                       General Linear Models Procedure

                          E = Error SS&CP Matrix

                               Q1                Q2

           Q1          408.30824182       74.603217758
           Q2          74.603217758       706.94116552
```

```
                                                                    2


                       General Linear Models Procedure
                       Multivariate Analysis of Variance

      Partial Correlation Coefficients from the Error SS&CP Matrix / Prob > |r|

                   DF = 22           Q1           Q2

                   Q1          1.000000     0.138858
                                0.0001       0.5176

                   Q2          0.138858     1.000000
                                0.5176       0.0001




                       General Linear Models Procedure
                       Multivariate Analysis of Variance

                    H = Type III SS&CP Matrix for STORE

                               Q1                Q2

           Q1          223.83267344       93.801152319
           Q2          93.801152319       155.09933793


            Characteristic Roots and Vectors of: E Inverse * H, where
           H = Type III SS&CP Matrix for STORE   E = Error SS&CP Matrix

        Characteristic    Percent        Characteristic Vector  V'EV=1
            Root
                                              Q1           Q2

          0.5736382915      78.23        0.04622384   0.00941459
          0.1596032187      21.77       -0.01899048   0.03679295



                 Manova Test Criteria and F Approximations for
                   the Hypothesis of no Overall STORE Effect
           H = Type III SS&CP Matrix for STORE   E = Error SS&CP Matrix

                        S=2      M=1     N=10

    Statistic                    Value          F     Num DF   Den DF   Pr > F

    Wilks' Lambda            0.54800645    1.5437        10       44   0.1564
    Pillai's Trace           0.50216601    1.5422        10       46   0.1553
    Hotelling-Lawley Trace   0.73324151    1.5398        10       42   0.1594
    Roy's Greatest Root      0.57363829    2.6387         5       23   0.0501

         NOTE: F Statistic for Roy's Greatest Root is an upper bound.
               NOTE: F Statistic for Wilks' Lambda is exact.



                     H = Type III SS&CP Matrix for DAY

                               Q1                Q2

           Q1          433.09686996       461.05064188
           Q2          461.05064188       614.4088834
```

(continued on next page)

(continued from previous page)

```
              Characteristic Roots and Vectors of: E Inverse * H, where
              H = Type III SS&CP Matrix for DAY   E = Error SS&CP Matrix

       Characteristic    Percent        Characteristic Vector  V'EV=1
            Root
                                                Q1              Q2

          1.6070877570    93.18            0.03517603      0.02300242
          0.1176654552     6.82           -0.03549548      0.03021993


                  Manova Test Criteria and F Approximations for
                     the Hypothesis of no Overall DAY Effect
              H = Type III SS&CP Matrix for DAY   E = Error SS&CP Matrix

                        S=2      M=1      N=10

     Statistic                  Value           F      Num DF    Den DF    Pr > F

     Wilks' Lambda            0.34318834     3.1108       10        44     0.0044
     Pillai's Trace           0.72170813     2.5971       10        46     0.0137
     Hotelling-Lawley Trace   1.72475321     3.6220       10        42     0.0015
     Roy's Greatest Root      1.60708776     7.3926        5        23     0.0003

         NOTE: F Statistic for Roy's Greatest Root is an upper bound.
               NOTE: F Statistic for Wilks' Lambda is exact.
```

```
                                                                              3

                      H = Type III SS&CP Matrix for P1

                               Q1              Q2

             Q1      538.16885116      -212.5196287
             Q2     -212.5196287        83.922717744


              Characteristic Roots and Vectors of: E Inverse * H, where
              H = Type III SS&CP Matrix for P1   E = Error SS&CP Matrix

       Characteristic    Percent        Characteristic Vector  V'EV=1
            Root
                                                Q1              Q2

          1.5770193008   100.00            0.04805513     -0.01539025
          0.0000000000     0.00            0.01371082      0.03472026


                  Manova Test Criteria and Exact F Statistics for
                     the Hypothesis of no Overall P1 Effect
              H = Type III SS&CP Matrix for P1   E = Error SS&CP Matrix

                        S=1      M=0      N=10

     Statistic                  Value           F      Num DF    Den DF    Pr > F

     Wilks' Lambda            0.38804521    17.3472        2        22     0.0001
     Pillai's Trace           0.61195479    17.3472        2        22     0.0001
     Hotelling-Lawley Trace   1.57701930    17.3472        2        22     0.0001
     Roy's Greatest Root      1.57701930    17.3472        2        22     0.0001


                      H = Type III SS&CP Matrix for P2

                               Q1              Q2

             Q1       39.542251923      -183.5850939
             Q2     -183.5850939         852.34110489
```

```
              Characteristic Roots and Vectors of: E Inverse * H, where
              H = Type III SS&CP Matrix for P2    E = Error SS&CP Matrix

          Characteristic    Percent          Characteristic Vector   V'EV=1
              Root
                                                    Q1              Q2

            1.4248902960     100.00           -0.01960102        0.03666503
            0.0000000000       0.00            0.04596827        0.00990107


                  Manova Test Criteria and Exact F Statistics for
                       the Hypothesis of no Overall P2 Effect
              H = Type III SS&CP Matrix for P2    E = Error SS&CP Matrix

                          S=1      M=0      N=10

      Statistic                   Value          F       Num DF    Den DF   Pr > F

      Wilks' Lambda             0.41238979    15.6738       2         22    0.0001
      Pillai's Trace            0.58761021    15.6738       2         22    0.0001
      Hotelling-Lawley Trace    1.42489030    15.6738       2         22    0.0001
      Roy's Greatest Root       1.42489030    15.6738       2         22    0.0001
```

For the STORE effect, none of the statistics produce significant results. This is not totally consistent with univariate results where sales of the first type of oranges are nearly significant at the 5% level.

The DAY effect is quite significant according to all statistics, although there is a considerable difference in the level of significance (Pr > F) among the statistics. Also, there is one dominant eigenvalue, indicating that the trend in sales over days is roughly parallel for the two types of oranges. This can be verified by printing and plotting the least-squares means.

The results for the PRICE effects are relatively straightforward. Even though both P1 and P2 are significant for only one dependent variable in the univariate analyses, the multivariate analysis indicates that their effects are substantial enough to be significant overall.

7.7 Contrasts in Multivariate Analyses

Chapter 2, "Analysis of Variance for Balanced Data," discusses how specialized questions concerning certain levels of factors in univariate analyses can be answered by using the CONTRAST statement to define an hypothesis to be tested. This same technique can be useful in multivariate analyses of variance. The GLM procedure prints output for CONTRAST statements as part of its multivariate analysis. As an example, consider the study described in Section 7.6, "Multivariate Analysis of Covariance." Assume you want to know if Saturday sales differ from weekday sales, averaged across the two types of oranges. Because the levels for day are coded as 1 through 6 corresponding to Monday through Saturday, you need to construct a contrast that compares the average of the first five levels of DAY to the sixth. The following SAS statement is required:

```
contrast 'SAT. vs. WEEKDAYS' day .2 .2 .2 .2 .2 -1;
```

The label SAT. vs. WEEKDAYS appears in the output to identify the contrast. If this CONTRAST statement is appended to the program of the previous section, preceding the MANOVA statement, then Output 7.10 is produced.

Output 7.10
Results of
Multivariate
Analysis:
CONTRAST
Statement

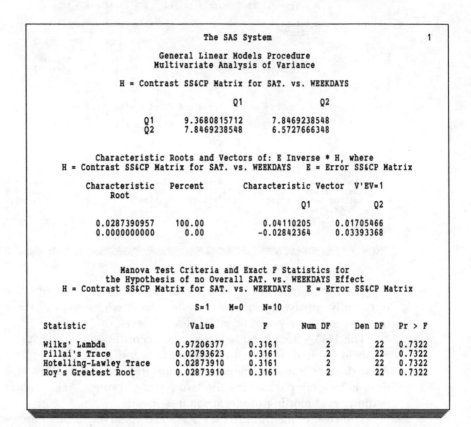

```
                              The SAS System                              1

                         General Linear Models Procedure
                         Multivariate Analysis of Variance

                H = Contrast SS&CP Matrix for SAT. vs. WEEKDAYS

                                    Q1              Q2

                    Q1        9.3680815712    7.8469238548
                    Q2        7.8469238548    6.5727666348


              Characteristic Roots and Vectors of: E Inverse * H, where
       H = Contrast SS&CP Matrix for SAT. vs. WEEKDAYS  E = Error SS&CP Matrix

           Characteristic    Percent        Characteristic Vector  V'EV=1
               Root
                                                   Q1              Q2

           0.0287390957      100.00         0.04110205      0.01705466
           0.0000000000        0.00        -0.02842364      0.03393368


                    Manova Test Criteria and Exact F Statistics for
                   the Hypothesis of no Overall SAT. vs. WEEKDAYS Effect
           H = Contrast SS&CP Matrix for SAT. vs. WEEKDAYS   E = Error SS&CP Matrix

                         S=1     M=0     N=10

       Statistic                 Value          F      Num DF    Den DF    Pr > F

       Wilks' Lambda          0.97206377    0.3161       2         22      0.7322
       Pillai's Trace         0.02793623    0.3161       2         22      0.7322
       Hotelling-Lawley Trace 0.02873910    0.3161       2         22      0.7322
       Roy's Greatest Root    0.02873910    0.3161       2         22      0.7322
```

The results of the multivariate tests indicate no significant overall difference between the Saturday and weekday sales for the two types of oranges (Pr > F=0.7322).

Chapter 8 Repeated-Measures Analysis of Variance

8.1 *Introduction   265*

8.2 *Multivariate Repeated-Measures Analysis Using the MANOVA Statement   266*

8.3 *Multivariate Repeated-Measures Analysis Using the REPEATED Statement   269*

8.4 *Univariate Repeated-Measures Analysis As a Split-Plot Design   272*

8.5 *Univariate Repeated-Measures Analysis Using the REPEATED Statement   274*

8.6 *Contrasts among Dependent Variables: SUMMARY Option   278*

8.7 *Two Repeated-Measures Factors: Multivariate and Univariate Analysis   282*

8.1 Introduction

Chapter 7, "Multivariate Linear Models," discusses experiments in which several measurements are taken on each subject or experimental unit. For example, Section 7.4, "A Two-Factor Factorial," presents an experiment involving production in cotton plants. Weights of seed, lint, and bract were measured on plants of different varieties planted with different spacings. Because measurements in situations like this are correlated, multivariate techniques are used to take the correlations among the dependent variables (the weights of the seed, lint, and bract) into account while testing the hypotheses of interest; in this case, does the variety or spacing of cotton plants affect the production of seed, lint, and bract? Notice that there is no interest in hypotheses *within* the measurements of individual plants, for example, whether plants produce a different amount of seed than bract. If questions about changes across the various measurements taken on an individual subject or experimental unit are important, then you are dealing with *repeated-measures* data. Note that what distinguishes repeated-measures data from any other multivariate data is not so much the existence of the repeated measurements but the desire to examine changes in the measurements taken on each subject. These changes are therefore known as *within-subjects effects*.

Repeated-measures designs arise in a variety of disciplines and experimental settings. For example, you may ask consumers about each of several different products or measure test scores before, during, and after a training program. In agriculture, samples from the same location in a field may be looked at over time in an attempt to see if yields are changing. In an industrial setting, you may want to know if the output of a particular type of machine changes depending on the day of the week. In each case, the interest in changes from measurement to measurement within the same subject is what distinguishes these as repeated-measures designs.

A simple example of a repeated-measures design is presented in Section 7.3, "Hotelling's T^2 Test." Weight gain is measured on several rats, each four times. The question of interest is whether weight gains changed over the course of the experiment. A simple transformation of the dependent variables solves the problem, and, as shown below, this method can be applied to more complex designs, allowing tests of hypotheses involving within-subjects effects. Furthermore, this approach provides a way to calculate quantities necessary for a univariate approach to repeated-measures designs, which is statistically similar to the analysis of split-plot designs in Section 3.5, "Split-Plot Experiments."

8.2 Multivariate Repeated-Measures Analysis Using the MANOVA Statement

As mentioned earlier, transformations of the dependent variables can be used to test hypotheses about within-subjects effects from a multivariate point of view. The following example illustrates this point.

Three weight-lifting training programs (PROGRAM) are investigated in an exercise therapy study. These programs include a control (CONT), a program in which the amount of the weight is increased (WI), and a program in which the number of repetitions of each exercise is increased (RI). Several subjects are assigned to each group, and each subject's strength is measured every other day for two weeks. These strength measurements are called S1 through S7 in a SAS data set named EXERCISE. The data appear in Output 8.1.

Output 8.1
Data for
Multivariate
Repeated-Measures
Design

```
                              The SAS System                              1

      OBS     PROGRAM    S1    S2    S3    S4    S5    S6    S7

        1     CONT       85    85    86    85    87    86    87
        2     CONT       80    79    79    78    78    79    78
        3     CONT       78    77    77    77    76    76    77
        4     CONT       84    84    85    84    83    84    85
        5     CONT       80    81    80    80    79    79    80
        6     CONT       76    78    77    78    78    77    74
        7     CONT       79    79    80    79    80    79    81
        8     CONT       76    76    76    75    75    74    74
        9     CONT       77    78    78    80    80    81    80
       10     CONT       79    79    79    79    77    78    79
       11     CONT       81    81    80    80    80    81    82
       12     CONT       77    76    77    78    77    77    77
       13     CONT       82    83    83    83    84    83    83
       14     CONT       84    84    83    82    81    79    78
       15     CONT       79    81    81    82    82    82    80
       16     CONT       79    79    78    77    77    78    78
       17     CONT       83    82    83    85    84    83    82
       18     CONT       78    78    79    79    78    77    77
       19     CONT       80    80    79    79    80    80    80
       20     CONT       78    79    80    81    80    79    80
       21     RI         79    79    79    80    80    78    80
       22     RI         83    83    85    85    86    87    87
       23     RI         81    83    82    82    83    83    82
       24     RI         81    81    81    82    82    83    81
       25     RI         80    81    82    82    82    84    86
       26     RI         76    76    76    76    76    76    75
       27     RI         81    84    83    83    85    85    85
       28     RI         77    78    79    79    81    82    81
       29     RI         84    85    87    89    88    85    86
       30     RI         74    75    78    78    79    78    78
       31     RI         76    77    77    77    77    76    76
       32     RI         84    84    86    85    86    86    86
       33     RI         79    80    79    80    80    82    82
       34     RI         78    78    77    76    75    75    76
       35     RI         78    80    77    77    75    75    75
       36     RI         84    85    85    85    85    83    82
       37     WI         84    85    84    83    83    83    84
       38     WI         74    75    75    76    75    76    76
```

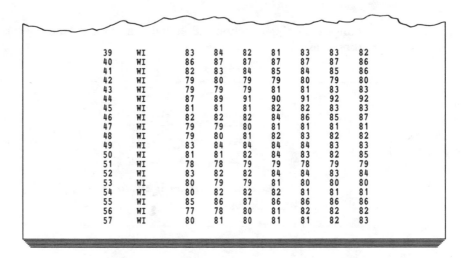

```
39    WI       83    84    82    81    83    83    82
40    WI       86    87    87    87    87    87    86
41    WI       82    83    84    85    84    85    86
42    WI       79    80    79    79    80    79    80
43    WI       79    79    79    81    81    83    83
44    WI       87    89    91    90    91    92    92
45    WI       81    81    81    82    82    83    83
46    WI       82    82    82    84    86    85    87
47    WI       79    79    80    81    81    81    81
48    WI       79    80    81    82    83    82    82
49    WI       83    84    84    84    84    83    83
50    WI       81    81    82    84    83    82    85
51    WI       78    78    79    79    78    79    79
52    WI       83    82    82    84    84    83    84
53    WI       80    79    79    81    80    80    80
54    WI       80    82    82    82    81    81    81
55    WI       85    86    87    86    86    86    86
56    WI       77    78    80    81    82    82    82
57    WI       80    81    80    81    81    82    83
```

If you consider the strength measurements as being entirely different measurements, then the methods described in Chapter 7 enable you to answer this question: Does the training program affect the overall strength of the subjects across the different times? However, if you want to know if there is a difference in strength over time (the within-subjects factor) or if these differences depend on the different programs employed (an interaction between a between-subjects factor and a within-subjects factor), then you have a repeated-measures design, and the methods described in this chapter are more appropriate.

This section describes how you can use the MANOVA statement to obtain an analysis of repeated-measures data. Section 8.3, "Multivariate Repeated-Measures Analysis Using the REPEATED Statement," shows you how to obtain this type of analysis more directly with the REPEATED statement. It is not necessary to read Section 8.3 if you understand how multivariate computation works with the REPEATED statement.

To implement the repeated-measures analysis using the MANOVA statement, you need to transform the dependent variables S1 through S7. To determine if there is a difference in strength at the different times, you need a transformation that produces variables that have a mean of 0 if the strength is the same each time it is measured but not 0 otherwise. You can achieve such a transformation by subtracting the last measurement from each of the other measurements; if the differences between each measurement and the last measurement are all 0, then there is no change in strength over time. You can examine this by testing the INTERCEPT effect for the transformed variables using the following SAS statements:

```
proc glm data=exercise;
   class program;
   model s1 s2 s3 s4 s5 s6 s7=program / nouni;
   manova h=intercept m=s1-s7,s2-s7,s3-s7,s4-s7,s5-s7,s6-s7 / short;
```

The SHORT option in the MANOVA statement prints the multivariate test statistics and the associated F statistics in a condensed form. The results of the analysis appear in Output 8.2. You can see that the INTERCEPT effect is highly significant ($F=6.456$, $p<0.0001$), and this means that the strength measurements did change over time. Section 8.3 contains a more detailed description of the hypothesis tested.

Output 8.2
Multivariate
Analysis of
Repeated-Measures
Design Using the
MANOVA
Statement

```
                           The SAS System                              1

                     General Linear Models Procedure
                         Class Level Information

                   Class      Levels     Values

                   PROGRAM       3       CONT RI WI


            Number of observations in data set = 57
```

```
                                                                       2



                     General Linear Models Procedure
                     Multivariate Analysis of Variance

                  M Matrix Describing Transformed Variables


                 S1      S2      S3      S4      S5      S6      S7

       MVAR1      1       0       0       0       0       0      -1
       MVAR2      0       1       0       0       0       0      -1
       MVAR3      0       0       1       0       0       0      -1
       MVAR4      0       0       0       1       0       0      -1
       MVAR5      0       0       0       0       1       0      -1
       MVAR6      0       0       0       0       0       1      -1
```

```
                                                                       3



                     General Linear Models Procedure
                     Multivariate Analysis of Variance

           Characteristic Roots and Vectors of: E Inverse * H, where
          H = Type III SS&CP Matrix for INTERCEPT   E = Error SS&CP Matrix

                 Variables have been transformed by the M Matrix

    Characteristic   Percent          Characteristic Vector   V'EV=1
         Root
                                       MVAR1          MVAR2          MVAR3
                                       MVAR4          MVAR5          MVAR6

      0.7905690339   100.00         0.15658690    -0.11837823     0.02617175
                                   -0.06784808     0.00934707     0.03742981

      0.0000000000     0.00         0.05550883    -0.04626320    -0.13809927
                                    0.11479268    -0.00709963     0.04173246

      0.0000000000     0.00         0.01241154     0.00176060    -0.02342527
                                    0.00537127     0.12999167    -0.10348500

      0.0000000000     0.00        -0.03288271     0.08951569    -0.06556267
                                   -0.01301445     0.01215419     0.09568045

      0.0000000000     0.00         0.01694942    -0.09383769     0.08049642
                                   -0.09265154     0.08277518     0.04986859

      0.0000000000     0.00        -0.01434132    -0.06010924     0.10535467
                                    0.08216175    -0.10722388     0.06886449
```

```
                  Manova Test Criteria and Exact F Statistics for
                      the Hypothesis of no Overall INTERCEPT Effect
                  on the variables defined by the M Matrix Transformation
           H = Type III SS&CP Matrix for INTERCEPT   E = Error SS&CP Matrix

                        S=1    M=2    N=23.5

        Statistic               Value         F       Num DF    Den DF   Pr > F

        Wilks' Lambda           0.55848168    6.4563       6        49   0.0001
        Pillai's Trace          0.44151832    6.4563       6        49   0.0001
        Hotelling-Lawley Trace  0.79056903    6.4563       6        49   0.0001
        Roy's Greatest Root     0.79056903    6.4563       6        49   0.0001
```

8.3 Multivariate Repeated-Measures Analysis Using the REPEATED Statement

In Section 8.2, "Multivariate Repeated-Measures Analysis Using the MANOVA Statement," the hypothesis that a within-subjects factor has no effect is tested by using the M= option in the MANOVA statement to transform the dependent variables to a set of variables that have means of 0 if the within-subjects factor has no effect. This is achieved by examining the test statistics for the hypothesis of no INTERCEPT effect. There are two drawbacks to this method. First, the output is not labeled appropriately; it is hard to remember that the test statistics for the hypothesis of no INTERCEPT effect are really for the hypothesis of no change in strength over time. Second, specifying the transformation by hand can be tedious, especially if the repeated-measures factor has many levels. The REPEATED statement overcomes both of these problems and provides other useful features.

The following SAS statements use the REPEATED statement in its simplest form to perform an analysis equivalent to the analysis described in Section 8.2:

```
proc glm data=exercise;
   class program;
   model s1 s2 s3 s4 s5 s6 s7=program / nouni;
   repeated time / nou short;
```

The name TIME in the REPEATED statement associates a name with the factor defined by the variability across the dependent variables for an observation. In this example, the strength of the subjects is measured at several different times, so the factor defined across the variables is named TIME. The NOU option in the REPEATED statement suppresses the univariate analysis of the repeated-measures effects. The SHORT option in the REPEATED statement prints the multivariate test statistics and the associated F statistics in a condensed form. The condensed form produced by the SHORT option is the default for Version 6 and subsequent releases of the SAS System. The output for the REPEATED statement appears in

Output 8.3. Although not used in this example, the **M** matrix used by the REPEATED statement can be printed by using the PRINTM option.

Output 8.3
Multivariate
Analysis of
Repeated-Measures
Design Using the
REPEATED
Statement

```
                         The SAS System                              1

                   General Linear Models Procedure
                      Class Level Information

              Class      Levels    Values

              PROGRAM        3      CONT RI WI


           Number of observations in data set = 57


                   General Linear Models Procedure
                  Repeated Measures Analysis of Variance
                  Repeated Measures Level Information

  Dependent Variable       S1     S2     S3     S4     S5     S6

      Level of TIME          1      2      3      4      5      6

  Dependent Variable       S7

      Level of TIME          7
```

```
Manova Test Criteria and Exact F Statistics for the Hypothesis of no TIME Effect
       H = Type III SS&CP Matrix for TIME    E = Error SS&CP Matrix

                        S=1    M=2    N=23.5

  Statistic               Value           F      Num DF   Den DF   Pr > F

  Wilks' Lambda         0.55902276      6.4422       6       49    0.0001
  Pillai's Trace        0.44097724      6.4422       6       49    0.0001
  Hotelling-Lawley Trace 0.78883592     6.4422       6       49    0.0001
  Roy's Greatest Root   0.78883592      6.4422       6       49    0.0001
```

```
               Manova Test Criteria and F Approximations for
                 the Hypothesis of no TIME*PROGRAM Effect
        H = Type III SS&CP Matrix for TIME*PROGRAM   E = Error SS&CP Matrix

                        S=2    M=1.5    N=23.5

  Statistic               Value           F      Num DF   Den DF   Pr > F

  Wilks' Lambda         0.73167437      1.3808      12       98    0.1880
  Pillai's Trace        0.28188936      1.3672      12      100    0.1943
  Hotelling-Lawley Trace 0.34819029     1.3928      12       96    0.1827
  Roy's Greatest Root   0.28259027      2.3549       6       50    0.0442

          NOTE: F Statistic for Roy's Greatest Root is an upper bound.
             NOTE: F Statistic for Wilks' Lambda is exact.
```

```
                   General Linear Models Procedure
                  Repeated Measures Analysis of Variance
               Tests of Hypotheses for Between Subjects Effects

  Source         DF      Type III SS      Mean Square    F Value    Pr > F

  PROGRAM         2        419.43526        209.71763       3.07     0.0548

  Error          54       3694.69005         68.42019
```

Note that the results of the tests for the factor TIME are exactly the same as for INTERCEPT in the previous example.

Denote by μ_{ij} the population mean for PROGRAM=i at TIME=j. Then the null hypotheses for the TIME effect is

$$H_0: \bar{\mu}_{.1} = \bar{\mu}_{.2} = \ldots = \bar{\mu}_{.7}$$

where

$$\bar{\mu}_{ij} = \frac{(\mu_{ij} + \mu_{2j} + \mu_{3j})}{3} \quad .$$

The tests for TIME*PROGRAM tell you if the effect of the within-subjects factor changes for the different levels of the between-subjects factors. The null hypothesis is

$$H_0: \mu_{11} - \mu_{17} = \mu_{21} - \mu_{27} = \mu_{31} - \mu_{37},$$
$$\mu_{12} - \mu_{17} = \mu_{22} - \mu_{27} = \mu_{32} - \mu_{37},$$
$$\vdots$$
$$\mu_{16} - \mu_{17} = \mu_{26} - \mu_{27} = \mu_{36} - \mu_{37} \quad .$$

One additional test provided by the REPEATED statement is labeled Tests of Hypotheses for Between Subjects Effects, and it tests the hypothesis that these effects (in this example, the different weight training programs) have no effect on the dependent variables, ignoring the within-subjects effects in the design. The null hypothesis is

$$H_0: \bar{\mu}_{1.} = \bar{\mu}_{2.} = \bar{\mu}_{3.}$$

where

$$\bar{\mu}_{i.} = \frac{\mu_{i1} + \ldots + \mu_{i7}}{7} \quad .$$

Since these tests ignore the effects that exist across the dependent variables, they are constructed by simply adding together the dependent variables and performing an analysis on the sum. (Actually, the analysis is performed on the sum divided by the square root of the number of dependent variables.) Thus, the between-subjects tests differ from the corresponding multivariate tests in that they do not attempt to account for correlation among the dependent variables. They only tell you whether these factors are important when averaged over the dependent variables representing the within-subjects effects. In this case, the F value of 3.07 with a probability of 0.0548 indicates that the PROGRAM effect on strength is of borderline significance when averaged over the different times when strength is measured.

The results of the two multivariate tests indicate that TIME has a clear effect on strength, as indicated by the F value of 6.456 and p value of 0.0001 for all the multivariate tests. However, the TIME*PROGRAM interaction effect is less clear. Only one of the multivariate tests yields a p value of less than .05. This is discussed later in Section 8.5, "Univariate Repeated-Measures Analysis Using the REPEATED Statement." The only assumption required for the validity of the tests is that the strength measurements at the different times (S1 through S7) have a multivariate normal distribution with a common covariance matrix for the subjects within each PROGRAM.

8.4   Univariate Repeated-Measures Analysis As a Split-Plot Design

As mentioned previously, the univariate analysis of repeated-measures designs is similar to the split-plot analysis outlined in Section 3.5. The split-plot model specifies that pairs of observations on the same unit are equally correlated. With repeated-measures data, pairs of observations on the same unit are not necessarily equally correlated. Measurements close in time are usually more highly correlated than measurements far apart in time. Since the unequal correlation between the repeated measurements is ignored in a split-plot analysis, the univariate tests derived in this manner may not be valid. However, in cases where many repeated-measurement observations are missing, this might be the only way of analyzing a repeated-measures design, because the REPEATED statement (like the MANOVA statement) ignores cases where any of the repeated measurements are missing. In general, the univariate tests are more capable of detecting existing differences than their multivariate counterparts. In this section, a univariate repeated-measures analysis of the data set EXERCISE is performed using the MODEL statement in the GLM procedure for a split-plot design. In Section 8.5, the REPEATED statement is used to perform the same analysis more efficiently. In addition, the REPEATED statement also provides a test for the covariance structure of the repeated measures required for the split-plot analysis of variance. It also provides approximate F tests that take the covariance structure of the repeated measures into account.

The first step in analyzing a repeated-measures design in the fashion of a split plot is to organize the data in the appropriate form. In Output 8.1, all seven repeated measurements for an individual appear on one line, and there is no need to explicitly define a variable corresponding to the subject on which the measurement was taken. To use the split-plot approach, each repeated measure must be a separate observation in the data set. The following SAS statements achieve this goal:

```
data split;
   set exercise;
   array s{7} s1-s7;
   subject + 1;
   do time=1 to 7;
      strength=s{time};
      output;
   end;
   drop s1-s7;
run;
```

The statement

```
subject+1;
```

creates a variable called SUBJECT and increments its value by 1 for each observation in the EXERCISE data set. In this experiment, PROGRAM is the whole plot treatment (since it is applied to an entire subject), TIME is the sub-plot treatment, SUBJECT(PROGRAM) serves the role of replication, and STRENGTH is the dependent variable. The following SAS statements are used for the analysis:

```
proc glm data=split;
   class time program subject;
   model strength=program subject(program) time time*program;
   test h=program e=subject(program);
```

The results appear in Output 8.4.

Output 8.4
Univariate Analysis of Repeated-Measures Design Using the MODEL Statement

```
                             The SAS System                              1

                       General Linear Models Procedure
                           Class Level Information

   Class     Levels   Values

   TIME         7     1 2 3 4 5 6 7

   PROGRAM      3     CONT RI WI

   SUBJECT     57     1 2 3 4 5 6 7 8 9 10 11 12 13 14 15 16 17 18 19 20 21 22
                      23 24 25 26 27 28 29 30 31 32 33 34 35 36 37 38 39 40 41
                      42 43 44 45 46 47 48 49 50 51 52 53 54 55 56 57


                   Number of observations in data set = 399
```

```
                                                                         2

                       General Linear Models Procedure

   Dependent Variable: STRENGTH
                                 Sum of            Mean
   Source                 DF    Squares          Square    F Value    Pr > F

   Model                  74   4210.0528643   56.8926063     47.53    0.0001

   Error                 324    387.7867347    1.1968726

   Corrected Total       398   4597.8395990

                   R-Square          C.V.        Root MSE      STRENGTH Mean

                   0.915659      1.350972       1.0940167          80.979950


   Source                 DF    Type I SS    Mean Square    F Value    Pr > F

   PROGRAM                 2    419.4352623   209.7176311    175.22    0.0001
   SUBJECT(PROGRAM)       54   3694.6900510    68.4201861     57.17    0.0001
   TIME                    6     52.9273183     8.8212197      7.37    0.0001
   TIME*PROGRAM           12     43.0002327     3.5833527      2.99    0.0005

                                             (continued on next page)
```

```
(continued from previous page)

Source              DF      Type III SS     Mean Square   F Value    Pr > F

PROGRAM              2       419.4352623     209.7176311   175.22     0.0001
SUBJECT(PROGRAM)     54      3694.6900510    68.4201861    57.17      0.0001
TIME                6       53.3542637      8.8923773     7.43       0.0001
TIME*PROGRAM         12      43.0002327      3.5833527     2.99       0.0005

Tests of Hypotheses using the Type III MS for SUBJECT(PROGRAM) as an error term

Source              DF      Type III SS     Mean Square   F Value    Pr > F

PROGRAM              2       419.43526226    209.71763113  3.07       0.0548
```

You should remember that, because of the unequal correlations between pairs of observations taken on the same subject, the results in Output 8.4 might not be valid. The TEST statement specifies that the test for PROGRAM uses SUBJECT (PROGRAM) as an error term. The results in Output 8.4 indicate that TIME has a significant effect (Pr > F=0.0001), agreeing with the conclusion of the multivariate analysis. In addition, the test for PROGRAM effect using SUBJECT(PROGRAM) as an error term results in the same test as the between-subjects hypothesis test obtained from the REPEATED statement. This is true because this test is produced by averaging over the repeated measurements; therefore, unequal correlations present no problem.

8.5 Univariate Repeated-Measures Analysis Using the REPEATED Statement

To implement the univariate repeated-measures analysis using the REPEATED statement, simply replace the NOU option in the REPEATED statement in Section 8.3 with the NOM option; NOM requests univariate tests only, not multivariate tests. In addition, if you add the PRINTE option after the slash, you also get (among other output) a test of the hypothesis that the covariance structure of the repeated measurements is such that the probabilities from the ordinary F tests are correct. This test is known as a test of sphericity of a set of orthogonal components, which are simply a set of transformed variables that meet certain mathematical conditions (Huynh and Feldt 1970). The sphericity test itself is concerned with the pattern of correlations of the orthogonal components; specifically, it tests the hypothesis that the orthogonal components are uncorrelated and have equal variance. If the hypothesis of sphericity of orthogonal components is true, then the probabilities provided by the univariate F tests are correct. If the hypothesis of sphericity of the orthogonal components is false, then remedial steps should be taken. Either use the multivariate tests for the TIME and PROGRAM*TIME effects, or make adjustments to the univariate tests. The univariate analysis of the REPEATED statement provides two approximations. Each one attempts to account for the unequal correlations among pairs of the repeated measurements by deflating the numerator and denominator degrees of freedom for the F tests involving the within-subjects (repeated-measures) effect.

The statements used for the univariate analysis are as follows:

```
proc glm data=exercise;
   class program;
   model s1 s2 s3 s4 s5 s6 s7=program / nouni;
   repeated time / nom printe;
```

The results appear in Output 8.5.

Output 8.5
Univariate
Repeated-Measures
Analysis Using the
REPEATED
Statement

```
                           The SAS System                        1

                   General Linear Models Procedure
                       Class Level Information

               Class     Levels    Values

               PROGRAM       3     CONT RI WI


          Number of observations in data set = 57
```

```
                                                                 2

                   General Linear Models Procedure
                 Repeated Measures Analysis of Variance
                 Repeated Measures Level Information

Dependent Variable         S1      S2      S3      S4      S5      S6

    Level of TIME           1       2       3       4       5       6

Dependent Variable         S7

    Level of TIME           7
```

```
                                                                 3

                   General Linear Models Procedure
                 Repeated Measures Analysis of Variance

     Partial Correlation Coefficients from the Error SS&CP Matrix / Prob > |r|

DF = 53        S1        S2        S3        S4        S5        S6        S7

S1        1.000000  0.960210  0.924649  0.871580  0.842113  0.809118  0.796771
          0.0001    0.0001    0.0001    0.0001    0.0001    0.0001    0.0001

S2        0.960210  1.000000  0.939585  0.876990  0.859610  0.827336  0.791740
          0.0001    0.0001    0.0001    0.0001    0.0001    0.0001    0.0001

S3        0.924649  0.939585  1.000000  0.955591  0.937237  0.897542  0.875517
          0.0001    0.0001    0.0001    0.0001    0.0001    0.0001    0.0001

S4        0.871580  0.876990  0.955591  1.000000  0.960087  0.909447  0.887424
          0.0001    0.0001    0.0001    0.0001    0.0001    0.0001    0.0001

S5        0.842113  0.859610  0.937237  0.960087  1.000000  0.951369  0.916529
          0.0001    0.0001    0.0001    0.0001    0.0001    0.0001    0.0001

S6        0.809118  0.827336  0.897542  0.909447  0.951369  1.000000  0.953077
          0.0001    0.0001    0.0001    0.0001    0.0001    0.0001    0.0001

S7        0.796771  0.791740  0.875517  0.887424  0.916529  0.953077  1.000000
          0.0001    0.0001    0.0001    0.0001    0.0001    0.0001    0.0001

                                           (continued on next page)
```

(continued from previous page)

E = Error SS&CP Matrix

TIME.N represents the contrast between the nth level of TIME and the last

	TIME.1	TIME.2	TIME.3	TIME.4	TIME.5	TIME.6
TIME.1	251.43988	235.58393	164.42202	132.20357	86.79881	46.61905
TIME.2	235.58393	259.63036	176.67321	137.58214	100.43929	59.57143
TIME.3	164.42202	176.67321	161.47560	128.48929	97.12024	49.47619
TIME.4	132.20357	137.58214	128.48929	145.84286	102.73571	49.42857
TIME.5	86.79881	100.43929	97.12024	102.73571	112.18810	56.19048
TIME.6	46.61905	59.57143	49.47619	49.42857	56.19048	62.95238

4

General Linear Models Procedure
Repeated Measures Analysis of Variance

Partial Correlation Coefficients from the Error SS&CP Matrix
of the Variables Defined by the Specified Transformation / Prob > |r|

DF = 53	TIME.1	TIME.2	TIME.3	TIME.4	TIME.5	TIME.6
TIME.1	1.000000	0.922042	0.815999	0.690373	0.516801	0.370544
	0.0001	0.0001	0.0001	0.0001	0.0001	0.0054
TIME.2	0.922042	1.000000	0.862858	0.707036	0.588508	0.465966
	0.0001	0.0001	0.0001	0.0001	0.0001	0.0003
TIME.3	0.815999	0.862858	1.000000	0.837280	0.721577	0.490723
	0.0001	0.0001	0.0001	0.0001	0.0001	0.0001
TIME.4	0.690373	0.707036	0.837280	1.000000	0.803166	0.515857
	0.0001	0.0001	0.0001	0.0001	0.0001	0.0001
TIME.5	0.516801	0.588508	0.721577	0.803166	1.000000	0.668626
	0.0001	0.0001	0.0001	0.0001	0.0001	0.0001
TIME.6	0.370544	0.465966	0.490723	0.515857	0.668626	1.000000
	0.0054	0.0003	0.0001	0.0001	0.0001	0.0001

Test for Sphericity: Mauchly's Criterion = 0.0009992
Chisquare Approximation = 357.70745 with 20 df   Prob > Chisquare = 0.0000

Applied to Orthogonal Components:
Test for Sphericity: Mauchly's Criterion = 0.0403737
Chisquare Approximation = 166.18471 with 20 df   Prob > Chisquare = 0.0000

5

General Linear Models Procedure
Repeated Measures Analysis of Variance
Tests of Hypotheses for Between Subjects Effects

Source	DF	Type III SS	Mean Square	F Value	Pr > F
PROGRAM	2	419.43526	209.71763	3.07	0.0548
Error	54	3694.69005	68.42019		

```
                                                                    6
                          General Linear Models Procedure
                        Repeated Measures Analysis of Variance
                  Univariate Tests of Hypotheses for Within Subject Effects

   Source: TIME
                                                                Adj  Pr > F
        DF         Type III SS        Mean Square   F Value  Pr > F   G - G     H - F
         6         53.35426371        8.89237729      7.43   0.0001  0.0003   0.0002

   Source: TIME*PROGRAM
                                                                Adj  Pr > F
        DF         Type III SS        Mean Square   F Value  Pr > F   G - G     H - F
        12         43.00023272        3.58335273      2.99   0.0005  0.0130   0.0104

   Source: Error(TIME)

        DF         Type III SS        Mean Square
       324        387.78673469        1.19687264

                     Greenhouse-Geisser Epsilon = 0.4233
                         Huynh-Feldt Epsilon = 0.4624
```

Pages 1 and 2 of the output (the class level and repeated-measures level information) is identical to that for the multivariate tests. Page 3 presents the partial correlations of the original (untransformed) dependent variables, in this case, the strength measurements at the seven times. These correlations are corrected for all the independent variables in the model. Because these correlations are for the original variables, they are sometimes easier to interpret than the correlations of the transformed variables that appear later in the output. Note that correlations generally decrease as the time interval increases. Next, the error sums of squares matrix and partial correlations are printed for the transformed variables, in this case, the default transformation that subtracts the measurement representing the last level of time (S7) from each of the other levels of time. After this, two sphericity tests are presented; the first for the particular transformation being used and the second for a set of orthogonal components. The test applied to the orthogonal components is the one that is important in determining whether the univariate F tests for the within-subjects effects are valid. In this case, the hypothesis that the F tests are valid is rejected because the reported probability is 0.0001. (When there are only two levels of a within-subjects effect, there is only one transformed variable, and a sphericity test is not needed and cannot be preformed.)

Page 5 of the output shows that the tests of hypotheses for between-subjects effects are identical to those tests produced previously using the multivariate approach. In both cases, these tests represent an average over the repeated measure. Finally, the univariate tests for the within-subjects effects appear on Page 6. The sums of squares and F values for these tests are the same as those obtained through the split-plot approach, but two additional columns appear in the ANOVA tables; these columns present two adjusted probabilities that attempt to correct for the unequal correlations among pairs of repeated measures. Both of the tests are carried out by estimating a quantity known as ε (epsilon) and then multiplying the numerator and denominator degrees of freedom by this estimate before determining the significance level for the test labeled Adj Pr > F in the output. The first test is labeled G - G in the output, which stands for Greenhouse-Geisser, the two authors who proposed the technique of deflation of degrees of freedom for use in repeated-measures experiments (Greenhouse and Geisser 1959). The second test is labeled H - F in the output, which stands for Huynh-Feldt, two authors who proposed an alternative estimator for epsilon that provides tests that are not as conservative as the Greenhouse-Geisser tests (Huynh and Feldt 1976).

The true value of epsilon must be between 0 and 1, but the Huynh-Feldt estimator sometimes produces values greater than 1. In these cases, no adjustment is made to the degrees of freedom or to the resultant significance levels. (As with the sphericity tests, no adjustments are possible or needed when there are only two levels of a within-subjects effect.) In practice, the Huynh-Feldt estimators are often 1 or greater in those cases where the hypothesis of sphericity of orthogonal components is not rejected. They provide a reasonable adjustment to the probabilities for the F tests for moderate to large samples. You should note that even when the value of the H - F epsilon is greater than 1 in the output, a value of 1 (no adjustment) is used for calculating probabilities. In Output 8.5, both the G - G epsilon value of 0.4233 and the H - F epsilon value of 0.4624 indicate that some adjustment may be necessary to ensure that the probability levels are corrected to account for the correlation of the within-subjects factor. Since the G - G estimator tends to give a conservative test (that is, one that might sometimes fail to reject the null hypothesis even when it should be rejected), it is up to the experimenter to decide whether or not the adjustment should be used. In this case, even the G - G adjusted probability indicates significance for the TIME effect at the 0.0003 level. Of interest here is the fact that the univariate test for the TIME*PROGRAM effect is significant at the (corrected) 0.0130 p level, even though the multivariate tests showed probabilities of approximately 0.19. This is because the univariate approach, if appropriate, is more powerful than its multivariate counterpart. Strictly speaking, the univariate tests are appropriate only when the measurements conform to the pattern tested by the sphericity test discussed above. Even though corrections are applied to the probabilities, the univariate tests may be too liberal (that is, they might reject the null hypothesis even though it is true more often than the stated probabilities) when the data do not conform to this pattern. In a case where the sphericity test is rejected so dramatically ($p<0.0001$), the univariate tests should be interpreted cautiously.

8.6 Contrasts among Dependent Variables: SUMMARY Option

Chapter 7 shows contrasts among the dependent variables in a multivariate analysis using the M= option in the MANOVA statement. There are some common contrasts that have proven to be extremely useful in repeated-measures analysis of variance which can be generated automatically by the REPEATED statement in PROC GLM. The most common use of these contrasts is through the examination of ANOVA tables for each transformed variable to gain insight into the nature of a repeated-measures effect. There are several contrasts available in the REPEATED statement. In this section, the POLYNOMIAL contrasts are used because the levels of TIME represent a quantitative factor whose effect can often be explained through polynomial relations. For descriptions of the other transformations available, see "Transformations Used in Repeated Measures Analysis of Variance," in Chapter 24, "The GLM Procedure," in the *SAS/STAT User's Guide, Version 6, Fourth Edition, Volume 2*. Keep in mind that the univariate and multivariate statistics and probabilities that are presented earlier are not affected by the choice of contrast; only the elements of the matrices involved in the tests and the ANOVA tables produced by the SUMMARY option change when a different transformation is used.

To produce the ANOVA tables for the polynomial contrasts in the strength example, you need to replace the REPEATED statement used in Section 8.5 with the following statement:

```
repeated time polynomial / summary nom nou;
```

Both the NOU and NOM options suppress redundant output. Any additional options, such as PRINTM or PRINTE, can also be used. The keyword POLYNOMIAL signals that a POLYNOMIAL transformation is requested. Output 8.6 shows the output from this REPEATED statement.

Output 8.6
Analysis of Variance of Transformed Variables Using the POLYNOMIAL Keyword

```
                        The SAS System                          1
                 General Linear Models Procedure
                     Class Level Information

              Class     Levels    Values

              PROGRAM      3      CONT RI WI


        Number of observations in data set = 57



                 General Linear Models Procedure
              Repeated Measures Analysis of Variance
               Repeated Measures Level Information

Dependent Variable      S1      S2      S3      S4      S5      S6

    Level of TIME        1       2       3       4       5       6

Dependent Variable      S7

    Level of TIME        7




                 General Linear Models Procedure
              Repeated Measures Analysis of Variance
           Tests of Hypotheses for Between Subjects Effects

Source              DF      Type III SS      Mean Square   F Value    Pr > F

PROGRAM              2       419.43526       209.71763      3.07      0.0548

Error               54      3694.69005        68.42019




                 General Linear Models Procedure
              Repeated Measures Analysis of Variance
            Analysis of Variance of Contrast Variables

      TIME.N represents the nth degree polynomial contrast for TIME

Contrast Variable: TIME.1

Source              DF      Type III SS      Mean Square   F Value    Pr > F

MEAN                 1      40.51445294      40.51445294    9.85      0.0028
PROGRAM              2      40.39136233      20.19568117    4.91      0.0110

Error               54     222.18758503       4.11458491

Contrast Variable: TIME.2

Source              DF      Type III SS      Mean Square   F Value    Pr > F

MEAN                 1      10.57713133      10.57713133    8.64      0.0048
PROGRAM              2       1.42410491       0.71205245    0.58      0.5626

Error               54      66.13395692       1.22470291

                                          (continued on next page)
```

(continued from previous page)

Contrast Variable: TIME.3

Source	DF	Type III SS	Mean Square	F Value	Pr > F
MEAN	1	1.31320035	1.31320035	2.55	0.1163
PROGRAM	2	0.03999060	0.01999530	0.04	0.9620
Error	54	27.83720238	0.51550375		

Contrast Variable: TIME.4

Source	DF	Type III SS	Mean Square	F Value	Pr > F
MEAN	1	0.00000000	0.00000000	0.00	1.0000
PROGRAM	2	0.53719750	0.26859875	0.39	0.6798
Error	54	37.31675557	0.69105103		

Contrast Variable: TIME.5

Source	DF	Type III SS	Mean Square	F Value	Pr > F
MEAN	1	0.69325639	0.69325639	2.19	0.1451
PROGRAM	2	0.20663265	0.10331633	0.33	0.7234
Error	54	17.12670068	0.31716112		

Contrast Variable: TIME.6

Source	DF	Type III SS	Mean Square	F Value	Pr > F
MEAN	1	0.00000000	0.00000000	0.00	1.0000
PROGRAM	2	0.40094473	0.20047237	0.63	0.5365

General Linear Models Procedure
Repeated Measures Analysis of Variance
Analysis of Variance of Contrast Variables

TIME.N represents the nth degree polynomial contrast for TIME

Contrast Variable: TIME.6

Source	DF	Type III SS	Mean Square	F Value	Pr > F
Error	54	17.18453412	0.31823211		

The legend above the ANOVA tables describes the transformation of the original dependent variables that the contrast variables represent. In Output 8.6, TIME.1 represents the first-degree (linear) polynomial, TIME.2 represents the second-degree (quadratic) polynomial, and so on. The exact combinations of the original dependent variables that are used can be printed using the PRINTM option. The line labeled MEAN tests the hypothesis that, averaged over all the observations, the mean of the specified contrast variable is 0. Thus, the significant ($F=9.85$, $p<0.0028$) MEAN effect for the contrast TIME.1 indicates that the linear component of TIME is significantly different from 0. Likewise, the F value of 8.64 ($p<0.0048$) for the MEAN effect on TIME.2 implies that the quadratic effect of TIME is also important. The quadratic component of the effect would appear as a curve on a plot of TIME versus STRENGTH. The test labeled PROGRAM tests the hypothesis that the mean of the contrast variable is the same for each level of PROGRAM tested. The significant PROGRAM effect for TIME.1 shows that the slopes of the lines describing the STRENGTH*TIME relationship are different for the three programs tested. To produce a plot allowing an examination of these effects, the data are first summarized as means using PROC

SUMMARY. This produces three observations, one for each level of PROGRAM, with variables named MWT1 through MWT7. Next, each observation is expanded to produce an observation for each level of TIME. Finally, the data are plotted using the value of PROGRAM as the plotting symbol. The following SAS statements produce the plot in Output 8.7:

```
proc summary nway data=exercise;
   class program;
   var s1-s7;
   output out=new mean=mwt1-mwt7;
data plot;
   set new;
   array mwt(7) mwt1-mwt7;
   do time=1 to 7;
      strength=mwt(time);
      output;
   end;
   drop mwt1-mwt7;
proc plot;
   plot strength*time=program;
```

The MEAN effect for TIME.1 (the linear component) can be seen as a general tendency for strength to increase with time, whereas the MEAN effect for TIME.2 (the quadratic component) results from the bend in each of the lines around time 4 or 5. Finally, the PROGRAM effect for the linear component is evident in the steeper slope of the **WI** (W) and **RI** (R) lines as compared to the **CONT** (C) line.

Output 8.7
Plot of
Repeated-Measures
Data

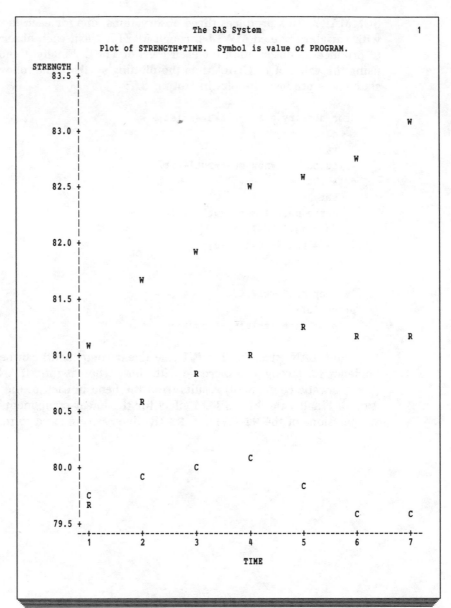

8.7 Two Repeated-Measures Factors: Multivariate and Univariate Analysis

The methods described in previous sections are applicable when there is more than one repeated-measures factor involved, as the next example using simulated data illustrates.

In an experiment concerned with growth of soybeans, each of several plants from planting beds of three different heights is tested for moisture at four different depths in the morning and once again in the afternoon, forming a 4×2 pattern of two factors. Thus, there were eight measurements taken on each plant.

The moisture measurements, made at depths of 10, 20, 40, and 50 centimeters, are represented by the variables M10_AM, M10_PM, M20_AM, M20_PM, M40_AM, M40_PM, M50_AM, and M50_PM, where the _AM and the _PM indicate whether the measurement was taken in the morning or the afternoon. The three BED heights are labeled LOW, MED, and HIGH. In this case, BED is a between-subjects factor, and both DEPTH and TIMEDAY are within-subjects factors. Notice that TIMEDAY is nested within DEPTH because each DEPTH measurement has two measurements associated with it, one taken in the morning and one taken in the afternoon. Output 8.8 shows the data.

Output 8.8
Data with Two Repeated-Measures Factors

```
                               The SAS System                                    1

  OBS  BED   M10_AM  M10_PM  M20_AM  M20_PM  M40_AM  M40_PM  M50_AM  M50_PM

   1   LOW    12.3    13.4    13.7    15.0    16.4    15.6    16.4    17.0
   2   LOW    12.0    12.8    13.5    14.3    14.4    13.4    14.9    14.1
   3   LOW    11.7    12.2    12.2    12.7    13.3    14.1    13.6    14.0
   4   MED    12.2    13.4    13.2    14.0    15.5    15.4    16.7    16.4
   5   MED     9.6     9.9    12.0    12.9    14.3    14.0    16.2    16.9
   6   HIGH   16.5    15.2    17.6    18.1    21.2    21.2    22.7    22.1
   7   HIGH   14.3    15.2    18.7    16.8    18.9    20.1    23.0    22.5
   8   HIGH   12.8    12.2    14.5    16.9    17.3    18.5    19.5    19.4
```

This experiment is different from a true nested design (see Section 3.2, "Nested Classifications") because the levels of the nested factor (TIMEDAY) are the same for each level of the factor within which they are nested (DEPTH). This experiment is common for observations with more than one within-subjects factor. Some of the questions of interest in the study are listed below:

1. Were there overall changes in moisture over the depths sampled?

2. Are the changes in moisture over depth different depending on the bed height?

3. Is there a difference in moisture level in the morning and afternoon?

4. Are changes due to time of day the same for the different bed heights?

5. Are changes due to time of day the same for the different depths at which moisture measurements were taken?

Questions 1, 3, and 5 involve only the within-subjects factors; questions 2 and 4 are addressed by studying interactions of the within-subjects factors with between-subjects factors. Appropriate tests for both kinds of hypotheses are automatically generated when you use the REPEATED statement in PROC GLM. The SAS statements for performing the analysis are as follows:

```
proc glm data=moisture;
   class bed;
   model m10_am m10_pm
         m20_am m20_pm
         m40_am m40_pm
         m50_am m50_pm=bed / nouni;
   repeated depth 4, timeday 2 / short;
```

The SHORT option in the REPEATED statement prints the multivariate test statistics and the associated *F* statistics in a condensed form. The condensed form produced by the SHORT option is the default for Version 6 and subsequent releases of the SAS System. Since there are two repeated-measures factors, their labels and number of levels are separated by a comma. Output 8.9 shows the output.

Output 8.9

Repeated-Measures Analysis with Two Within-Subjects Factors Using the REPEATED Statement

```
                              The SAS System                              1

                       General Linear Models Procedure
                          Class Level Information

                     Class     Levels    Values

                     BED          3      HIGH LOW MED


               Number of observations in data set = 8

                     General Linear Models Procedure
                   Repeated Measures Analysis of Variance
                    Repeated Measures Level Information

Dependent Variable     M10_AM  M10_PM  M20_AM  M20_PM  M40_AM  M40_PM

      Level of DEPTH       1       1       2       2       3       3
      Level of TIMEDAY     1       2       1       2       1       2

Dependent Variable     M50_AM  M50_PM

      Level of DEPTH       4       4
      Level of TIMEDAY     1       2


                  Manova Test Criteria and Exact F Statistics for
                      the Hypothesis of no DEPTH Effect
              H = Type III SS&CP Matrix for DEPTH   E = Error SS&CP Matrix

                          S=1     M=0.5    N=0.5

Statistic                      Value          F      Num DF    Den DF   Pr > F

Wilks' Lambda               0.02925461    33.1827       3         3     0.0084
Pillai's Trace              0.97074539    33.1827       3         3     0.0084
Hotelling-Lawley Trace     33.18265135    33.1827       3         3     0.0084
Roy's Greatest Root        33.18265135    33.1827       3         3     0.0084


                  Manova Test Criteria and F Approximations for
                    the Hypothesis of no DEPTH*BED Effect
          H = Type III SS&CP Matrix for DEPTH*BED   E = Error SS&CP Matrix

                          S=2     M=0     N=0.5

Statistic                      Value          F      Num DF    Den DF   Pr > F

Wilks' Lambda               0.11826219     1.9079       6         6     0.2258
Pillai's Trace              1.10448637     1.6445       6         8     0.2516
Hotelling-Lawley Trace      5.57227331     1.8574       6         4     0.2858
Roy's Greatest Root         5.21081042     6.9477       3         4     0.0459

            NOTE: F Statistic for Roy's Greatest Root is an upper bound.
                 NOTE: F Statistic for Wilks' Lambda is exact.
```

```
                                                                    2

                    General Linear Models Procedure
                    Repeated Measures Analysis of Variance

              Manova Test Criteria and Exact F Statistics for
                  the Hypothesis of no TIMEDAY Effect
          H = Type III SS&CP Matrix for TIMEDAY   E = Error SS&CP Matrix

                    S=1    M=-0.5    N=1.5

Statistic                  Value         F      Num DF    Den DF   Pr > F

Wilks' Lambda            0.58242023    3.5849       1         5    0.1169
Pillai's Trace          0.41757977    3.5849       1         5    0.1169
Hotelling-Lawley Trace  0.71697333    3.5849       1         5    0.1169
Roy's Greatest Root     0.71697333    3.5849       1         5    0.1169


              Manova Test Criteria and Exact F Statistics for
                 the Hypothesis of no TIMEDAY*BED Effect
          H = Type III SS&CP Matrix for TIMEDAY*BED   E = Error SS&CP Matrix

                    S=1    M=0    N=1.5

Statistic                  Value         F      Num DF    Den DF   Pr > F

Wilks' Lambda            0.86079103    0.4043       2         5    0.6875
Pillai's Trace          0.13920897    0.4043       2         5    0.6875
Hotelling-Lawley Trace  0.16172214    0.4043       2         5    0.6875
Roy's Greatest Root     0.16172214    0.4043       2         5    0.6875


              Manova Test Criteria and Exact F Statistics for
                 the Hypothesis of no DEPTH*TIMEDAY Effect
          H = Type III SS&CP Matrix for DEPTH*TIMEDAY   E = Error SS&CP Matrix

                    S=1    M=0.5    N=0.5

Statistic                  Value         F      Num DF    Den DF   Pr > F

Wilks' Lambda            0.50087348    0.9965       3         3    0.5011
Pillai's Trace          0.49912652    0.9965       3         3    0.5011
Hotelling-Lawley Trace  0.99651219    0.9965       3         3    0.5011
Roy's Greatest Root     0.99651219    0.9965       3         3    0.5011
```

```
                                                                    3

                    General Linear Models Procedure
                    Repeated Measures Analysis of Variance

              Manova Test Criteria and F Approximations for
                the Hypothesis of no DEPTH*TIMEDAY*BED Effect
      H = Type III SS&CP Matrix for DEPTH*TIMEDAY*BED   E = Error SS&CP Matrix

                    S=2    M=0    N=0.5

Statistic                  Value         F      Num DF    Den DF   Pr > F

Wilks' Lambda            0.25360305    0.9857       6         6    0.5067
Pillai's Trace          0.75468509    0.8080       6         8    0.5912
Hotelling-Lawley Trace  2.91048865    0.9702       6         4    0.5374
Roy's Greatest Root     2.89921609    3.8656       3         4    0.1122

       NOTE: F Statistic for Roy's Greatest Root is an upper bound.
            NOTE: F Statistic for Wilks' Lambda is exact.
```

(continued on next page)

(continued from previous page)

```
                                                                          4
                        General Linear Models Procedure
                      Repeated Measures Analysis of Variance
                   Tests of Hypotheses for Between Subjects Effects

    Source              DF      Type III SS      Mean Square    F Value    Pr > F

    BED                  2      270.1016667      135.0508333     10.85     0.0152

    Error                5       62.2433333       12.4486667
```

```
                                                                          5
                        General Linear Models Procedure
                      Repeated Measures Analysis of Variance
                  Univariate Tests of Hypotheses for Within Subject Effects

    Source: DEPTH
                                                                  Adj  Pr > F
         DF      Type III SS      Mean Square    F Value   Pr > F   G - G    H - F
          3     217.76535714      72.58845238     90.22    0.0001   0.0001   0.0001

    Source: DEPTH*BED
                                                                  Adj  Pr > F
         DF      Type III SS      Mean Square    F Value   Pr > F   G - G    H - F
          6      35.13291667       5.85548611      7.28    0.0009   0.0060   0.0009

    Source: Error(DEPTH)
         DF      Type III SS      Mean Square
         15      12.06833333       0.80455556

                      Greenhouse-Geisser Epsilon = 0.6403
                        Huynh-Feldt Epsilon = 1.4470


    Source: TIMEDAY
                                                                  Adj  Pr > F
         DF      Type III SS      Mean Square    F Value   Pr > F   G - G    H - F
          1       1.23857143       1.23857143      3.58    0.1169    .        .

    Source: TIMEDAY*BED
                                                                  Adj  Pr > F
         DF      Type III SS      Mean Square    F Value   Pr > F   G - G    H - F
          2       0.27937500       0.13968750      0.40    0.6875    .        .

    Source: Error(TIMEDAY)
         DF      Type III SS      Mean Square
          5       1.72750000       0.34550000

    Source: DEPTH*TIMEDAY
                                                                  Adj  Pr > F
         DF      Type III SS      Mean Square    F Value   Pr > F   G - G    H - F
          3       1.23500000       0.41166667      0.88    0.4722   0.4288   0.4722

    Source: DEPTH*TIMEDAY*BED
                                                                  Adj  Pr > F
         DF      Type III SS      Mean Square    F Value   Pr > F   G - G    H - F
          6       2.51270833       0.41878472      0.90    0.5212   0.4901   0.5212

    Source: Error(DEPTH*TIMEDAY)
         DF      Type III SS      Mean Square
         15       6.99416667       0.46627778

                      Greenhouse-Geisser Epsilon = 0.5460
                        Huynh-Feldt Epsilon = 1.1010
```

On Page 1 of the output, after the class level information, note that the repeated-measures level information shows which dependent variable corresponds to each level of the within-subjects effects. In this example, M10_AM and M10_PM both represent level 1 of DEPTH, and levels 1 and 2, respectively, of

TIMEDAY. This pattern repeats itself for the other dependent variables; that is, each time pair (for example, M20_AM and M20_PM), represents the same level of DEPTH, and 1 and 2, respectively, of TIMEDAY. It is important to remember the way the REPEATED statement expects the dependent variables to be ordered when there is more than one within-subjects factor: the last factor (in this case TIMEDAY) always changes most rapidly as you go through the dependent variables. The repeated-measures level information confirms that the variables are ordered properly.

The multivariate tests indicate that only DEPTH has a significant effect ($p<0.0084$). The univariate test for DEPTH agrees with this finding, but the univariate test for the DEPTH*BED interaction is also significant, indicating that the effect of planting DEPTH on moisture level is different for at least one of the beds. In addition, the test for the between-subjects factor, BED, is also significant ($p<0.0152$), indicating that, averaged over the depths sampled, the moisture level is different depending upon the height of the planting bed. To get an idea of where these differences are coming from, a plot of the data similar to the one in the previous section can be generated. The TIMEDAY effect is ignored to simplify the plot because it is not declared significant. Because the depths do not have equal spacing and because the TIMEDAY effect is being eliminated, some modifications to the program in the previous section are necessary. The following program first separates the data into eight observations per plant and then uses PROC SUMMARY to generate the necessary means:

```
data one;
   set moisture;
   array m{8} m10_am--m50_pm;
   k=1;
   do depth=10,20,40,50;
      do timeday=1 to 2;
         moisture=m{k};
         k=k+1;
         output;
      end;
   end;
   keep depth bed moisture;
proc summary nway;
   class depth bed;
   var moisture;
   output out=plot mean=moisture;
proc plot;
   plot moisture*depth=bed;
run;
```

Output 8.10 shows the plot.

Output 8.10
Interaction Plot for
Repeated-Measures
Analysis with Two
Within-Subjects
Factors

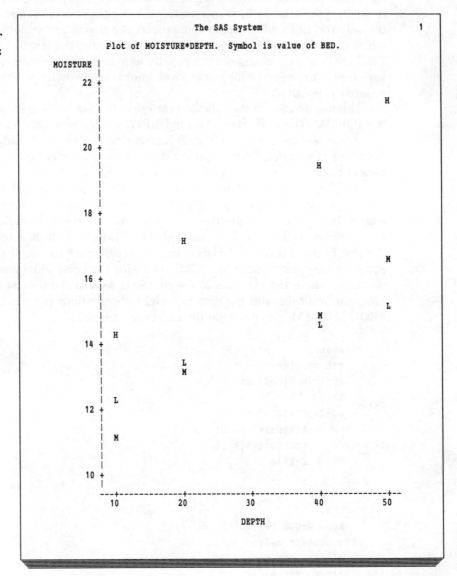

The main effect for the between-subjects factor, BED, is expressed on the plot by the appearance of a separate line for the measurements taken from plants with high (H) planting beds; the moisture levels for these plants appear to be higher than those for the low and medium bed plants. The main effect for the within-subjects factor, DEPTH, is seen as an overall trend (for all groups) for moisture levels to rise as DEPTH increases; that is, the lines have a marked positive slope and do not remain parallel to the horizontal axis. You can see that the change in moisture levels over depth is somewhat more pronounced for the high planting beds than for the beds of other heights. This effect is an indication of the DEPTH*BED interaction. It is important not to confuse the main effect for BED, which is evidenced by the overall level of the lines on the plot, with the DEPTH*BED interaction, which is evidenced by the changes in the slope of the lines. Because DEPTH is a quantitative measure, it is useful to examine the analyses of the contrast variables produced by a POLYNOMIAL transformation.

When a POLYNOMIAL transformation is used, however, the REPEATED statement assumes that the values of the repeated-measures effect are equally spaced. Since this is not the case in the current example (the values of DEPTH are 10, 20, 40, and 50), the spacing must be given in parentheses after the number of levels. The following SAS statement produces the required analyses. Both the NOM and NOU options are specified to eliminate redundant output:

```
repeated depth 4(10 20 40 50) polynomial, timeday / summary nom nou;
```

Since no transformation keyword is provided for TIMEDAY, a default CONTRAST transformation is used, which compares all but the last level of the effect with the last level. In this case, with only two levels of TIMEDAY, the choice of transformation is unimportant because all transformations simply compare the first level to the second level. Output 8.11 shows selected output from this statement.

Output 8.11
Analysis of Variance of Transformed Variables Using the SUMMARY Option

```
                               The SAS System                          1

                        General Linear Models Procedure
                           Class Level Information

                    Class     Levels     Values

                    BED          3        HIGH LOW MED


               Number of observations in data set = 8



                        General Linear Models Procedure
                      Repeated Measures Analysis of Variance
                       Repeated Measures Level Information

   Dependent Variable   M10_AM   M10_PM   M20_AM   M20_PM   M40_AM   M40_PM

       Level of DEPTH      10       10       20       20       40       40
       Level of TIMEDAY     1        2        1        2        1        2

   Dependent Variable   M50_AM   M50_PM

       Level of DEPTH      50       50
       Level of TIMEDAY     1        2
```

```
                                                                        2
                        General Linear Models Procedure
                      Repeated Measures Analysis of Variance
                   Tests of Hypotheses for Between Subjects Effects

   Source           DF     Type III SS     Mean Square    F Value    Pr > F

   BED               2     270.1016667     135.0508333     10.85     0.0152

   Error             5      62.2433333      12.4486667
```

(continued on next page)

(continued from previous page)

```
                                                                    3
                        General Linear Models Procedure
                       Repeated Measures Analysis of Variance
                       Analysis of Variance of Contrast Variables

            DEPTH.N represents the nth degree polynomial contrast for DEPTH

     Contrast Variable: DEPTH.1

     Source              DF      Type III SS      Mean Square     F Value    Pr > F

     MEAN                 1     426.22288095     426.22288095     153.56     0.0001
     BED                  2      67.85804167      33.92902083      12.22     0.0119

     Error                5      13.87783333       2.77556667

     Contrast Variable: DEPTH.2

     Source              DF      Type III SS      Mean Square     F Value    Pr > F

     MEAN                 1       1.76095238       1.76095238       4.13     0.0978
     BED                  2       0.77208333       0.38604167       0.91     0.4617

     Error                5       2.13166667       0.42633333

     Contrast Variable: DEPTH.3

     Source              DF      Type III SS      Mean Square     F Value    Pr > F

     MEAN                 1       7.54688095       7.54688095       4.64     0.0837
     BED                  2       1.63570833       0.81785417       0.50     0.6323

     Error                5       8.12716667       1.62543333


      TIMEDA.N represents the contrast between the nth level of TIMEDAY and the last

     Contrast Variable: TIMEDA.1

     Source              DF      Type III SS      Mean Square     F Value    Pr > F

     MEAN                 1       9.90857143       9.90857143       3.58     0.1169
     BED                  2       2.23500000       1.11750000       0.40     0.6875

     Error                5      13.82000000       2.76400000


            DEPTH.N represents the nth degree polynomial contrast for DEPTH
       TIMEDA.N represents the contrast between the nth level of TIMEDAY and the last

     Contrast Variable: DEPTH.1*TIMEDA.1

     Source              DF      Type III SS      Mean Square     F Value    Pr > F

     MEAN                 1       1.72288095       1.72288095       4.30     0.0927
     BED                  2       1.49504167       0.74752083       1.87     0.2480

     Error                5       2.00183333       0.40036667
```

```
                                                                        4

                       General Linear Models Procedure
                      Repeated Measures Analysis of Variance
                     Analysis of Variance of Contrast Variables

           DEPTH.N represents the nth degree polynomial contrast for DEPTH
       TIMEDA.N represents the contrast between the nth level of TIMEDAY and the last

  Contrast Variable: DEPTH.2*TIMEDA.1

  Source                 DF      Type III SS      Mean Square    F Value    Pr > F

  MEAN                    1       0.32595238       0.32595238      0.40     0.5553
  BED                     2       2.24166667       1.12083333      1.37     0.3349

  Error                   5       4.08333333       0.81666667

  Contrast Variable: DEPTH.3*TIMEDA.1

  Source                 DF      Type III SS      Mean Square    F Value    Pr > F

  MEAN                    1       0.42116667       0.42116667      0.27     0.6277
  BED                     2       1.28870833       0.64435417      0.41     0.6855

  Error                   5       7.90316667       1.58063333
```

The contrast variables corresponding to single repeated-measures effects (such as DEPTH.1 and DEPTH.2) are interpreted as described above. The interaction variables are interpreted similarly to interactions in the usual analysis of variance; thus, DEPTH.1*TIMEDA.1 represents the interaction of the linear effect of DEPTH with the difference between the two levels of TIMEDAY. DEPTH.1*TIMEDA.1 also addresses the question of differences in the linear effect of DEPTH between the two levels of TIMEDAY. In this example, the significant effect ($F = 153.56$, $p < 0.0001$) of the MEAN for DEPTH.1 is a formalized test for the hypothesis that, averaged across the three heights of beds studied, there is no linear effect of depth. Naturally, the hypothesis of no linear effect can be rejected. The significant effect ($F = 12.22$, $p < 0.0119$) of BED for DEPTH.1 indicates that the linear effect of DEPTH is different across the three bed heights, as you can see in the plot in Output 8.10. Keep in mind that these tests on contrast variables are vulnerable to inaccuracies of the probabilities due to multiple comparisons and should be limited to a small number of comparisons, preferably decided upon before the results of the analysis are examined. Nevertheless, they often prove useful in exploratory analyses of repeated-measures designs.

Appendix Example Code

Chapter 1 293

Chapter 2 296

Chapter 3 301

Chapter 4 304

Chapter 5 307

Chapter 6 311

Chapter 7 314

Chapter 8 317

This appendix contains the SAS code needed to produce the output in this book with Release 6.06 of the SAS System. The DATA steps, including the raw data, that are needed to produce the output are shown here. The PROC statements that you must use are presented in the appropriate chapter in the context of the discussion.

This appendix is divided into sections that correspond to chapter numbers to help you quickly locate the example code you need. Before each DATA step, there is a sentence telling you what output that DATA step corresponds to.

Chapter 1

Use the following DATA step to produce Output 1.1 through 1.3.

```
data methane;
   input stortime gas;
   cards;
1  8.2
1  6.6
1  9.8
2  19.7
2  15.7
2  16.0
3  28.6
3  25.0
3  31.9
4  30.8
4  37.8
4  40.2
5  40.3
5  42.9
5  32.6
;
```

Use the following DATA step to produce Output 1.6.

```
data methane;
   input stortime gas;
   cards;
1  8.2
1  6.6
1  9.8
2  19.7
2  15.7
2  16.0
3  28.6
3  25.0
3  31.9
4  30.8
4  37.8
4  40.2
5  40.3
5  42.9
5  32.6
2.5 .
;
proc reg;
   id stortime;
   model gas=stortime / p clm cli;
run;
```

Use the following DATA step to produce Output 1.15 and 1.18.

```
data newmeth;
   set methane;
   storsq=stortime**2;
data phony;
   do stortime=1 to 5 by .1;
      storsq=stortime**2;
      output;
   end;
data both;
   set newmeth phony;
```

Note: You must use the raw data used to produce Output 1.1 through 1.3 to produce Output 1.15 and 1.18.

Use the following DATA step to produce Output 1.4 and 1.5, 1.7 through 1.12, and 1.17.

```
data auction;
   input mkt cattle calves hogs sheep cost volume type $;
   cards;
1  3.437   5.791  3.268   10.649  27.698  23.145  O
2  12.801  4.558  5.751   14.375  57.634  37.485  O
3  6.136   6.223  15.175  2.811   47.172  30.345  O
4  11.685  3.212  0.639   0.694   49.295  16.230  B
5  5.733   3.220  0.534   2.052   24.115  11.539  B
```

```
 6  3.021   4.348   0.839   2.356    33.612  10.564   B
 7  1.689   0.634   0.318   2.209     9.512   4.850   O
 8  2.339   1.895   0.610   0.605    14.755   5.449   B
 9  1.025   0.834   0.734   2.825    10.570   5.418   O
10  2.936   1.419   0.331   0.231    15.394   4.917   B
11  5.049   4.195   1.589   1.957    27.843  12.790   B
12  1.693   3.602   0.837   1.582    17.717   7.714   B
13  1.187   2.679   0.459  18.837    20.253  23.162   O
14  9.730   3.951   3.780   0.524    37.465  17.985   B
15 14.325   4.300  10.781  36.863   101.334  66.269   O
16  7.737   9.043   1.394   1.524    47.427  19.698   B
17  7.538   4.538   2.565   5.109    35.944  19.750   B
18 10.211   4.994   3.081   3.681    45.945  21.967   B
19  8.697   3.005   1.378   3.338    46.890  16.418   B
;
```

Note: In Output 1.10, you must use the following assignment statement in the DATA step to get the correct output:

```
hs=hogs+sheep;
```

Use the following DATA step to produce Output 1.13 and 1.14.

```
data newmeth;
   input stortime gas;
   storsq=stortime**2;
   storcu=stortime**3;
   cards;
1   8.2
1   6.6
1   9.8
2  19.7
2  15.7
2  16.0
3  28.6
3  25.0
3  31.9
4  30.8
4  37.8
4  40.2
5  40.3
5  42.9
5  32.6
;
```

Use the following DATA step to produce Output 1.16.

```
data weighgas;
   input stortime gas;
   storsq=stortime**2;
   ww=1/storsq;
   cards;
1  8.2
1  6.6
1  9.8
2  19.7
2  15.7
2  16.0
3  28.6
3  25.0
3  31.9
4  30.8
4  37.8
4  40.2
5  40.3
5  42.9
5  32.6
;
```

Use the following DATA step to produce Output 1.19.

```
data resplot;
  set resplot;
  if type='B' then bcost=cost;
  else bcost=.;
```

Note: You must use the raw data presented earlier to produce Output 1.4 with this DATA step, along with the appropriate PROC REG statements given in the chapter, to produce Output 1.19.

Chapter 2

Use the following DATA step to produce Output 2.1.

```
data peppers;
  input angle @@;
cards;
3 11 -7 2 3 8 -3 -2 13 4 7
-1 4 7 -1 4 12 -3 7 5 3 -1
9 -7 2 4 8 -2
 ;
```

Use the following DATA step to produce Output 2.2.

```
data pulse;
  input pre post;
  d=pre-post;
cards;
62 61
63 62
58 59
64 61
64 63
61 58
68 61
66 64
65 62
67 68
69 65
61 60
64 65
61 63
63 62
;
```

Use the following DATA step to produce Output 2.3.

```
data bullets;
  input powder velocity;
cards;
1 27.3
1 28.1
1 27.4
1 27.7
1 28.0
1 28.1
1 27.4
1 27.1
2 28.3
2 27.9
2 28.1
2 28.3
2 27.9
2 27.6
2 28.5
2 27.9
2 28.4
2 27.7
;
```

Use the following DATA step to produce Output 2.4 through 2.12.

```
data veneer;
   input brand $ wear;
cards;
ACME 2.3
ACME 2.1
ACME 2.4
ACME 2.5
CHAMP 2.2
CHAMP 2.3
CHAMP 2.4
CHAMP 2.6
AJAX 2.2
AJAX 2.0
AJAX 1.9
AJAX 2.1
TUFFY 2.4
TUFFY 2.7
TUFFY 2.6
TUFFY 2.7
XTRA 2.3
XTRA 2.5
XTRA 2.3
XTRA 2.4
;
proc print data=veneer;
run;
```

Use the following DATA step to produce Output 2.13 through 2.16.

```
data pestcide;
input block blend $ pctloss;
cards;
1 B 18.2
1 A 16.9
1 C 17.0
1 E 18.3
1 D 15.1
2 A 16.5
2 E 18.3
2 B 19.2
2 C 18.1
2 D 16.0
3 B 17.1
3 D 17.8
3 C 17.3
3 E 19.8
3 A 17.5
;
```

Use the following DATA step to produce Output 2.17 and 2.18.

```
data garments;
input run pos mat $ wtloss shrink;
cards;
2 4 A 251 50
2 2 B 241 48
2 1 D 227 45
2 3 C 229 45
3 4 D 234 46
3 2 C 273 54
3 1 A 274 55
3 3 B 226 43
1 4 C 235 45
1 2 D 236 46
1 1 B 218 43
1 3 A 268 51
4 4 B 195 39
4 2 A 270 52
4 1 C 230 48
4 3 D 225 44
;
```

Use the following DATA step to produce Output 2.19.

```
data grasses;
input method $ 1 variety 2 y1-y6 trt $ 1-2;
y1=y1/10; y2=y2/10; y3=y3/10; y4=y4/10; y5=y5/10; y6=y6/10;
cards;
A1 221 241 191 221 251 181
A2 271 151 206 286 151 246
A3 223 258 228 283 213 183
A4 198 283 268 273 268 268
A5 200 170 240 225 280 225
B1 135 145 115  60 270 180
B2 169 174 104 194 119 154
B3 157 102 167 197 182 122
B4 151  65 171  76 136 211
B5 218 228 188 213 163 143
C1 190 220 200 145 190 160
C2 200 220 255 165 180 175
C3 164 144 214 199 104 214
C4 245 160 110  75 145 155
C5 118 143 213  63  78 138
;
```

Use the following DATA step to produce Output 2.20 through 2.29.

```
data fctorial;  set grasses;  drop y1-y6;
yield=y1; output;
yield=y2; output;
yield=y3; output;
yield=y4; output;
```

```
yield=y5; output;
yield=y6; output;
run;
```

Note: You must use the raw data presented in Output 2.19 to produce Output 2.20 through 2.29.

Use the following DATA step to produce Output 2.30 and 2.31.

```
data splplot;
input rep cult $ inoc $ drywt;
cards;
1  A  CON  27.4
1  A  DEA  29.7
1  A  LIV  34.5
1  B  CON  29.4
1  B  DEA  32.5
1  B  LIV  34.4
2  A  CON  28.9
2  A  DEA  28.7
2  A  LIV  33.4
2  B  CON  28.7
2  B  DEA  32.4
2  B  LIV  36.4
3  A  CON  28.6
3  A  DEA  29.7
3  A  LIV  32.9
3  B  CON  27.2
3  B  DEA  29.1
3  B  LIV  32.6
4  A  CON  26.7
4  A  DEA  28.9
4  A  LIV  31.8
4  B  CON  26.8
4  B  DEA  28.6
4  B  LIV  30.7
;
```

Use the following DATA step to produce Output 2.32 through 2.34.

```
data nested;
input package sample srct;
cards;
1  1  3.4641
1  1  3.7417
1  2  5.1962
1  2  5.9161
1  3  4.8990
1  3  7.9363
1  4  9.2195
1  4  6.0828
2  1  23.5160
2  1  19.9499
2  2  6.8557
```

```
2  2   7.6158
2  3  14.4914
2  3  19.6214
2  4  64.8895
2  4  29.1548
3  1   9.7980
3  1   8.6603
3  2  14.1774
3  2  12.5300
3  3   7.2801
3  3   7.9373
3  4   9.2195
3  4  14.3875
4  1   7.9373
4  1   8.5440
4  2   9.2736
4  2   9.2195
4  3   4.4721
4  3   6.3246
4  4   9.0000
4  4   6.0828
5  1  14.1774
5  1  15.9060
5  2  20.5670
5  2  17.5214
5  3  22.4499
5  3  24.5967
5  4  29.6142
5  4  23.2164
;
```

Chapter 3

Use the following DATA steps to produce Output 3.1 through 3.7.

```
data microbgs;
  do package=1 to 20;
   p=rannor(111); drop p;
    s1=rannor(1111); s2=rannor(1112); s3=rannor(1113);
     drop s1 s2 s3;
   lgct11=5 + p + .7* s1 + .3*rannor(11111); ct11=4**lgct11;
   lgct12=5 + p + .7* s1 + .3*rannor(11111); ct12=4**lgct12;
   lgct21=5 + p + .7* s2 + .3*rannor(11111); ct21=4**lgct21;
   lgct22=5 + p + .7* s2 + .3*rannor(11111); ct22=4**lgct22;
   lgct31=5 + p + .7* s3 + .3*rannor(11111); ct31=4**lgct31;
   lgct32=5 + p + .7* s3 + .3*rannor(11111); ct32=4**lgct32;
  output;
end;
data microbgs; set microbgs;
keep package ct11 ct12 ct21 ct22 ct31 ct32;
  ct11=round(ct11);
  ct12=round(ct12);
```

```
     ct21=round(ct21);
     ct22=round(ct22);
     ct31=round(ct31);
     ct32=round(ct32);
run;
data logbgs; set microbgs;
   drop ct11 ct12 ct21 ct22 ct31 ct32;
     sample=1; logct=log10(ct11); output;
     sample=1; logct=log10(ct12); output;
     sample=2; logct=log10(ct21); output;
     sample=2; logct=log10(ct22); output;
     sample=3; logct=log10(ct31); output;
     sample=3; logct=log10(ct32); output;
run;
data bugs; set logbgs;
   ct=10**logct;
```

Use the following DATA steps to produce Output 3.8 through 3.11.

```
 data grasses;
    input method $ variety y1-y6;
      y1=y1/10; y2=y2/10; y3=y3/10; y4=y4/10; y5=y5/10; y6=y6/10;
 cards;
 A 1 221 241 191 221 251 181
 A 2 271 151 206 286 151 246
 A 3 223 258 228 283 213 183
 A 4 198 283 268 273 268 268
 A 5 200 170 240 225 280 225
 B 1 135 145 115  60 270 180
 B 2 169 174 104 194 119 154
 B 3 157 102 167 197 182 122
 B 4 151  65 171  76 136 211
 B 5 218 228 188 213 163 143
 C 1 190 220 200 145 190 160
 C 2 200 220 255 165 180 175
 C 3 164 144 214 199 104 214
 C 4 245 160 110  75 145 155
 C 5 118 143 213  63  78 138
 ;
 data fctorial;  set grasses;  drop y1-y6;
   yield=y1; output;
    yield=y2; output;
    yield=y3; output;
    yield=y4; output;
    yield=y5; output;
    yield=y6; output;
  run;
```

Use the following DATA step to produce Output 3.12 through 3.16.

```
data chips;
  input resista et wafer pos;
 cards;
5.22 1 1 1
5.61 1 1 2
6.11 1 1 3
6.33 1 1 4
6.13 1 2 1
6.14 1 2 2
5.60 1 2 3
5.91 1 2 4
5.49 1 3 1
4.60 1 3 2
4.95 1 3 3
5.42 1 3 4
5.78 2 1 1
6.52 2 1 2
5.90 2 1 3
5.67 2 1 4
5.77 2 2 1
6.23 2 2 2
5.57 2 2 3
5.96 2 2 4
6.43 2 3 1
5.81 2 3 2
5.83 2 3 3
6.12 2 3 4
5.66 3 1 1
6.25 3 1 2
5.46 3 1 3
5.08 3 1 4
6.53 3 2 1
6.50 3 2 2
6.23 3 2 3
6.84 3 2 4
6.22 3 3 1
6.29 3 3 2
5.63 3 3 3
6.36 3 3 4
6.75 4 1 1
6.97 4 1 2
6.02 4 1 3
6.88 4 1 4
6.22 4 2 1
6.54 4 2 2
6.12 4 2 3
6.61 4 2 4
```

```
6.05 4 3 1
6.15 4 3 2
5.55 4 3 3
6.13 4 3 4
;
```

Use the following DATA step to produce Output 3.17 and 3.18.

```
  data inoc;
    input rep cult $ inoc $ drywt;
cards;
1 A CON 27.4
1 A DEA 29.7
1 A LIV 34.5
1 B CON 29.4
1 B DEA 32.5
1 B LIV 34.4
2 A CON 28.9
2 A DEA 28.7
2 A LIV 33.4
2 B CON 28.7
2 B DEA 32.4
2 B LIV 36.4
3 A CON 28.6
3 A DEA 29.7
3 A LIV 32.9
3 B CON 27.2
3 B DEA 29.1
3 B LIV 32.6
4 A CON 26.7
4 A DEA 28.9
4 A LIV 31.8
4 B CON 26.8
4 B DEA 28.6
4 B LIV 30.7
;
```

Chapter 4

Use the following DATA step to produce Output 4.1 through 4.6.

```
  data teachers;
    input teach $ score1 score2;
    cards;
JAY    69 75
JAY    69 70
JAY    71 73
JAY    78 82
JAY    79 81
JAY    73 75
PAT    69 70
PAT    68 74
```

```
PAT     75 80
PAT     78 85
PAT     68 68
PAT     63 68
PAT     72 74
PAT     63 66
PAT     71 76
PAT     72 78
PAT     71 73
PAT     70 73
PAT     56 59
PAT     77 83
ROBIN   72 79
ROBIN   64 65
ROBIN   74 74
ROBIN   72 75
ROBIN   82 84
ROBIN   69 68
ROBIN   76 76
ROBIN   68 65
ROBIN   78 79
ROBIN   70 71
ROBIN   60 61
;
```

Use the following DATA step to produce Output 4.7 through 4.12, and Output 4.15.

```
data bulls;
   input a b y;
   cards;
1  1 5
1  1 6
1  2 2
1  2 3
1  2 5
1  2 6
1  2 7
1  3 3
2  1 2
2  1 3
2  2 8
2  2 8
2  2 9
2  3 4
2  3 4
2  3 6
2  3 6
2  3 7
;
```

Use the following DATA step to produce Output 4.13, 4.14, and 4.16.

```
data bullmiss;
   input a b y;
   cards;
1 1 5
1 1 6
1 2 2
1 2 3
1 2 5
1 2 6
1 2 7
2 1 2
2 1 3
2 2 8
2 2 8
2 2 9
2 3 4
2 3 4
2 3 6
2 3 6
2 3 7
;
```

Use the following DATA step to produce Output 4.19 through 4.21.

```
data irrigate;
   input irrig reps cult $ yield;
   cards;
1 1 A 1.6
1 1 B 3.3
1 2 A 3.4
1 2 B 4.7
1 3 A 3.2
1 3 B 5.6
2 1 A 2.6
2 1 B 5.1
2 2 A 4.6
2 2 B 1.1
2 3 A 5.1
2 3 B 6.2
3 1 A 4.7
3 1 B 6.8
3 2 A 5.5
3 2 B 6.6
3 3 A 5.7
3 3 B 4.5
;
```

Chapter 5

Use the following DATA step to produce Output 5.1 through 5.3.

```
data confound;
   input rep blk a b c y;
   ca=-(a=0)+(a=1);
   cb=-(b=0)+(b=1);
   cc=-(c=0)+(c=1);
   cards;
1 1 1 1 1   3.99
1 1 1 0 0   1.14
1 1 0 1 0   1.52
1 1 0 0 1   3.33
1 2 1 1 0   2.06
1 2 1 0 1   5.58
1 2 0 1 1   2.06
1 2 0 0 0  -0.17
2 1 1 1 1   3.77
2 1 1 0 1   6.69
2 1 0 1 0   2.17
2 1 0 0 0  -0.01
2 2 1 1 0   2.43
2 2 0 1 1   1.22
2 2 1 0 0   0.37
2 2 0 0 1   2.06
3 1 1 1 1   4.53
3 1 0 1 1   1.90
3 1 1 0 0   1.62
3 1 0 0 0  -0.70
3 2 1 1 0   1.56
3 2 1 0 1   5.99
3 2 0 1 0   1.44
3 2 0 0 1   2.42
;
```

Use the following DATA step to produce Output 5.4 through 5.6.

```
data bibd;
   input blk trt y;
   cards;
1 1   1.2
1 2   2.7
2 3   7.1
2 4   8.6
3 1   7.1
3 3   9.7
4 2   8.8
4 4  15.1
5 1   9.7
```

```
5 4 17.4
6 2 13.0
6 3 16.6
;
```

Use the following DATA step to produce Output 5.7 through 5.9.

```
data resdefct;
   retain ptrtment ' ';
   input cow period trtment $ square milk;
   resid='O'; if period ne 1 then resid = ptrtment;
   ptrtment=trtment;
   drop ptrtment;
   resida=0; residb=0;
   if resid='A' then resida=1;
   if resid='C' then resida=-1;
   if resid='B' then residb=1;
   if resid='C' then residb=-1;
   cards;
1 1 A 1  38
1 2 B 1  25
1 3 C 1  15
2 1 B 1 109
2 2 C 1  86
2 3 A 1  39
3 1 C 1 124
3 2 A 1  72
3 3 B 1  27
4 1 A 2  86
4 2 C 2  76
4 3 B 2  46
5 1 B 2  75
5 2 A 2  35
5 3 C 2  34
6 1 C 2 101
6 2 B 2  63
6 3 A 2   1
;
```

Use the following DATA step to produce Output 5.10 through 5.12.

```
data monofil;
   input source $ amt ts;
   cards;
A 1  11.5
A 2  13.8
A 3  14.4
A 4  16.8
A 5  18.7
B 1  10.8
B 2  12.3
B 3  13.7
B 4  14.2
```

```
B 5   16.6
C 1   13.1
C 2   16.2
C 3   19.0
C 4   22.9
C 5   26.5
;
```

Use the following DATA step to produce Output 5.13 and 5.14.

```
data monofil;
    input source $ amt ts;
    cards;
A 1   11.5
A 2   13.8
A 3   14.4
A 4   16.8
A 5   18.7
B 1   10.8
B 2   12.3
B 3   13.7
B 4   14.2
B 5   16.6
C 1   13.1
C 2   16.2
C 3   19.0
C 4   22.9
C 5   26.5
;
data zeroamt;
    input source $ amt ts;
    cards;
C 0   10.1
C 0   10.2
C 0    9.8
C 0    9.9
C 0   10.2
;
data monofil; set monofil zeroamt;
```

Use the following DATA step to produce Output 5.15 through 5.17.

```
data pots;
input trt pot plant y;
cards;
1  1 1   15
1  1 2   13
1  1 3   16
1  2 1   17
1  2 2   19
1  3 1   12
2  1 1   20
2  1 2   21
```

```
2   2 1   20
2   2 2   23
2   2 3   19
2   2 4   19
3   1 1   12
3   1 2   13
3   1 3   14
3   2 1   11
3   3 1   12
3   3 2   13
3   3 3   15
3   3 4   11
3   3 5    9
;
```

Use the following DATA step to produce Output 5.18 through 5.22.

```
data sires;
input line sire agedam steerno age intlwt avdlygn;
cards;
1 1 3 1   192 390 2.24
1 1 3 2   154 403 2.65
1 1 4 3   185 432 2.41
1 1 4 4   193 457 2.25
1 1 5 5   186 483 2.58
1 1 5 6   177 469 2.67
1 1 5 7   177 428 2.71
1 1 5 8   163 439 2.47
1 2 4 9   188 439 2.29
1 2 4 10  178 407 2.26
1 2 5 11  198 498 1.97
1 2 5 12  193 459 2.14
1 2 5 13  186 459 2.44
1 2 5 14  175 375 2.52
1 2 5 15  171 382 1.72
1 2 5 16  168 417 2.75
1 3 3 17  154 389 2.38
1 3 4 18  184 414 2.46
1 3 5 19  174 483 2.29
1 3 5 20  170 430 2.30
1 3 5 21  169 443 2.94
2 4 3 22  158 381 2.50
2 4 3 23  158 365 2.44
2 4 4 24  169 386 2.44
2 4 4 25  144 339 2.15
2 4 5 26  159 419 2.54
2 4 5 27  152 469 2.74
2 4 5 28  149 379 2.50
2 4 5 29  149 375 2.54
2 5 3 30  189 395 2.65
2 5 4 31  187 447 2.52
2 5 4 32  165 430 2.67
2 5 5 33  181 453 2.79
```

```
2 5 5 34 177 385 2.33
2 5 5 35 151 414 2.67
2 5 5 36 147 353 2.69
3 6 4 37 184 411 3.00
3 6 4 38 184 420 2.49
3 6 5 39 187 427 2.25
3 6 5 40 184 409 2.49
3 6 5 41 183 337 2.02
3 6 5 42 177 352 2.31
3 7 3 43 205 472 2.57
3 7 3 44 193 340 2.37
3 7 4 45 162 375 2.64
3 7 5 46 206 451 2.37
3 7 5 47 205 472 2.22
3 7 5 48 187 402 1.90
3 7 5 49 178 464 2.61
3 7 5 50 175 414 2.13
3 8 3 51 200 466 2.16
3 8 3 52 184 356 2.33
3 8 3 53 175 449 2.52
3 8 4 54 178 360 2.45
3 8 5 55 189 385 1.44
3 8 5 56 184 431 1.72
3 8 5 57 183 401 2.17
3 9 3 58 166 404 2.68
3 9 4 59 187 482 2.43
3 9 4 60 186 350 2.36
3 9 4 61 184 483 2.44
3 9 5 62 180 425 2.66
3 9 5 63 177 420 2.46
3 9 5 64 175 440 2.52
3 9 5 65 164 405 2.42
;
```

Chapter 6

Use the following DATA step to produce Output 6.1 through 6.4.

```
data oysters;
   input  trt rep initial final;
   cards;
1      1      27.2      32.6
1      2      32.0      36.6
1      3      33.0      37.7
1      4      26.8      31.0
2      1      28.6      33.8
2      2      26.8      31.7
2      3      26.5      30.7
2      4      26.8      30.4
3      1      28.6      35.2
3      2      22.4      29.1
3      3      23.2      28.9
```

```
3         4         24.4      30.2
4         1         29.3      35.0
4         2         21.8      27.0
4         3         30.3      36.4
4         4         24.3      30.5
5         1         20.4      24.6
5         2         19.6      23.4
5         3         25.1      30.3
5         4         18.1      21.8
;
```

Use the following DATA step to produce Output 6.5, 6.6, and 6.10.

```
data oranges;
   input  store week day p1 p2 q1 q2;
   cards;
1         1         1    37   61   11.3208   0.0047
1         1         2    37   37   12.9151   0.0037
1         1         3    45   53   18.8947   7.5429
1         1         4    41   41   14.6739   7.0652
1         1         5    57   41    8.6493  21.2085
1         1         6    49   33    9.5238  16.6667
2         1         1    49   49    7.6923   7.1154
2         1         2    53   53    0.0017   1.0000
2         1         3    53   45    8.0477  24.2176
2         1         4    53   53    6.7358   2.9361
2         1         5    61   37    6.1441  40.5720
2         1         6    49   65   21.7939   2.8324
3         1         1    53   45    4.2553   6.0284
3         1         2    57   57    0.0017   2.0906
3         1         3    49   49   11.0196  13.9329
3         1         4    53   53    6.2762   6.5551
3         1         5    53   45   13.2316  10.6870
3         1         6    53   53    5.0676   5.1351
4         1         1    57   57    5.6235   3.9120
4         1         2    49   49   14.9893   7.2805
4         1         3    53   53   13.7233  16.3105
4         1         4    53   45    6.0669  23.8494
4         1         5    53   53    8.1602   4.1543
4         1         6    61   37    1.4423  21.1538
5         1         1    45   45    6.9971   6.9971
5         1         2    53   45    5.2308   3.6923
5         1         3    57   57    8.2560  10.6679
5         1         4    49   49   14.5000  16.7500
5         1         5    53   53   20.7627  15.2542
5         1         6    53   45    3.6115  21.5442
6         1         1    53   53   11.3475   4.9645
6         1         2    53   45    9.4650  11.7284
6         1         3    53   53   22.6103  14.8897
6         1         4    61   37    0.0020  19.2000
6         1         5    49   65   20.5997   2.3468
6         1         6    37   37   28.1828  17.9543
;
```

Use the following DATA step to produce Output 6.7 through 6.9.

```
data cotton;
   input var spac plt boll lint;
   cards;
 37        30       3       8.4      2.9
 37        30       3       8.0      2.5
 37        30       3       7.4      2.7
 37        30       3       8.9      3.1
 37        30       5       5.6      2.1
 37        30       5       8.0      2.7
 37        30       5       7.6      2.5
 37        30       5       5.4      1.5
 37        30       5       6.9      2.5
 37        40       3       4.5      1.3
 37        40       3       9.1      3.1
 37        40       3       9.0      3.1
 37        40       3       8.0      2.3
 37        40       3       7.2      2.2
 37        40       3       7.6      2.5
 37        40       3       9.0      3.0
 37        40       3       2.3      0.6
 37        40       3       8.7      3.0
 37        40       5       8.0      2.6
 37        40       5       7.2      2.5
 37        40       5       7.6      2.4
 37        40       5       6.9      2.2
 37        40       5       6.9      2.5
 37        40       5       7.6      2.4
 37        40       5       4.7      1.4
213        30       3       4.6      1.7
213        30       3       6.8      1.7
213        30       3       3.5      1.3
213        30       3       2.4      1.0
213        30       3       3.0      1.0
213        30       5       2.8      0.5
213        30       5       3.6      0.9
213        30       5       6.7      1.9
213        40       0       7.4      2.1
213        40       0       4.9      1.0
213        40       0       5.7      1.0
213        40       0       3.0      0.7
213        40       0       4.7      1.5
213        40       0       5.0      1.3
213        40       0       2.8      0.4
213        40       0       5.2      1.2
213        40       0       5.6      1.0
213        40       3       4.5      1.0
213        40       3       5.6      1.2
213        40       3       2.0      0.7
213        40       3       1.2      0.2
```

```
213      40      3      4.2      1.2
213      40      3      5.3      1.2
213      40      3      7.0      1.7
;
```

Chapter 7

Use the following DATA step to produce Output 7.1 and 7.2.

```
data tests;
   input teach $ score1 score2;
   cards;
JAY     69  75
JAY     69  70
JAY     71  73
JAY     78  82
JAY     79  81
JAY     73  75
PAT     69  70
PAT     68  74
PAT     75  80
PAT     78  85
PAT     68  68
PAT     63  68
PAT     72  74
PAT     63  66
PAT     71  76
PAT     72  78
PAT     71  73
PAT     70  73
PAT     56  59
PAT     77  83
ROBIN   72  79
ROBIN   64  65
ROBIN   74  74
ROBIN   72  75
ROBIN   82  84
ROBIN   69  68
ROBIN   76  76
ROBIN   68  65
ROBIN   78  79
ROBIN   70  71
ROBIN   60  61
;
```

Use the following DATA step to produce Output 7.3 and 7.4.

```
data wtgain;
   input gain1-gain4;
   cards;
29 28 25 33
33 30 23 31
```

```
25 34 33 41
18 33 29 35
25 23 17 30
24 32 29 22
20 23 16 31
28 21 18 24
18 23 22 28
25 28 29 30
;
```

Use the following DATA step to produce Output 7.5 through 7.8.

```
data cotton;
   input variety spacing plant seed lint bract;
   cards;
213          30        3   3.1    1.7    2.0
213          30        3   1.5    1.7    1.4
213          30        5   3.0    1.9    1.8
213          30        5   1.4    0.9    1.3
213          30        6   2.3    1.7    1.5
213          30        6   2.2    2.0    1.4
213          30        8   0.4    0.9    1.2
213          30        8   1.7    1.6    1.3
213          30        9   1.8    1.2    1.0
213          30        9   1.2    0.8    1.0
213          40        0   2.0    1.0    1.9
213          40        0   1.5    1.5    1.7
213          40        1   1.8    1.1    2.1
213          40        1   1.0    1.3    1.1
213          40        2   1.3    1.1    1.3
213          40        2   2.9    1.9    1.7
213          40        3   2.8    1.2    1.3
213          40        3   1.8    1.2    1.2
213          40        4   3.2    1.8    2.0
213          40        4   3.2    1.6    1.9
 37          30        1   3.2    2.6    1.4
 37          30        1   2.8    2.1    1.2
 37          30        2   3.6    2.4    1.5
 37          30        2   0.9    0.8    0.8
 37          30        3   4.0    3.1    1.8
 37          30        3   4.0    2.9    1.5
 37          30        5   3.7    2.7    1.6
 37          30        5   2.6    1.5    1.3
 37          30        8   2.8    2.2    1.2
 37          30        8   2.9    2.3    1.2
 37          40        1   4.1    2.9    2.0
 37          40        1   3.4    2.0    1.6
 37          40        3   3.7    2.3    2.0
 37          40        3   3.2    2.2    1.8
 37          40        4   3.4    2.7    1.5
 37          40        4   2.9    2.1    1.2
 37          40        5   2.5    1.4    0.8
```

```
37        40        5        3.6      2.4        1.6
37        40        6        3.1      2.3        1.4
37        40        6        2.5      1.5        1.5
;
```

Use the following DATA step to produce Output 7.9 and 7.10.

```
data oranges;
   input  store week day p1 p2 q1 q2;
   cards;
1        1        1        37       61       11.3208       0.0047
1        1        2        37       37       12.9151       0.0037
1        1        3        45       53       18.8947       7.5429
1        1        4        41       41       14.6739       7.0652
1        1        5        57       41        8.6493      21.2085
1        1        6        49       33        9.5238      16.6667
2        1        1        49       49        7.6923       7.1154
2        1        2        53       53        0.0017       1.0000
2        1        3        53       45        8.0477      24.2176
2        1        4        53       53        6.7358       2.9361
2        1        5        61       37        6.1441      40.5720
2        1        6        49       65       21.7939       2.8324
3        1        1        53       45        4.2553       6.0284
3        1        2        57       57        0.0017       2.0906
3        1        3        49       49       11.0196      13.9329
3        1        4        53       53        6.2762       6.5551
3        1        5        53       45       13.2316      10.6870
3        1        6        53       53        5.0676       5.1351
4        1        1        57       57        5.6235       3.9120
4        1        2        49       49       14.9893       7.2805
4        1        3        53       53       13.7233      16.3105
4        1        4        53       45        6.0669      23.8494
4        1        5        53       53        8.1602       4.1543
4        1        6        61       37        1.4423      21.1538
5        1        1        45       45        6.9971       6.9971
5        1        2        53       45        5.2308       3.6923
5        1        3        57       57        8.2560      10.6679
5        1        4        49       49       14.5000      16.7500
5        1        5        53       53       20.7627      15.2542
5        1        6        53       45        3.6115      21.5442
6        1        1        53       53       11.3475       4.9645
6        1        2        53       45        9.4650      11.7284
6        1        3        53       53       22.6103      14.8897
6        1        4        61       37        0.0020      19.2000
6        1        5        49       65       20.5997       2.3468
6        1        6        37       37       28.1828      17.9543
;
```

Chapter 8

Use the following DATA step to produce Output 8.1 through 8.3, and to produce Output 8.5 and 8.6.

```
data weights;
   input program $ s1-s7;
   cards;
CONT   85 85 86 85 87 86 87
CONT   80 79 79 78 78 79 78
CONT   78 77 77 77 76 76 77
CONT   84 84 85 84 83 84 85
CONT   80 81 80 80 79 79 80
CONT   76 78 77 78 78 77 74
CONT   79 79 80 79 80 79 81
CONT   76 76 76 75 75 74 74
CONT   77 78 78 80 80 81 80
CONT   79 79 79 79 77 78 79
CONT   81 81 80 80 80 81 82
CONT   77 76 77 78 77 77 77
CONT   82 83 83 83 84 83 83
CONT   84 84 83 82 81 79 78
CONT   79 81 81 82 82 82 80
CONT   79 79 78 77 77 78 78
CONT   83 82 83 85 84 83 82
CONT   78 78 79 79 78 77 77
CONT   80 80 79 79 80 80 80
CONT   78 79 80 81 80 79 80
RI     79 79 79 80 80 78 80
RI     83 83 85 85 86 87 87
RI     81 83 82 82 83 83 82
RI     81 81 81 82 82 83 81
RI     80 81 82 82 82 84 86
RI     76 76 76 76 76 76 75
RI     81 84 83 83 85 85 85
RI     77 78 79 79 81 82 81
RI     84 85 87 89 88 85 86
RI     74 75 78 78 79 78 78
RI     76 77 77 77 77 76 76
RI     84 84 86 85 86 86 86
RI     79 80 79 80 80 82 82
RI     78 78 77 76 75 75 76
RI     78 80 77 77 75 75 75
RI     84 85 85 85 85 83 82
WI     84 85 84 83 83 83 84
WI     74 75 75 76 75 76 76
WI     83 84 82 81 83 83 82
WI     86 87 87 87 87 87 86
WI     82 83 84 85 84 85 86
WI     79 80 79 79 80 79 80
WI     79 79 79 81 81 83 83
WI     87 89 91 90 91 92 92
```

```
WI      81 81 81 82 82 83 83
WI      82 82 82 84 86 85 87
WI      79 79 80 81 81 81 81
WI      79 80 81 82 83 82 82
WI      83 84 84 84 84 83 83
WI      81 81 82 84 83 82 85
WI      78 78 79 79 78 79 79
WI      83 82 82 84 84 83 84
WI      80 79 79 81 80 80 80
WI      80 82 82 82 81 81 81
WI      85 86 87 86 86 86 86
WI      77 78 80 81 82 82 82
WI      80 81 80 81 81 82 83
;
```

Use the following DATA step to produce Output 8.4.

```
data split;
   set weights;
   array s{7} s1-s7;
   subject + 1;
   do time=1 to 7;
      strength=s{time};
      output;
   end;
   drop s1-s7;
```

Note: You must use the raw data needed for Output 8.1 through 8.3 to produce Output 8.4.

Use the following DATA step to produce Output 8.7.

```
data plot;
   set new;
   array mwt(7) mwt1-mwt7;
   do time=1 to 7;
      strength=mwt(time);
      output;
   end;
   drop mwt1-mwt7;
```

Note: You must use the raw data needed for Output 8.1 through 8.3 with the PROC SUMMARY statement presented in the chapter before using this DATA step.

Use the following DATA step to produce Output 8.8 and 8.9.

```
data moisture;
   input bed $ m10_am m10_pm m20_am m20_pm m40_am m40_pm
                 m50_am m50_pm;
   cards;
LOW     12.3   13.4   13.7   15.0   16.4   15.6   16.4   17.0
LOW     12.0   12.8   13.5   14.3   14.4   13.4   14.9   14.1
LOW     11.7   12.2   12.2   12.7   13.3   14.1   13.6   14.0
MED     12.2   13.4   13.2   14.0   15.5   15.4   16.7   16.4
```

```
MED     9.6    9.9   12.0   12.9   14.3   14.0   16.2   16.9
HIGH   16.5   15.2   17.6   18.1   21.2   21.2   22.7   22.1
HIGH   14.3   15.2   18.7   16.8   18.9   20.1   23.0   22.5
HIGH   12.8   12.2   14.5   16.9   17.3   18.5   19.5   19.4
;
```

Use the following DATA step to produce Output 8.10.

```
data one;
   set moisture;
   array m{8} m10_am--m50_pm;
   k=1;
   do depth=10,20,40,50;
      do timeday=1 to 2;
         moisture=m{k};
         k=k+1;
         output;
      end;
   end;
   keep depth bed moisture;
```

Note: You must use the raw data needed in Output 8.8 and 8.9 to produce Output 8.10.

References

Bancroft, T.A. (1968), *Topics in Intermediate Statistical Methods*, Ames: Iowa State University Press.

Belsley, D.A., Kuh, E., and Welsch, R.E. (1980), *Regression Diagnostics*, New York: John Wiley & Sons, Inc.

Chew, V. (1976), "Uses and Abuses of Duncan's Multiple Range Test," *Proceedings of Florida State Horticultural Society*, 89, 251—253.

Cochran, W.G. and Cox, M.G. (1957), *Experimental Designs*, New York: John Wiley & Sons, Inc.

Duncan, D.B. (1955), "Multiple Range and Multiple F-Tests," *Biometrics*, 11, 1—42.

Freund, R.J. (1980), "The Case of the Missing Cell," *The American Statistician*, 34, 94—98.

Freund, R.J. and Littell, R.C. (1991), *SAS System for Regression, Second Edition*, Cary, NC: SAS Institute Inc.

Freund, R.J. and Minton, P.D. (1979), *Regression Methods*, New York: Marcel Dekker, Inc.

Goodnight, J.H. (1978), "Tests of Hypotheses in Fixed Effects Linear Models," SAS Technical Report R-101, Cary, NC: SAS Institute Inc.

Graybill, F.A. (1976), *Theory and Application of the Linear Model*, Belmont, CA: Wadsworth Publishing Co.

Greenhouse, S.W. and Geisser, S. (1959), "On Methods in the Analysis of Profile Data," *Psychometrika*, 32(3), 95—112.

Hartley, H.O. and Searle, S.R. (1969), "A Discontinuity in Mixed Model Analysis," *Biometrics*, 25, 573—576.

Harvey, W.R. (1975), "Least Squares Analysis of Data," Washington, DC: U.S. Department of Agriculture, ARS-H-4, February.

Heck, D.L. (1960), "Charts of Some Upper Percentage Points of the Distribution of the Largest Characteristic Root," *Annals of Mathematical Statistics*, XXXI, 625—642.

Hicks, C.R. (1973), *Fundamental Concepts in the Design of Experiments*, New York: Holt, Rinehart & Winston.

Hocking, R.R. (1973), "A Discussion of the Two-Way Mixed Model," *The American Statistician*, 27, 148—152.

Hocking, R.R. and Speed, F.M. (1975), "A Full-Rank Analysis of Some Linear Model Problems," *Journal of the American Statistical Association*, 70, 706—712.

Hocking, R.R. and Speed, F.M. (1980), "The Cell Means Model for the Analysis of Variance," Twenty-Fourth Annual Technical Conference, Cincinnati, OH: 23—24.

Huynh, H. and Feldt, L.S. (1970), "Conditions under Which Mean Square Ratios in Repeated Measurements Designs Have Exact F-Distributions," *Journal of the American Statistical Association*, 65, 1582—1589.

Huynh, H. and Feldt, L.S. (1976), "Estimation of the Box Correction for Degrees of Freedom from Sample Data in the Randomized Block and Split Plot Designs," *Journal of Educational Statistics*, 1, 69—82.

Little, T.U. (1978), "If Galileo Published in HortiScience," *HortiScience*, 13, 504—506.

Morrison, D.F. (1967), *Multivariate Statistical Methods*, New York: McGraw-Hill Book Co.

Morrison, D.F. (1976), *Multivariate Statistical Methods, Second Edition*, New York: McGraw-Hill Book Co.

Peterson, R.G. (1977), "Use and Misuse of Multiple Comparison Procedures," *Agronomy Journal*, 69, 205—208.

Pillai, K.C.S. (1960), *Statistical Tables for Tests of Multivariate Hypotheses*, Manila: The Statistical Center, University of the Philippines.

Rao, C.R. (1965), *Linear Statistical Inference and Its Applications*, New York: John Wiley & Sons, Inc.

SAS Institute Inc. (1990), *SAS/GRAPH Software: Reference, Version 6, First Edition, Volume 1* and *Volume 2*, Cary, NC: SAS Institute Inc.

SAS Institute Inc. (1990), *SAS/IML Software: Usage and Reference, Version 6, First Edition*, Cary, NC: SAS Institute Inc.

SAS Institute Inc. (1990), *SAS Language: Reference, Version 6, First Edition*, Cary, NC: SAS Institute Inc.

SAS Institute Inc. (1990), *SAS Procedures Guide, Version 6, Third Edition*, Cary, NC: SAS Institute Inc.

SAS Institute Inc. (1990), *SAS/STAT User's Guide, Version 6, Fourth Edition, Volume 2*, Cary, NC: SAS Institute Inc.

Satterthwaite, F.W. (1946), "An Approximate Distribution of Estimates of Variance Components," *Biometrics Bulletin*, 2, 110—114.

Searle, S.R. (1971), *Linear Models*, New York: John Wiley & Sons, Inc.

Snee, R.D. (1973), "Some Aspects of Nonorthogonal Data Analysis," *Journal of Quality Technology*, 5, 67—69.

Speed, F.M., Hocking, R.R., and Hackney, O.P. (1978), "Methods of Analysis of Linear Models with Unbalanced Data," *Journal of the American Statistical Association*, 73, 105—112.

Steel, R.G.B. and Torrie, J.H. (1980), *Principles and Procedures of Statistics, Second Edition*, New York: McGraw-Hill Book Co.

Waller, R.A. and Duncan, D.B. (1969), "A Bayes Rule for the Symmetric Multiple Comparison Problem," *Journal of the American Statistical Association*, 64, 1484—1499.

Index

A

ABSORB statement
  ANOVA procedure 63
  GLM procedure 222–227
absorption 220–221
adjusted means 149, 165, 233
adjusted R-SQUARE 18
ALPHA= option
  MEANS statement (ANOVA) 79
analysis of covariance 229–230
  assumptions 243
  contrasts 234
  multiple covariates 235
  multivariate 260–263
  one-way structure 230
  two-way structure with interaction 238–243
  two-way structure without interaction
    235–238
analysis of variance 59–61
  crossed-nested classification 122
  empty cells 178–190
  factorial experiment 87
  Latin square 83–86
  mixed model 115–119
  multivariate 249–252
  nested classification 109–111, 112–114
  one-way classification 64, 138
  overspecified model 139, 163
  randomized-blocks design 77–78
  repeated-measures 265–266
  split-plot design 191
  split-plot experiment 131
  split-split-plot experiment 134
  two-way with unbalanced data 153
ANOVA procedure 57, 59, 69, 109, 150,
    155, 248–256
  ABSORB statement 62–63
  BY statement 62–63, 91–93
  CLASS statement 216
  compared with PROC GLM 143
  dummy-variable model 138
  FREQ statement 62–63
  Hotelling's T^2 test 255–256
  MANOVA statement 62–63, 253–258
  MEANS statement 69, 94–95
  MODEL statement 66, 90–91
  multiple comparisons 63, 78–83
  options 78–83
  RANDOM statement 132
  REPEATED statement 62–63
  split-split-plot experiment 134–135
  TEST statement 62, 132, 133, 191,
    255–258
  unbalanced data 153–155
approximate confidence intervals 130
approximate F tests 129, 193
approximate t tests 57, 58
AUTOREG procedure 9

B

balanced data 153
balanced incomplete blocks design 203–205
blocks 76, 107
BY statement
  ANOVA procedure 62–63, 91–93
  GLM procedure 148
  MEANS procedure 52

C

CALIS procedure 8
canonical correlation 249
CATMOD procedure 8
cell means 96
characteristic roots 249
characteristic vectors 249
CLASS statement
  ANOVA procedure 62, 66, 77–78, 85, 95,
    132, 216
  dummy variables 209–214
  GLM procedure 69, 95–102, 144–146,
    167–168, 206–207, 215–216, 229,
    231–232, 244
  MEANS procedure 52
  NESTED procedure 109
  TTEST procedure 57–58
CLDIFF option
  MEANS statement (ANOVA) 82–83
CLI option
  MODEL statement (GLM) 148
  MODEL statement (REG) 17–20
CLM option
  MEANS statement (ANOVA) 68
  MODEL statement (GLM) 148
  MODEL statement (REG) 17–20
coefficient of variation 12
collinearity 50
complete model 3–4
components of variance 109
  estimates 110–111
  expected mean squares 110, 113
  hypothesis testing 112
confidence intervals
  means 53, 129
  regression coefficients 5
confidence limits 19–20

CONTRAST statement
 diagrammatic method 103–104
 GLM procedure 63, 68–74, 95–102,
   117–118, 122–129, 143, 149, 151–152,
   164–178, 185–193, 200–201, 226,
   234–235, 263–266
CONTRAST transformation
 REPEATED statement (GLM) 289–291
contrasts 151–152, 167, 177, 234, 278–282
 interaction 167
 main effects 167
 nonestimability 187
CORRB option
 MODEL statement (REG) 30
correction for the mean 21
covariables 229
covariance analysis 229–230
 assumptions 243
 contrasts 234
 multiple covariates 235
 multivariate 260–263
 one-way structure 230
 two-way structure with interaction 238–243
 two-way structure without interaction
   235–238
COVB option
 MODEL statement (REG) 30
creating data sets
 REG procedure 39–40
crossed-nested classification 120–121
 analysis of variance 122
crossover design 205–209
cubic model 31–33

D

DATA= option
 PROC REG statement 11, 27, 31
degrees of freedom 59
 interaction effect 61
 main effect 60
 nested effect 61
 Satterthwaite's formula 128–130
DEPONLY option
 MEANS statement (GLM) 233
diagnostic measures 49–50
dummy-variable model 138–153
 analysis-of-variance model 139
 matrix notation 140
dummy variables 138–153, 157, 209–214
DUNCAN option
 CONTRAST statement (GLM) 191
 MEANS statement (ANOVA) 79
 MEANS statement (GLM) 191, 233
Duncan's multiple-range test 63, 133
Duncan's new multiple range test 79

E

E option
 CONTRAST statement (GLM) 176, 185–186
 ESTIMATE statement (GLM) 176, 185–186
 LSMEANS statement (GLM) 150, 176,
   185–186
 MODEL statement (GLM) 149, 169–171
E= option
 CONTRAST statement (GLM) 117–118, 123
 LSMEANS statement (GLM) 150
effect 205
effects model 64–65
eigenvalues 249
eigenvectors 249
empty cells 178
error 65
error rates
 comparisonwise 63
 experimentwise 63
estimable functions 7, 143, 148, 169–170
 estimates 175–176
 general form 149, 169
ESTIMATE statement
 diagrammatic method 103–104
 GLM procedure 63, 74–76, 95–102, 143,
   149–152, 164–178, 185–190, 208,
   212–213, 226, 234–235, 242–243, 245
 options (GLM) 234
ETYPE= option
 LSMEANS statement (GLM) 150
exact collinearity 48–49
example code 293–319
expected mean squares 193–197
 crossed-nested classification 124–125, 127
 mixed model 117
 nested classification 112–114
 variance components 110, 113
experimental error 118

F

F ratios 59–60
F tests 12
 all parameters 5, 16
 for equal variances 57
 for polynomial model 33
 for regression model 4–5, 22
 linear function of parameters 7, 22–24
 subset of parameters 5
 Type I (sequential) 22, 33
 Type II (partial) 22
factorial experiments 86–87, 101–104
 analysis of variance 87
 confounding 199–202
 lack of fit 216

multiple comparisons 91, 94
preplanned comparisons 95–97
FREQ statement
   ANOVA procedure 62–63
   GLM procedure 148
   MEANS procedure 52

G

generalized inverse 6–7, 143, 148
GLM procedure 22, 59, 91, 109, 137–138,
   141–143, 164, 248
   ABSORB statement 221–227
   analysis of variance 143–148
   BY statement 148
   CLASS statement 69, 95–102, 144–146,
      167–168, 206–207, 215–216, 229,
      231–232, 244
   computing sums of squares 155–157
   CONTRAST statement 70, 72, 190
   dummy variables 162–164
   empty cells 178–190
   estimable functions 149–153
   ESTIMATE statement 190
   expected mean squares 112–114
   FREQ statement 148
   generalized inverse 6–7, 143, 148
   heterogeneity of slopes 243–246
   ID statement 143–144, 148
   LSMEANS statement 190
   MANOVA statement 266–269
   MEANS statement 63, 150–151, 165–166,
      191, 219–220, 233
   MODEL statement 33, 135
   multiple comparisons 63, 78–83
   options 78–83
   OUTPUT statement 54
   RANDOM statement 106, 114–118,
      122–127, 143–144, 194–197
   REPEATED statement 267, 269–272,
      274–278, 283–289
   sums of squares 3–4
   TEST statement 114–118, 123–127,
      191–193, 239–241, 273–274
   unbalanced nested structure 216–220
   WEIGHT statement 143–144, 148
GPLOT procedure 43
grand mean 142
Greenhouse-Geisser test 277–278
group effects 142

H

heterogeneity of slopes 243–246
Hotelling-Lawley trace 249
Hotelling's T^2 test 252–255
Huynh-Feldt test 277–278
hypothesis testing 4–6
   crossed-nested classification 122, 125, 127
   for equal variances 57, 58
   linear combination of means 69–71

linear combinations of coefficients 22–24
mean 54
mixed model 117
paired samples 55
preplanned comparisons 69–71
simultaneous contrasts 72–73, 100–101
subsets of coefficients 22–24
two independent samples 56–57
variance components 112

I

I option
   MODEL statement (GLM) 146–147
   MODEL statement (REG) 28–30
ID statement
   GLM procedure 143–144, 148
   MEANS procedure 52
   REG procedure 19
independent samples 56–58
influential observations 50
interaction effects 60–61, 153, 162, 164, 165,
   188
   analysis of covariance 238
   factorial experiments 101–102
interaction parameters 164, 188
INTERCEPT argument
   CONTRAST statement (GLM) 75
   ESTIMATE statement (GLM) 75

K

k ratio 79
KRATIO= option
   MEANS statement (ANOVA) 79

L

lack-of-fit analysis 214–216
latin square design 83–86
least significant difference (LSD) 63, 67–68,
   79
least squares
   estimates 2
   ordinary 37
   weighted 37
least-squares means 149, 152, 165
   analysis of covariance 233
LIFEREG procedure 8
linear combination of means 69–71, 103–104
linear combination of parameters 72,
   103–104
   confidence intervals 75
   estimating 74
linear combinations of mean squares 128–130
linear dependency 48–49
linear functions of parameters
   estimable functions 7
   estimates 4
   tests 7, 22–24
   variance 4, 7

LOGISTIC procedure 8
LSD option
  MEANS statement (ANOVA) 79
LSMEANS statement
  GLM procedure 63, 143, 149–151, 153,
     164–178, 185–191, 208–209, 220, 226,
     233
L95= option
  OUTPUT statement (REG) 43
L95M= option
  OUTPUT statement (REG) 43

M

M= option
  MANOVA statement (ANOVA) 253, 269,
     278
main effect comparisons 96, 99
main effects 60, 165
MANOVA statement
  ANOVA procedure 62–63, 253–258
  GLM procedure 266–269
marginal means 154
mean 52
mean squares 59, 193
  crossed-nested classification 124–125, 127
  error 3
  mixed model 117
  nested classification 110, 112–114
  synthetic 128–130
means model 64, 138, 159–161, 166
MEANS procedure 52–54, 55–56, 264
  BY statement 52
  CLASS statement 52
  FREQ statement 52
  ID statement 52
  OUTPUT statement 52, 54, 88
  VAR statement 52
  WEIGHT statement 52
  WHERE statement 52
MEANS statement
  ANOVA procedure 62, 63, 67, 69, 133,
     258
  GLM procedure 63, 150–151, 165–166,
     191, 219–220, 233
misspecification 50
mixed models 115, 191
  analysis of variance 115–119
  expected mean squares 117
MNAMES= option
  MANOVA statement (ANOVA) 253–254
model parameters 72, 74–76, 96, 103
MODEL procedure 9
MODEL statement 251, 252–254
  ANOVA procedure 62, 66–67, 77–78, 85,
     89, 95, 132, 134, 135, 216, 251–254
  GLM procedure 30, 69, 72, 95–102, 114,
     123, 144–146, 150, 156, 158–161, 163,
     169–175, 188–190, 200–202, 206–207,
     215–216, 235, 239–241, 245, 272–274
  multiple models 30

options (GLM) 148
options (REG) 27–30, 43–44
REG procedure 9, 11, 23, 25–26, 30–31,
    33, 37, 40–43, 48–49
multicollinearity 50
multiple comparisons 63, 78–79
  as confidence intervals 82–83
  Duncan 63, 79, 133
  factorial experiment 91, 94
  least significant difference (LSD) 63, 67–68,
    79
  repeated-measures designs 291
  Tukey's HSD 79
  Waller-Duncan 79
multiple models 30
multivariate analysis 248–249
  contrasts 263–264
  two-factor factorial 255–260
multivariate analysis of covariance 260–263
multivariate analysis of variance 249–252

N

nested classifications 106
  analysis of variance 109–111, 112–114
  optimum sampling plan 111–112
  repeated-measures design 282–283
  unbalanced 216–220
  variances of means 111–112
nested effect 61
NESTED procedure 59, 109–111, 216, 220
  CLASS statement 109
NLIN procedure 8
NOINT option
  MODEL statement (REG) 11, 25–27
NOM option
  REPEATED statement (GLM) 274, 279, 289
NOPRINT option
  PROC MEANS statement 88
normal equations 2, 6, 141, 142
NOU option
  REPEATED statement (GLM) 269, 274,
    279, 289
NOUNI option
  MODEL statement (ANOVA) 250, 253
  MODEL statement (GLM) 260–263

O

one-way classification 64, 138
  estimable functions 148
  normal equations 140, 141, 142
  overspecification 139
  parameter estimates 141–143, 147
ORDER= option
  PROC GLM statement 69
ordinary least squares 37
orthogonal contrasts 73–74
ORTHOREG procedure 8
outliers 50

OUTPUT statement
GLM procedure 143–144, 148
MEANS procedure 52, 54, 88
REG procedure 48
overspecification 139, 163

P

P option
MODEL statement (GLM) 148
MODEL statement (REG) 17–20
p value 12, 13
paired samples 55–56
parameters 1, 2
estimates 2, 12, 138
less-than-full-rank models 141
linear functions 4
restrictions 141, 158
sequential estimates of 34
standard errors 13
tests 7, 13, 17
partial sums of squares 21
PDIFF option
LSMEANS statement (GLM) 150, 233
PDLREG procedure 9
Pillai's trace 249
PLOT procedure 43, 89
plotting regression curves 41–43
plotting residuals 40–41
polynomial models 31–37
POLYNOMIAL specification
REPEATED statement (ANOVA) 278–280
POLYNOMIAL transformation
REPEATED statement (GLM) 288–289
pooled variance estimate 56–57
predicted values 17–19
confidence interval for individual 19
confidence interval for mean 19
estimates 6
standard error 19
variance 6
predicting to a different set of data 44–47
preplanned comparisons 68–72
factorial experiment 95–97
PRINT procedure 53, 56, 58
PRINTE option
MANOVA statement (ANOVA) 251
REPEATED statement (GLM) 274, 279
PRINTH option
MANOVA statement (ANOVA) 251
PRINTM option
REPEATED statement (GLM) 270, 279, 280
PROBIT procedure 8
PROC ANOVA statement 62–63
See also ANOVA procedure
PROC AUTOREG statement 9
PROC CALIS statement 8
PROC CATMOD statement 8
PROC GLM statement 8
See also GLM procedure
PROC LIFEREG statement 8
PROC LOGISTIC statement 8

PROC MEANS statement 53–54, 88
See also MEANS procedure
PROC MODEL statement 9
PROC NESTED statement
See NESTED procedure
PROC NLIN statement 8
PROC ORTHOREG statement 8
PROC PDLREG statement 9
PROC PROBIT statement 8
PROG REG statement 8, 27
See also REG procedure
PROC RSREG statement 9
PROC SUMMARY statement
See SUMMARY procedure
PROC SYSLIN statement 9
PROC TRANSREG statement 9
PROC TTEST statement 57–58
PROC UNIVARIATE statement 52
PROC VARCOMP statement 59, 109

Q

Q option
RANDOM statement (GLM) 124–125, 194
quadratic forms 119, 191, 194–197
quadratic model 31, 34–36

R

R-SQUARE statistic 12
random effects 106, 115, 191
random models 191
RANDOM statement 113–114
ANOVA procedure 132
GLM procedure 106, 114–118, 122–127,
143–144, 194–197
randomized-blocks design 76
reduced (restricted) model 3–4, 25–27
reduction notation 3–4, 21–22, 157–159
REG procedure 9–30, 45, 54
diagnostic measures 49–50
generalized inverse 6–7
ID statement 19
linear dependency 48–49
MODEL statement 9, 11, 23, 25–26,
30–31, 33, 37, 40–43, 48–49
one independent variable 10–13
OUTPUT statement 48
plotting regression curves 41–43
plotting with transformed variables 47–48
RESTRICT statement 25–27
several independent variables 15–17
sums of squares 3–4
TEST statement 22–24
WEIGHT statement 11, 37–39
regression analysis 1–50
complete model 3
cubic models 31–33
least squares 2
one independent variable 10–14
plotting regression curves 41–43

regression analysis (*continued*)
  polynomial models 31–37
  predicting to a different data set 44–47
  quadratic models 31, 34–36
  qualitative and quantitative variables
     210–211, 213
  reduced model 3
  restricted model 25–27
  several independent variables 15–17
  transformed variables 47–48
  weighted least squares 37–39
REPEATED statement
  ANOVA procedure 62–63
  GLM procedure 267, 269–272, 274–278,
     283–289
repeated-measures data 265
  contrasts 278–282
  multiple factors 282–283
  multivariate analysis 266–272
  univariate analysis 274–278
residual plots 40–41
RESTRICT statement
  REG procedure 25–27
restrictions method 141–143
Roy's Maximum Root 249
RSREG procedure 9

S

SAS/ETS software 7, 9
SAS/GRAPH software 43
SAS/STAT software 7–9
Satterthwaite's approximation 58
Satterthwaite's formula 128–130
SEQB option
  MODEL statement (REG) 34
sequential sums of squares 20, 33
SHORT option
  MANOVA statement (ANOVA) 251
  MANOVA statement (GLM) 267
  REPEATED statement (GLM) 269, 284–286
simple effect comparisons 96, 97–99
SIMPLE option
  PROC REG statement 27, 30
simultaneous contrasts 72–73, 99–100
SINGULAR= option
  LSMEANS statement (GLM) 150
SOLUTION option 175
  MODEL statement (GLM) 145–146, 148,
     162–164, 231–232
sorting data 88, 91, 109, 152
sources of variation 59
sphericity of a set of orthogonal components
    274
sphericity test 274, 277
split-plot design 191
split-plot experiment 130
  analysis of variance 131
  Duncan's test 133
  repeated-measures design 272–274
split-split-plot experiment 134–135

SS1 option
  MODEL statement (GLM) 156, 160,
    162–164
  MODEL statement (REG) 20–22
SS2 option
  MODEL statement (GLM) 156, 160,
    162–164
  MODEL statement (REG) 20–22
SS3 option
  MODEL statement (GLM) 156, 160
SS4 option
  MODEL statement (GLM) 156, 160,
    162–164
standard deviation 52
standard error of the mean 52
standardizing variables 28
STB option
  MODEL statement (REG) 27–28
STDERR option
  LSMEANS statement (GLM) 150, 233
Student's t statistic 52
subpopulation mean 5–6
SUMMARY option
  MANOVA statement (ANOVA) 253
  REPEATED statement (GLM) 278–282
SUMMARY procedure 52, 280–281, 287
sums of squares
  adjusted treatment 204, 232
  basic identity 3
  error 12
  interaction effect 60–61, 62
  interpreting 157–161
  interpreting using estimable functions
    170–175
  main effect 60
  means model notation 159–161
  model 3, 12
  multivariate linear models 248
  nested effect 61
  partial 21
  reduction notation 157–159
  regression (model) 3, 12
  residual (error) 3, 6, 59
  sequential 20, 33
  total 3, 59
  Type I (sequential) 20–22, 33, 155–156,
    160, 161, 171–172, 232
  Type II (partial) 20–22, 156, 160–161,
    172–173
  Type III 156, 161, 173, 183, 232
  Type IV 156, 161, 183
  unadjusted treatment 204, 232
synthetic mean square 128–130
SYSLIN procedure 9

T

t tests
  approximate 57, 58
  for independent samples 56–57, 58
  for one sample 54
  for paired samples 55

for polynomial model 33
for regression model 4–5, 22
several independent variables 17
simple linear model 13
TEST option
  RANDOM statement (GLM) 114, 116, 123,
     126–127
TEST statement
  ANOVA procedure 62, 132, 133, 191,
     255–258
  GLM procedure 114–118, 123–127,
     191–193, 239–241, 273–274
  REG procedure 22–24
TOLERANCE option
  MODEL statement (GLM) 148
transformed variables 47–48
TRANSREG procedure 9
TTEST procedure 57–58
  CLASS statement 57–58
  VAR statement 57–58
TUKEY option
  MEANS statement (ANOVA) 79
Tukey's honest significant difference (HSD)
  63, 79
two-way classification 153, 159
Type I error 100
Type II error 100

U

unbalanced data 137, 153–155
UNIVARIATE procedure 52
USSCP option
  PROC REG statement 27, 30
U95= option
  OUTPUT statement (REG) 43
U95M= option
  OUTPUT statement (REG) 43

V

VAR statement
  MEANS procedure 52
  TTEST procedure 57–58
VARCOMP procedure 59, 109
variance components
  estimates 110–111
  expected mean squares 110, 113
  hypothesis tests 112
variance stabilizing transformations 107

W

WALLER option
  MEANS statement (ANOVA) 79
  MEANS statement (GLM) 233
Waller-Duncan test 79
WEIGHT statement
  GLM procedure 143–144, 148
  MEANS procedure 52
  REG procedure 11, 37–39

weighted cell means 160, 166
weighted least squares 37–39
WHERE statement
  MEANS procedure 52
Wilks' criterion 249
within-subjects effects 265

X

XPX option
  MODEL statement (GLM) 144, 146–147
  MODEL statement (REG) 28–30

Y

Yates' weighted squares of means analysis 156